Subject-Oriented
Business Process Management

T0212347

Albert Fleischmann • Werner Schmidt •
Christian Stary • Stefan Obermeier •
Egon Börger

Subject-Oriented Business Process Management

 Springer

Albert Fleischmann
Pfaffenhofen
Germany

Christian Stary
Wien
Austria

Egon Börger
Calci
Italy

Werner Schmidt
Altmannstein-Schamhaupten
Germany

Stefan Obermeier
Oberasbach
Germany

ISBN 978-3-642-44095-3   ISBN 978-3-642-32392-8 (eBook)
DOI 10.1007/978-3-642-32392-8
Springer Heidelberg New York Dordrecht London

ACM Computing Classification (1998): J.1, H.4, K.6

© 2011 by Carl Hanser Verlag, München
Title of the German original: Subjektorientiertes Prozessmanagement
ISBN 978-3-446-42707-5
All rights reserved.

Preface

Numerous success stories on Business Process Management exist, however probably just as many reports of failure. In many cases, Business Process Management is an endless topic that people associate with paper, large drawings on the walls, endless discussions, etc. Based on these results, the IT departments of an organization generally receive an order to develop an IT-supported process. But workflows developed in this way typically do not have much in common with the original setting and its models, and therefore, they are rarely accepted by the involved stakeholders. Hence, so far the result of all these efforts is often unsatisfactory. Consequently, many executives still criticize Business Process Management. However, you find processes in every kind of organization—whether it is an industrial enterprise or a nonprofit animal breeding farm. Only when these processes are continuously scrutinized and optimized can redundant work in Business Process Management be avoided and the ultimate survival of the organization ensured.

Margot Berghaus writes in her book, "Luhmann easy to grasp" ["Luhmann leicht gemacht"]: "Social systems operate through communication, they are communication systems." and organizations are social systems (Berghaus 2004). In other words:

Organization = Communication.

(A corresponding Internet search with Google delivered 269 hits on June 2, 2011). Activities in organizations performed by their members are coordinated according to organizational goals. As a precondition for this, members of an organization need to communicate with each other.

There exists a natural language sentence structure in all known languages. It is composed of three components: subject, predicate, and object. The subject is the starting point of activities, the predicate is the action on the object, and the object is affected by the action. Following this structure, everyone is well prepared to think in a process-oriented way and to model processes.

The subject-oriented approach to Business Process Management, which is presented in this book, is based on these simple, however, fundamental considerations. Actors (subjects) with their actions and their communication behavior are in the center of attention. A process is established by structuring the actions of each actor and the necessary coordination of the required communication among the actors.

This book should be understood as an invitation to capture, reflect, and stimulate discussion around many different aspects of the design of organizations. All interested persons should be encouraged to simply try this pragmatic approach to Business Process Management. There are already many companies and institutions that have been trying it successfully, and they have been surprised that their processes have become intelligible to stakeholders.

It is an ambitious undertaking to write about an interdisciplinary topic, taking into account technical, psychological, economic, mathematical, and organizational aspects. We have tried to consider all these different aspects and their intertwining. However, we are convinced there is still much to be done and to be written about this topic.

While working on the book, we have enjoyed a team spirit allowing everyone to bring in his different background and experience, both in terms of theory and practice. Our intense collaboration allowed us to come up with a comprehensive picture of subject orientation. We experienced the struggle of streamlining structure and content as a constructive and inspiring moment of our cooperation. We hope the readers are still able to grasp it, in particular when reflecting the systemic nature of Subject-Oriented Business Process Management.

For helping us to be successful, we want to thank:
- Our families, supporting our endeavor more or less voluntarily
- All interested persons who have been waiting until we finished our work and have kept us under friendly pressure by their steady inquiries
- Metasonic AG for providing resources
  The customers of Metasonic AG for the numerous suggestions from the field
- Hanser Verlag for granting us the rights to publish the English version of our German book
- Springer-Verlag GmbH, particularly Ms. Ford and Mr. Gerstner, for their constructive cooperation
- The proofreaders
- Deutsche Bahn for providing notebook-compatible trains in which even books can be written
- Richard Wright who converted our long German sentences with English words into real English. Nevertheless, the authors still take responsibility for any awkward sentences.
- Carina Busse who brought the manuscript into the right format
- Larissa Weitenthaler who made all the drawings

Special thanks go to Anna Fleischmann for providing her graphic design. This includes the design of the "To Go's", which help the reader to grasp the individual chapters or major sections of the chapters. The "To Go's" represent fictional dialogs among the various stakeholders in Subject-Oriented Business Process Management projects in an entertaining style. As an illustration of the roles, we have chosen essential elements of fast food: food to go bags and cups. The reader can easily take these to a place of his choice and quickly consume their contents. From the chapter "Subject-Oriented Process Analysis" onwards, they represent the different actors operating in the open life cycle of Subject-Oriented Business Process Management. Each cup and bag has a badge with the first character of the name of the role, such as F for Facilitator.

A note on "gender": For better readability, we typically use the masculine form in the text. The female form is always considered to be included, and vice versa. When designing the fast-food bags and cups, we also took care to maintain a balance between the sexes.

In case the readers are keen on working with the introduced method, we refer to the Web site of the nonprofit organization Institute of Innovative Process Management e.V. (see also http://www.i2pm.net). There, interested persons will find material and tools currently available. Every person interested in driving Business Process Management forward outside of over-trodden paths, especially by bringing in his knowledge and valuable experiences, can become a member of the Institute of Innovative Process Management.

Spring, 2012

Albert Fleischmann
Werner Schmidt
Christian Stary
Stefan Obermeier
Egon Börger

Acknowledgments: The research leading to these results has received funding from the European Commission within the Marie Curie Industry and Academia Partnerships & Pathways (IAPP) programme under grant agreement n° 286083.

Reference

Berghaus, M.; Luhmann leicht gemacht; Köln/Weimar/Wien, 2004.

Contents

Thinking of Business Processes Systematically

1

1.1   To Go

Why should I read this book and work in a subject-oriented way? What is special about it? Is it not just another book, new wine in old bottles, enriched with more or less helpful examples and pretty pictures? What is special about subjects?

You find a lot of literature on business processes, considering processes as sequences of activities. If you take a closer look, it is never at all mentioned who performs these activities. However, the activities of the processes are performed by the involved stakeholders, which we call subjects. Subjects exist in all business processes. They have not been invented by this book. They are rather taken for granted—to such an extent that they might need to be revisited—in particular when they are considered implicit or secondary process information. Once we move the subject to the center of a process, the entire perspective on the process changes. And many open issues that could not be previously clarified can be resolved immediately. Amazingly, subject-oriented process models can be directly transformed into technology-supported workflows. See for yourself!

A. Fleischmann et al., *Subject-Oriented Business Process Management*,
DOI 10.1007/978-3-642-32392-8_1, © The Author(s) 2012

1.2   Introduction

Today, the success of organizations is not only based on their products and services but rather on their capability to (re)design their business processes in a flexible and dynamic way (Scheer et al. 2007). In this respect we need to take different influencing factors into account:

- *Globalization.* Through the worldwide opening of goods, labor, and information markets, the dynamics of business activities has steadily increased. Markets are not only reinvented, which generates additional growth, but they also lead to a continuous redesign of jobs, dynamically changing portfolios and reorganized business operations. Any small change can have a far-reaching impact in a networked organization. The division of labor exceeds corporate and national boundaries.
- *Stakeholder Orientation.* In addition to procurement and sales, other actors and interests on the market affect the company directly or indirectly. For listed companies, the shareholders have a strong influence. The management is committed to them and tries to satisfy their striving for increasing profit. In addition, organizations need to comply with more and more regional, national, European, and other international laws and regulations, such as requirements for implementing risk management systems. In this context, mandatory equity agreements, e.g., Basel II, govern the granting of loans to organizations with a rating system.
- *Progressive Penetration* of the business community with information and communication technologies: in particular, internet technologies are driving forces for organizational and technical changes in almost all economic and business-relevant sectors of society. The transmission and communication platforms enable partial (if not complete) support, processing, and maintenance of exchange processes by means of electronic communication networks. Exchanging goods and services comprises the transfer of tangible and intangible elements, accompanied with configurable structure description languages such as Extensible Markup Language (XML). The latter allow the exchange of technical information across system boundaries, adapted to the respective interaction partner.

Each of these factors is directly or indirectly related to the organization and implementation of business processes or work processes. At the same time, these factors are interdependent and cannot be considered in isolation from each other. The mastery of complex business processes is one of the major challenges of every business. However, it requires concepts to deal with these challenges in a structured way (Heracleous 2003).

Accordingly, the continuous design of business processes and thereby, business process management (BPM) is of crucial importance for the success of organizations. It comprises the implementation of strategies and business models in organizational processes. As such, it goes beyond traditional management activities, resulting in cyclic planning, organization, management, and control of organizations. This has for example been vividly described by Liappas:

"Companies often have inhomogeneous business operations. Different types of business require different types of organization. The organization needs to be geared to the market and customer requirements" (Liappas in Scheer et al. 2007, p. 44). The management of an organization is interested in two views: financial figures are generally used for looking to the past; BPM provides a means for looking to the future (Gilbert 2010).

Apparently, BPM has primarily to do with the business of a company. It is no coincidence that the word "Business" precedes Process Management. Processes are considered as leverage to operate a business according to its strategy or to align an organization according to its (public) mandate (cf. Liappas in Scheer et al. 2007, p. 44).

> Subject-oriented process orientation means moving from profit orientation per se to sustainable income. The latter can be only achieved through high stakeholder satisfaction.

Two examples from consulting practices (Scheer et al. 2007):

- A market-leading chemical company has identified cost leadership as the most important success factor in its business. Product and process costs are the two key leverages for this purpose. The production network, which has been responsible for product manufacturing, guaranteed low product cost. The company decided to focus its efforts on developing an effective, efficient process landscape. It should, on the one hand both simplify and automate the customer interaction with the company and, on the other hand, ensure that the organization acts in compliance with the business model it has adopted.
- A European authority has decided to use business processes as a means of implementing its strategy and optimizing its resources. As a basis for subsequent activities, a business process model was created that reflected the statutory mandate to that authority. Based on this model, several design projects have been set up successfully, such as zero-based budgeting, optimization in various areas of the organization, and the introduction of a new ERP (enterprise resource planning) system.

Public service organizations often ask whether they can use the same methods as companies with market orientation. The only difference between the two of them is the purpose of the organization: one wants to earn money, and the other has to administer the law. However, the approach to the fulfillment of each objective can be the same in both cases.

These cases show tangible connections between business processes and their impact on organizations. Nevertheless, handling business processes at a high level of abstraction is the greatest risk for BPM today: the trivialization of dealing with processes. It is challenging to deal simultaneously with the company's business model, the processes, the planning and control systems, rules of conduct, information technology, and personnel matters.

Lack of knowledge about business processes can lead to wrong decisions with negative consequences for the organization.

Managers have to deal with the planning, monitoring, and controlling of business processes. Such a traditional focus on business-relevant processes is often chosen in practice; however, this results in unsatisfying outcome and low acceptance of BPM. Even when organizations publish their process descriptions on the intranet, these pages are rarely visited. Why? Since the process documentation is already memorized, or nobody is actually interested in it? "Processes cannot be decoupled from the business!" (Liappas in Scheer et al. 2007). They rather control what happens in the organization.

Another problem is the generally known fact that process issues are pursued by various stakeholders. Processes of an organization are actively incorporated and modeled by business departments, as well as by IT departments. However, IT departments take a different, more technical perspective on the processes. When stakeholders involved in the processes are interviewed, they do not speak the same language as process modelers or organization developers. A major government agency has reported that the process of attaining a thorough understanding causes most of the effort in process management. This is already mirrored in the terms business process and workflow. The business processes of individual departments are mainly implemented using information technologies. A business process is technically refined and becomes a workflow. The latter is often described using different methods than those used for describing business processes, leading to incoherent and inconsistent specifications. Hence, such a transformation can lead to a significant loss of information, due to the mapping and translations. In addition, process descriptions are usually not detailed sufficiently by concerned members of the organization to be transferred without further effort into a workflow system. This causes additional effort for a successful implementation, including making assumptions about the actual work procedures.

The design of business processes should be in line with the business intelligence of an organization (Kemper et al. 2004). It bundles relevant information about organizations. By modeling business processes, organizations can build up business intelligence, i.e., they can collect their knowledge to achieve organizational goals and transparent models for the targeted processing. Information and communication technologies play a major role in the presentation, imaging, and processing of information.

Moreover, the organization has to be recognized as a system consisting of people and their communication relationships. The individual stakeholders are responsible for implementing the business processes. Their qualifications and motivation are crucial for the success of the business. System thinking helps to recognize the mutual relationships of all relevant elements and their relationships within an organization (which is then considered a system).

> The more organizational changes are triggered through models, the more important the explicit consideration of contextual information becomes, so-called system thinking.

The generation of added value, therefore, requires an integrated BPM approach that takes into account many different aspects in a balanced way. To this end, a number of different capabilities are required, in particular product orientation, customer (or market) orientation, system thinking, and abstract thinking in terms of models:

- *Product orientation.* A market-driven orientation toward partners and products (Lehner et al. 2007) includes services and software and represents one of the key factors of process design. The use of corporate resources (information, materials, skills, etc.) should be aligned with the life cycle of products.
- *Customer orientation.* In addition to product orientation, customer orientation is the major trigger for the design and change management of an organization. The life cycle of a product has to be aligned with customer expectations (cf. debate about climate change) and is subject to changes according to customer behavior. Nevertheless, development, production, and distribution of products or services have to comply with the principles of economic efficiency.
- *System thinking* requires explicit recognition of context of all processes of an organization and linking of information across system boundaries, especially for decision-making purposes.
- *Abstract thinking in terms of models,* as a principle to approach capabilities and problems, allows focusing on relevant events and structures of the world as observed by humans. It strives for the "essence" without losing target-specific context.

The primary area of design for change management in integrated BPM is represented by organizations being seen as increasingly self-regulated socio-technical systems (Exner et al. 2010). IT systems, especially systems supporting the operational flow, such as workflow management systems, are embedded in the context of a work organization and need to be adapted according to economic benefits and human work requirements. Models, methods, and tools need to be applied accordingly.

Systemic BPM is context sensitive in two respects: on the one hand, organizational, technical, and human–social factors are considered, including their mutual relationships; on the other, these factors, along with their mutual dependencies, form the context for all BPM activities (ranging from the acquisition of work knowledge to evaluation and execution).

A comprehensive method for the concrete implementation of an integrated BPM-oriented approach is subject-oriented business process management (S-BPM). It brings the subject of a process to the center of attention. In doing so, it considers business processes and their organizational environment from a new perspective, meeting organizational requirements in a much better way.

At the S-BPM-ONE Conference in 2009, Hagen Buchwald differentiated between three different phases of perspectives in computer science, starting with flowcharts (predicate orientation) in 1970 (Buchwald 2010, p. 20f). This changed around 1990 by the paradigm shift to object orientation. And, again 20 years later, in 2010, a further change occurred, the shift to subject orientation.

> Integration is more than the sum of its parts. The subject-oriented management process is not only results-oriented but rather substantially reshapes modeling as a comprehensive construction process; in the long run, managers trust their staff to reflect business processes interactively and to (re)construct them dynamically.

S-BPM provides a coherent procedural framework of reference to manage business processes of an organization: its focus is on the cooperation of those involved in the strategic, tactical, and operational issues, sharing their knowledge in a networked structure of the organization. Thus, S-BPM is an integrated approach to organizational design and development of an organization. Regardless of the complexity of a case at hand, it can be handled on a technological basis, as all validated behavior models can be directly executed. Moreover, the concept and precise prescription of technological behavior allow the seamless integration of S-BPM models into existing, and heterogeneous IT landscapes.

The only requirement for acquiring S-BPM competence is a good command of natural language. Hence, based on the findings of developmental psychology and linguistics, we first explain in Chap. 2 that for complete S-BPM specifications sentence natural language semantics has to be used. In this way, business process owners are able to ensure that business requirements of internal and external stakeholders are entirely met. All involved people, regardless of their functional roles, are able to learn how to model in a subject-oriented way, because this approach is closely tied to operational actions and provides a direct reference to existing information exchange processes between stakeholders. Hence, in this chapter, we also explain how information systems can be developed using S-BPM, in order to meet different requirements on the implementation level in a straightforward way.

In the Chap. 3.5 we detail the procedures behind S-BPM when developing organizations on the basis of subject-oriented business process models. The process model is coherent and justifies its practicality. Its development has been based on widespread experiences with the use of S-BPM. Chapters 4–11 detail the various bundles of activities of the S-BPM method. Starting out with analysis, we demonstrate how subject orientation can develop and be experienced by gradually focusing on communication for service provision. The subject-oriented perspective is also of benefit for real-time execution of specifications as well as for solving complex problems due to the simple, networked modeling structure of S-BPM. In Chap. 12, we provide a formal specification of the modeling method. In Chap. 13, we illustrate how each of the previously described activity bundles can be supported through the use of appropriate software tools.

In the final part of the book, we show in Chap. 15 a typical round-trip from current S-BPM practice. We also mutually contrast existing formal methods for modeling business processes in the Chap. 14. The approaches are described on the basis of their fundamental concepts. We also explain what relationship natural languages have with formal languages of computer science in general, and how the subject-oriented modeling method could be developed out of the structure of natural language. These considerations complete our round-trip that started with discussing natural language capabilities required for subject-oriented modeling in the course of human-centered design of socio-technical systems.

Each chapter begins with a summary of key findings with respect to the addressed topic, called "To Go": in a fictional dialog of actors relevant for S-BPM the content of each chapter is addressed in an engaging and entertaining form.

The glossary and index at the end of the book should facilitate profound discussions and serve as a quick reference to S-BPM concepts and operational methods.

References

Buchwald H (2010) The Power of 'As-Is' Processes, Springer CCIS 85, pp. 13–23, 2010.

Exner, A., Exner, H., Hochreiter, G., Unternehmens(Selbst)Steuerung - Ein praktikables Managementmodell, in: Organisationsentwicklung - Zeitschrift für Unternehmensentwicklung und Change Management, No. 2, S. 56–65, 2010.

Gilbert, P., The next decade of BPM, in: Hull, R., Mendling, J., Tai, S. (Eds.), Business Process Management, Springer LNCS 6336, Berlin 2010.

Heracleous L., Strategy and Organization - Realizing Strategic Management, Cambridge/UK 2003.

Kemper, H.-G., Mehanna, W., Unger, C., Business Intelligence - Grundlagen und praktische Anwendungen, Wiesbaden 2004.

Lehner, F., Wildner, S., Scholz M., Wirtschaftsinformatik - Eine Einführung, München 2007.

Scheer, A.-W., Kruppke, H., Jost, W., Kindermann, H. (Hrsg.), Agilität durch ARIS-Geschäftsprozessmanagement, Jahrbuch Business Process Excellence 2006/2007, Berlin 2007.

From Language Acquisition to Subject-Oriented Modeling

2

2.1 To Go

Everybody is able to talk in natural language, well, more or less: Why would we like to describe processes in natural language? Since we already know how to do it, without the need to learn some strange language, such as that of IT people, which nobody can really relate to. Is S-BPM now the next hype? Another lingo? How does subject orientation help? And how is it related to natural language?

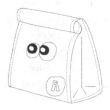

A business process is a highly complex bundle of communication in an organization. Humans have learned to communicate using language. Given that fact, it makes sense to describe processes entirely through natural language. Complete sentences are composed of subject, predicate, and object. At least, to my knowledge, all languages have this structure, and I have asked people of highly different origins. There might be differences in arranging the terms within a sentence, but with respect to their category they remain the same across different languages. Looking into existing BPM approaches, most of them are incomplete—they may lack the subject, the predicate, the object or some combination of these. In particular, subjects, if they are included at all, may be expressed indirectly or implicitly, e.g., using passive voice. Traditionally, processes are described by lists of predicates—we call them functions. Take, e.g., object-oriented methods: Besides predicates there are objects on which developers carry out operations. We tend to avoid expressing explicitly WHO is doing what. However, once we recognize that nothing happens without being triggered by someone, we have to move the subjects to the focus.

A. Fleischmann et al., *Subject-Oriented Business Process Management*, DOI 10.1007/978-3-642-32392-8_2, © The Author(s) 2012

In this chapter, we first reflect the origin and development of human thinking, acting, and natural language. Then, we introduce subject-oriented business process modeling by describing its main features and constructs intended to support organizational development steps. The focus of S-BPM modeling is on subjects as these are the active actors or systems in organizational development processes. Such a focus allows expressing knowledge in terms of natural language sentence semantics, as we do in natural language: a sentence consists of a subject, a predicate, and an object. Subject-oriented business process models can be directly derived from such natural language representations. Language is a complex communication system, using arbitrarily chosen symbols that can be combined in countless ways to achieve a single goal: conveying information.

In the following, we offer an overview of basic elements of natural language and show the transition of natural language representations to subject-oriented models. We start with significant findings on language acquisition and then discuss the developmental relationships between speech and action. We focus on language features and language development as detailed by Zwisler (1999).

For this reason, we deal first with the natural language semantics of sentences, which subsequently enable us to step directly into subject-oriented modeling of business processes without further effort. We then discuss the relationship of formal languages to natural language in order to clarify some differences. This discussion should help avoiding problems, primarily with respect to modeling, and subsequently with respect to implementing S-BPM models.

2.2   Acquiring Language and Dealing with Its Structure

Not only does the acquisition of language appear to be intrinsically motivated, but also its use, and thus, how to deal with distinct language structures. People intend to convey information and deliver meaningful messages when using language. Children are in particular interested in using voice communication: they find out very early how to influence their environment by acting. While improving their actions, they try to imitate the language of their parents. They learn that opening and closing the mouth twice when saying "ma" results in "mama" which not only delights their environment but also allows them to influence the behavior of their parents. Children experiment and play with language, and they quickly recognize that it is indeed useful to speak the same language as their parents. This insight has been conceptually explained as follows: "The foundation of language is based on a common understanding on the combination of sounds into meaningful units, and the combination of words into sentences. Phonemes are the sounds that make up the language. Morphemes are the smallest meaningful units" (Zwisler 1999).

Language therefore is governed by certain rules and hence structures the communication and interaction between people. While the syntactic dimension determines the relationship between linguistic symbols, the semantic dimension determines the relationship of symbols to nonlinguistic realities. Finally, the pragmatic dimension determines the relationship of symbols to speakers and listeners.

Language itself can therefore be regarded as a formal system. Within this system, distinct syntactic and semantic elements can be put into mutual context by way of rules. The most important basic semantic unit is a sentence. Language description and explanation are thus reduced to the description and explanation of sentences; the use of language is excluded. However, according to Chomsky, when using language, speakers and listeners generate some cognitive effort (while perception is learned prior to the production of language) (Chomsky 1986):

- They can judge sentences on their grammatical correctness.
- They recognize semantically equivalent sentences.
- They check ambiguities and can resolve them through paraphrasing content.
- They are able to repeatedly form new sentences and understand their meaning— they show linguistic creativity.

From the first three observations, Chomsky concluded that the perceivable forms of sentences are based on construction plans constituting actual meaning. He distinguishes between a surface structure and a deep structure of sentences. The deep structure determines which grammatical categories a sentence contains, which grammatical relations exist between the categories, and which lexical units can be used for the grammatical categories. The deep structure is allocated according to a semantic interpretation, which determines its semantic structure. By means of transformation rules, the deep structure is transferred into surface structure. Finally, sentences are pronounced correctly using the phonological component (Chomsky 1986).

Adolescents develop an individual language specific to their peer group or social environment. This language is generally characterized by simple sentences, revealing the sufficiency of natural language sentence semantics for effective communication.

Later, we show that the mapping of natural language sentences to an S-BPM model is comprehensive. Consequently, subject-oriented models enable effective communication, conveying complete information.

> Language as a formal system contains the grammar as a fundamental means for the formation of expressions, sentences, and stories.

2.3   Talking and Acting: Functional Alignment of Sentences

People do not produce sentences per se; they use them intentionally and purposefully. Linguistic competence, in terms of being able to understand meaning, includes the ability to know what to say in a certain social context, the skill to formulate content according to expectations of listeners, and the ability to recognize when it is perhaps better to conceal something. People learn the socio-normative rules of communication, i.e., communicative competence, through communication, not because they master a set of grammatical rules. People acquire the structure of sentences through the use of language, which in turn empowers them to explore its further usage. Hence, function and structure are mutually intertwined.

Language in its functional orientation enables speech. Talking represents a kind of action, with the speech act being constituent of the mutual relationship of the communication partners. The speech act can succeed or fail, just as any other activity. Bühler, with emphasis on the action character of language, interpreted language as a tool "to tell somebody something about things" (Bühler 1937). Thus, three constituent components of language can be distinguished:

- The subjective component: "oneself" (expression)
- The intersubjective component: "the other" (appeal)
- The objective component "of things" (presentation)

This distinction emphasizes the importance of separating presentation from content. It is reflected by the respective categories of symbols:

- Symbols by virtue of their relationship to objects and situations (objective component).
- Symptoms by virtue of their dependence on the speaker's intention, therefore, from the sender (subjective component).
- Signals by virtue of their appeal to the listener whose behavior they control (intersubjective component).

Therefore, a speech act always concurrently serves as a means for presentation, expression, and appeal. Usually, in a speech act, one of these functions moves to the foreground. Similarly, model building in BPM is aligned to a specific function.

2.4 Language Proficiency: The Transmission of Meaning

Being capable to use a certain (modeling) language means for a person to be able to master the grammatical rule set on the one hand. On the other hand, it means being able to make other people understand, to talk about items and issues, and—where appropriate—to reach an agreement. The first functional aspect is also known as "linguistic competence," while the second one is termed "communicative competence" due to its orientation toward action. In the context of modeling a business process, the functional aspect refers to the appropriateness of representation, from scratch to a complete and therefore coherent representation. The action aspect refers to adequately representing a situation by using a modeling language.

Language proficiency goes beyond the knowledge and application of the grammar of a language to convey meaning. People can only interpret information correctly when knowing its overall context. The conveyed meaning of a sequence of words can only be determined when knowing who the receiver is and what the concrete situation the sender and the receiver are part of involves. These dependencies of intended meaning determine, among other things, the cultural evolution:

- Semanticity: the utterance of a word is not necessarily linked to the presence of the signified object.
- Productivity: utterances that have never been expressed are possible.

• Substitutability: communication can occur independently of space and time.

When applying this knowledge to S-BPM and the development of organizations, organizational development using models of business processes is driven by the following characteristics: semanticity means that models based on the structure of language (as representations of the observable or anticipated reality) express organizational development opportunities. Productivity refers to situations achievable in the future. Substitutability implies the possibility of holding on to ideas that may become productive (in terms of the preceding sentence).

Consequently, the capability of speaking and articulating in natural language enables stakeholders, according to their relation to cultural evolution to actively participate in organizational development.

> Language allows the mapping of context with its own resources. Humans use their knowledge about language to describe processes and their embodiment in organizations.

2.5   Learning to Coordinate Speech, Thought, and Action

According to the findings of developmental psychology, the ability of individuals to learn a language is biologically determined. The environment only helps to trigger the biological potential. The receptor and articulation mechanisms of language according to their anatomical and physiological basis are already operational at the moment of birth. However, the brain regions required for the actual functioning of these mechanisms yet need to go through a further maturation process after birth. According to Chomsky, a speaker can only learn a language, when he has extracted the respective rules to construct linguistic utterances out of the abundance of utterances surrounding him as a child. These rules specify how the surface structure of a language is connected to the underlying deep structure. Mastering of all these rules has been referred to by Chomsky as linguistic competence. It is however an ideal claim, which will not be encountered in actual life. The actual speech capability is then speech performance.

According to Chomsky, there are universal principles that determine the types of grammatical regularities in the different languages; these should be innate to a child for language acquisition. What is to be determined by biology is a set of rules consisting of universal principles of structuring, which guide and channel the acquisition of grammar in the process of socialization. This control apparatus is called "LAD" (language acquisition device). It allows the child to induce general rules on how to form hypotheses from individual experiences with the language of its environment. In this way, it acquires a command of the grammar for that particular language. The constructive activity of the child in language learning comes to the foreground. Language is thus acquired in a long-lasting process. Since the child is fully engaged in the dynamic flow of the listener and speaker, it is able to understand what is meant by the (adult) speaker. Once the child knows what the speaker means, it can recognize and explore the meaning of what this person says. The child therefore does not learn what a word means, but rather how an existing meaning, or a term or concept, can be described verbally. The anchoring of language learning is provided through recognizing the intention of the speaker.

Up to a certain point, the development of thought and language proceed separately. But then, approximately at the age of two, they meet: thinking becomes language, and language becomes intellectual. "There is indeed no way to make achievements of thought visible without language" (Zwisler 1999).

The development of language itself involves several steps, which are of importance for the recognition of semantics. The following are particularly important:

- The one-word stage (age 1–2 years): The child uses single words to express whole phrases or sentences. The meaning of the words is understood by the adults because of the context. The child understands much of what it hears, as can be observed from the fact that it carries out correlated actions.
- The spurt in the development of words (at the age of two): The vocabulary is growing from about 300 words at 24 months to 1,000 words at 36 months. Two- and three-word sentences are formed by the child's own rules, which are not copied from the grown-ups' language.
- The sentence period (at the age of three): At this time the child uses sentences that contain grammatical features of the grown-ups' language. The child can use functionally complete, but grammatically incomplete sentences.
- To 5 years of age: The child uses sentences of each type: incomprehensible sentences; functionally complete but grammatically incomplete sentences; simple sentences; connected sentences; complex sentences; and mixed forms of the latter two.

Sentences, in which the actual subject is not explicitly named, are hard to understand for children ("At night, a black cat is hard to see"—Who sees the cat here? The subject "any person" has to be added with cognitive effort). Chomsky used a doll in his investigations which he blindfolded. Then he posed the question: "Is the doll easy to see or hard to see?" Only children at the age of 7 years gave correct answers at a high enough rate to indicate that this was not coincidental. The latter is particularly significant because linking displayed content to the respective actors seems to be of high importance for understanding.

Equally important is the sentence structure. In a sentence, words are put into mutual relation. The two most important keys to understanding sentences are the sequences of words and their inflection. The child begins with the word that has the most importance and includes the focus on what it wants to say (-> semantics). One of the most difficult grammatical forms seems to be the passive sentence. Often children are not able to use it correctly until the age of seven. For its understanding, they need to reverse their thoughts.

Semantic development occurs initially through vocalizations. In this way, the child can achieve targets. The child only knows that a particular verbal behavior can lead to desirable consequences; the actual meaning of a particular word is still not known to him. Semantics is achieved by inductive extrapolation: the child takes those speech utterances from the environment which it hears frequently and considers relevant for his needs and demands. These statements are memorized as best as possible and recalled in this form. Due to the variable use of these forms, the child then gradually recognizes that their individual positions can be taken by different words. The words in identical positions are turned into categories, and from their sequences syntactic rules for word positioning are derived.

A child does not operate only on the level of words, but also, and just at the beginning of language, with larger units. It is not only a cognitively motivated analyzer, but also, and primarily, a socially and emotionally motivated impersonator. The language rule sets do not only stem from internal but also external sources. The child does not learn the syntax in a direct way, but rather through conveyance of nonlinguistic conceptual information and linguistic semantic information; language acquisition is a highly active procedure.

These findings on language acquisition clarify which achievements are cognitively necessary for a successful language proficiency, even if they are intrinsically motivated. Active language acquisition lays the ground for the capability of people to interact, and ultimately for their coexistence in all systems of the society. These findings can be used to generate models of business processes and to contribute to organizational development. Considering the process of acquiring language skills, however, we have to recognize the inverse nature of S-BPM modeling through language constructs. The conscious use of syntax already allows the generation of meaningful content of models as shown in the sequel.

2.6 Models and Natural Language Semantics of Sentences

Models are representations of the perceived reality of humans. They can be formulated by means of natural language, even when they are processed by IT systems. The advantage of natural language descriptions is that they can be immediately understood by all people. And they are in line with natural language sentence semantics, as they contain subject, predicate, and object. What we call here natural language sentence semantics is considered the second level of sentence semantics in linguistics, with the semantic roles agent, predication, and theme ("Max plays the ball"). Level one corresponds to statements like "The ball is round." The third and last level is equivalent to the semantic structures within parts of sentences ("Peter's enjoyment of football brought luck"). For details, see Schmidt et al. (2005).

Natural language sentence semantics is familiar to all of us, as we invariably use it to communicate. However, natural languages have the disadvantage that they are frequently used in an incomplete and not sufficiently precise way. The results are different interpretations and misunderstandings.

The following illustrative example can be found in several Internet forums (Fig. 2.1):

A software engineer (programmer) and his wife:

Wife: Darling, we don't have any bread at home. Would you please go to the super market and buy a loaf? And if they have eggs, buy six!
Husband: Sure, darling.

After a while, he comes back with six loaves of bread.

Wife: Why did you buy six loaves, dear?!?
Husband: They had eggs…

Fig. 2.1 Example of a linguistic misunderstanding

What happened here? The woman has formulated her request incompletely. However, in ordinary settings, most people understand what she wants. But not the man, as his interpretation stems from language use that is neither common nor usual. Consequently, the result is curious. This example follows a pattern many jokes are built on. People interpreting the request of the wife in a syntactically correct way should actually come to the same conclusion the man did. They would have to buy seven loaves which, however, is not significant for the purpose of the story. This small example rather shows the limitations of colloquial use of formalizations.

Formal languages, in contrast to natural languages, have unique word semantics. Formal models are intended to convey abstract information. For the sake of a nonambiguous interpretation, they have reduced sentence semantics. Each model still can be interpreted in natural language by individuals. People are used communicating in complete sentences of the form subject, predicate, and object. If sentences are incomplete, problems in understanding occur. Therefore, sentences have to be complete in order to convey their entire meaning.

In modeling, essential aspects are differentiated from accidental or random aspects. Essential aspects describe the necessary elements for the formation of sentences. Such a distinction is also reflected in natural language: passive sentences are used when an action is in the foreground, without necessarily having to name the acting agent. Note: this sentence has also been written in passive voice, as the related subject, "a writer" is meaningless in this context. In order to form intelligible, complete sentences, it is advisable to create formal modeling languages that employ full natural language sentence semantics. This helps to avoid problems of comprehension and understanding.

Natural language sentences have the structure "subject–predicate–object" for conveying meaning. For instance, "I am writing a book" basically describes a meaningful situation through this kind of structure. It allows subject-oriented business process modeling.

Natural languages are used for communication between people. In terms of business processes, models describe the activities and communications of the people involved, application systems, machines, data, and other aids or tools. A business process is the medium to produce a reference for all participants to the activities they perform and techniques they use. On the one hand, there are actors or users who express how they (should) perform their activities. On the other hand, there are developers who integrate certain application programs in a process, and other stakeholders, who, e.g., assess the business process. A business process model provides all stakeholders with a common understanding of business operations. Such models must thus be understood not only by the experts who create them, but also by those who later (are expected to) work according to the model, and who should enrich it by providing additional information.

There is a description language for models that humans are generally familiar with, and which is basically sufficient for a first description of business activities: the natural language. The advantage is that it is known to all stakeholders and can be immediately understood and used. Task or process descriptions are therefore almost always initially documented in natural language statements and complemented with diagrams. Natural languages have three major semantic components. These are the subject of an action as a starting point, the predicate as the action being performed, and the object as the target of the action. These three elements define a complete sentence with the appropriate natural language sentence semantics. This facilitates the description of business processes, since in processes there are also actors who perform actions on certain objects.

In Fig. 2.2, a business trip process is broken down into to its components: subject, predicate, and object.

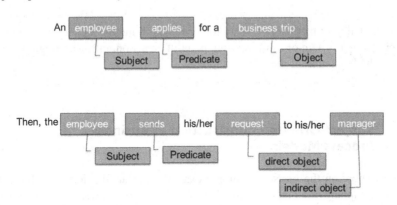

Fig. 2.2 Process description in natural language

2.7   Formal Languages and Natural Language

In theoretical computer science, the theory of formal languages plays a central role. It has been proved that programming languages are formal languages, which can be processed by a machine (Hopcroft et al. 2001). This is one of the most important statements of theoretical computer science. Yet natural languages cannot be fully described by formal languages, as natural languages have greater expressive power.

The relationship between formal and natural languages is also the subject of linguistics. Here, "langue" as a convention in a language system is distinguished from "parole" as content that is dynamic and context dependent. In the 1980s, Chomsky has continued to develop the terms further and introduced the names i-language for internal language and e-language for external language (Chomsky 1986). In a linguistic sense, the natural language sentence semantics is an i-language and more powerful than a formal language in the classical sense of computer science. We all are familiar with it, since it is used in daily communication.

As already described, natural language however also contains elements of e-language, which can be interpreted differently and may cause misunderstandings. Formal languages, in contrast, have a fixed (and thus possibly reduced) word semantics. In addition, in formal models a reduced set of semantics is used. This facilitates the automated processing of expressions in a certain language.

In modeling, one or even two of the standard sentence parts subject, object, and predicate are often omitted. For instance, when using flowcharts, only predicates (actions) are considered. Subjects and objects can be added as comments on the individual actions. But as such they are not fully integrated in the model. Data structure descriptions consider only objects, without dwelling on the actions or the starting point of the actions.

Formal models can be interpreted differently in business process modeling and software development. To avoid misunderstandings and ensure clarity, they also have to be translated into natural language, even when a reduced word or sentence semantics is used.

> For modeling, it may be necessary to once again bring the subject, as acting element in a system or as the starting point of an action, into the foreground, or to the beginning of the flow of thoughts.

2.8 Subject-Oriented Construction of Business Process Models

We now show on the basis of a simple example—an application for a business trip—the mapping of a language-based representation to a subject-oriented model. In doing so, the subject moves to the focus of attention. This method is the core of S-BPM. We show which parts of the standard semantics subject, predicate, or object are essential and which are accidental, and how the sample process is described in the respective modeling style.

Figure 2.3 shows the natural language description of a business trip application process.

An employee applies for a business trip. His manager checks the request and informs the employee whether he approves or rejects the request. The approved request is forwarded to the travel office which does all the travel arrangements.

Fig. 2.3 Natural language description of the business trip application process

The subject-oriented description of a process starts with the identification of process-specific roles involved in the process, the subjects, and the messages exchanged between them. When sending messages, the required data is transmitted from the sender to the receiver. Thus, with the message "business trip request" sent by the employee to the supervisor, among other things the start and end date are transmitted.

Figure 2.4 shows the interaction structure of the process.

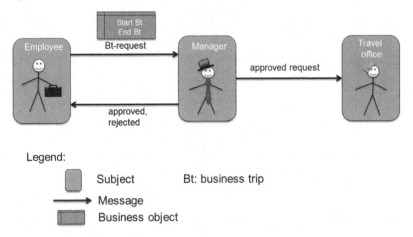

Fig. 2.4 The application process with the involved subjects and their interactions

In a further refinement step, it is now described which activities and interactions the subjects have to perform during the execution of the process and in which order, i.e., the behavior of individual subjects is defined.

We first consider more closely the behavior of the employee from his perspective. This can be formulated in natural language, as exemplified in Fig. 2.5.

> The *employee* fills out the **request form for business trips**. After that,
>
> the *employee* sends the **request** form to his/her **manager**. After that,
>
> if the *employee* receives the **approval** from his/her **manager**, then
>
> > *he/she* does the **business trip**; After that,
> >
> > *he/she* does **nothing** any more
>
> if the *employee* receives the **rejection** from his/her **manager**, then
> > *he/she* does **nothing**

Legend:
Subject   (e.g. employee)
Predicate/action (e.g. fill out)
Predicate/communication   (send or receive)
Direct object   (e.g. request form for business trips)
Indirect object (receiver in send action or sender in receive action)

Fig. 2.5 Natural language description of the behavior of the subject employee when applying for a business trip

The phrases used are bumpy and the process can be decomposed into alternative paths, so that a pictorial representation appears clearer. In the following, we will therefore use a graphical representation. Figure 2.6 shows the order in which the employee sends and receives messages, or executes internal actions, and in what states he is in during the corresponding action.

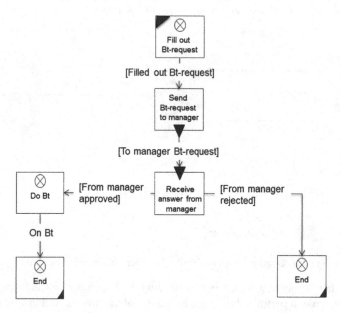

Fig. 2.6 Graphical representation of employee behavior when applying for a business trip

The initial state is marked by a triangle in the upper left corner. It is a function state in which the employees complete their business trip request. Then they come by way of the state transition "request completed" in a send state in which they send the application to the manager, before entering the receive state, in which an answer is received from the manager. Here, the applicants wait for the response of the manager. In case they receive a rejection message from the manager, the process is complete. In case the employees receive the message "approval" from the manager, they go on the trip on the agreed date and the business trip application process is completed.

The behavior of the manager is complementary to that of the employee (see Fig. 2.7). Messages sent by the employee are received by the manager, and vice versa. The manager therefore waits first in a receiving state for a business trip request from the employee. After receiving the application, he goes to a state of checking which leads either to the approval or rejection of the request. In the second case, a send state follows to send the refusal to the employee. In the first case, the manager moves first to a send state for transmitting the approval to the applicant and proceeds then into a state of informing the travel office about the approved business trip request.

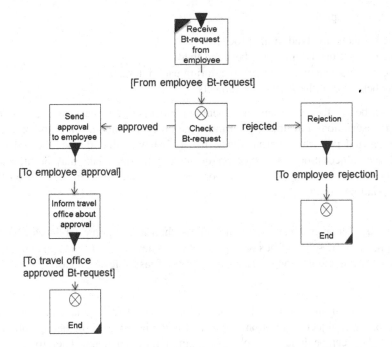

Fig. 2.7 Graphical representation of the behavior of managers when handling a business trip request

Figure 2.8 shows the behavior of the travel office. It receives the approved business trip request and stores it. Then its process terminates.

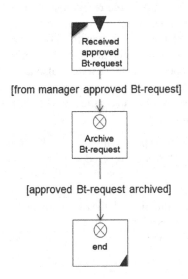

Fig. 2.8 Graphical representation of the behavior of the travel office when processing the application

In this example:

- The subjects involved in the process
- The interactions taking place between them
- The messages they send or receive during each interaction
- The behavior of the individual subjects

are described as they represent the essential elements of a subject-oriented model.

The description of a subject determines the order in which it sends and receives messages and performs internal functions. Its behavior thus defines the order in which the subject processes which predicates (operations). This may be the standard predicates sending or receiving, or other predicates that are defined on the corresponding objects.

> Although subjects constitute organizations, their interaction establishes what happens in the sense of business processes. So never forget the exchange of messages that goes along with the exchange of task-relevant data.

Therefore, an operation needs to be assigned to each individual state and state transition in a subject description, whereas it is not important how the operation is defined. This can be done by an object or using natural language. Therefore, in the following explanations for function, send, and receive states, we do not use the term method or operation but rather the general term service:

- Function state: An internal function is assigned to a service. Upon reaching this state, the associated service is executed. The end conditions of the executed service correspond to the exits of the respective internal state function.
- Send state: The output of a send state is associated with a service via a message name. This is triggered before the transmission process and determines the values of message parameters which are to be transmitted with the message.
- Receive state: Each output of a receive state is also associated with a service via the message name. Once a message is accepted, this service is initiated as intended in the state. The service takes the message received with the parameter values and processes them.

Services are used to assign a specific meaning to the individual steps captured by a subject behavior model. They are triggered synchronously, i.e., a subject does not enter the corresponding next state, unless the used service has been also completely processed.

Using the example of the employee behavior in the business trip request, Fig. 2.9 exemplifies how the predicates addressed in a subject can be defined using an object (class definition in the sense of object-oriented representations).

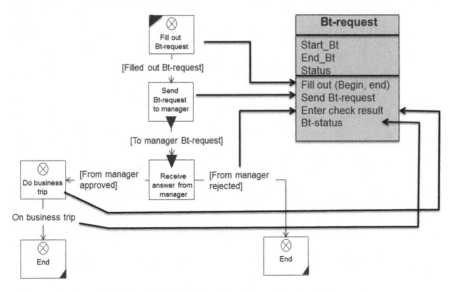

Fig. 2.9 Predicate definition in the behavior of a subject using an object

References

Bühler, Ch.: Kind und Familie: Untersuchungen der Wechselbeziehungen des Kindes mit seiner Familie, Jena 1937.

Chomsky, N., Knowledge of Language, New York 1986.

Hopcroft, J.E.; Motwani, R.; Ullman, J.D.: Introduction to Automata Theory, Languages, and Computation Second Edition, Upper Saddle River 2001.

Schmidt J.E.; Rabanus S.; Vilmos A.: Syntax, http://web.uni-marburg.de/dsa//Direktor/Rabanus/SS2005/Grundlagen.pdf, 2005.

Zwisler, R (1999): Sprachentwicklung, http://www.psychologie.uni-regensburg. de/~zwr02102/scripts/Sprachentwicklung.html (99-07-01), Download on August 13, 2010.

The Integrated S-BPM Process Model

3

3.1 To Go

Now I have gotten the message from the last two chapters that language plays a prominent role for the documentation and modeling of business processes. I also understood that subjects have to be at the center of processes, since acting requires actors. However, the introduction of processes could also be performed here along the usual BPM procedure—analysis, modeling, and implementation: Why do we need a specific process model to implement S-BPM?

The concept of S-BPM could actually be implemented along the traditional way of introducing or improving business processes. Nevertheless, the procedure to follow in S-BPM is subject-oriented in itself. The creation of a process is also a process driven by a stakeholder—a process cannot be created by itself. When implementing S-BPM consequently, we leave behind our traditional BPM hierarchical arrangement of organizational roles and identify four categories of actors that drive S-BPM, regardless of their positions in organizations. These categories are aligned in accordance with S-BPM process requirements, and their activities are already well known. We call them activity bundles, as they bundle actions that are selected according to requirements and work processes at hand. In this way, we are able to demonstrate how S-BPM meets the requirements of an integrated method.

Subject-oriented business process management does not only include the opportunity to transfer information expressed in natural language with minimal effort into a model. It also allows a continuous change of business processes in a

A. Fleischmann et al., *Subject-Oriented Business Process Management*,
DOI 10.1007/978-3-642-32392-8_3, © The Author(s) 2012

structured way. The S-BPM method itself is subject-oriented, with actors (subjects) at the focus. In the following, we explain the coordinated S-BPM activity bundles (predicates) that are executed by the respective actors. The object in S-BPM is the process itself. In this way, the S-BPM process model can be fully specified by its inherent elements and logic of description. This self-referentiality reflects the consistency of the approach.

First, we introduce the process understanding required for S-BPM. We then address the importance of S-BPM for organizations and introduce the various S-BPM stakeholders and activity bundles. Thereafter, the methodological framework of S-BPM is detailed. And finally, we show the multiple integrated nature of S-BPM.

3.2   Concept of Processes in S-BPM

The concept of processes for S-BPM is consistent with the concept commonly used to define business processes in traditional BPM (cf. Becker et al. 2008, p. 6; Schmelzer and Sesselmann 2010, p. 61ff; Fischermann 2006).

We therefore understand a business process as a set of interrelated activities (tasks), which are handled by active entities (people or systems performing work tasks) in a logical (with respect to business) and chronological sequence, and which use resources (material and information) to work on a business object for the purpose of satisfying a customer need (to thus contribute an added value), and which have a defined start and input, as well as a defined end state and result.

Business objects as such are those objects, which are economically relevant for shaping the business and which include the communication relationships in the course of task accomplishment. In S-BPM therefore, those objects are considered which are relevant during the exchange of messages between subjects, and which are also relevant for the individual activities of the subjects.

3.3   S-BPM Stakeholders

S-BPM is driven by several active roles. Governors (people caring for, taking responsibility for, or driving processes) create the conditions under which Actors operate. These Actors manage work tasks, and in doing so, cooperate with specialists (Experts) when needed. Governors are also responsible for organizational development. The respective stages of development are supported by Facilitators, who again involve Experts where needed. S-BPM does not require a hierarchical structuring of these actors and in turn does not require explicit management structures. It rather dissolves the classic distinction between business and IT people. Representatives from both areas can be found in all of the roles relevant for S-BPM.

3.3.1   Governors (People Caring for, Taking Responsibility for, or Driving Processes)

Governors are subjects who have responsibility for environmental factors and who take influence on the respective work and development processes. Governors should bridge the gap in the organizational development between executive officers and the operational business. They are not responsible for the technical control of work processes. They rather ensure that processes meet certain quality standards. Consequently, each process needs to be considered in the context of its organizational embodiment. In order for a process to become productive, requirements of corporate governance have to be provided. They need to be implemented under the responsibility of the Governor (business and IT compliance).

In the context of modeling, the organizational design or development department is in the role of the Governor. It implements the rules of how models shall be generated (in terms of modeling methods, types of models, tools, etc.). This department also takes care of accompanying process workers (Actors when modeling processes) by methods specialists (Experts) of its unit.

A Governor may need to handle several influencing factors simultaneously in a responsible way. In addition, different players may take differential influence on the organizational development, leading to additional or changing constraints. Typical examples are:

- Management: Definition of business/domain strategy
- Middle management: Definition of functional strategies (tactics)
- IT management: Definition of the IT strategy
- Organizational design department: Specification of methods, tools, and conventions
- Process owner: Definition of process metrics and target values

Accordingly, the task profile of Governors is diverse. Their profile is detailed later on when introducing the S-BPM activity bundles.

> Helplessness of managers does not protect organizations from harm—alternatives to existing behavior patterns need to be brought up in such situations. This is what the Governor is for—he helps to trigger creative and reflective processes. And he needs to take responsibility for them.

3.3.2   Actors (Active Participants in a Process)

Actors run work processes. They are empowered through S-BPM to participate actively in (re-) developing their organization of work. They correspond to subjects and become part of subject-oriented process models when their behavior needs to be represented.

In accordance with the objectives of S-BPM, Actors are active elements and simultaneously the points of reference, primarily in the analysis, modeling, optimization, and implementation of business process models. Actors are supported by Experts and Facilitators.

For instance, Actors can identify weaknesses in their work process and, where appropriate, in consultation with the responsible Governor and supported by Facilitators and Experts, eliminate by themselves deficiencies in the organization of work in a responsible way.

> Without time, money, and individually invested energy, there can be no S-BPM—working actors (Actors) need time, skills, confidence, and distance, in order to engage in change processes with the required intensity.

3.3.3   Experts (Specialists in a Specific Field)

Once expertise in a certain domain or situation is required, experts are needed. They are activated either by the Actors, the Governor, or the Facilitator. They are expected to deliver solutions to recognized problems. Typical examples of experts are:

- Internal and external process consultants
- Organizational developers
- IT architects
- Domain experts, such as software developers or database specialists

> Options for organizing work can neither be prescribed nor reinvented by a single person—domain experts and managers shape work processes together with those accomplishing tasks.

3.3.4   Facilitators (People Accompanying Organizational Development)

Facilitators support Actors when initiating organizational development steps, when taking action within a bundle of activities or development step, and during transition from one step (activity) or bundle to another step or bundle. They accompany the introduction or adaptation of a business process toward stakeholder needs. They influence organizational development processes through specific recommendations. For instance, once a particular part of a process has been modeled successfully, the Facilitator advises the involved Actors to validate the current model before proceeding with modeling.

Structural persistence is usually characterized by a lack of communication. In this case, the Facilitators explore opportunities for stakeholder communication. They create the necessary interaction pathways and support stakeholders in the context of design and reflection processes. The Facilitators also control and support the communication of Actors and Experts. For instance, they recognize when another Actor or Expert needs to be involved.

Thus, we regard the Facilitators as a catalyst when developing an organization. They should succeed in qualifying Actors professionally and personally. Typical examples of Facilitators, performing different support services, are:

- Members of middle management
- Project managers
- Organizational developers
- Coaches
- Service desk staff

It is the inner commitment that leads to changes. If an organization does not recognize that conditions of operation are changing and how they are changing, then it cannot accomplish its mission and is "doomed to die" sooner or later. It requires a team including Governor, Facilitator, Actor, and Expert to empower people to commonly develop and share inner commitment on the organizational level.

3.4 S-BPM Activity Bundles

The different activity bundles (cf. Schmidt et al. 2009, p. 52f) are the topic of main chapters following later. They are therefore just briefly described here:

- Analysis: The first step in S-BPM is usually the analysis. In this phase, a process is examined while being decomposed into parts. In addition, its operational context and rationale is made transparent. The object of concern is on the one hand derived from the organization's strategy to structure work and its S-BPM strategy. On the other hand, analysis activities can also be triggered by feedback stemming from another bundle of activity, especially monitoring, for instance to identify causes of deviations from desired process performance.
- Modeling: Modeling in Business Administration means reducing the complexity of the reality through mapping observations to a specific medium (Meyer 1990, p. 16). Before doing so, a self-contained set of characteristic items and relationships needs to be identified and abstracted from the observed reality. Modeling of business processes is essentially a matter of representing which subjects (humans and machines as actors) perform which activities (tasks and

functions) on which objects (as a rule, information which is bound to specific carriers) using which tools (e.g., IT systems), and how they interact to achieve the desired process goals and outcomes. Initially, an abstract process model is created. This model is still independent of the specific actors. These are then added in the course of the organizational and IT implementation of business process models.

- Validation: Validation in the context of S-BPM means checking whether a process is effective, i.e., whether it yields the expected output in the form of a product or service. The subject of validation is the observed business process itself or its model. Through validation, a process model can be evaluated to see whether it corresponds to the intended representation.
- Optimization: While the goal of validation is to ensure the effectiveness of business processes, the target of optimization is the efficiency of the same processes. Process efficiency can be expressed in terms of process attributes concerning the consumption of resources, such as duration, costs, and frequency of use. Optimization means to adjust a process and its subprocesses with respect to specific (resource) parameters (in the sense of achieving an organizational goal by meeting corresponding parameter values, such as cost limits).
- Organization-specific implementation: When embodying processes, validated and optimized processes are embedded into an existing or novel organizational environment according to its specific settings.
- IT implementation: The IT implementation of a process means the technical introduction of a business process into an organization, namely as an IT-based workflow including the integration of a suitable user interface, business logic, and the required IT systems.
- Monitoring: Once optimized and implemented, processes become productive (go live) in an organization. They are executed within the work structure of the organization and its IT environment in daily operations. In the course of monitoring process execution, data are collected and recorded. They are calculated to provide accurate actual values to be compared with previously defined performance targets. The results are processed through reporting according to the need of target groups and made available to the intended recipients. The evaluation of the results, when comparing actual performance data to plan data, may lead back to the analysis of causes in case of undesirable deviations, and depending on the nature of the perceived need for action, to the iteration of a downstream S-BPM activity bundle.

3.5   The Open Control Cycle of S-BPM Activity Bundles

The modeling of business processes is an essential part of business process management. In its basic features, it represents a traditional management process. When accomplishing its tasks, the management deals with business processes. Management activities are carried out along a feedback control cycle composed of the phases: analysis, modeling, validation, optimization, organization-specific implementation, IT implementation, operation, and monitoring. The phases follow the logic of BPM, whereby information about business processes and their design is accumulated progressively during cycle time.

The S-BPM activity bundles correspond to a great extent to these management activities of traditional BPM approaches. However, in contrast to traditional BPM approaches, as a rule they are not necessarily performed sequentially. We therefore speak of an open feedback control cycle, driven by people in the S-BPM roles that we have identified in Sect. 3.3 (see Fig. 3.1). The S-BPM activity bundles can be performed in the logic of S-BPM along a complete organizational development step as described is Sect. 3.4. However, the sequence of execution may also differ from this linear procedure. A nonlinear sequence is triggered by events in the individual activity bundles requiring such different paths, as detailed in the respective subchapters.

> The control loop of cybernetics teaches us to think in terms of feedback systems. S-BPM reflects the diversity of organizational interventions. Despite the central position of modeling activities, organizational development can be started in a continuous process from controlling (e.g., optimization), implementation (e.g., IT implementation), or analysis (e.g., validation).

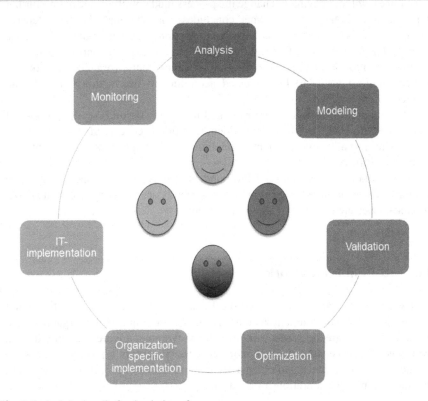

Fig. 3.1 Activity bundle for the design of a process

In BPM practice, the activities of the bundles, or even bundles out of the cycle, often cannot be clearly distinguished from each other. Quite often, organizations move back and forth between them without disruption. For instance, in case stakeholders identify ambiguities during the modeling of the process, they could switch to an upstream process step and consult the stakeholder involved in that process step for analysis. Once the issue is settled, they continue modeling their process. During the validation, the involved stakeholders can recognize obvious potential for optimization, embody it in their current model, and validate it again.

In this way, activity bundles are iterated and the process is enriched successively with information, until the process specification is complete and sufficiently detailed to meet the project target. Stepping back to a previous activity always leads to an analysis state, and, depending on the results of this analysis, back to another downstream activity bundle. This applies in particular to the feedback from monitoring activities. When modifications of the model follow, each downstream activity bundle after modeling has to be completely performed subsequently. Otherwise, it is possible to skip steps. For instance, when process owners recognize during monitoring a negative deviation from a target value, they initiate a causal chain analysis. In case this analysis results in recognizing a lack of work force handling the particular case, this deficiency can be removed through another organizational implementation of the process (simply by providing additional work force), without having to change the process model itself. There are no further steps required. If the process owner concludes from the analysis that extensive throughput times are caused by lacking possible parallel execution of process steps, the model needs to be modified and revalidated. In this case, the implementation of the process into the organization and the IT infrastructure (organization-specific implementation) needs to be reviewed according to the modified model, and adapted where required.

Which bundles of activities are executed iteratively depends on the purpose of each project. In case only the process documentation is concerned, e.g., for certification within quality management, modeling and description of the current processes are sufficient.

Before detailing the various S-BPM bundles of activities in distinct chapters, let us clarify the conditions under which the activities are performed, and also how these activities are affected by those conditions.

3.6   S-BPM Framework

Business process management based on the described bundles of activities is not independent of its environment in an organization. It is embedded in organizational frameworks that are designed primarily by Governors. Figure 3.2 provides an overview of various framework conditions, the Governors typically responsible for these conditions, and the affected activity bundles (see Fig. 3.2). Then, we detail the main framework conditions of S-BPM.

Framework conditions	Potentials governors	Affected activity bundles
Business system of an organization	Business management	Analysis
IT in the organization (IT strategy, architecture, development)	IT management (CIO)	IT implementation
BPM governance (methodology)	Organization department	All activity bundles (metaprocess)
BPM governance (Modeling principles / -conventions)	Organization department	Modeling
BPM governance (tool use)	Organization department	All activity bundles
BPM vision	Business management, organization department, IT management	All activity bundles
BPM strategy	Business management, organization department, IT management	All activity bundles
BPM culture	All, initiated by the organization department	All activity bundles

Fig. 3.2 Design of framework conditions through Governors

3.6.1 Business System of an Organization

The vision of an organization frames the formulation of its objectives. The strategy defines ways to achieve these objectives, such as the product–market combination for competitive positioning or the influencing of cost structures.

For implementing the strategy, i.e., the actual operation of a business, the design and execution of business processes, including their support by appropriate IT systems, are required. In this triad of strategy, processes, and information systems (cf. Österle and Winter 2003, p. 3ff; Schmidt 2010a, p. 37ff), Business Process Management is positioned according to its integrative meaning (see Sect. 3.7). As a management concept, it has close, usually complementary relationships with other management tools, such as Balanced Scorecard (BSC), Six Sigma, Total Quality Management (TQM), or the Model of the European Foundation for Quality Management (EFQM) (cf. Schmelzer and Sesselmann 2010, p. 14ff; Fischer et al. 2006, p. 21ff).

The entire business operation is subjected to Corporate Governance, a management system for corporate control and monitoring which is oriented toward long-term value creation, while following both legal frameworks and ethical principles (cf. RDCGK 2010, Preamble; Schmidt 2010b, p. 355). The foundation for this is based on (inter-)national regulations, such as the German Corporate Governance Code, the Law on Control and Transparency (KonTraG), and the Accounting Law Modernization Act (BilMoG) (cf. Klotz and Dorn 2008, p. 6).

The issues raised in this context are usually in the responsibility of management as Governor and are relevant primarily for the S-BPM analysis.

3.6.2 IT of an Organization

In the sense of IT/Business Alignment, IT vision and IT strategy have to be derived from their counterparts at the organizational level (company level), as detailed in the previous section (cf. Schmidt 2010a, p. 75ff). The IT, for its part, provides impulses for business operation, e.g., by enabling new business models.

IT governance, when derived from the Corporate Governance, should ensure with appropriate leadership and corresponding organizational structures and processes that IT supports the achievement of business goals (and contributes an added value). Hereby, resources should be responsibly used and risks properly monitored (cf. ITGI 2003, p. 11ff; Schmidt 2010b, p. 355ff; Johannsen and Goeken 2007, p. 21f).

IT delivers its value proposition from a strategic perspective by enabling competitive advantages and from an operational perspective by optimally supporting the business processes required to implement the business strategy. In the latter context, the technical dimension of S-BPM comes into play (see Sect. 3.7).

The vision, strategy, architecture, and governance of IT are essential conditions for the IT implementation of business processes. The role of Governor for the definition of these is usually taken by the head of IT (CIO) in an organization.

3.6.3   Business Process Management in an Organization

The business system and the IT of an organization lay the framework for Business Process Management. BPM in turn should create an environment in which the BPM process model is embedded. Essentially, it is about developing a vision and strategy, which are connected to the corporate culture and from which governance for business process management can be derived. These conditions usually have a long-term perspective, but need to be modified to reflect feedback from the activity bundles or changing environmental conditions (e.g., a change in corporate strategy). Particularly in the case of S-BPM, impulses may come from the operational work force. They influence vision and strategy in the long term.

3.6.3.1 Development of an S-BPM Vision

A vision is an attractive representation, which a person can identify with, of future reality (Wittmann et al. 2004, p. 16). The vision does not anticipate this future situation by specifically describing it. Rather, it should lead to a creative tension between the present state (as-is state) and a desired target (to-be state), and in this way serve as a management and motivational tool. Visions are usually formulated at the corporate level (see Sect. 3.6.3) and decomposed to organizational units (e.g., IT) and projects. The key elements of an S-BPM vision for introducing and operating business process management are summarized in Fig. 3.3.

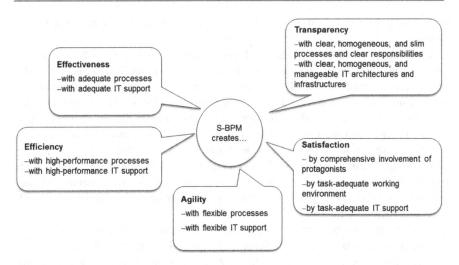

Fig. 3.3 Possible S-BPM vision (Schmidt 2009, p. 7)

With its focus on processes for implementing a strategy and associated IT support, the S-BPM vision is closely related to the overall corporate vision and IT vision. As a result, the management, the organization department, and the IT management can be derived in the role of Governor.

An S-BPM vision needs to be communicated throughout an organization, in order to achieve stakeholder-oriented participation in organizational development processes.

No S-BPM vision, no strategy development—it highlights the different roles required for organizational development in a concerted fashion. Consequently, diversity and complexity can be handled in a constructive way.

3.6.3.2 Development of an S-BPM Strategy

The first step of a strategic controlling process is the development of an S-BPM strategy (strategic process planning)—see Sect. 11.1. In the course of initially formulating the S-BPM strategy, first of all, specific organizational objectives are determined for action fields on the basis of the S-BPM vision (cf. Schmelzer and Sesselmann 2010, p. 231ff). Besides the vision, both impulses from the competitive environment (stimuli from outside), as well as, once S-BPM is implemented, feedback from executing the S-BPM process model (internal impulses) can be incorporated in the sense of a continuous improvement process. The next task is to identify the processes that need to be considered (cf. Becker et al. 2008, p. 123ff). This starts with the representation of the existing and the envisioned value chain. Afterward, existing processes are classified based on a first process map. In this way, processes can be grouped and evaluated with regard to actual and target values.

Under the participation of stakeholders, process groups are ranked and those groups with the highest potential are first selected for further evaluating cost-effectiveness. Hereby, special attention is given to the existing and potential IT support and process automation. The results of this analysis lay the ground for prioritizing the processes that ultimately form the subject matter of BPM. This allows process owners of the so identified processes to proceed with detailed planning in regard to project realization. Based on this prioritization, an economically sound standing roadmap for implementing an S-BPM strategy is created. Just like the vision, strategy and roadmap need to be communicated throughout the organization by all responsible stakeholders, in order to ensure transparency and acceptance (Schmidt 2009, p. 8).

The presented strategic planning process includes use of instruments, such as the Balanced Scorecard (BSC) and Strategy Maps and completes the first step to strategic process controlling. Once the BSC is transformed into scorecards with key performance indicators concerning business processes of an organization or its units, the implementation of the S-BPM strategy can be reviewed within the strategic process monitoring and control.

An analysis checking the discrepancy of target values (to-be values) of performance parameters to those actual values (as-is values) collected periodically (e.g., quarterly) from the current operation allows the identification of strategic gaps and needs for further action (cf. Schmelzer and Sesselmann 2010, p. 231ff). In addition, the assessment of the maturity of processes using respective models can give indications for the further development of the S-BPM strategy (see Sect. 11.2).

Of particular interest is the learning perspective, as it reveals development potential with respect to organizational change, customer structure, and finances. In S-BPM, executives and staff are enabled to generate business processes from their individual perspective. The resulting models can be reflected and further developed as part of a collective learning process. The latter ultimately lead to a modified process map of an organization.

The value chain and the associated derived process classes are mainly influenced by the corporate strategy. Therefore, the outlined approach ensures to a large extent the consistency of the S-BPM vision and strategy with the corporate vision and strategy. Thus, it is likely that in the case of a cost leadership strategy, the process groups moving to the focus of interest differ from those in the case of a differentiation strategy. With the recognition of the importance of IT support and automation in S-BPM, the reference to the IT strategy is also established. S-BPM strategy and vision thus form a connecting link between corporate vision and strategy and IT vision and strategy, and therefore significantly contribute to IT/Business Alignment (see Sect. 3.6.2).

The Governor's role to establish the S-BPM strategy as a framework is taken by corporate management, the organization department, and IT management (cf. S-BPM vision).

3.6.3.3 Development and Promotion of an S-BPM Culture

S-BPM vision and strategy contribute to the development of an S-BPM culture and to its establishment in a sustainable way in an organization. Such a culture is also a result of the S-BPM process model, as well as its critical success factor (Schmidt 2009, p. 9).

For achieving an S-BPM culture, it is indispensable that senior management is committed to process orientation in general, and the massive support of S-BPM projects exists in particular. Without this backing, there is the risk that the sustainable establishment of S-BPM is hindered by more or less strong resistance to change of the organization.

For successful S-BPM, it is necessary to promote the acceptance of managers and employees for S-BPM projects at all levels, and, ideally, to motivate them to participate actively. Appropriate Facilitators are the early, regular, and reflected:

- Increasing awareness of the importance of S-BPM
- Communication of S-BPM vision and strategy
- Information about specific S-BPM projects
- Involvement of affected people and institutions ("making concerned parties to engaged ones")
- Qualification of participants (situational)
- Communication of working results of S-BPM activities ("success stories")

In this way, organizations can develop a culture that provides orientation for staff members and reduces uncertainty and fears of change. An ambience focusing on learning facilitates engaging promoters and especially opponents of S-BPM in a constructive discourse.

Incentives, such as a reward system aligned with results of process execution (e.g., a bonus for the achievement of targets for key performance indicators, such as the average processing time) and a proposal scheme for rewarding suggestions for process-related improvements, can bring about a willingness to change.

3.6.3.4 Development of an S-BPM Governance

S-BPM governance should be interpreted in this context largely in analogy to IT governance, namely as leadership behavior, organizational structures, and rules. These factors ensure that S-BPM supports the corporate strategy and organizational objectives in an optimal way while carefully considering the risks involved. Leadership behavior and organizational structures are primarily represented by the anchoring of S-BPM in the organization. Rules become evident, e.g., by the definition of S-BPM standards.

For instance, before implementing S-BPM projects, a variety of general regulations should be set up and documented in an obligatory standard guide for modeling. This also needs to be communicated as such to become effective (Schmidt 2009, p. 10). Such a standard or style guide should contain:

- Process model: Prescription of a uniform approach (BPM process), e.g., according to the S-BPM-model.

- Modeling principles: Specification of constraints when modeling, such as the Principles of Proper Modeling (PoPM) given in Fig. 3.4 (cf. GoM in Becker et al. 2008, p. 47ff).
- Modeling conventions: Specification of concrete rules to be followed when modeling, e.g., how to use methods and model types, descriptions, layout, etc.
- Specification of a previously carefully selected tool environment for modeling, and other S-BPM activity bundles when needed.

Basic principle	Meaning
Correctness	Correct reproduction of the facts
Systematic structure	Well-defined interface between sub-models
Clearness	Comprehensibility for the adressees, if possible, without a profound knowledge of the method
Comparability	Similar modeling in different projects by compliance of comprehensive convetions
Relevance	Only illustration of facts, which are necessary for the model description
Economy	Appropriate cost-benefit ratio

Fig. 3.4 Principles of Proper Modeling (PoPM)

In practice, convention manuals often include 100 and more pages. Consequently, they may not be accepted by modelers, as they regulate too much or in a far too pedantic way. As we will show later, for subject-oriented modeling only a few conventions are required, since the method can be used by mastering just a few symbols.

The outlined standards need to be periodically reviewed and adjusted if required according to practical experiences. They are handled by organizational departments, which take the Governor role here.

> For S-BPM governance, the principle of systems thinking and acting is essential. In addition to classical economic parameters, organization-specific factors (information infrastructure, task profiles, communication structures, etc.) and their interdependencies have to be taken into account.

3.6.4 Governance, Risk, Compliance Triad (GRC-Triad)

A comprehensive condition for Business Process Management is the so-called Governance, Risk, Compliance Triad. The term expresses the close interdependence of the three aspects and their increasing relevance for running businesses (Klotz and Dorn 2008, p. 7).

In the previous sections, we have detailed governance at the corporate, IT, and S-BPM levels. It has thereby been shown that governance encompasses as a major component the handling of risks and the associated conflict potential, which implies the establishment of a sound standing risk management in organizations. A significant part of business risks stem from the increasing amount of regulations organizations need to follow.

Here, compliance comes into play, aiming to prevent risks from violation of external and internal regulations by ensuring their implementation at the operational level (cf. Klotz and Dorn 2008, p. 5 et seq.). Compliance is not about the apparent obedience to existing laws, but about identifying possible violations of regulations as risks subject to the regime of risk management which need to be encountered with appropriate organizational, technical, and personnel measures (cf. Klotz and Dorn 2008, p. 7). Examples of such measures are the design and implementation of respective processes (such as workflows for approval), the careful nurturing of awareness, the informing and qualifying of staff, and the regular monitoring, control, and documentation of compliance to regulations, including sanctions in case of violation.

As with governance, we can consider IT compliance as a subset of corporate compliance. With such a comprehensive understanding, they both refer not only to compliance with legal regulations, such as the Federal Data Protection Act (BDSG), the Digital Signature Act (SigG), or the Principles of Access to Data and Verifiability of Digital Documents (GDPdU), but also to meet other external regulations, such as contracts and service level agreements or frameworks like the IT Infrastructure Library (ITIL), as well as internal corporate compliance requirements, e.g., self-imposed rule sets such as an IT security policy. The binding effect (commitment) and the risks of noncompliance are higher for external regulations and decrease accordingly when dealing with internal standards (cf. Klotz and Dorn 2008, pp. 8).

The cooperation of corporate compliance and IT compliance can be interpreted as compliance for Business Process Management (BPM compliance). In the context of corporate compliance, i.e., on the business level, it is important to identify compliance-related processes and to formulate respective compliance requirements. S-BPM facilitates meeting these requirements through an appropriate process design, e.g., incorporation of control steps (cf. Schmelzer and Sesselmann 2010, p. 40). The IT compliance then covers the abidance to IT-related regulations through the technology support of business processes. In the development and maintenance of processes, especially the responsible Governor ensures that the requirements are incorporated into the respective processes.

1. Governance–2. Risk–3. Compliance—not vice versa. A livable holistic organizational model cannot emerge from standardization efforts.

3.7   S-BPM for the Integrated Development of an Organization

S-BPM is a methodology that enables integration in multiple ways in an organization. In order to demonstrate this capability, we first consider the business and technical aspect of S-BPM—two dimensions which traditionally allow the term Business Process Management to be grasped (BPM) (cf. Bucher and Winter 2009, p. 6; Becker et al. 2009, p. 3; Schmelzer and Sesselmann 2010, p. 5). The original exclusive economic point of view refers to an integrated management approach for documentation, design, optimization, implementation, control, and further development of management, core, and support processes in organizations. It is intended to meet the needs of stakeholders, especially to satisfy customers and to achieve business objectives.

Moreover, the term BPM in science and industry is also often associated with its technical dimension of IT support of business processes. This ranges from tools for documenting and modeling of processes, to workflow engines for the execution of process instances while using functionalities of application software (such as services of an ERP system), to business intelligence applications to evaluate the performance of processes. Solutions with a high degree of coverage of these aspects are referred to as Business Process Management Systems (BPMS) or, preferably by software vendors as business process management suites. An example of such is the Metasonic Suite, which already covers the modeling and validation of process specifications based on executable models.

S-BPM integrates the business and technical point of view by focusing on business processes from the perspective of all stakeholders. It provides them with a tool, which enables them to express their respective views of these processes effectively and efficiently. S-BPM is a role-centric and communication-centric tool for the development of organizations. Unlike other BPM approaches, it does not put the development of functional processes in the foreground, but rather the parties involved, i.e., the subjects and their interactions. Thus, development is equally enabled on both the organizational and personal level.

The organizational aspect of work does not only come to bear from the technological operational perspective, but rather already when dealing with the respective work profiles, in the context of which stakeholders in the operational business ultimately need to be supported by information technology. In S-BPM, subjects determine the roles of Actors that are relevant to the achievement of organizational objectives. Subsequently, their respective behavior is defined, and synchronized through the exchange of messages when performing tasks.

Unlike many BPM approaches, a model developed with S-BPM is directly executable. This means that in each step of development, models can be processed without further transformation. Thus, for the first time, a coherent development process based on subject-oriented modeling can be established (seamless round-trip engineering). With this approach, modeling and implementation can be directly interconnected.

In addition, the S-BPM process model comprises a procedure that allows the dynamic integration of activity bundles with each other. Going beyond classical life cycle approaches, parallel and branched activities can be triggered—depending on what is currently required according to the business process. Feedback between the activity bundles can occur, which leads to successive transitions, not only forward and backward between business logic states, but also skipping intermediate states.

Finally, S-BPM itself can be described in a subject-oriented way using the available tools. The item to be represented in a model, i.e., the process, can be grasped by using subject–predicate–object descriptors (i.e., modeling), just as the process of developing a process model itself can be described by using subject–predicate–object sequences (see Fig. 3.1). The core is the modeling process, which is embedded in an organization-specific development process based on modeling.

> S-BPM is coherent: It is the stakeholders who are involved in S-BPM-specific interaction, either as Governor, Actor, Expert, or Facilitator. They are the subjects that act (predicate), which leads to changes in organizational processes (objects). Consequently: Always think in complete sentences for S-BPM projects!

References

Becker, J., Mathas, C., Winkelmann, Geschäftsprozessmanagement, Berlin 2009.

Becker, J., Kugeler, M., Rosemann, M. (Hrsg.): Prozessmanagement, 6. Auflage, Berlin 2008.

Bucher, T., Winter, R., Geschäftsprozessmanagement – Einsatz, Weiterentwicklung und Anpassungsmöglichkeiten aus Methodiksicht, HMD 266, S. 5-15.

Fischer, H., Fleischmann, A. und Obermeier, S., Geschäftsprozesse realisieren, Wiesbaden 2006.

Fischermann G., Praxishandbuch Prozessmanagement, ibo Schriftenreihe Band 9, Gießen 2006.

ITGI, IT Governance Institute, IT Governance für Geschäftsführer und Vorstände, 2. Ausgabe 2003, http://www.itgi.org/Template_ITGI. cfm?Section=Recent_Publications&CONTENTID=14529 &TEMPLATE=/ContentManagement/ContentDisplay.cfm, Download am 19.01.2007.

Johannsen, W., Goeken, M., Referenzmodelle für IT-Governance, Heidelberg, 2007.

Klotz, M., Dorn, D., IT-Compliance – Begriff, Umfang und relevante Regelwerke, in: HMD - Praxis der Wirtschaftsinformatik, Heft 263, 2008, S. 5-14.

Meyer 1990. Operations Research – Systemforschung, 3. Auflage, Stuttgart 1990.

Österle, H. und Winter, R., Business Engineering, in: Österle, H. und Winter, R. (Hrsg.), Business Engineering, 2. Auflage, Berlin 2003, S. 3-20.

Regierungskommission Deutscher Corporate Governance Kodex, Deutscher Corporate Governance Kodex in der Fassung vom 26. Mai 2010, http://www.corporate-governance-code. de/ger/download/kodex_2010/D_CorGov_Endfassung_Mai_2010.pdf, Download am 15.02.2011.

Schmelzer, H., Sesselmann, W.: Geschäftsprozessmanagement in der Praxis, 7. Auflage, München 2010.

Schmidt, W., IT-Strategie, in: Hofmann, J. und Schmidt, W. (Hrsg.), Masterkurs IT-Management, Wiesbaden 2010, S. 11-92.

Schmidt, W., IT-Governance, in: Hofmann, J. und Schmidt, W. (Hrsg.), Masterkurs IT-Management, Wiesbaden 2010, S. 355-403.

Schmidt, W., Fleischmann, A. und Gilbert, O., Subjektorientiertes Geschäftsprozessmanagement, HMD – Praxis der Wirtschaftsinformatik, Heft 266, S. 52-62, 2009.

Schmidt, W., Integrierter Business-Process-Management-Zyklus, Arbeitsberichte (Working Papers) der Hochschule Ingolstadt, Heft Nr. 16, 2009

Wittmann, R., Littwin, A., R., Reuter, M. u. Sammer, G., Unternehmensstrategie und Businessplan, Frankfurt 2004.

Subject-Oriented Process Analysis

4

4.1 To Go

What do I need an analysis for? I know the organization here like the back of my hand! I know how it works. Good that my colleagues and I will now also be asked.

We do not want to just accumulate existing facts—our success is not measured in terms of the "number of ring binders" when we gather documents. We rather need to consider our objectives and act in a goal-directed way—where are we headed and what does the effort result in?

Moreover, we do not want to only refer to the knowledge of one specific individual—this is the reason that many process analysis projects fail. We want to involve anybody who can make a contribution to the process.

Therefore, analysis is an overarching process, which possibly needs to involve a larger part of the organization in a suitable manner. Process analysis enables us to proceed in this way, without compromising the overall picture.

A. Fleischmann et al., *Subject-Oriented Business Process Management*,
DOI 10.1007/978-3-642-32392-8_4, © The Author(s) 2012

Process analysis is a central bundle of activities of the S-BPM process model. Once an S-BPM project is started, analysis is paramount. It denotes a purposeful collection and evaluation of relevant process information in preparation for the next steps of the process model. Such process information includes existing descriptions of business processes, current process specifications (e.g., ARIS diagrams), measurements, and analyses of key performance indicators, or other documentation for quality assurance. Process definitions describe specific business processes to achieve organizational goals. We have already presented the major components of process definitions in Sect. 3.2 while introducing the concept of processes in S-BPM.

In case in the analysis for these elements no significant data could be collected or important information is missing, other activity bundles of the integrated S-BPM approach may be affected. In such cases, the analysis has to be repeated for refinement. The unique characteristic of the subject-oriented analysis is its focus on subjects and thus on the process actors. It implements system thinking by using acquired information about business processes to identify roles or actors that serve as reference points for further specification. Therefore, S-BPM differs from conventional BPM. For instance, in ARIS-based BPM, analysis can be performed using a context-free function tree representation (Scheer 1998). In doing so, important questions remain open, e.g., the communication relationships between Actors required for task accomplishment. The respective information needs to be added later on, which causes an increased amount of effort.

The key benefit for organizations when analyzing according to S-BPM is that work performers (Actors) and responsible managers (Governors) can be directly involved in the acquisition and analysis process. They need no special training, since they are assumed to have already mastered the natural language semantics of natural language sentences. Therefore, we can start introducing the tasks the various S-BPM stakeholders need to perform in the course of analysis.

In the following, we detail the various points of reference of subject-oriented process analysis. They represent the context for the analysis methodology explained subsequently.   .

4.2   S-BPM Stakeholders Involved in Process Analysis

The analysis process can be viewed from the perspective of the four specific S-BPM roles. Each of the four roles deals with different tasks.

The guidelines for the individual work performers resulting from process analysis should trigger the adaptation of work processes to human needs and capabilities.

4.2.1   Actors

In a process, usually multiple Actors (work performers) are involved. They analyze which parts of the process are already known and how their interaction can best be represented. The central questions of the Actors are oriented toward standard sentences semantics of natural language. They deal with roles and systems (subjects), actions (predicates), business objects, and the communication between subjects for accomplishing tasks. The Actors of a process also usually know best where deficiencies occur, and how these might be resolved.

4.2.2   Facilitators

A Facilitator analyzes the best possible process to follow in BPM projects. He supports Actors in finding relevant contacts or consulting experts. He handles the communication between the involved parties in the project. In particular, he ensures that the objectives associated with adjusting a process are sufficiently communicated by the Governor, and that their relationship to the objectives of an organization is explained to Actors and Experts.

> Actors should come to a constructive dialog with each other through the Facilitator. Experts can help to bring an external perspective to existing processes, which enables Governors to completely focus on organization-specific developments.

4.2.3   Governors

A Governor ensures that the constraints of an organization are complied to. He takes care that the objectives of a process at hand or a process to be defined are in accordance with the overall goals of an organization. In particular, he influences the performance indicators of a process, how they should be measured, and what targets should be pursued.

> Scoping is always required—in particular for organization-wide S-BPM. By limiting the initial scope to an area that Governors can handle in a transparent way, such as the production unit of an organization, explicit interfaces can be identified which can then be subsequently addressed in their own specific context, such as that of product development.

4.2.4   Experts

Experts are specialists who are either directly or indirectly involved in a process. They have background information that is crucial for the process design. When needed, Experts contribute data, information, and knowledge about the process, reference process models, etc. for analysis. For instance, if within the scope of an analysis the efficiency of a current process is to be measured, appropriate specialists could be brought in. As a general rule, it makes sense to involve external Experts in order to efficiently encounter the tunnel vision often associated with daily routine work.

4.3   Reference Points

After describing the tasks of the S-BPM stakeholders throughout analysis, we are going to highlight the frame of reference for performing process analysis. It includes the following conditions, which we will then describe in more detail:

*   Process analysis is a form of system analysis.
*   Process analysis is a kind of knowledge management.
*   Process analysis includes the analysis of an organization.
*   Process analysis requires stringent procedures.

4.3.1   Systems Theory

The roots of systems theory can be found in biology. In addition, it is now used in many other areas, such as physics, chemistry, sociology, etc. (von Bertalanffy 1969). Systems theory is an interdisciplinary model of knowledge, in which systems are used to describe and explain phenomena of various complexities. A system consists of elements, which refer to each other and interact in such a way that they can be considered a single unit with regard to a specific task, purpose, or meaning. They can be distinguished in this respect from their surrounding environment. As an interdisciplinary field, systems analysis has also found use in many other sciences, including organizational theory (cf. Häfele 1990, Morgan 2002).

In system thinking, causal relationships are replaced by associative ones and, where appropriate, also by circular explanations, and isolated elements become tightly coupled system elements. By systems analysis, the elements of a system with their most important causal relationships can be identified and described. There are not only linear "if-then" chains, but also feedback loops (Krallmann et al. 1999, Simon 2011). The integrated S-BPM process model considers not only fundamental system contexts, such as the implementation of compliance rules in business processes but also dedicated opportunities for feedback. The subject with its outward bound communication relationships stands in the foreground.

Therefore, process analysis is a special form of systems analysis applied to business processes. Elements and relationships can be applied to process management through the interpretation of a process as a set of actors, activities, subprocesses, etc. As discussed in Sect. 3.2, activities or tasks, work performers, materials, and information are essential components of processes. These elements can be related causally. Usually, tasks are linked through successor or predecessor relationships. An activity can be related to a resource through a "used" relation. The relation "executes" defines which actor is responsible for the execution of a certain task. Depending on the type and depth of the process analysis, elements and causal relationships can be designed in different levels of detail. A structuring of the analysis results is required in order to be able to implement them later in a process model.

For instance, if we consider the basic requirements of a modeling language according to Mielke, the element "activity" with its relationships (e.g., the sequence) stands at the center of attention (Mielke and Balzert 2002). They are only secondarily linked to objects, relations, and roles. This is consistent with most traditional BPM approaches. In subject-oriented process analysis, however, the element "subject" including its relations with other subjects is at the center of interest. This allows transparent stakeholder orientation and role-oriented communication flows as opposed to function-oriented sequence specification.

Another aspect of systems analysis is to define a system boundary and the system environment (scoping). Thus, the focus of analysis represents a certain universe of discourse. Process analysis, as a special form of systems analysis, reveals a special feature, since the scope of a process and thus the system boundary is not necessarily identical with the boundary of an organizational structure. Processes can represent cross-organizational work or information flows (Fischer et al. 2006, p. 3f).

Consequently, people (work performers) and IT systems (resources) could be part of processes, even though they are not part of the organization at hand—the system boundary for process management can be a dynamic gray zone (Rosenkranz 2006). For this reason, a process analysis should always include the organizational environment. This means: Stakeholders who are not part of the organizational structure, which is initiating and held responsible for BPM, may be involved in the analysis process. For instance, the paradigm shift in strategic process management of CRM (customer relationship management) includes customers. Customers in fact are not part of the internal organization; however, all the processes need to be aligned to them. In CRM, their knowledge determines the development of products.

Therefore, Actors need a context-sensitive understanding of their duties to successfully accomplish their tasks. This allows structuring the various elements and relations in such a way that subjects of a process can work with them to accomplish their tasks.

4.3.2 Knowledge Management

When performing a process analysis, knowledge of an organization is acquired in a targeted way, namely, by obtaining relevant information about a process

(Gronau et al. 2004). In doing so, we have to differentiate between explicit and tacit knowledge (Krallmann et al. 1999).

Explicit knowledge is already documented information about a process and an organization. The analysis should filter out the information that is relevant for the considered process.

The counterpart of explicit knowledge is tacit knowledge. The latter is not available in documented form. Tacit knowledge is (still) in the minds of work performers. Questions not immediately obvious to outsiders and questions which possibly are even impossible to document in their detailed complexity are: How is a task accomplished in a certain way? Why does it only work in that way? The collection of tacit knowledge and its transformation to explicit knowledge starts with stakeholders directly involved and affected. Surveys in this regard lead to detailed requirements for processes or parts of processes, and to dependencies and communication structures between the involved stakeholders that have previously not been documented. Subject-oriented analysis is focused on the subject, i.e., role-relevant application of tacit knowledge and its documentation.

Knowledge management in S-BPM means first and foremost to identify and localize the knowledge about the processes of an organization (Riempp 2004). An essential factor is the role of Experts acting as knowledge carriers. In addition, the other stakeholders of the S-BPM process model are also knowledge carriers. The identification of Actors through subjects facilitates the documentation of knowledge, since along with the function or activity relationships, actors and responsible stakeholders become transparent in the course of acquiring process-relevant information. When a process is designed from scratch, then usually no stakeholders with appropriate experience, who could be consulted or involved, are available. In this case, it is the task of the Actors to conceive this role and design a communicable behavior specification emphasizing the necessity of its existence.

4.3.3 Organization

To better cope with complex relationships, the traditional concept of "organization" comprises a distinction between structural elements and process elements. This dates back to Nordsieck (1934), Seidel (1972), and Kosiol (1976, p. 32f) and describes two sides of the same object. The organizational structure statically places organizational units at the center of attention, and subtasks, representing the respective objects of process design, are only considered secondarily.

Job descriptions define which tasks are performed by which parts of an organization. Today, IT systems are regarded as part of the organizational structure (Fischermann 2006). They are considered not only as detached material resources, but also as media to convey information "at the right time at the right place." Meanwhile, they are of crucial importance for the accomplishment of tasks.

An organizational structure also represents an identity creating structure of an organization. Each employee can identify himself with his responsibilities and a particular unit (Fischer et al. 2006, Vahr 2009). For many organizations, org charts are still their "business cards" to external partners and their main structural elements to organize their work internally. The business cards of most employees of an organization include their position within the structural organization.

Once the focus is placed on the performance-relevant processes, running in space and time, among the work force, we speak of a flow-oriented or process organization. This constitutes the dynamic view of an organization (Picot et al. 2005). In such organizations, the tasks are at the center of attention, and most importantly, how these tasks are arranged. An essential question is how organizational units are mutually related to accomplish a correct temporal order when executing tasks. Processes are the actual implementation of organizing workflows in practice (Fischer et al. 2006). "The sum of all processes composes the process organization" (Fischermann 2006). Processes can be mapped to workflows by IT support and at least partially automated.

Both points of view of an organization contain valuable information. Hence, always both organizational dimensions should be considered in the context of subject-oriented process analysis. In organization theory, a paradigm shift has occurred in recent years. This is also reflected in organizational research. While in the past organizational charts, job descriptions, etc. have been put to the foreground, today we speak of the "primacy of the process organization" (Gaitanides 1983). It is not an organization's structure that stands in the foreground, but rather processes, also known as "structure follows process" (Fischermann 2006).

The primacy of process organization is emphasized by the rapidly growing need for interdivisional and cross-company collaboration. The generation of organizational value creation through isolated services is decreasing more and more. The division of labor for generating services and products has been extended over the entire globe in many cases (Hirzel et al. 2008). Collaboration can be effectively described through processes and efficiently supported by IT.

However, if the orientation toward the flow of work tasks is predominately one sided, several issues are likely to have to be addressed:

- The responsibility for employees, tasks, goals, and budget is still primarily held by people in the line of the organizational hierarchy. This can lead to conflicting process and organizational goals.
- Stakeholders are identified in an organization primarily by their position in the structural hierarchy, not by processes. In the scope of a process, even employees holding positions in higher levels of the hierarchy are traditionally handling simple tasks, such as approvals. When running processes, the focus is on collaboration and less on the hierarchy. It is difficult for many managers to accept this shift.
- Thinking in terms of processes is generally more difficult than thinking in terms of a familiar static organizational structure (Fischermann 2006).

Process analysis therefore is a special form of organizational analysis. This means, conversely, that it should also take into account the organizational structure in an appropriate way. The processes have to be aligned to the corresponding organization and embedded in existing hierarchical structures. In other words: "In the practical organization of work, the organizational structure is often a requirement, so that the flow follows the limits of the organizational structure, which cannot be changed" (Steinbuch et al. 1997). For these reasons, both organizational views have to converge. Fischermann recommends a process-oriented organizational hierarchy (Fischermann 2006).

In subject-oriented process management, the process can be guided by the organizational hierarchy. Therefore, we also refer to S-BPM as process management oriented toward the static structure of an organization. The S-BPM role of the Governor represents the driver (e.g., management, organization development) for integrating business processes within an organization.

4.4   Choice of Approach

In traditional process analysis, basically two approaches can be followed: top-down and bottom-up (cf. Österle, 1995):

> The predominant pattern of thinking of an organization guides process analysis, either toward a top-down, bottom-up, or middle-out approach (combination of the first two).

The *top-down approach* focuses on the corporate strategy and vision of an organization for the analysis. The so-called FAU-process model (F for "Fuehrung" or Management/A for "Ausfuehrung" or Execution/U for "Unterstuetzung" or Support) identifies three distinct types of processes (Fischermann 2006):

- Management processes are processes for creating a strategy, planning, and control. They may also be referred to as meta-processes for process management, which as such affect other processes, in particular execution and support processes.
- Execution processes (core processes and value-adding processes) describe the actual operational processes. Traditionally, they are aligned to the production or supply of services. Modern CRM strategies recommend the alignment to the customer. Each process should lead to a measurable value for customers. According to Hammer and Champy (1996), there should be no more than ten core processes in any organization.
- Support processes (auxiliary processes) are required to provide the resources needed for the management and execution processes. These include for instance staff management, financial management, or IT management.

Representatives of each type of process at the top level are progressively detailed and structured in the top-down approach. Process analysis is correspondingly understood as a stepwise refinement of the processes of a coarse representation to a more detailed description level (Gaitanides 1983). This step can be iterated any number of times, right down to the description of individual actions. In associated literature, several recommendations for decomposing business processes can be found. For instance, Buchner et al. (1999) distinguish between corporate processes, business processes, subprocesses, workflows, partial workflow, subworkflows, and activities.

A simpler variant (Fischermann 2006) decomposes business processes into subprocesses and tasks of different degrees. Both of the above-mentioned approaches to detailing a process leave open at what level of detail processes need to be initially specified before starting refinements, and how to design the interface between different levels of detail. Different stakeholders will approach this issue in different ways. In practice, therefore, systematic guidelines seem difficult. The analyst and the stakeholders involved in the collection and evaluation of data may interpret differently for each case at what level of abstraction a process needs to be positioned. Certification, software development, or process cost accounting, etc. have different objectives and subjective assessments with regard to the process level. Taking their respective perspectives may lead to specific abstraction levels. It is the duty of the Governor to establish a common view among those involved in the process development.

The advantage of top-down analysis is that the process goals are easy to anchor in the organization's objectives, as they represent the starting point of analysis.

In the *bottom-up approach*, however, the process is constructed from the "base" upwards. The starting point is the individual actions that are linked together to form processes and procedures. The survey could start by identifying elementary actions involved in task accomplishment followed by composing those actions to a process specification. The disadvantage of the bottom-up approach is the assumption that each action is also required on its own. Only in case of an optimization, individual steps can be combined or omitted. Moreover, in this approach to analysis, the objective of a process could get lost in the details. The advantage still, however, is that the process is successively constructed from detailed factual steps.

The advantage of a bottom-up approach when involving operative stakeholders concerns the initial selection of an abstraction level, which corresponds to their perception. Analysis will consequently lead to collecting and describing only those processes that match the perceived reality. Another advantage of this approach is that participative organizational learning is triggered, once individual perspectives on events can be communicated effectively (cf. Stary and Fleischmann et al. 2011).

The subject-oriented analysis combines the advantages of the top-down and bottom-up approach. It starts with analyzing the active subject. According to the particular objective, either a top-down analysis is required, namely when identifying how subjects communicate with each other, or a bottom-up analysis is more appropriate, when considering certain operations in detail. Both approaches are not contradictory and can even be combined. In case it is required to represent certain aspects in detail, the respective subject is detailed accordingly, while other subjects such as the customer can remain abstract.

4.5   Determine the Context of a Process

Before a process can be described in detail, the goal of process analysis needs to be formulated. In order to do so, fundamental information about the process context needs to be obtained, including, e.g., a unique process name and internal and external conditions influencing process execution. These are detailed in the following.

4.5.1   Target of Analysis

An important prerequisite for a successful survey and evaluation of processes is to determine the objective to be achieved when performing the analysis. It is not sufficient to collect just any type of information about the process, especially if the analysis phase is the result of previous step of the S-BPM process model. In this case, the analysis has a very concrete target. For instance, a need for optimization has been identified and needs to be detailed. This could require obtaining additional information, since previously collected information from existing analysis may not be sufficient.

4.5.2   Initial Information

In order to describe a process, the following fundamental information needs to be acquired:

- *Process name*. The process needs to have a unique name in the organization. The analysis should determine whether the same process is used in another context with a different name. If so, the "twin process" needs to be included in the analysis.
  Example: The accompanying sample process handling a business trip request is termed "business trip application."
- *Type of process*. In Sect. 4.4, fundamental process types have been described. For each process, it has to be determined whether it is a management, execution, or support process.
  Example: The process "business trip application" is a support process of an organization; it usually does not contribute to the value creation of the organization.
- *Process objective*. Each process has one or more targets that should be achieved for the organization as a result of its implementation. These targets play an important role in determining appropriate metrics and approaches to optimization.
  Example: The process "business trip application" should allow carrying out a coordinated and unified travel preparation for all employees.

- *Objective of the S-BPM project.* The client (Governor) has different requirements on an S-BPM project. In general, participants or managers expect either improvement in the efficiency or effectiveness of processes.
  Example: The Governor mainly expects from the process "business trip application" an improvement in effectiveness, because the error rate so far has been quite high.
- *Process metrics.* Metrics of a process usually are defined very early—in this context, they are termed KPIs (key performance indicators) (see Sect. 11.4.2).
  Example: In the process "business trip application," a KPI is the processing time. If it is too high, no short-term travels can be approved.
- *Process owner.* The Governor assigns the responsibility for a process to a specific person (termed process owner). The process owner himself usually has a Governor role. He is responsible for accepting the process model and is in charge of its implementation. During operation, process change requests must be approved by the process owner. He takes care of regular monitoring of the process and its optimization, if necessary.
  Example: For the process "business trip application," the department head of HR (human resources) takes the role of process owner and Governor.
- *Existing process models.* It needs to be checked whether the process has already been (partly) modeled with a tool (e.g., ARIS), as this may influence the modeling path—existing process descriptions might possibly be reused.
  Example: The process "business trip application" has not yet been modeled.
- *Supporting IT systems.* It needs to be documented whether IT tools for process execution are already in use.
  Example: For the process "business trip application," an Excel spreadsheet was developed in which the personnel department documented all business trips so far.
- *Super/subordinate process.* Does the process need to be considered in context with other processes?
  Example: The process "business trip application" is closely related to the processes "booking" and "absence management."
- *Process map.* In a process map, a rough overview of the relationships of the process to other processes and the organization is represented. According to Schmelzer et al. (2010), relationships with customers and partners need to be included.
  Example: Figure 4.1 shows how the "business trip application" is embodied into the process map of an organization.

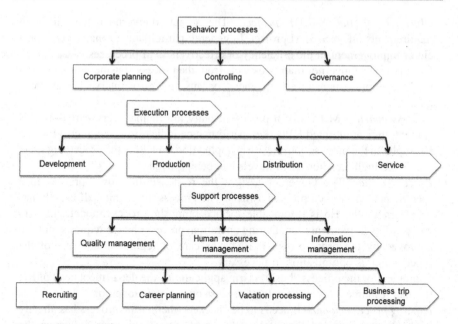

Fig. 4.1 Example of a process map including the "business trip application"

- *Maturity*. In a first estimate, the maturity of the process can be determined. Well-known approaches are the Object Management Group's Business Process Maturity Model (BPMM) and the Process Assessment Models for Business Processes (PAB) and Enterprises (PAE), which are based on the model of the European Foundation for Quality Management (EFQM) (cf. Hogrebe and Nüttgens 2009; OMG 2008; Schmelzer et al. 2010, pp. 288ff). Figure 4.2 exemplifies the maturity levels of BPMM.

Level 1: Initial — wherein business processes are performed in inconsistent sometimes ad hoc ways with results that are difficult to predict.

Level 2: Managed — wherein management stabilizes the work within local work units to ensure that it can be performed in a repeatable way that satisfies the workgroup's primary commitments. However, work units performing similar tasks may use different procedures.

Level 3: Standardized — wherein common, standard processes are synthesized from best practices identified in the work groups and tailoring guidelines are provided for supporting different business needs. Standard processes provide an economy of scale and a foundation for learning from common measures and experience.

Level 4: Predictable — wherein the capabilities enabled by standard processes are exploited and provided back into the work units. Process performance is managed statistically throughout the workflow to understand and control variation so that process outcomes can be predicted from intermediate states.

Level 5: Innovating — wherein both proactive and opportunistic improvement actions seek innovations that can close gaps between the organization's current capability and the capability required to achieve its business objectives.

Fig. 4.2 Maturity levels of BPMM (OMG 2008)

Example: The process of handling business trip requests is already implemented in most companies. The employees largely follow the same principles when applying for business trips. They can find instructions for submitting a request for business trips in the organization's intranet. However, these are not obligatory and leave many options open. According to OMG's level model, the process can be assigned to level 2 (managed).

4.5.3   Internal Constraints

Internal constraints of the analysis are internal organizational factors, which influence the course of survey and evaluation (see Sect. 3.6).

- *S-BPM strategy*. An S-BPM strategy, which is derived from the business strategy, is a set of concepts and standards provided by top management which describe how processes are managed in the organization (see Sect. 3.6.3.2).
  Example: All standard administrative processes have to be unified and supported with a common tool. This requirement also forces the examination of the "business trip application" process within the scope of an S-BPM project.
- *S-BPM culture*. This reflects how an organization informally handles process orientation (see Sect. 3.6.3.3).
  Example: It is common practice to assign the management of processes to external consultants. The resulting costs can be justified since the development of a common solution usually takes a long time. The employees are accustomed to participate actively in changes. Hence, targets cannot always be achieved in a timely manner. The process "business trip application" is therefore initially investigated by a neutral party.
- *S-BPM Governance*. This is understood as a control of how processes are to be implemented in an organization (see Sect. 3.6.3.4).
  Example: The design of the process "business trip application" follows the process model of S-BPM.
- *Budget/Household*. An assessment of the current financial situation is crucial. In times of scarce financial and human resources, a complete reengineering of many processes may not be appropriate. In this case, emphasis is likely to be put on a cost-effective optimization.
  Example: In the budget plan, a budget of 25,000 Euros was allocated to the process "business trip application."
- *Projects*. As part of multiproject management, it needs to be checked whether other projects are in progress which may affect the S-BPM project directly or indirectly. The process is possibly already under investigation in another project. In this case, synergy effects could be used.
  Example: The company is currently introducing an ERP system. However, this has no functionality to implement the "business trip application" process.

4.5.4   External Constraints

The procedure to follow for process analysis concerns the context of the subject matter at hand (Sect. 4.3.1). In order to recognize this context, the external conditions of the process have to be considered.

- *Market situation.* There may be the need to clarify in how far the described process is influenced by the situation on the market.
  Example: Due to the strong market growth in Eastern Europe, the sales department is intensifying its activities in this region. For this purpose, the travel budget has been increased by 50 %. It can be assumed that this will lead to a respective increase in applications for business travels.
- *Competitors.* Especially for customer processes, the competitors' process should be investigated as far as possible in order to check whether possible business advantages and disadvantages can be derived. A typical competitive advantage would be offering a faster, more transparent, and more customer-oriented process than competitors.
  Example: The travel expenses of the consultants of the organization are added to the customer rates. It is known that one of the competitors handles this in a failure-prone way, as the billings are apparently arbitrary and not comparable. Setting up the "business trip application" process should ensure that business trip requests are handled in a uniform way. This could be a competitive advantage.

> Learn from the best! Do you know why your competitors outperform you? Do you know what constitutes the competition in your market segment? If not, you should reflect the frame of reference for your market segment!

4.6   Process Descriptions in Natural Language

As mentioned in Chap. 2, a process can be described using major elements of natural language—subject, predicate, and object. The objective of analysis is to work out this set of elements from available information (Buchner et al. 1999, p. 84f). Analogous to the questions on the sentence building blocks ("Who or what?"), there are three fundamental questions, as shown in Fig. 4.3.

Subject view	Predicate view	Object view
Who acts?	What does the subject?	What edits the subject?

Fig. 4.3 Elements of sentences

Below, we describe the procedure to follow for subject-oriented process analysis based on these questions.

4.6.1 Identification of Subjects

Point of origin and center of interest of subject-oriented analysis is the subject with the question: "Who is acting?" In a process, subjects are abstract actors, and they represent specific roles. In this way, a subject is independent of actual people.

Essential questions:

- Who (or actually, what role) is active in the process?
- Who is passively involved in the process (e.g., as a source of information)?
- Who has to communicate, and with whom?
- Which organizational units are involved?

Result. The names of the identified subjects are documented together with a brief description. The subject name should be a unique and generally accepted name of a role in the organization. In case the name has been used multiple times or exists in several variations, a naming convention needs to be determined.

Example: The subject "travel office" is used in several contexts. There is a unit for domestic travel and another for foreign travel.

> The reluctance of stakeholders to model processes can be eliminated by teaching them to reflect their assertions within the framework of communication processes by using complete natural language sentences. This could even lead to the establishment of a novel communication culture.

4.6.2 Identification of Activities

After identifying the subjects, their activities need to be determined. In the context of subject orientation, an activity is defined as behavior. This stresses the fact that an activity never occurs by itself; there is always an actor: the subject. Hereby, two types of behavior are distinguished: Either the subject communicates with other subjects, or it performs its own tasks, possibly with the help of Business Objects, which are specified in the third step.

Essential questions:

- With whom does the subject communicate?

  - From whom does the subject receive information?
  - To whom does the subject send information?
- Which activities does the subject perform by himself?

  - What tasks does the job description of the subject contain?
  - In which sequence are these tasks being accomplished?
  - Do these tasks depend on other events?
  - Are there specific waiting periods?
  - What other prerequisites for running the activities must be met?

Again, the natural language serves as a guideline for the analysis. The dative is usually used to describe communication partners ("the subject x passes the document to subject y"), and the accusative to describe one's own actions ("the subject x works on the task").

Result. The subject descriptions are supplemented by the respective behavior descriptions.

Quantitative and qualitative assessment: There may be a demand to measure the behavior. In this case, in the analysis certain key figures need to be defined (see Sect. 11.4):

- Process execution metrics (performance parameters): In view of later process calculations, it can be useful to determine performance parameters early. As such, a minimum or maximum duration can be determined for an action.
- Qualitative requirements for an activity: Instructions need to be specified, such as "compliance to quality standards according to ISO 9000 has to be assured," or "requirements according to process manual must be adhered to," etc.

4.6.3 Identification of Business Objects

Once the subjects and their behavior have been identified, in the third step, the tools, objects, or also products that are handled by the subject, used, or passed on to others have to be specified. Business objects are all objects or tools a subject needs to execute a process. They can be both: tangible or intangible (Allee 2002). They usually refer to actions for communication and the subject's own individual activities.

Essential questions:

- Are physical or electronic documents or forms created, processed, or forwarded in the process?
- How are these structured?
- Which elements do they contain, and what is their structure and format?
- Are there physical or electronic documents being used for completing the process?
- What IT support, such as through a content management system or transactions of an ERP system, is provided?
- What input masks are used in the process?
- What data is used hereby, in terms of reading or writing information?
- What role does information from the Internet play for handling the process?

Result. The result is a collection of materials, such as a list of documents, electronic forms, data entry screens of applications being used, as well as data record and data element descriptions, etc.

Who performs what, using what, and when? W-questions can help to attain complete natural language sentences.

4.6.4 Example

As a result of the analysis, a first documentation in natural language of the "business trip application" process is given in Fig. 4.4.

When it's necessary for an employee to do a business trip they fill in a business trip request.
He then collects the following data:

- Name and personnel number of the employee
- Travel destination
- Aim of the trip
- Date/time of the outward trip and return trip
- Favoured means of transport
- Request for the necessary accommodation
- Advice to other trip members
- Date and signature

He presents the business trip request (Word document) to his manager, who initials it and either gives it back to the employee in case of a rejection, or passes it to the travel office. They book the hotel and the transportation and the tickets are shipped to the employee.

Subject view	Predicate view	Object view
Who acts?	What is done?	What is edited?
•Employee •Manager •Travel office	•Present •Initial •Give it back •Pass it •book •Ship it	•Business trip request (with fields) •Hotel •Means of transport •Ticket

Fig. 4.4 Working out the elements of sentences in the analysis using the example of the "business trip application"

4.6.5 Documentation Guidelines

When documenting requirements in natural language, the following guidelines may help to describe these more accurately (cf. Pohl et al. 2009, Dori 2004):

- *Do not use passive voice.* Processes are often described using passive voice. In these cases, the subject is missing; it is no longer known who is actually responsible for an action. Instead, sentences should be written in active form, or passive sentences should be extended with adverbial enhancements.
  Example: "Then, the data is entered into the system." Better: "The clerk then enters the data using the "personal data" form of the human resource management system."
- *Do not nominalize predicates.* Predicates used as nouns often conceal relevant information. An associated resolution and a more detailed explanation are often helpful.
  Example: "(. . .) Then the forwarding of the "business trip application" is done." Better: "The employee forwards his "business trip application" as an e-mail attachment to his manager."
- *Do not use universal quantifiers.* Universal quantifiers do not reflect requirements accurately. It is better to provide concrete details.

Example: "In general, the application is completed by doing so." Better: "By filing the application form, the process enters the state "temporarily closed." There, it remains until the end of the 4-week objection period. In case an objection comes up during this period, the status is set to "in progress," otherwise to "completed.""

- *Fully specify conditions*. Conditions that are relevant for decision making must be clearly formulated.
  Example: "If all the necessary inputs are provided, the process can be completed."
  Better: "The process can be completed once the travel office has entered the following data:

  - First name and last name
  - A syntactically correct personal identification number which was verified using the last name
  - A start date and end date for the travel in which the end date is later than or equal to the start date, and taking into consideration that the travel data entry may not occur earlier than three months prior to departure"

4.6.6 Elicitation and Documentation of Implicit Knowledge

The above-detailed procedure is applicable to the collection of explicit knowledge, which is available in existing process manuals, forms, reports, software manuals, and other documents. Tacit knowledge is not documented; however, it is in the minds of the knowledge holders, who should therefore participate in the documentation process. Organizational developers design approaches for the transformation of implicit knowledge into explicit knowledge. Some conventional methods for transformation are given below:

- *Questioning techniques*. A standardized questionnaire, a survey on knowledge, or interviews with predefined questions allows the collection of a variety of information in the same form. The advantage here is the target specific data collection. Stakeholders are no longer tempted to provide irrelevant information. The disadvantage of this approach is the fact that because of the specific formulation of the questions, certain results are predetermined, or respectively, certain aspects are excluded. This can be partially overcome through the inclusion of open questions.
- *Creativity techniques*. Various methods, such as the well-known brainstorming, allow accumulating valuable knowledge in the course of analysis. An interesting approach is the so-called six-hat-thinking (de Bono 2006). Each stakeholder has to play six different roles and should try to describe these roles from their individual perspectives. This allows the widening of potentially limited subjective views. Other well-known creativity techniques, which can be used for analysis, are mind-mapping, the 6-3-5 method, the morphological box, the stimulus word analysis, or the Osborne checklist (cf. Backerra et al. 2007).
- *Observation techniques*. In cases in which collaboration with stakeholders is difficult due to cost or time constraints, the analyzer can himself observe.

However, this should be done using an appropriate technique; otherwise, the analysis runs the risk of delivering an individual target concept without a sound absorbing of relevant knowledge. An effective method for the latter is "apprenticing". The analyzer learns the tasks of a stakeholder involved in the process, runs these tasks himself, and captures his associated experience. This technique however will only work with manageable units of work, which do not require additional training, as needed for expert activities.

The results are usually documented in natural language.

> Do not collect data for the sake of collecting. A strategy aimed at the target reflection should guide the collection of data for analysis.

4.7 Evaluate and Decide

At the end of an analysis, a preliminary assessment has to be done. An analysis is not a mere collection of data, but rather clearly reveals the following:

- Which results are well structured, and which are confusing and require clarification?
- Which subjects have a clearly described field of operation, and which subject descriptions lead to the impression that not everything was documented, although this would be a requirement for achieving the objectives (e.g., workflow definition)?
- Which phases of the process most likely need support, and which do not?

These observations have to be documented conclusively, in addition to the process constraints and the language-oriented analysis.

Finally, the Facilitator needs to clarify how to proceed. The determination of the maturity level can help to identify further steps along the path of the S-BPM process model.

The analysis is considered complete as soon as sufficient material could be collected, structured, and evaluated according to the original objective, so that further S-BPM bundles of activities can be processed.

References

Allee, V., The Future of Knowledge - Increasing Prosperity Through Value Networks, Butterworth Heineman, New York 2002.
Backerra, H., Malorny, C., Schwarz, W., Kreativitätstechniken - kreative Prozesse anstoßen, Innovationen fördern, 3rd edition, München 2007.
von Bertalanffy, L., General System Theory, New York 1969
Buchner, D., Hofmann, U., Magnus, S., Prozess-Power, Wiesbaden 1999.
De Bono E., Six Thinking Hat, London 2006.

Dori D., System Model Acquisition from requirements text, in: BPM Conference 2004, Potsdam 2004.

Fischer H., Fleischmann A., Obermeier S., Geschäftsprozesse realisieren, Wiesbaden 2006.

Fischermann G., Praxishandbuch Prozessmanagement, ibo Schriftenreihe Band 9, Gießen 2006.

Gaitanides, M., Prozessorganisation. Entwicklung, Ansätze und Programme prozessorientierter Organisationsgestaltung, München 1983.

Gronau N., Weber E., Management of knowledge intensive business processes in: BPM Conference 2004, Potsdam 2004.

Häfele W., Systemische Organisationsentwicklung, Frankfurt 1990.

Hammer M., Champy J., Business Reengineering. 6th edition, Frankfurt am Main 1996.

Hirzel, M., Kühn, F., Gaida, I., Prozessmanagement in der Praxis, Wiesbaden 2008.

Hogrebe, F., Nüttgens, M., Business Process Maturity Model (BPMM): Konzeption, Anwendung und Nutzenpotenziale, HMD – Praxis der Wirtschaftsinformatik, Vol. 266, 2009, pp. 17-25

Kosiol E., Organisation der Unternehmung, 2nd edition, Wiesbaden 1976.

Krallmann H., Frank H., Gronau N., Systemanalyse im Unternehmen, München 1999.

Mielke, K., Balzert, H. (Hrsg.), Geschäftsprozesse - UML - Modellierung und Anwendungsgenerierung, Heidelberg, 2002.

Morgan, G., Bilder der Organisation, Stuttgart 2002.

Nordsieck, F., Grundlagen der Organisationslehre, Stuttgart 1934.

Object Management Group, Business Process Maturity Model (BPMM), Version 1.0, http://www.omg.org/spec/BPMM/1.0, Download on 13.07.2010. 2008

Österle H., Prozessanalytik, Oldenburg-Verlag, München 1995.

Picot A., Dietl H., Franck E., Organisation, eine ökonomische Perspektive, Stuttgart 2005.

Pohl K., Rupp C., Basiswissen Requirements Engineering, Heidelberg 2009.

Riempp G., Integrierte Wissensmanagementsysteme, Berlin 2004.

Rosenkranz, F., Geschäftsprozesse, Springer, Berlin 2006.

Scheer A.-W., ARIS – Modellierungsmethoden, Metamodelle, Anwendungen, Berlin 1998.

Seidel K., Betriebsorganisation, Berlin 1972.

Schmelzer, H., Sesselmann, W., Geschäftsprozessmanagement in der Praxis, 7th edition, München 2010.

Simon, F., Einführung in Systemtheorie und Konstruktivismus, 5th edition, Heidelberg 2011.

Stary, Ch., Fleischmann, A., Evidence-based Interactive Management of Change, in: Knowledge Management & E-Learning, 2011.

Steinbuch, P., Organisation, Ludwigshafen 1997.

Vahr, D., Organisation, Stuttgart 2009.

Modeling Processes in a Subject-Oriented Way

5

5.1 To Go

Our processes are sometimes quite complicated. I would like for this high complexity to actually get implemented, and for everything to nevertheless remain well structured. As simple as possible, but not simpler, as Albert Einstein once said.

If we want to solve complex problems, we need to look for proper structuring possibilities. The best case would be to have just a handful of symbols to describe the process structure and the dynamics. It would also help if we could use a small number of additional complementary symbols to represent constantly recurring behavior sequences in a compact and structured way.

Everybody should be able to understand the basic constructs and these should be based on what we do. What are we really doing? We communicate with colleagues to exchange information and synchronize tasks, and we use the information or things which we receive from others to do something.

Yes, this is exactly the type of reality that we find in processes. We can capture this perceived reality through models. Such process models describe who is communicating with whom, and how stakeholders interact.

A. Fleischmann et al., *Subject-Oriented Business Process Management*,
DOI 10.1007/978-3-642-32392-8_5, © The Author(s) 2012

In the following, we will discuss the S-BPM bundle of modeling activities in detail.

As the distinction between design time and runtime of models is essential to the understanding of modeling, we first distinguish between models and instances. Then, we explain what role S-BPM stakeholders play in the course of modeling. Subsequently, the individual modeling constructs are described. We distinguish here between basic and extension constructs.

Using basic constructs, processes can be described completely from a subject-oriented perspective. However, for the compact and concise representation of complex affairs of humanly perceived reality, the subject-oriented method has been extended with corresponding constructs. These allow a much shorter and more transparent representation (notation) of certain constellations in processes. These constructs are not fundamental extensions enriching the expressiveness of the S-BPM specification language, but rather merely a means of simplifying the notation to handle complex cases, as each extension can be expressed completely using the basic constructs. The extension constructs result from practical experiences with the subject-oriented approach. While continuing S-BPM practice, it may be useful to add other constructs as well. However, such extensions have always to be traceable to basic constructs.

5.2   Process Models and Process Instances

In business process management, there is a distinction between process models and process instances. Subject-oriented process models describe the behavior of parties involved in business transactions, in particular, which activities are performed by whom to yield a result of value. Such models represent generalized situations, in particular, of how a business transaction is managed and which tasks need to be accomplished. Subjects are abstract resources, which represent active agents in a process.

For instance, a process model describing the request for a business trip contains the subjects involved, what the people responsible for those subjects do and in what order, and how they communicate to achieve a result.

However, a process instance is a concrete occurrence of the process described by the model. It is created when a transaction is actually triggered. For example, a process instance is initiated in the case of the business trip application when an employee, e.g., Mr. Schulz, submits a respective request.

Process instances contain concrete data: actors, activities, and affected business objects, as well as messages that are exchanged between actors for accomplishing a task. All of these are described in abstract form in process models.

A process model is created independently of specific organizational units or actors. Similarly, the model is independent of the tools or application programs that are available to execute the process. Thus, a business trip application may be submitted by any employee of an organization. The activities to be carried out are usually the same for all: they are performed in the roles/subjects "employee" (applicant), "manager" (approver), and "travel office" (clerk). In addition, different IT support for the same process could be used. A central organization could manage business trip requests with an SAP system, while in remote offices homegrown applications could be used.

A process model is therefore implemented on the one hand several times in the organization and on the other hand possibly in different computing environments. Although this complicates the aim of many organizations to achieve standardization and homogenization, it corresponds to reality, since heterogeneous organizational and system landscapes, which have either grown historically or are the result of corporate mergers often, have to be taken into consideration. A process model should therefore be largely independent of these environmental conditions.

The initiation of process instances can be done in different ways. In a first variant, a user creates an instance by interacting with an IT system. For example, employee Schulz creates a business trip request because he needs to visit a client. This process instance is executed in accordance with the process model and with the help of the specific people and respective tools assigned while embedding the process model into the organizational and IT environment. A second variant is the instantiation according to time constraints. For example, every Thursday a business trip request is automatically generated for a regular meeting in the branch office. A third possibility is the instantiation as a result of certain constellations of data. For instance, if the negative account balance of a checking account exceeds the associated overdraft line of credit for this account, an appropriate handling process is instantiated. Or in another example, the trigger could be a certain stock price: if the value falls below a certain mark and a bank customer is assigned to a certain risk class, a process is automatically initiated to respond to this situation. This is realized by a so-called complex event processing system.

In the following, we introduce the S-BPM-conform description of models. In subsequent chapters, we discuss the embedding into the organizational and IT environment of an organization, as well as the formation and execution of process instances of models.

5.3 Modeling Procedure

A subject-oriented process model describes, in contrast to existing approaches to BPM modeling, business processes primarily from the perspective of communicating actors or systems. It captures which tasks of a business process have to be performed by whom using which tools, what result is produced in doing so, and for whom the result is intended.

A process model is considered a basic pattern that enables generating process instances for specific situations. A model of the process "business trip application" captures how the process basically works, while an instance of the process, e.g., Mr. Schulz's application for a business trip, reflects the actual execution of his specific trip request, pursuant to the process model.

When modeling according to the subject-oriented approach, subjects are in the center of attention. They represent participating actors in a process. The modeling procedure essentially is a sequence of the following steps in which the associated level of detail increases moving forward:

- Identification of processes in an organization: The result is a process map with the processes and their mutual relationships.
- Specification of the communication structure: Based on the identification of the subjects and their interactions, in this step the communication structure of a business process is specified including the messages exchanged between the subjects.
- Specification of the behavior of the subjects involved in the process: The steps for accomplishing individual tasks of the subjects and the rules to follow thereby are specified.
- Description of the information all subjects involved in the process edit locally and mutually exchange via messages.

Actually, an organization is an ongoing process, a continuous chain of communication, regardless of whether both partners are coordinated in time or not (i.e., interacting synchronously or asynchronously).

Since the identification of processes and their constituent elements have already been discussed in the context of subject-oriented process analysis (see Chap. 4), we will detail the procedure from step 2 onwards in the following. The model constructs used for modeling are exemplified in the process "business trip application" of an organization.

This chapter reveals the fundamental constructs of S-BPM, namely subjects, their interactions via messages, their behavior, and the business objects they handle and exchange via messages. For each of the constructs, a diagrammatic symbol is available. This set of basic constructs is sufficient to model settings observed in perceived reality.

5.4   S-BPM Modeling Stakeholders

5.4.1   To Go

May I remind you that every endeavor requires specific roles. Hence, I see it as my duty to make you familiar with the various hats stakeholders are wearing when performing S-BPM activities. The roles help to clarify responsibilities. Each person is assigned to a role or receives a corresponding sticker.

An old story, in the end there is chaos anyway.

Thanks to de Bono, we know that four hats are sufficient for a balanced procedure.

Alongside myself as Governor, the Facilitator will interact with Experts and Actors in S-BPM.

I have my doubts whether the job will be easier then.

Yes and No, on the one hand, all stakeholders wear only one hat at a certain point in time. But when they try to simultaneously wear more than one hat, we need intervention and clarification. This actually depends on the state of affairs as reflected by the Facilitator. This explains his function quite well.

... I wish it would be that easy for me!

In principle, it is that easy: Actors are the key figures. Their communication behavior determines the success of the business of an organization. Without them, an S-BPM project cannot be legitimized.

If we need special methods to represent knowledge, or rather require domain-specific information, experts can help us. With their cooperation, we can pursue the goal of an organization following S-BPM.

Various stakeholders are involved with different levels of intensity in the activity bundle "modeling", as already indicated in the previous section. In the following, we detail their tasks along the various activities.

5.4.2   Governors

The Governors (drivers and managers) determine the constraints for a process, and thus the rules for creating and maintaining process models. The Governors determine above all the process scope stakeholders need to consider in the project, and which methodology and tools they should use.

Specifications of the scope for modeling include process boundaries, i.e., how a process (domain) is distinct to others, and the representational structure, namely in which subprocesses a process should be decomposed. In addition, it should be specified which results from a previous activity bundle (e.g., analysis or monitoring) should be mainly addressed when revising or rebuilding a model. This ultimately represents a prioritization.

Finally, a Governor decides, whether and when a model is complete and should be passed on to the activity bundle "validation" or another one.

Consequently, Governors set standards for different aspects of modeling. Thus, for the scope, depending on the importance of the process, top management or middle management takes responsibility, while the method and tool guidelines often stem from the Organization Department. Affected stakeholders traditionally encounter standards set by other bodies with mixed feelings, and with different, often insufficient levels of acceptance. Therefore, in particular with regard to rules which have been defined by the executive board level, but for which this in itself is not enough to grant them a strong binding effect, at least the moral support from top management is required to increase acceptance.

5.4.3   Actors

The Actors (work performers) are the active agents in the process. They can either be people in specific roles or machines that perform the individual actions in the respective processes and process instances. Process descriptions are essential for Actors because they indicate their behavior in the process or in its sub processes, i.e., what activities they perform and when.

S-BPM enables the Actors to create this description, within the guidelines specified by the Governor, themselves, and thus to actively design the development of the respective processes. Since, in principle, each employee of an organization is involved in at least one process as an Actor, this holds for every member of the organization. The behavioral specification for an Actor in a process corresponds to his subject description. Hence, in modeling, all directly and indirectly involved stakeholders, representing the process as such, have to be incorporated. They usually know well, what they have to do in a process, when they have to do it and in what order, and also how they can perform their work tasks effectively and efficiently. The Actors also know with whom they need to communicate during the execution of a process instance, and what data they need to exchange to enable a smooth process flow.

If necessary, the Actors or the Facilitator ask Experts to assist in coordination and modeling.

No Actors—no process description. S-BPM models should be semantically correct—models should reflect the work for each stakeholder in a coherent way.

5.4.4   Experts

An Expert (specialist) supports the Governor, Actor, and Facilitator with methodological and technical knowledge (see Sect. 9.4.3). Experts are consulted on specific
technical or functional issues to introduce effective and efficient solutions. By
selecting and using appropriate methods, they can help to find solutions to
problems.

Experts can assist Governors in the formulation of modeling requirements, such
as convention manuals. On request of a Facilitator, Experts can also perform
method and tool trainings to qualify Actors.

Experts can also help Actors with modeling of processes, for instance by using
reference process models. In such cases, the experience of an Expert can help to
describe specific task sequences in a transparent and understandable way and to
ensure compliant modeling.

The addressed expert competence in modeling and tool handling is often
concentrated in the organization department of an organization.

Finally, the implementation of processes or parts of processes often requires the
help of IT Experts.

5.4.5   Facilitators

Facilitators (guide during development) coordinate the various tasks within the
activity bundle of modeling. This means they manage the communication between
the Governor, Actors, and the Experts. They ensure that the Governor provides the
required modeling guidelines in time, and that all Actors understand them.

If necessary, the Facilitator identifies the appropriate Experts for specific tasks
and then puts in a request for their support, e.g., a tool specialist might be requested
for solving a problem with the modeling tool.

The Facilitator ensures that the Actors' communicate with their colleagues and
that they coordinate their activities in the course of modeling. The Facilitator also
checks repeatedly by himself, or with the help of Experts, whether a model meets
the requirements of the Governor, and whether the requirements resulting from a
previous activity bundle are incorporated. Ambiguities are clarified together with
responsible Governors and involved Actors.

Together with the Governors of the organizational development, the Facilitator
guides the transition from modeling to validation, and thus initiates the subsequent
activity bundle. Facilitators mostly belong to the organization department or the
middle management and have temporarily taken on the function of a project
manager for a process change project. They may be responsible for a complete
process change or be appointed only for a particular activity, such as the modeling
bundle. In this case, the role of a person as Facilitator is completed with the
transition to validation. Such a scenario is especially common in modeling because
here the Facilitator is often also the Expert for the modeling methodology.

S-BPM managers should signal from the very beginning to their coworkers their desire to communicate, point out to them the objectives of change processes, and inform them in the course of development of each step.

5.5 Basic Constructs of Subject-Oriented Modeling

5.5.1 To Go

I regularly receive requests to deliver data or to collaborate in modeling of processes. What does this mean?

The Governor has started a project.

What is the goal of the project?

The objectives have been defined by the Governor. We want to improve some of our processes.

We want to check whether our existing business
processes correspond to our actual work tasks, which
should help us to improve our processes in a targeted
way.

And you want me to contribute?

Not before we have clarified to what extent and
how to proceed. Actors should have a clear
understanding of their involvement in processes.

5.5.2 Subject

In the simple scenario of the business trip application, we can identify three
subjects, namely the employee as applicant, the manager as the approver, and the
travel office as the travel arranger.

The definition of which subjects should be part of a process is a leadership
decision—this is why the Governor needs to be involved. On the one hand, the
necessary subjects result from the actual (as-is) situation, as it has for example
already been described in the process analysis. On the other hand, the subject
scoping, i.e., the question of what subjects there are and what tasks they roughly
perform, can be adjusted to the envisioned or desired (to-be) situation.

Depending on the required or desired division of labor in a process, a
corresponding number of subjects are necessary. This division is a design decision
that must be taken in accordance with business needs. It influences the necessary
granularity of a process model (see Sect. 5.5.6).

In case there are many specialized subjects involved in a process, it may lead to
many potentially complex interactions between the subjects. This can be a problem,
since the communication between process participants always carries the risk of
delays and misunderstandings. In case of few subjects, however, the subject carriers
often cover a too wide a range of activities, which puts high demands on the

participants. The decision with respect to subject scoping therefore has far-reaching consequences. It is complex, represents a major challenge, and requires extensive experience and care.

5.5.3 Subject-to-Subject Communication

After the identification of subjects involved in the process (as process-specific roles), their interaction relationships need to be represented. These are the messages exchanged between the subjects. Such messages might contain structured information—so-called business objects (see Sect. 5.5.7).

The result is a model structured according to subjects with explicit communication relationships, which is referred to as a Subject Interaction Diagram (SID) or, synonymously, as a Communication Structure Diagram (CSD) (see Fig. 5.1).

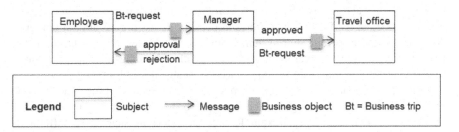

Fig. 5.1 Subject interaction diagram for the process "business trip application"

Messages represent the interactions of the subjects during the execution of the process. We recommend naming these messages in such a way that they can be immediately understood and also reflect the meaning of each particular message for the process. In the sample "business trip application", therefore, the messages are referred to as "business trip request", "rejection", and "approval".

Messages serve as a container for the information transmitted from a sending to a receiving subject. There are two options for the message content:

- Simple data types: Simple data types are string, integer, character, etc. In the business trip application example, the message "business trip request" can contain several data elements of type string (e.g., destination, reason for traveling, etc.) and of type number (e.g., duration of trip in days).
- Business Objects: Business Objects in their general form are physical and logical "things" that are required to process business transactions. We consider data structures composed of elementary data types, or even other data structures, as logical business objects in business processes. For instance, the business object "business trip request" could consist of the data structures "data on applicants", "travel data", and "approval data"—with each of these in turn containing multiple data elements.

5.5.4 Synchronization of the Technical Message Exchange

In the previous section, we have stated that messages are transferred between subjects and have described the nature of these messages. What is still missing is a detailed description of how messages can be exchanged, how the information they carry can be transmitted, and how subjects can be synchronized. These issues are addressed in the following subsections.

5.5.4.1 Synchronous and Asynchronous Exchange of Messages

In the case of synchronous exchange of messages, sender and receiver wait for each other until a message can be passed on. If a subject wants to send a message and the receiver (subject) is not yet in a corresponding receive state, the sender waits until the receiver is able to accept this message. Conversely, a recipient has to wait for a desired message until it is made available by the sender.

The disadvantage of the synchronous method is thus a close temporal coupling between sender and receiver. This raises problems in the implementation of business processes in the form of workflows, especially across organizational borders. As a rule, these also represent system boundaries across which a tight coupling between sender and receiver is usually very costly. For long-running processes, sender and receiver may wait for days, or even weeks, for each other.

Using asynchronous messaging, a sender is able to send anytime. The subject puts a message into a message buffer from which it is picked up by the receiver. However, the recipient sees, for example, only the oldest message in the buffer and can only accept this particular one. If it is not the desired message, the receiver is blocked, even though the message may already be in the buffer, but in a buffer space that is not visible to the receiver. To avoid this, the recipient has the alternative to take all of the messages from the buffer and manage them by himself. In this way, the receiver can identify the appropriate message and process it as soon as he needs it. In asynchronous messaging, sender and receiver are only loosely coupled. Practical problems can arise due to the in reality limited physical size of the receive buffer, which does not allow an unlimited number of messages to be recorded. Once the physical boundary of the buffer has been reached due to high occupancy, this may lead to unpredictable behavior of workflows derived from a business process specification. To avoid this, the input pool concept has been developed for S-BPM (see Sect. 5.5.5.2).

A typical example of a message exchange is the business trip as a business transaction. It is triggered by an event such as a scheduled customer visit. The application for the business trip can take place far in advance of the actual commencement of the journey. Before this, a hotel needs to be booked and travel arrangements need to be made—processes that can run in parallel or interlocked.

Once the trip starts, the process has not yet been completed. Billing and application for reimbursement may still need to be requested. A permanent synchronization of all the steps is not only expensive but usually not necessary because a coherent processing scheme for business trips can be derived according to the causality given in the business process specification "business trip". This represents an ideal scenario for an asynchronous message exchange.

5.5.4.2 Exchange of Messages via the Input Pool

To solve the problems outlined in asynchronous message exchange, the input pool concept has been developed. Communication via the input pool is considerably more complex than previously shown; however, it allows transmitting an unlimited number of messages simultaneously. Due to its high practical importance, it is considered as a basic construct of S-BPM.

> Consider the input pool as a mail box of work performers, the operation of which is specified in detail.

Each subject has its own input pool. It serves as a message buffer to temporarily store messages received by the subject, independent of the sending communication partner. The input pools are therefore inboxes for flexible configuration of the message exchange between the subjects. In contrast to the buffer in which only the front message can be seen and accepted, the pool solution enables picking up (= removing from the buffer) any message. For a subject, all messages in its input pool are visible.

The input pool has the following configuration parameters (see Fig. 5.2):

- Input pool size: The input pool size specifies how many messages can be stored in an input pool, regardless of the number and complexity of the message parameters transmitted with a message. If the input pool size is set to zero, messages can only be exchanged synchronously.
- Maximum number of messages from specific subjects: For an input pool, it can be determined how many messages received from a particular subject may be stored simultaneously in the input pool. Again, a value of zero means that messages can only be accepted synchronously.
- Maximum number of messages with specific identifiers: For an input pool, it can be determined how many messages of a specifically identified message type (e.g., invoice) may be stored simultaneously in the input pool, regardless of what subject they originate from. A specified size of zero allows only for synchronous message reception.
- Maximum number of messages with specific identifiers of certain subjects: For an input pool, it can be determined how many messages of a specific identifier of a particular subject may be stored simultaneously in the input pool. The meaning of the zero value is analogous to the other cases.

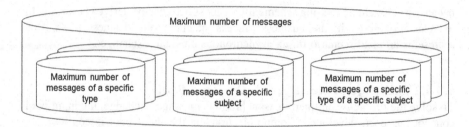

Fig. 5.2 Configuration of input pool by parameters

By limiting the size of the input pool, its ability to store messages may be blocked at a certain point in time during process runtime. Hence, messaging synchronization mechanisms need to control the assignment of messages to the input pool. Essentially, there are three strategies to handle the access to input pools:

- Blocking the sender until the input pool's ability to store messages has been reinstated: Once all slots are occupied in an input pool, the sender is blocked until the receiving subject picks up a message (i.e., a message is removed from the input pool). This creates space for a new message. In case several subjects want to put a message into a fully occupied input pool, the subject that has been waiting longest for an empty slot is allowed to send. The procedure is analogous if corresponding input pool parameters do not allow storing the message in the input pool, i.e., if the corresponding number of messages of the same name or from the same subject has been put into the input pool.
- Delete and release of the oldest message: In case all the slots are already occupied in the input pool of the subject addressed, the oldest message is overwritten with the new message.
- Delete and release of the latest message: The latest message is deleted from the input pool to allow depositing of the newly incoming message. If all the positions in the input pool of the addressed subject are taken, the latest message in the input pool is overwritten with the new message. This strategy applies analogously when the maximum number of messages in the input pool has been reached, either with respect to sender or message type.

5.5.4.3 Sending Messages

Before sending a message, the values of the parameters to be transmitted need to be determined. In case the message parameters are simple data types, the required values are taken from local variables or business objects of the sending subject, respectively. In case of business objects, a current instance of a business object is transferred as a message parameter.

The send process attempts to send the message to the target subject and store it in its input pool. Depending on the described configuration and status of the input pool, the message is either immediately stored or the sending subject is blocked until a delivery of the message is possible.

In the sample business trip application, employees send completed requests using the message "send business trip request" to the manager's input pool. From a send state, several messages can be sent as an alternative. The following example shows a send state in which the message M1 is sent to the subject S1, or alternatively the message M2 is sent to S2, therefore referred to as alternative sending (see Fig. 5.3). It does not matter which message is attempted to be sent first. If the send mechanism is successful, the corresponding state transition is executed. In case the message cannot be stored in the input pool of the target subject, sending is interrupted automatically, and another designated message is attempted to be sent. A sending subject will thus only be blocked if it cannot send any of the provided messages.

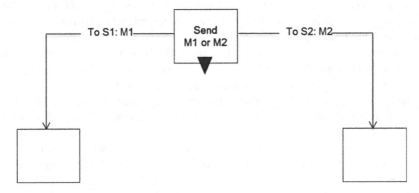

Fig. 5.3 Example of alternative sending

By specifying priorities, the order of sending can be influenced. For example, it can be determined that the message M1 to S1 has a higher priority than the message M2 to S2. Using this specification, the sending subject starts with sending message M1 to S1 and then tries only in case of failure to send message M2 to S2. In case message M2 can also not be sent to the subject S2, the attempts to send start from the beginning.

The blocking of subjects when attempting to send can be monitored over time with the so-called timeout. The example in Fig. 5.4 shows with "Timeout: 24 h" an additional state transition, which occurs when within 24 h one of the two messages cannot be sent. If a value of zero is specified for the timeout, the process immediately follows the timeout path when the alternative message delivery fails completely.

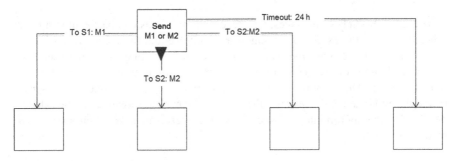

Fig. 5.4 Send using time monitoring

5.5.4.4 Receiving Messages

Analogously to sending, the receiving procedure is divided into two phases, which run inversely to send.

The first step is to verify whether the expected message is ready for being picked up. In case of synchronous messaging, it is checked whether the sending subject offers the message. In the asynchronous version, it is checked whether the message has already been stored in the input pool. If the expected message is accessible in either form, it is accepted, and in a second step, the corresponding state transition is performed. This leads to a takeover of the message parameters of the accepted message to local variables or business objects of the receiving subject. In case the expected message is not ready, the receiving subject is blocked until the message arrives and can be accepted.

In a certain state, a subject can expect alternatively multiple messages. In this case, it is checked whether any of these messages is available and can be accepted. The test sequence is arbitrary, unless message priorities are defined. In this case, an available message with the highest priority is accepted. However, all other messages remain available (e.g., in the input pool) and can be accepted in other receive states.

Figure 5.5 shows a receive state of the subject "employee" which is waiting for the answer regarding a business trip request. The answer may be an approval or a rejection.

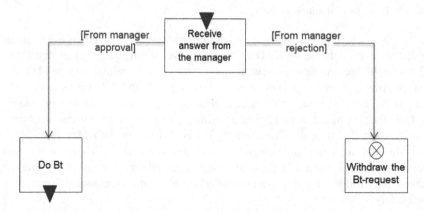

Fig. 5.5 Example of alternative receiving

Just as with sending messages, also receiving messages can be monitored over time. If none of the expected messages are available and the receiving subject is therefore blocked, a time limit can be specified for blocking. After the specified time has elapsed, the subject will execute the transition as it is defined for the timeout period. The duration of the time limit may also be dynamic, in the sense that at the end of a process instance the process stakeholders assigned to the subject decide that the appropriate transition should be performed. We then speak of a manual timeout.

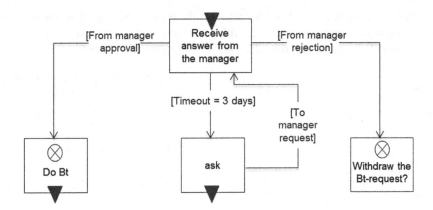

Fig. 5.6 Time monitoring for message reception

Figure 5.6 shows that, after waiting 3 days for the manager's answer, the employee sends a corresponding request.

Instead of waiting for a message for a certain predetermined period of time, the waiting can be interrupted by a subject at all times. In this case, a reason for abortion can be appended to the keyword "breakup". In the example shown in Fig. 5.7, the receive state is left due to the impatience of the subject.

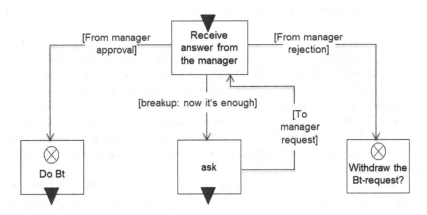

Fig. 5.7 Message reception with manual interrupt

5.5.5 Subject Behavior

The possible sequences of a subject's actions in a process are termed subject behavior. States and state transitions describe what actions a subject performs and how they are interdependent. In addition to the communication for sending and receiving, a subject also performs so-called internal actions or functions.

States of a subject are therefore distinct: there are actions on the one hand, and communication states to interact with other subjects (receive and send) on the other hand. This results in three different types of states of a subject:

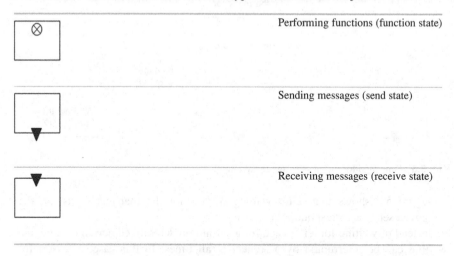

Performing functions (function state)

Sending messages (send state)

Receiving messages (receive state)

In S-BPM, work performers are equipped with elementary tasks to model their work procedures: sending and receiving messages and immediate accomplishment of a task (function state).

In case an action associated with a state (send, receive, and do) is possible, it will be executed, and a state transition to the next state occurs. The transition is characterized through the result of the action of the state under consideration: For a send state, it is determined by the state transition to which subject what information is sent. For a receive state, it becomes evident in this way from what subject it receives which information. For a function state, the state transition describes the result of the action, e.g., that the change of a business object was successful or could not be executed.

The behavior of subjects is represented by modelers using Subject Behavior Diagrams (SBD). Figure 5.8 shows the subject behavior diagram depicting the behavior of the subjects "employee", "manager", and "travel office", including the associated states and state transitions.

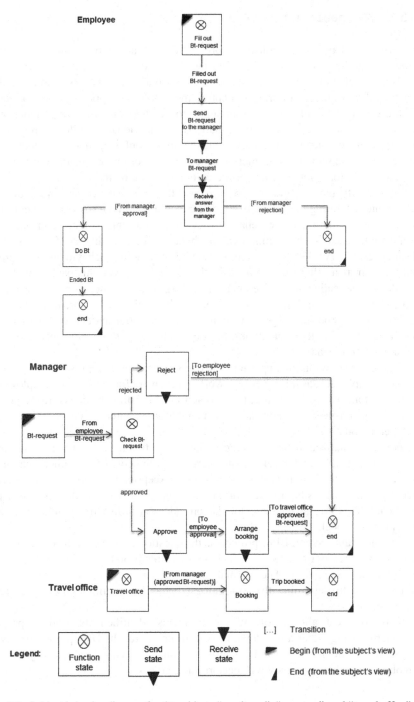

Fig. 5.8 Subject behavior diagram for the subjects "employee", "manager", and "travel office"

5.5.6   Normalization

The default behavior of a subject is represented by its action behavior (performing functions) and communication behavior (sending and receiving messages).

Action behavior can in principle contain many internal functions to be performed in sequence, in order to capture the individual work steps of a subject. In these sequences of internal functions, no sending and receiving nodes are included. This is crucial as work regulations for individuals or roles representing a subject but can lead to extensive and therefore confusing behavior diagrams. Moreover, these sequences of internal functions are not important for communication, and therefore, not relevant for the communication partners.

To simplify the presentation, we can use the fact that neighboring subjects, which interact during the course of process execution with the subject momentarily under consideration, and the behavior of which is currently being described, are mainly interested in the communication behavior of this subject (Do I get the desired result?) and less in its action behavior. The action behavior is of interest only insofar as it affects the communication behavior. Given this background, we can define a so-called normalized behavior, merging a sequence of functions into a larger function. By hiding functional details, the subject behavior, from the perspective of neighboring subjects, becomes much more transparent, without having to change the, for those neighboring subjects so important, description of the communication behavior.

Figure 5.9 shows in the upper half the detailed behavioral representation for the subject "employee", as it is given as a work requirement for the affected employees. In the bottom half of the figure, the two actions "withdraw business trip request" and "change business trip request" (with a double-lined border) were combined into a larger action.

For a normalized behavior, in principle, any function states between their encompassing send and receive states can be combined to form other ones that remain visible to their neighboring subjects. Exceptions are end states. Consequently, it is not possible in the example to group the functions "do business trip" and "end". This normalized behavior also provides indications for the level of detail of a process model.

An important issue in BPM projects is the question of the level of detail needed to describe the steps of a process. This issue was already addressed in the chapter on analysis (see Sect. 4.4). The normalization of subject-oriented modeling is a suitable tool to determine that normalized behavior is sufficient for complete representations.

This construct allows solving the problems identified for finding proper granularity using either a top-down or bottom-up approach. The appropriate level of granularity in modeling can be determined, once it is known which subjects are involved and what tasks they will perform in a process.

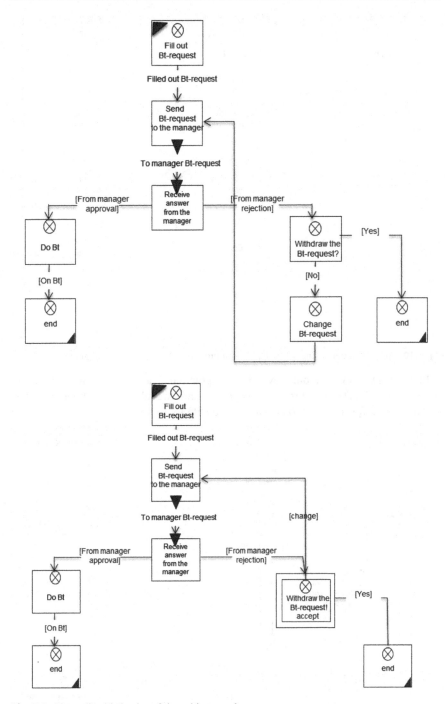

Fig. 5.9 Normalized behavior of the subject employee

To illustrate this issue, we use again the business trip as an example. Its resulting activities are shown in Fig. 5.10 in different levels of granularity.

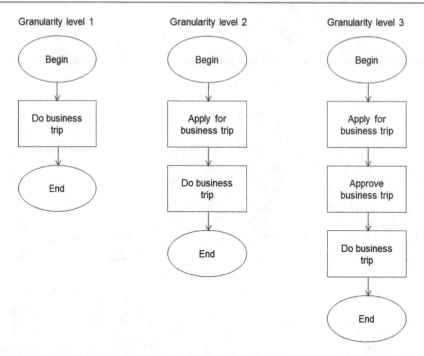

Fig. 5.10 Actions in the business trip application process in different levels of granularity

Figure 5.11 shows that only level three of granularity allows assigning activities to the three subjects "employee", "manager", and "travel office". Otherwise, the activities were formulated too coarsely to be able to do this.

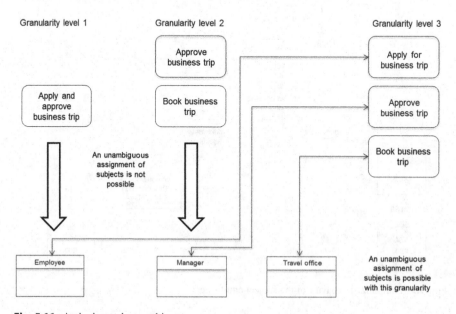

Fig. 5.11 Assigning tasks to subjects

The example illustrates that the granularity of actions in a process description is defined by the parties, or the active agents, involved in the process. The individual actions need to be clearly assigned to active agents.

The normalization thus determines the crudest possible description of a process as well as the minimal required granularity of process descriptions. The normalization of subjects is also required to identify the observable behavior of a process (see Sect. 5.6.7).

> Discover matching processes; establish them as the ultimate guide on how to accomplish tasks through normalization. This helps stakeholders with orientation.

5.5.7   Business Objects

5.5.7.1 Understanding of Business Objects

In natural language, sentences are usually composed of a subject, predicate, and object (e.g., "Robert plays ball"). An object is not mandatory for a grammatically correct sentence structure, although if the object is missing, the sentence lacks the information on what or whom the predicate is acting upon (e.g., "Robert plays, but using what?"). This is transferable to a process:

A business process consists of actors who perform specific actions in a certain sequence, so-called predicates, and objects on which the predicates are defined. In this particular case, sending and receiving represent special predicates with the message as a direct object, and the addressee and sender as indirect objects.

Business objects are those things that are needed to provide outcome of business processes. Consequently, they are things that are used in a process. Business objects are passive, i.e., they do not initiate interactions or actions. Business objects are processed by subjects (cf. Grässle et al. 2004). They can outlast the execution of a process instance and can be used in process instances initiated later on as sources of information.

In the following, we deal with modeling of business objects and operations, which are processed on them in the course of executing process instances. The focus is less on physical business objects (e.g., a product which is delivered) than on logical business objects (such as the associated information for service delivery or a business trip application).

5.5.7.2 Structures of Business Objects

A basic structure of business objects consists of an identifier, data structures, and data elements. The identifier of a business object is derived from the business environment in which it is used. Examples are business trip requests, purchase orders, packing lists, invoices, etc.

Business objects are composed of data structures. Their components can be simple data elements of a certain type (e.g., string or number) or even data structures themselves.

For better understanding, it is recommended to describe the semantics of the data elements in more detail, especially if these cannot be unequivocally deduced from the identifiers.

Figure 5.12 shows an example of a business trip request. It consists of the data structure "data of requester" (employee) with data elements for name, first name, and personnel number, and the structure "data of trip" with the data elements for the start, end, and purpose of the trip.

Data structure	Meaning	Data type	Can/must	Value range/Default
Data of requester				
Name	Last name	Character	M	
First name	First name	Character	M	
Personnel number	...	Integer	M	
Organizational unit	...		C	
Pay group	...		C	
Data of trip				
Start trip	...	Date	M	Within 1 year from current date/ current date
End trip	...	Date	M	Start trip plus 1 year/ start trip
International trip	...	Boolean?	C	y/n; n
Travel destination (city/country)	...	Character	M	...
Reason for traveling	...	Character	M	...
Desired advance money	...	Integer	C	...
Data of approval				
Approval	Approval comment	Boolean?	M	y/n; n
Cost center	...	Integer	M	...
Desired advance money	...	Integer	C	...

Fig. 5.12 Data structure of the business object "business trip request"

5.5.7.3 Status of Business Objects and Their Instances

In many cases, the semantics of a business object changes during process execution, such as when a delivery slip is transferred into an invoice. Therefore, for a business object several different statuses can be defined. If a status changes, only those data structures or data elements, which are required for the new status, are transferred from the previous status, and new components are added as needed, or existing removed if no longer necessary. This ensures that a subject receives only those data elements for its work that it really needs. This will facilitate compliance with data protection regulations.

In the example of the business trip application, the status "booking business trip" can be derived from the original status "business trip request" of the business object (see Fig. 5.12). In particular, data elements with internal information such as employee number, category of salary, reason for travelling, and the complete data structure for approval are removed. They should not be visible, e.g., outside the organization, and are not relevant for the (external) travel agent to book the trip. Therefore, as shown in Fig. 5.13, a new data structure "data of booking" is added. It contains data elements, which allow the travel agent to set a deadline for the latest possible receipt of the confirmation of booking while specifying certain hotel chains which have been contracted.

Data structure/ Data element	Meaning	Data type	Can/must	Value range/Default
Data of requester				
Name	Last name	Character	M	
First name	First name	Character	M	
Data of trip				
Start trip	...	Date	M	Within 1 year from current date/ current date
End trip	...	Date	M	Start trip plus 1 year/ start trip
Travel destination (city/country)	...	Character	M	...
Data of booking				
Contracted hotel chains	Approval comment	Character	M	...
Deadline of booking confirmation	...	Date	C	...
Booking confirmation	...	Date	M	y/n

Fig. 5.13 Business object "business trip request" in the status "booking business trip"

Using status information, a form template can be constructed. First of all, a status is defined as a business object type, from which different variants of business objects for use in other business process environments can then be derived. For instance, it would be conceivable that the travel office provides booking of private tours as a special service to staff members. In such a case, a business object "private travel booking" could be generated from the previous status of the business object "business trip request" by removing data fields irrelevant for private trips (e.g., reason for the trip, advance payments, etc.), and supplementing with others (e.g., in case a travel insurance is requested).

5.5.7.4 Views of Business Objects and Their Instances

Besides the definition of statuses for business objects and their instances, it may be necessary to define different views for different subjects. In contrast to status changes, in views the data structures or elements are not physically removed from a business object and its instances, but rather only different access rights are assigned to it. This is done for each subject in its respective process context, i.e., for the particular behavior status of the subject. As usual, read access (read) means that a subject can only see data elements and their content. In case of an assigned write permission, values can additionally be changed (read/write).

Figure 5.14 shows the views of the subjects "employee", "manager", and "travel office" in the status "business trip application" of the business object "business trip request". The applicant can read all the data elements but is not able to fill in approval data, the cost center, and the amount of an advance payment. This is reserved for the manager. The view of the travel office includes only read permissions, and not even these for certain data elements. Thus, the reason for the trip and the advance payment requested by the employee are not accessible for the travel office at all, as they are not relevant for the actions of this subject.

Data structure/ Data element	View of employee	View of manager	View of travel office
Data of requester			
Name	R/W	R	R
First name	R/W	R	R
Personnel number	R/W	R	R
Organizational unit	R/W	R	R
Pay group	R/W	R	R
Data of trip			
Start trip	R/W	R/W	R
End trip	R/W	R/W	R
International trip	R/W	R	R
Travel destination	R/W	R	R
Reason for traveling	R/W	R/W	-
Desired advance payment	R/W	R	-
Data of approval			
Approval	R	R/W	R
Cost center	R	R/W	R
Allowed advance payment	R	R/W	R

Fig. 5.14 Views on the business object "business trip request" in the status "business trip application"

Let us have a look at the views of the business object "business trip request" in the advanced status "trip booking" (see Fig. 5.15). This status is relevant to the travel office, as it monitors the receipt of the confirmation from travel agents, and if necessary, changes travel dates in case of availability problems. The employees, however, are only interested in information on whether the trip has already been successfully booked, whereas the manager does not need a view on this status at all.

Data structure/ Data element	View of employee	View of manager	View of travel office
Data of requester			
Name	R	-	R
First name	R	-	R
Data of trip			
Start trip	R	-	R/W
End trip	R	-	R/W
Travel destination	R	-	R
Data of booking			
Contracted hotel chains	-	-	R/W
Deadline of booking confirmation	-	-	R/W
Booking confirmation	R	-	R/W

Fig. 5.15 Views on the business object "business trip request" in the status "trip booking"

5.5.7.5 Access Privileges to Business Object Instances

For business object instances, the modeler can specify whether only a single subject, namely, the one initiating the instance, can access them directly, or also other subjects. Accordingly, we distinguish between local and global business objects.

Local Business Object (Private Business Object)

A subject creates a local instance of a business object. Its data elements can only be read or modified by the generating subject. Other subjects can acquire access to an instance of a business object when a copy of that instance has been explicitly sent to them in a message.

Local business objects are appropriate for business transactions with external partners, such as suppliers and customers, because external subjects should not have direct access to business objects for reasons of security. Changes that are required in accordance with a certain business logic can also be returned by message exchange and lead to controlled modification of the data of the private business object by the designated and authorized subject.

In Fig. 5.16, only the subject "employee" can access its copy of a business object "business trip request". The manager can only add his information once he has received the message with a copy of the business object. Similarly, the travel office can only handle the case after it has received a copy of the business object from the manager in the new status "business trip request approved". By sending or receiving messages, a copy of the required business object is transferred to the respective partner.

Fig. 5.16 Business trip request as a private business object of the subject "employee" (transmission via message)

Global Business Object (Shared Business Object)

A global business object, when being defined, can be assigned to several subjects simultaneously. All of these subjects ("object owner") can edit data elements in instances of the global business object according to their access rights controlled by views. A corresponding example is shown in Fig. 5.17.

Since all the involved subjects can access the business object "business trip request", it is sufficient that the employee fills in the form (business object) and then informs his manager by sending a message, without transferring the business object. The manager can then directly access the application request and make his amendments. This also applies in the later phases of processing the trip, e.g., by the travel office.

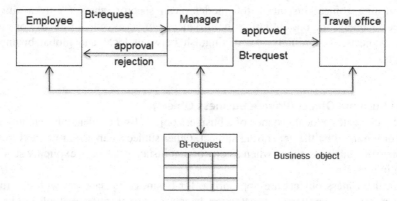

Fig. 5.17 Business trip application as a global business object of the subjects "employee", "manager", and "travel office"

Global business objects can be shared by any number of subjects of an organization in a complex process network (see Sect. 5.5.5). The benefit is that various subjects can access a common database with secure transactions, as there are not multiple copies of a business object in use. The disadvantage is that the subjects need to be able to access common business objects. In interorganizational processes, this often cannot be achieved without substantial effort.

However, using the concept of global business objects, complex access right issues can be clarified elegantly: a subject only has access to a business object when it has a task to accomplish within the process instance which is associated with the business object under consideration.

In the example of the business trip application, it is not necessary for the travel office to have access to all personal and trip data permanently. However, when using static structures, no other solution is possible. On the other hand, if the data access is implemented through a global business object, the travel office only has access to the data when this is required for processing their associated tasks. At the latest, the data is protected again upon completion of the process.

> Not all task performers need to see and manipulate all data. They should take a certain view of business objects. These "glasses" should reflect the information that they need to have to accomplish their tasks—no more and no less, but in association with time, namely just-in-time.

5.5.7.6 Operations on Business Objects

When executing business process instances, subjects perform operations on business object instances as part of their task and communication profile. Depending on the privileges of a subject, the following operations are possible:

- Generate business object instances: A subject can generate a business object instance by deriving it from the general business object definition, or copying it from an already existing instance.
- Assign values to business objects: Once business objects have been instantiated, the values required for the execution of the process need to be assigned to the individual elements by the authorized subjects. How these values are entered, shall be determined as part of the implementation of a process when being embedded in the organizational and IT environment. Examples include the identification and manual entry of data by people (e.g., quantity in an order position) or the saving of an automatically computed result by an IT system (e.g., VAT amount of an invoice).
- In case of the business trip process, for instance, a concrete object is generated from the specification of the business object "business trip request", once an employee requests a trip. When filing a request, it is conceivable that the employee himself manually enters his personnel number into an electronic form and the IT system uses this to determine his name, first name, and category of salary and automatically enter them into the appropriate fields.
- Duplicate business object instances: Business object instances can be duplicated, e.g., to preserve a certain status of a business object. In the example of the business trip, the status can remain the same after completion of the form by the employee, until, for instance, the manager performs changes, e.g., changes the date. Each duplicate is given a unique name in order to distinguish it from other instances. This is defined in the status in which the copy is created.

- Transfer data elements from a business object instance: From a business object instance, field values can be transferred to data elements in instances of other business objects. Only the types of the data elements need to match. Such a mapping of values must be defined in function states of the process description of a subject. In case there are already duplicates of the target instance, it must also be specified to which duplicates the mapping refers to.
- Change status of a business object instance: A status change in business objects has been introduced as a variation of the initial business object by means of dismissing and/or adding data elements. Here, in a function state at runtime, i.e., for business object instances, retained data elements are transferred with their values to the new status. Data items no longer needed are deleted along with their values for the new status, while added data elements are initially empty and waiting to be entered. Here too, it must be specified in case of multiple instances to which instance the change of status refers to.
- Send business object instance: This operation can be performed only in a send state. As a result, a copy of a business object instance is sent. In case there are multiple copies of the instance, it must be specified to which instance the send operation refers to.
- Receiving a business object instance: A subject as addressee of a message with a business object instance must be in a receive state to accept the message. Once it takes this message from the input pool, a uniquely identifiable copy of the business object instance is created.

How the respective operations will be run on a business object is specified in the context of the IT implementation of a business object (see Sect. 10.5.1). In the course of modeling, it is only specified which operations are performed on a business object and which of its content parts need to be changed when tasks are accomplished.

> With the view comes the privilege. The access rights to business objects are derived from the required task support. It has to be clarified whether a stakeholder requires access to a business object at all, and if so, whether he is only allowed to read it, or possibly even change it.

5.6   **Extension Constructs for Process Networks**

5.6.1   **To Go**

This sounds quite convincing. But what about complex processes involving a large number of subjects? I need to decompose them into related sub-processes.

We can decompose a large process into sub-processes, and each of the involved parties describes his sub-process.

In each of the processes, there are then subjects communicating with other subjects in other processes.

Yes, these are the interface subjects.

Does this mean I only need to know the interface
subject of another process?

Exactly, it is represented in your process as a so-
called external subject.

In this way, we can construct entire networks of
processes. We can recognize all the mutual
dependencies between processes in our organization.

5.6.2   Interface Subjects and Process Network

So far, we have considered only individual processes. However, processes are
generally mutually dependent, i.e., subjects in one process communicate with
subjects in other processes. In this way, networks of processes are created. Conversely, large and complex processes can be decomposed into smaller
subprocesses. In the following sections, we introduce the various concepts for the
formation of process networks.

> Networked organizations especially benefit from S-BPM. This approach
> enables the structuring of the flow of information in a transparent form across
> the boundaries of an organization, and the disclosure of those parts of
> participating organizations that are required by network partners for success-
> ful cooperation.

The process "business trip application" represents only a portion of the entire
business trip process. In reality, this process can consist of a whole series of small,
highly interrelated processes. For instance, after approval by the manager, a
subsequent process could address the travel office, booking through a travel agent
a train ticket and a hotel room for the employee (applicant). When modeling using

the basic S-BPM constructs, this results in the subject interaction diagram extended by the booking process, as shown in Fig. 5.18.

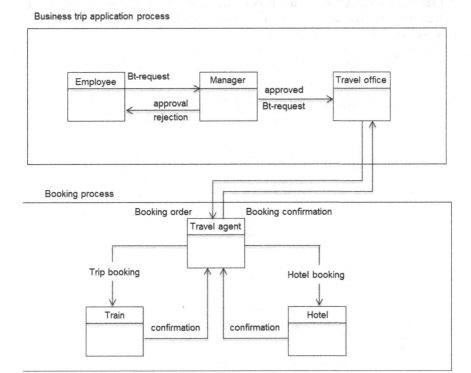

Fig. 5.18 Extended subject interaction diagram for the process "business trip application"

In order to structure and simplify the representation, the overall process can be decomposed into the two coupled subprocesses: "business trip application" and "booking". Subprocesses describe specific, logically self-contained aspects of a complex process. The overall process is denoted as a process network. In this network, it is required that subjects of the subprocesses are linked across their process boundaries and communicate with each other.

A link between two processes is represented through interface subjects that reference one another. The associated interface subject of the respective other process is represented in the considered process through a so-called external subject.

> Interface subjects regulate cooperation and facilitate the synchronization of processes of the network partners.

In the example, from the perspective of the subprocess "business trip application", the travel agent is the interface subject. In the subject interaction diagram in

Fig. 5.19, it is indicated by gray coloring as an external subject. The reference symbol also contains "booking process" as the name of the process which contains the referenced subject. From the perspective of the booking process, the travel office is the interface subject, and "business trip application process" indicates the process containing this external subject.

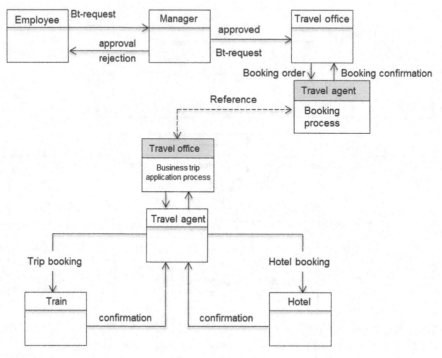

Fig. 5.19 Subprocesses "business trip application process" and "booking process" linked via interface subjects

Using mutual referencing, subject interaction diagrams (SIDs) can be consolidated into process network diagrams (PNDs), which only show processes linked in a process network and the messages exchanged across their borders. We refer to these as horizontal process networks. Such a network is presented in Fig. 5.20 as a Process Network Diagram for the entire business trip process in its currently developed form.

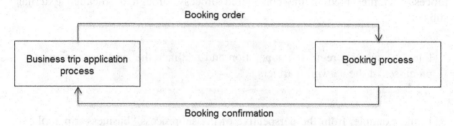

Fig. 5.20 Horizontal process network for the business trip process

5.6.3   Service Processes

In operational reality, there are (sub) processes which deliver defined results which can be encapsulated as a service process. Several other processes call this process to take advantage of its results.

For coupling the calling process with the service process, a so-called general external subject is introduced for the service process. It represents all the processes that use the service process. In this way, all sorts of calling subjects are implicitly referenced in the course of modeling, instead of setting explicit references to the respective subject in the calling process.

In the example of the business trip process, the booking process can be implemented as a reusable service process and thus made available to other calling processes. This could be useful, e.g., if an organization offers its employees booking of private tours through the travel office with special conditions. Then, the employees use the respective service process not only for booking business trips but also for vacation trips.

In such a service process, the utilizing process needs to know the interface subject of the service process. It will communicate with it as usual, so that nothing changes for the description of the behavior of the utilizing processes.

Figure 5.21 shows the booking process as a service process using "booking customers" as a general external subject.

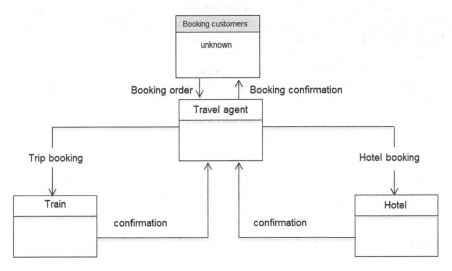

Fig. 5.21 Booking process as a service process with a general external subject

At the time of modeling, the service process neither knows the interface subject nor the utilizing process to which it belongs. Therefore, the external subject representing the interface subject in the processes calling the service process needs to be provided with a formal name. In this way, the messages, which are sent by the subjects of a service process to the utilizing processes, can be addressed.

In our example, the formal name "booking customers" is given. The process name "unknown" in the external subject identifies the considered process as a service process.

5.6.4   Multiprocesses

In a business process, there may be several identical subprocesses that perform certain similar tasks in parallel and independently. This is often the case in a procurement process, when bids from multiple providers are solicited. A process or subprocess is therefore executed simultaneously or sequentially multiple times during overall process execution. A set of type-identical, independently running processes or subprocesses are termed multiprocess. The actual number of these independent subprocesses is determined at runtime.

> Multiprocesses simplify process execution, since a specific sequence of actions can be used by different processes. They are recommended for recurring structures and similar process flows.

An example of a multiprocess can be illustrated as a variation of the current booking process. The travel agent should simultaneously solicit up to five bids before making a reservation. Once three offers have been received, one is selected and a room is booked. The process of obtaining offers from the hotels is identical for each hotel and is therefore modeled as a multiprocess.

As a result, the representation is changed first on the abstract level of the process network diagram as shown in Fig. 5.22, where the nesting expresses that the "hotel offer and booking process" is a multiprocess.

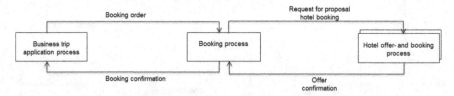

Fig. 5.22 Process network diagram "business trip application with hotel selection"

On the next level of detail, the subject interaction diagram, the nested symbol for the interface subject "hotel" shows that it belongs to a multiprocess (see Fig. 5.23). Every time the subject "travel agent" sends the message "request for proposal" to the subject "hotel" from the multiprocess "hotel offer and booking process", a new copy of this process is generated. Each copy corresponds to a specific hotel inquiry.

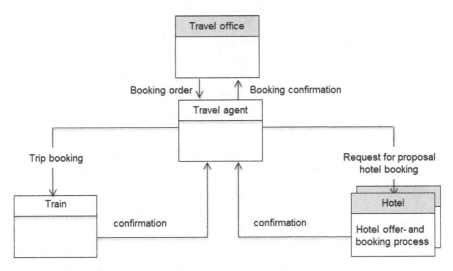

Fig. 5.23 Subject interaction diagram for the "booking process" with the "hotel offer and booking process" as a multiprocess

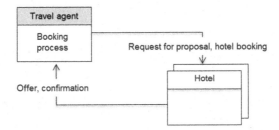

Fig. 5.24 Subject interaction diagram for the "hotel offer and booking process"

The "hotel offer and booking process" contains only the subject "hotel", which communicates with the external subject "travel agent" in the booking process (see Fig. 5.24).

Multiprocesses are described in the same way as other processes of a process network. A supplement is required for the commissioning subject that communicates with a subject of a multiprocess. It needs to know how many and which copies of a multiprocess it has produced. Therefore, when describing its behavior, the respective copies are indexed like elements of a field, in order to identify the relevant copy for process state transitions. In case a subject wants to communicate with a subject of a particular process copy from the multiprocess field, it specifies the proper index of the process copy when sending or receiving. In our example, in the action "select hotel" the index for the best bid is saved in the parameter "selected". This allows communication with the corresponding bidding hotel.

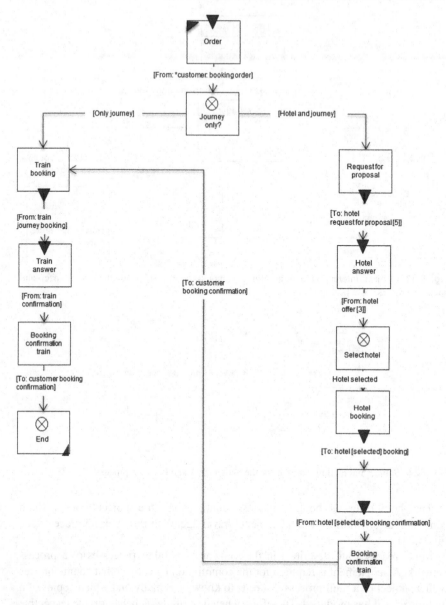

Fig. 5.25 Behavior of the subject "travel agent" with a multiprocess for selecting hotel

Figure 5.25 illustrates this situation with the state transitions [to: hotel request for proposal [5]] and [from: hotel offer [3]]. This specification expresses that offers from five hotels need to be obtained, and that a hotel will be selected and booked as soon as three bids have been received.

5.6.5   Complex Process Network Topologies

So far, we have mainly considered process networks with two or three processes and have illustrated the methods for linking processes. However, it is possible to expand networks to arbitrary complexity and to structure them hierarchically. Hereby, hierarchical structuring is not an extension of the means for representation, but rather a structured application of the previously described capabilities for linking processes. Process links in complex process topologies can be vertical or horizontal and can be constructed with "vertical" and "horizontal" subjects.

We will now demonstrate such a case for the "business trip application" process. It could be embedded into a more comprehensive process network termed

Fig. 5.26   Processes of the process network "customer care"

"customer care". In such a network, customer reports could be received and edited by the process "customer service". In some cases, to handle the customer request, a customer visit by a service employee could be required. This is initiated by sending the message "service order" triggering the process "business trip application". Figure 5.26 shows this process network.

Messages, according to the S-BPM methodology, are not exchanged between processes, but always between subjects in processes. This results in the example in a refinement in which the subject "service desk" from the process "customer service" sends the message "service order" to the subject "employee" of the process "business trip application" (see Fig. 5.27). Both subjects are external subjects from the respective viewpoint of the other process and are not interested in the behavior of

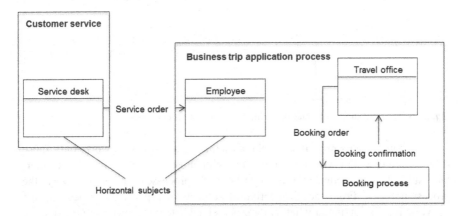

Fig. 5.27   Linking processes in process networks using interface subjects

their communication partner in the other process. Other subjects occurring in both processes, such as the manager in the business trip application process or a service dispatcher in the customer service process, therefore remain hidden at this level. These subjects are not visible from the respective perspective of the other process.

In the process "business trip application", the subject "travel office" sends the message "booking order" to the booking process and receives the message "booking confirmation" in return. The booking process is not visible to the process "customer service" as a whole; it will be encapsulated by the process "business trip application". This puts the booking process one level lower than the processes "customer service" and "business trip application", which are on the same hierarchical level and are connected by the subjects "service desk" and "employee" through horizontal communication relationships. Subjects communicating with subjects of other processes on the same level are called horizontal subjects.

A refinement of the booking process by introducing the subject "travel agent" as a communication partner to the travel office leads to the representation shown in Fig. 5.28. Due to their vertical communication relationship, the travel office and travel agent are referred to as vertical subjects. All subjects of a process which communicate with subjects in processes in a higher or lower hierarchical level are termed vertical.

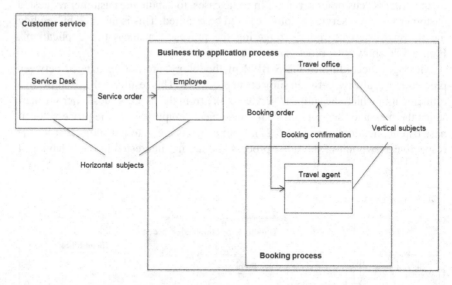

Fig. 5.28 External subjects in multilevel hierarchical process networks

Our example illustrates that for the structure of a process network, only those subjects are essential which communicate with subjects in other processes. Interface subjects thus define relationships between processes, and in this way, the process network. From the perspective of subjects of a particular process in the network, it does not matter whether their perceived external subjects are involved in

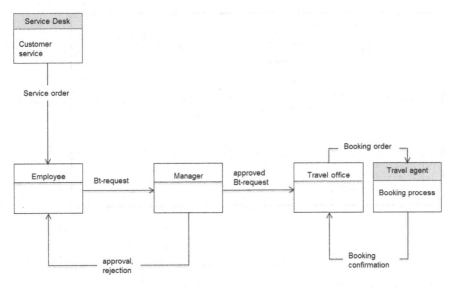

Fig. 5.29 Business trip application process with the associated external subjects

communication relations with other subjects of their process or not. In Fig. 5.29, this indifference becomes evident.

The previously presented concepts for the construction of hierarchical process networks will now be detailed using a complex, however abstract example. Figure 5.30 shows a process network with the three processes A, B, and C, with each of these in turn representing a process network in itself.

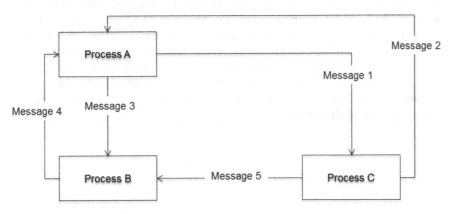

Fig. 5.30 Example of a complex process network

In the process network in Fig. 5.31, "process A" consists of the processes "A1" and "A2" and the external subjects (interface subjects) "SA1" to "SA4". The subjects "SA3" and "SA4" represent "process A" with respect to "process B" and

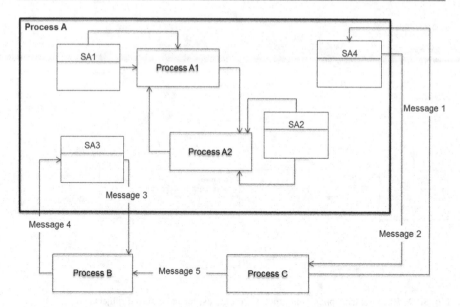

Fig. 5.31 Internal structure of a hierarchical level of a complex process network

"process C", while "SA1" and "SA2" communicate with "process A1" or "processA2", respectively.

In addition to the interface subjects, "process A" may contain other subjects which interact internally, but are not relevant for other processes, and therefore are hidden. In Fig. 5.32, the refined subject interaction diagram of process "process A" is shown. Instead of the partner processes "B" and "C", the corresponding external subjects "SB1" and "SC1" are included. The processes "A1" and "A2", which are only visible in "process A", are represented as the external subjects "SA11" and "SA21". The relationship between the processes "process A1" and "process A2" is not relevant for the subjects of "process A" and is therefore not included in Fig. 5.32. For reasons of intelligibility, in this figure, as well as in the subsequent diagrams, the messages exchanged between subjects are shown exclusively by arrows (without labeling them).

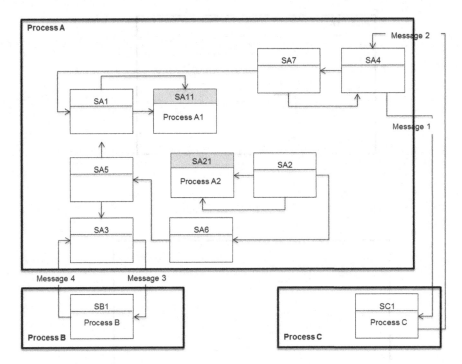

Fig. 5.32 Communication structure of "process A"

In Fig. 5.33, we take a closer look at the communication structure of "process A1" and "process A2". In the upper part, we see for "A1" that its partner "process A" is represented by the interface subject "SA1" (vertical relationship), and its partner "process A2" by the interface subject "SA23" (vertical relationship). Accordingly, in the lower part for "process A2", the interface subjects "SA2" and "SA12" connect it to its partner "process A" (vertical relationship) and "process A1" (vertical relationship).

After having detailed the individual sections of the network, Fig. 5.34 shows the hierarchy of the complex process system. It includes only those subjects which communicate with subjects from other processes. They are recognized as interface subjects in these processes.

"Process A" communicates via the horizontal subjects "SA3" and "SB1" with "process B", and via "SA4" and "SC1" with "process C", respectively. The processes "process A1" and "process A2" are subordinate to "process A". Subjects in these processes can therefore only be reached via processes of "process A", e.g., via the connections of the vertical subjects "SA1" and "SA11", or "SA2" and "SA21", respectively.

Figure 5.34 shows the external subjects of "process A".

Analogous to the hierarchical structuring of "process A", "process B", and "process C" can be further decomposed. Figure 5.35 shows the processes embedded in "process B" and "process C", and the associated horizontal and vertical subjects.

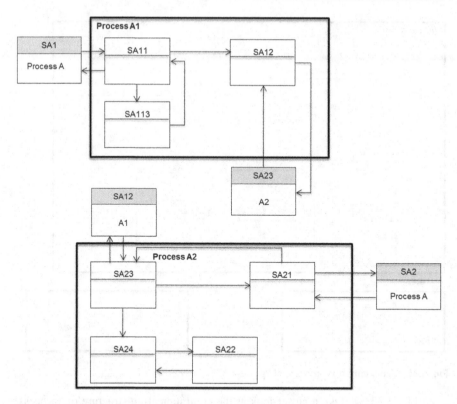

Fig. 5.33 Communication structure of "process A1" and "process A2"

Here, "process A" is again reduced to its external subjects from the perspective of processes "B" and "C".

The above-mentioned concepts have revealed the S-BPM capabilities to structure a complex process system in subsystems as efficiently as possible. If we combine Figs. 5.30 and 5.31, a communication structure of the complex process system emerges, including all horizontal and vertical subjects. A complete representation would additionally include all of the internal subjects, which are not visible to subjects of other processes and were therefore hidden.

Such a fully resolved structure is usually very confusing. For a compact overview of a complex hierarchical process network, we therefore introduce the Process Hierarchy Diagram (PHD). It allows the consolidation of the representation into the hierarchical and communication relationships between processes. Figure 5.36 shows the process hierarchy diagram for the example used.

We now consider subjects of processes, which are embedded in a process network. They can only indirectly communicate with the other subjects of the subject network. As seen in the process hierarchy diagram in the figure above, a subject of "process B1" can only communicate with a subject "C1" via a subject of "process B" and "process C".

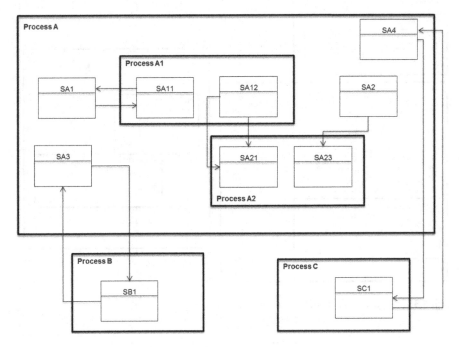

Fig. 5.34 External subjects of "process A"

5.6.6 Business Objects in Process Networks

What is the impact of hierarchical relationships of processes on the joint ownership (joint access rights) of subjects with respect to business objects? In the context of hierarchical process networks, Shared Business Objects can be defined as follows:

- Joint ownership of all subjects of a particular hierarchy level: All subjects of a certain process network on a particular hierarchy level can access a specific business object for reading and/or writing if views with appropriate access rights are available. This is not possible for subjects on levels above or below the addressed one. In Fig. 5.37, "Bo-1" is a Shared Business Object. It is in joint ownership of the subjects "SC1", "SC3", and "SC6", as well as of all other subjects at this level. The latter do not appear in the figure, as they are not interface subjects.
- Joint ownership of all subjects from a particular hierarchy level downwards: In this case, in addition, all subjects of the processes "process C1" and "process C2" are joint owners of the business object "Bo-1" in Fig. 5.37.
- Joint ownership of all subjects from a particular hierarchy level upwards: With such a definition, business object "Bo-2" in Fig. 5.37 is in the joint ownership of all subjects in the process "process C2" and all subjects of the parent process.
- Joint ownership of all subjects in the entire hierarchical process network: Each subject of the hierarchical process network has access to such a business object, according to its views.

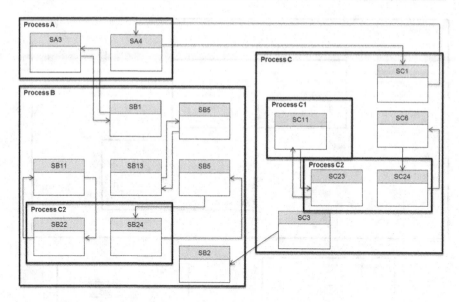

Fig. 5.35   Process hierarchy of "process A" and "process B"

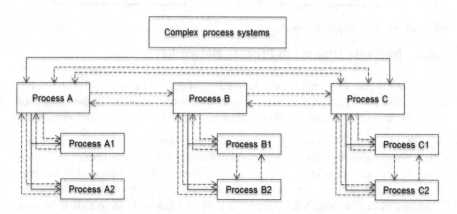

Fig. 5.36   Process hierarchy diagram

Intelligibility can be achieved by applying the following guiding principle during the modeling process: "As simple as possible, but as complex as necessary". Process networks may lead to a hierarchical structure. They facilitate "stepping through" by introducing generalization and refinement.

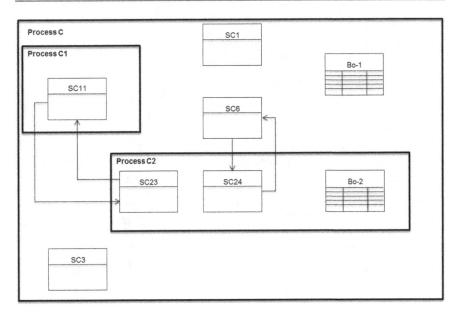

Fig. 5.37 Joint ownership of business objects in process networks

5.6.7   Reduction to Observable Behavior

Following the "as simple as possible" principle again, we can often reduce behavior to what is visible in the network.

The previously discussed simplifications when representing horizontal process networks refer to the interaction structure. In addition, even at the level of subjects, behavior representations are necessary to derive the externally visible behavior of an interface subject. In this context, we exploit the fact that subjects, which belong to different processes but yet are interacting with each other in process networks, are not interested in the internal behavior of the partner subject.

The functional behavior of an external communication partner and its interactions with other subjects in its native process are generally not relevant to subjects in linked processes. A subject is only interested in its partner's communication behavior in the other process to the extent that it is directly affected by this behavior. Therefore, the partner's behavior can be reduced to that interface when modeling. This is first done by replacing all those send and receive states of its communication partner used to simply interact with process-internal subjects with so-called pseudo-internal functions. In this way, the subject is shielded from communication behavior of the partner subject that does not directly affect it. In a second step, parts of the action behavior of the partner subject can be hidden by normalizing its behavior as shown in Sect. 5.5.6. Subject behavior reduced in this

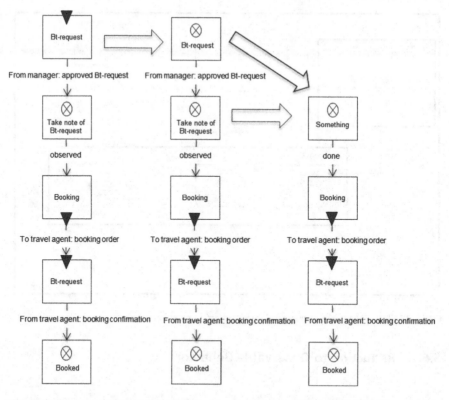

Fig. 5.38 Deriving interface behavior of the process "business trip application" with respect to the external subject "travel agent" from the behavior of the subject "travel office"

way is externally observable, and ultimately, represents the interface description of a process toward the partner process.

We introduce behavior reduction therefore as restriction on the behavior of a subject to aspects, which need to be recognizable by another subject in a linked process.

In the example, it is not relevant for the interface subject "travel agent" that the "travel office" communicates within its subprocess "business trip application" with the manager of the applicant. The travel agent is interested only in the communication behavior of the travel agency referring to him directly, i.e., the fact that they order him to book. The original behavior of the travel office, as shown in the left part of Fig. 5.38, can therefore be reduced from the view of the travel agent to the behavior visible in the far right part.

The first step is to replace the receive state "business trip request" by the pseudo-internal function "business trip request". The result is shown in the middle of the behavioral description. This can then be further simplified by normalization: Both internal states "business trip request" and "take note of business trip request" are summarized to the function "something". The right description emerges, representing the interface behavior of the process "business trip request" with respect to the subject "travel agent" in the booking process.

5.7   Extension Constructs for Subject Behavior Specifications

5.7.1   To Go

The structuring concepts for large process structures work quite well, but we still have problems describing complex subject behavior.

What do you mean by complex subject behavior? Can you provide concrete examples here?

Yes, take for instance recurring patterns of behavior - we have these for approvals, or when messages come in unexpectedly (out of sequence), such as cancelations. Basically, we can model such situations using existing constructs. However, such representations cannot be constructed in a straightforward way and they are not really transparent.

There are modeling capabilities to handle this. Macros can be used for similar behavior structures. And exception handling can be used in case reactions to specific messages need to be modeled.

That sounds good. Did it help you?

Yes, we could actually use macros for recurring behavior structures, and exception handling to represent proper reactions to important messages.

5.7.2 Behavior Macros

Quite often, a certain behavior pattern occurs repeatedly within a subject. This happens in particular, when in various parts of the process identical actions need to be performed. If only the basic constructs are available to this respect, the same subject behavior needs to be described many times.

Instead, this behavior can be defined as a so-called behavior macro. Such a macro can be embedded at different positions of a subject behavior specification as often as required. Thus, variations in behavior can be consolidated, and the overall behavior can be significantly simplified.

The brief example of the business trip application is not an appropriate scenario to illustrate here the benefit of the use of macros. Instead, we use an example for order processing. Figure 5.39 contains a macro for the behavior to process customer orders. After placing the "order", the customer receives an order confirmation; once the "delivery" occurs, the delivery status is updated.

As with the subject, the start and end states of a macro also need to be identified. For the start states, this is done similarly to the subjects by putting black triangles in the top left corner of the respective state box. In our example, "order" and "delivery" are the two correspondingly labeled states. In general, this means that a behavior can initiate a jump to different starting points within a macro.

The end of a macro is depicted by gray bars, which represent the successor states of the parent behavior. These are not known during the course of the macro definition.

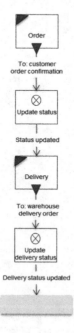

Fig. 5.39 Behavior macro "Order processing"

Figure 5.40 shows a subject behavior in which the modeler uses the macro "order processing" to model both a regular order (with purchase order), as well as a call order.

The icon for a macro is a small table, which can contain multiple columns in the first line for different start states of the macro. The valid start state for a specific case is indicated by the incoming edge of the state transition from the calling behavior. The middle row contains the macro name, while the third row again may contain several columns with possible output transitions, which end in states of the surrounding behavior.

The left branch of the behavioral description refers to regular customer orders. The embedded macro is labeled correspondingly and started with the status "order", namely through linking the edge of the transition "order accepted" with this start state. Accordingly, the macro is closed via the transition "delivery status updated".

The right embedding deals with call orders according to organizational frameworks and frame contracts. The macro starts therefore in the state "delivery". In this case, it also ends with the transition "delivery status updated".

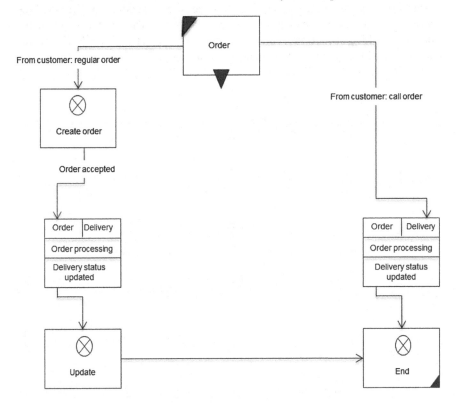

Fig. 5.40 Subject behavior for order processing with macro integration

Similar subject behavior can be combined into macros. When being specified, the environment is initially hidden, since it is not known at the time of modeling.

5.7.3   Behavior Macro Classes

The behavior macros presented in Sect. 5.7.2 enable multiple use of the description of similar sequences of behavior within a subject. There are also situations in which identical behavior sequences are required in several subjects. In order to avoid redundant modeling of this behavior, we introduce so-called behavior macro classes. These are descriptions of behavior that can be included multiple times in different subjects.

When defining a behavior macro class, the subjects involved in communication are not known. We use formal subject names to handle this. They represent subjects as part of internal macro communication. When embedded in a subject, the formal names for the other send and receive operations are replaced by the names of the subjects with which the calling subject communicates corresponding to the macro.

An example of the use of a behavior macro class in the course of modeling is a generic approval process. This runs the same way, regardless of what specific case (business trip request, vacation request, etc.) needs to be handled. In Fig. 5.41, the behavior macro class for the approval process is shown. The formal subject name "approver", which at runtime contains the concrete subject that should review the request, is set in angle brackets to mark it accordingly.

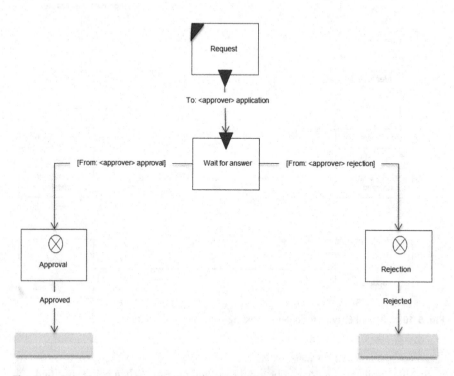

Fig. 5.41 Behavior macro class "request for approval"

Figure 5.42 exemplifies for "request for approval" how a macro of a behavior macro class can be integrated into a subject behavior. The formal name of the subject "<approver>" is replaced at runtime by the subject name "manager".

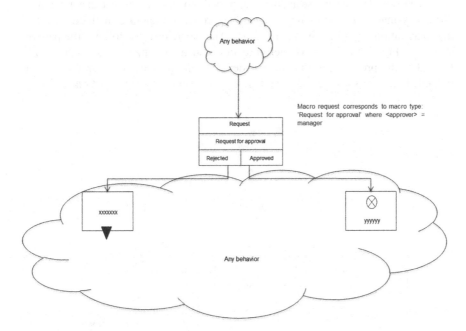

Fig. 5.42 Using a behavior macro class

Behavior macro classes improve the management of processes. For example, if the approval process needs to be fundamentally changed, it is sufficient to adapt the definition of the macro class. Consequently, all processes using this macro class have the revised behavior. However, it has to be ensured that the communication partners of a subject with a modified macro class are compatible to this modified behavior.

> Macro classes generalize subject behavior and establish behavior conventions in this way.

5.7.4 Subject Classes

In processes, there are sometimes subjects, which have the same behavior. To avoid redundant description of these subjects, subject classes can be defined.

A subject class is an abstract subject that is assigned a specific subject name at runtime.

As with behavior macro classes, at the time of modeling the subjects involved are not known, since these depend on the respective process. Therefore, also in this case, a formal subject name is used for sending and receiving operations.

As an example, we can use again the approval process. A subject can act in many different contexts as approving instance ("approver"). Examples include business trip or vacation requests, buying a PC, etc. The behavior often follows the pattern shown in Fig. 5.43, which is therefore modeled as a subject class "approver". Instead of the process-specific subject identifier, the formal name "applicant" set in angle brackets is used for the send and receive states in the subject class.

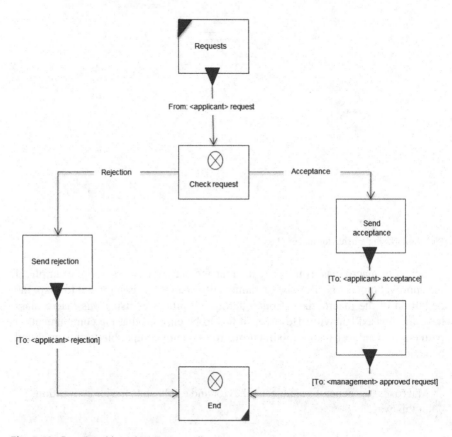

Fig. 5.43 Sample subject class "approver"

Figure 5.44 shows how subject classes can be used in processes. The defined subject class "approver" is used in both the process "business trip application" and in the process "PC purchase". In the process "business trip application", it represents the subject "manager" and in the process "PC purchase" the subject "controller". The formal name of the subject "applicant" is replaced in the case of the business trip application by the subject "employee" and in the case of the PC purchase by the subject "customer", respectively. The subject name of "management" is replaced by "manager" in the process "business trip application", and by "accounting" in the process "PC purchase".

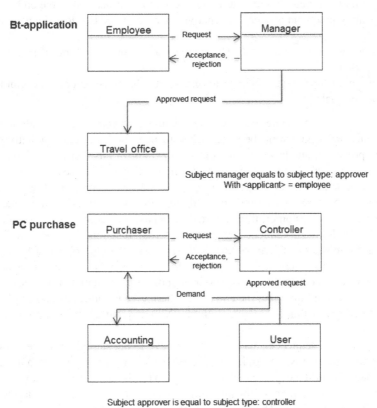

Fig. 5.44 Use of the subject class "approver"

5.7.5 Freedom of Choice

So far, the behavior of subjects has been regarded as a distinct sequence of internal functions, send and receive activities. In many cases, however, the sequence of internal execution is not important.

Certain sequences of actions can be executed overlapping. We are talking about freedom of choice when accomplishing tasks. In this case, the modeler does not specify a strict sequence of activities. Rather, a subject (or concrete entity assigned to a subject) will organize to a particular extent its own behavior at runtime.

The freedom of choice with respect to behavior is described as a set of alternative clauses, which outline a number of parallel paths. At the beginning and end of each alternative, switches are used: a switch set at the beginning means that this alternative path is mandatory to get started, a switch set at the end means that this alternative path must be completely traversed. This leads to the following constellations:

- Beginning is set/end is set: Alternative needs to be processed to the end.
- Beginning is set/end is open: Alternative must be started but does not need to be finished.
- Beginning is open/end is set: Alternative may be processed, but if so must be completed.
- Beginning is open/end is open: Alternative may be processed but does not have to be completed.

The execution of an alternative clause is considered complete when all alternative sequences, which were begun and had to be completed, have actually been entirely processed and have reached the end operator of the alternative clause.

Transitions between the alternative paths of an alternative clause are not allowed. An alternate sequence starts in its start point and ends entirely within its end point.

Figure 5.45 shows an example for modeling alternative clauses. After receiving an order from the customer, three alternative behavioral sequences can be started, whereby the leftmost sequence, with the internal function "update order" and sending the message "deliver order" to the subject "warehouse", must be started in any case. This is determined by the "X" in the symbol for the start of the alternative sequences (gray bar is the starting point for alternatives). This sequence must be processed through to the end of the alternative because it is also marked in the end symbol of this alternative with an "X" (gray bar as the end point of the alternative).

The other two sequences may, but do not have to be, started. However, in case the middle sequence is started, i.e., the message "order arrived" is sent to the sales department, it must be processed to the end. This is defined by an appropriate marking in the end symbol of the alternatives ("X" in the lower gray bar as the end point of the alternatives). The rightmost path can be started but does not need to be completed.

The individual actions in the alternative paths of an alternative clause may be arbitrarily executed in parallel and overlapping, or in other words: a step can be executed in an alternative sequence and then be followed by an action in any other sequence. This gives the performer of a subject the appropriate freedom of choice while executing his actions.

In the example, the order can thus first be updated, and then the message "order arrived" sent to sales. Now, either the message "deliver order" can be sent to the warehouse or one of the internal functions, "update sales status" or "collect data for statistics", can be executed.

The left alternative must be executed completely, and the middle alternative must also have been completed, if the first action ("inform sales" in the example) is executed. It can occur that only the left alternative is processed because the middle one was never started. Alternatively, the sequence in the middle may have already reached its end point, while the left is not yet complete. In this case, the process

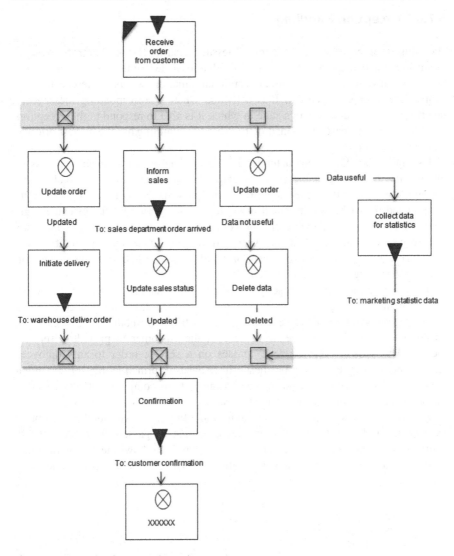

Fig. 5.45 Example of process alternatives

waits until the left one has reached its end point. Only then will the state "confirmation" be reached in the alternative clause. The right branch neither needs to be
started nor to be completed. It is therefore irrelevant for the completion of the
alternative construct.

The leeway for freedom of choice with regard to actions and decisions
associated with work activities can be represented through modeling the
various alternatives—situations can thus be modeled according to actual
regularities and preferences.

5.7.6   Exception Handling

Handling of an exception (also termed message guard, message control, message monitoring, and message observer) is a behavioral description of a subject that becomes relevant when a specific, exceptional situation occurs while executing a subject behavior specification. It is activated when a corresponding message is received, and the subject is in a state in which it is able to respond to the exception handling. In such a case, the transition to exception handling has the highest priority and will be enforced.

Exception handling is characterized by the fact that it can occur in a process in many behavior states of subjects. The receipt of certain messages, e.g., to abort the process, always results in the same processing pattern. This pattern would have to be modeled for each state in which it is relevant. Exception handlings cause high modeling effort and lead to complex process models, since from each affected state a corresponding transition has to be specified. In order to prevent this situation, we introduce a concept similar to exception handling in programming languages or interrupt handling in operating systems.

To illustrate the compact description of exception handlings, we use again the service management process with the subject "service desk" introduced in Sect. 5.6.5. This subject identifies a need for a business trip in the context of processing a customer order—an employee needs to visit the customer to provide a service locally. The subject "service desk" passes on a service order to an employee. Hence, the employee issues a business trip request. In principle, the service order may be canceled at any stage during processing up to its completion. Consequently, this also applies to the business trip application and its subsequent activities.

Below, it is first shown how the behavior modeling looks without the concept of exception handling. The cancelation message must be passed on to all affected subjects to bring the process to a defined end. Figure 5.46 shows the communication structure diagram with the added cancelation messages to the involved subjects.

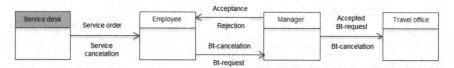

Fig. 5.46 Communication structure diagram (CSD) of the business trip application process including cancelation messages

A cancelation message can be received by the employee either while filling out the application, or while waiting for the approval or rejection message from the manager. With respect to the behavior of the subject "employee", the state "response received from manager" must also be enriched with the possible input message containing the cancelation and the associated consequences (see Fig. 5.47). The verification of whether filing the request is followed by a cancelation, is modeled through a receive state with a timeout. In case the timeout is zero,

there is no cancelation message in the input pool and the business trip request is sent
to the manager. Otherwise, the manager is informed of the cancelation and the
process terminates for the subject "employee".

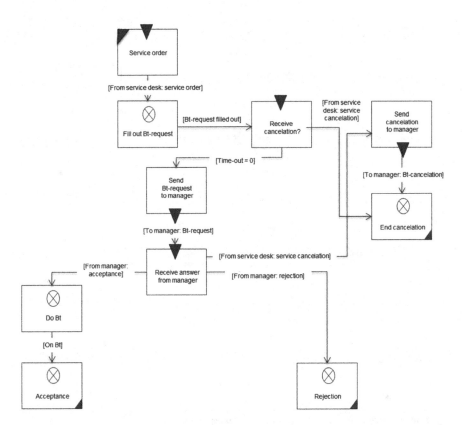

Fig. 5.47 Handling the cancelation message using existing constructs (without the concept of
exception handling)

A corresponding adjustment of the behavior must be made for each subject
which can receive a cancelation message, including the manager, the travel office,
and the interface subject "travel agent".

This relatively simple example already shows that taking such exception
messages into account can quickly make behavior descriptions confusing to understand. The concept of exception handling, therefore, should enable supplementing
exceptions to the default behavior of subjects in a structured and compact form.
Figure 5.48 shows how such a concept affects the behavior of the employee.

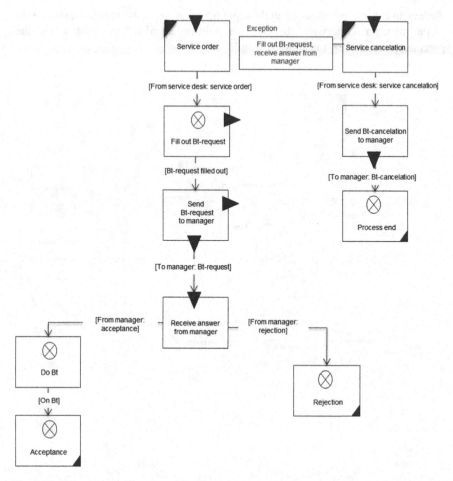

Fig. 5.48 Behavior of subject "employee" with exception handling

Instead of, as shown in Fig. 5.47, modeling receive states with a timeout zero and corresponding state transitions, the behavioral description is enriched with the exception handling "service cancelation". Its initial state is labeled with the states from which it is branched to, once the message "service cancelation" is received. In the example, these are the states "fill out Bt-request" and "receive answer from manager". Each of them is marked by a triangle on the right edge of the state symbol. The exception behavior leads to an exit of the subject, after the message "service cancelation" has been sent to the subject "manager".

A subject behavior does not necessarily have to be brought to an end by an exception handling; it can also return from there to the specified default behavior. Exception handling behavior in a subject may vary, depending on from which state or what type of message (cancelation, temporary stopping of the process, etc.) it is called. The initial state of exception handling can be a receive state or a function state.

Messages, like "service cancelation", that lead to exception handling always have higher priority than other messages. This is how modelers express that specific messages are read in a preferred way. For instance, when the approval message from the manager is received in the input pool of the employee, and shortly thereafter the cancelation message, the latter is read first. This leads to the corresponding abort consequences.

Since now additional messages can be exchanged between subjects, it may be necessary to adjust the corresponding conditions for the input pool structure. In particular, the input pool conditions should allow storing an interrupt message in the input pool.

> To meet organizational dynamics, exception handling and extensions are required. They allow taking not only discrepancies, but also new patterns of behavior, into account.

5.7.7 Behavior Extensions

When exceptions occur, currently running operations are interrupted. This can lead to inconsistencies in the processing of business objects. For example, the completion of the business trip form is interrupted once a cancelation message is received, and the business trip application is only partially completed. Such consequences are considered acceptable due to the urgency of cancelation messages. In less urgent cases, the modeler would like to extend the behavior of subjects in a similar way, however, without causing inconsistencies. This can be achieved by using a notation analogous to exception handling. Instead of denoting the corresponding diagram with "exception", it is labeled with "extension".

Behavior extensions enrich a subject's behavior with behavior sequences that can be reached from several states equivocally.

For example, the employee may be able to decide on his own that the business trip is no longer required and withdraw his trip request. Figure 5.49 shows that the employee is able to cancel a business trip request in the states "send business trip request to manager" and "receive answer from manager". If the transition "withdraw business trip request" is executed in the state "send business trip request to manager", then the extension "F1" is activated. It leads merely to canceling of the application. Since the manager has not yet received a request, he does not need to be informed.

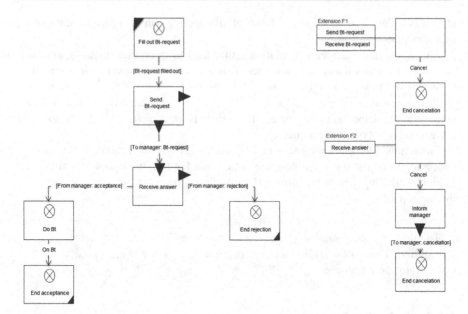

Fig. 5.49 Subject behavior of employee with behavior extensions

In case the employee decides to withdraw the business trip request in the state "receive answer from manager", then extension "F2" is activated. Here, first the supervisor is informed, and then the business trip is canceled.

5.7.8 Additional Semantics

Often it is necessary to record further information in a process, explaining what specific considerations have influenced modeling. This is possible with the so-called additional semantics. It allows specification of reasons for the existence of subjects or conditions to be added within the behavioral description.

For example, it may be necessary for reasons of compliance to include additional subjects in a process and to introduce additional interactions between subjects, in order to satisfy certain external or internal rules. Such requirements can, e.g., result from quality management systems like ISO 9001, environmental regulations, or rules affecting Internal Control Systems (ICS), such as the Sarbanes-Oxley Act (SOX) (see Sect. 3.6.4). They usually cause higher communication overhead and thus, often more complex processes. This poses the risk that the additionally modeled subjects and states are removed in the course of a subsequent optimization because the optimizer might no longer know the reasons why certain subjects or communication patterns had been installed. Therefore, such subjects and states should be provided with appropriate references to those regulations that justify their introduction.

Figure 5.50 shows the existing business trip application process with the addition of an internal control for international business trips. This states that, effective immediately, such trips must be approved by management, to better control travel costs in difficult economic times, and to reduce them where appropriate. In the modified process, there is now a new subject "management board". This subject will receive for approval all submitted requests for international travel. Its specification is therefore enriched with a corresponding comment, pointing out that it was introduced in the process for reasons of compliance in conjunction with the internal control system (ICS).

Fig. 5.50 Revised business trip application process including the management review of requests for international travel and their justification

Due to the introduction of the subject "management board" in the business trip application process, the behavior of the subject "manager" also needs to be adapted. The manager first checks whether an application has been made for international travel. If this is not the case, he will proceed as previously specified. In case of an international travel request, the trip request is forwarded for consideration to the board. This is specified by introducing the send state "request board review" and the corresponding receive state "board response". Both states are marked with "ICS request". Figure 5.51 shows the modified behavior of the subject "manager".

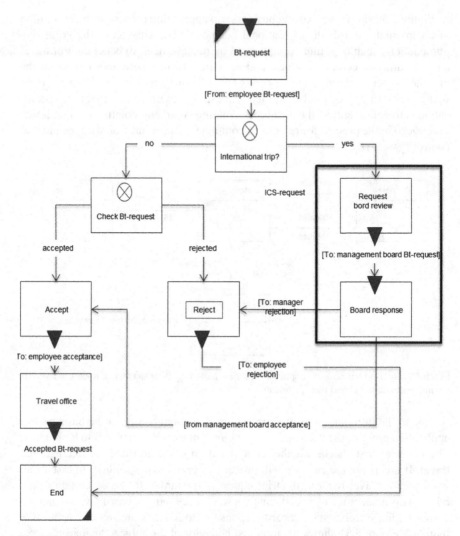

Fig. 5.51 Communication of manager with board

Although S-BPM-models are constructed in a systematic way (Who is involved? Who interacts with whom/with what? What information needs to be exchanged to perform tasks?), it is often necessary to provide additional information, on how a coherent result of the work can be achieved—this is when you should use the S-BPM feature "Additional Semantics".

References

Fleischmann, A.: Distributed Systems – Software Design and Implementation, Heidelberg 1995.

Grässle, P.; Baumann, H.; Baumann, P.: UML 2.0 projektorientiert – Geschäftsprozessmodellierung, IT-System-Spezifikation und Systemintegration mit der UML, Bonn 2004.

Subject-Oriented Modeling by Construction and Restriction

6

6.1 To Go

Now I've learned in the last chapter how to model what I want, but I dread getting started! It will take quite a while before I get something on paper.

Don't worry. This is not mandatory when using the subject-oriented method! It is possible to construct a process the 'other way around'. You can start with a process where every subject can do anything it wants, and everyone communicates with everyone else. Then, just remove what is not needed step-by-step, until only the essential elements remain.

This sounds like striptease!

Ha! Ha!   Ha! Ha!   Ha! Ha!

A. Fleischmann et al., *Subject-Oriented Business Process Management*,
DOI 10.1007/978-3-642-32392-8_6, © The Author(s) 2012

I like the idea! For my processes, I would like to have agility, not restrictions. My staff should not be spoon-fed, but rather guided in certain ways, and guidance should only be as tight as necessary.

This method is called restriction. The nice thing about restriction is that it is actually postmodern by its very nature—'anything goes ...' And this only works with S-BPM. However, in most projects, the traditional way is taken—which is also possible—it is called construction.

In the previous chapter, we have discussed modeling in detail. For this purpose, a variety of constructs are available. When putting them to practice, modelers can proceed along two fundamentally different ways: modeling by construction and modeling by restriction.

The method of construction is widely known: starting point is a process for which initially nothing has been clearly defined. It starts with a "blank sheet of paper", and then a process model is "constructed". The involved subjects, their activities, and the required business objects have to be introduced step by step. Traditional modeling approaches, such as Unified Modeling Language (UML), Business Process Model & Notation (BPMN), or event-driven process chains (EPCs), only support modeling by construction.

Modeling by restriction works differently. Its starting point is a "world" of subjects where, initially, every subject can do everything and is able to communicate with all other subjects. Modeling starts with an open model with predefined communication links between all subjects. The starting point for modeling by restriction corresponds to a picture in which, based on modern communications technology, each partner is able to exchange any information with any other partner, at any time, and at any place. This picture becomes reality, for instance, when each person can contact any other person by electronic mail (e-mail). In S-BPM, the starting point for modeling by restriction is a single "universal" process, where everyone communicates with everyone else. This process is then restricted step by step until only the desired communication relations remain. This is done by successively removing those elements, which are not required to accomplish tasks.

Figure 6.1 summarizes the fundamental modeling approaches possible with S-BPM.

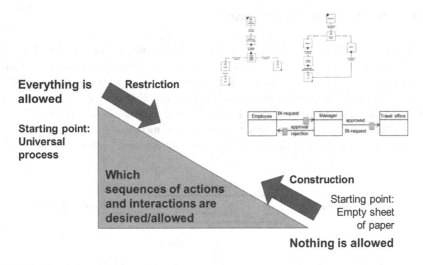

Fig. 6.1 Restriction and construction

6.2 Modeling by Construction

When designing a process model, the Actors begin with a "blank sheet of paper". Using the information from analysis, the process is described step by step. The activities required for the subject-oriented approach have already been presented and are summarized here briefly:

- Description of the processes and their relationships (process network)
- Identification of the process to be described
- Identification of subjects involved in the process
- Determination of messages exchanged between the subjects
- Description of the behavior of the individual subjects
- Definition of business objects and their use

These activities need not be carried out in a strictly sequential manner. It can occur, e.g., that during the course of describing the behavior of a subject, it is discovered that another message needs to be added or removed later on. In this way, the process model is continuously expanded.

Modeling by construction is common to most modeling techniques, such as EPCs, or BPMN. However, with these, it represents the only possible approach to build models.

Start with a blank screen or sheet of paper. You should use construction when there is nothing clearly defined yet in a process. Introduce step by step the involved subjects, their activities, and business objects.

6.3   Modeling by Restriction

In the process model of S-BPM, besides modeling by construction, the modeler can also use modeling by restriction. In doing so, he assumes a universal process model. In a universal process model, each subject participating in a process is able to send a message to any other involved subject at any time and also receive a message from any other subject at any time, respectively. This message is labeled "message" and can, in the case of business objects, transfer any media object. The result is a universal process that is characterized by the number of its subjects. Figure 6.2

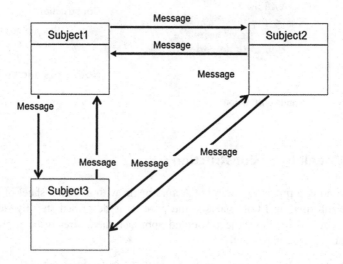

Fig. 6.2 Universal process with three subjects

shows a universal process with three subjects.

Each subject can send messages to any other subject at any time and also receive messages accordingly. This is indicated by the respective arrows between the subject boxes. Consequently, each subject has a similar initial behavior. This is shown in Fig. 6.3. The boxes represent states of the subject; the arrows transitions associated with activities, such as "receive" depicts the transition between the state "what do I do?" and the state "receive message".

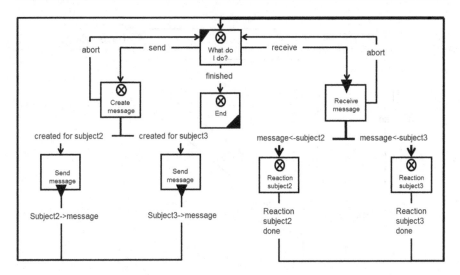

Fig. 6.3 Initial subject behavior of Subject1 in a universal process with three subjects

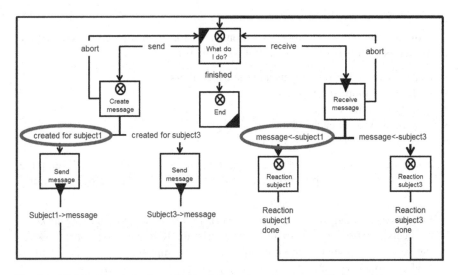

Fig. 6.4 Initial subject behavior of Subject2 in a universal process with three subjects

Subject2 and Subject3 have analogous behavior. Figure 6.4 shows the initial behavior of Subject2 as an example. The elliptical frame indicates that Subject2 was replaced by Subject1.

When more than three subjects are involved in a process, the behavioral descriptions are supplemented accordingly—a corresponding send or receive path for Subject4 is included into the behavior scheme, and so on and so forth.

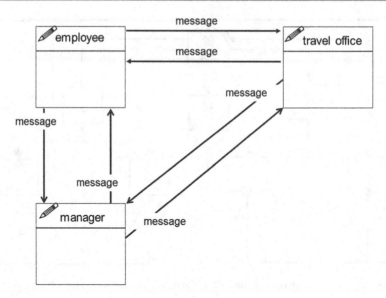

Fig. 6.5 Subject interaction diagram with subject identifiers

Based on the universal process (demonstrated for three subjects), modeling by restriction is then performed in the following five steps:

- Determine number of subjects and their identifiers
- Reduce communication paths
- Specify message types
- Adapt behavior of each subject accordingly
- Specify and refine business objects

These steps will now be detailed in the following sections. We will develop the process "business trip application" as a demonstration of modeling by restriction.

In case you already know all of the work performers accomplishing tasks (subjects), you are advised to model by restriction. Remove step by step those interaction relations that are not required for accomplishing tasks. This will lead you to an accurate specification of your organizational behavior.

6.3.1 Determine Number of Subjects and Subject Identifiers

We need the three subjects "employee", "manager", and "travel office" to model the process "business trip application". The abstract names Subject1, Subject2, and Subject3 are replaced by these concrete subject identifiers. Figure 6.5 shows the

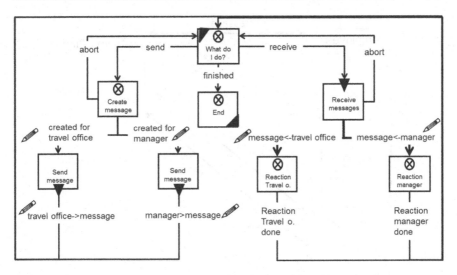

Fig. 6.6 Behavior of the subject "employee" with adaption of the subject names

subject interaction diagram in which the subjects have already been renamed. The modification is highlighted using the pencil icon.

After renaming the subjects, their behavior has to be adapted. Figure 6.6 shows the required changes for the subject "employee" (previously Subject1).

6.3.2 Reduce Communication Paths

So far, each subject is able to communicate with every other subject. In the target process, in order to achieve a work result, many of these communication relationships are not necessary. Therefore, they need to be removed from the process model. In the upper part of Fig. 6.7, the communication structure before elimination is shown. Below this, the new structure after removal of the communication relationships not required for handling business trip applications is illustrated.

Due to the removal of communication relationships, the behavior of the affected subjects also needs to be adjusted. Figure 6.8 shows the behavior of the subject "employee" prior to the change. The circled paths for sending and receiving messages to the subject "travel office" need to be removed.

Figure 6.9 shows the behavior after removal of the corresponding behavior paths.

6.3.3 Specify Message Types

In the next step, the messages are reduced to the necessary content. It is determined for each communication what information needs to be transmitted. The hitherto open transmission interface "message" is tailored to the content required for the process.

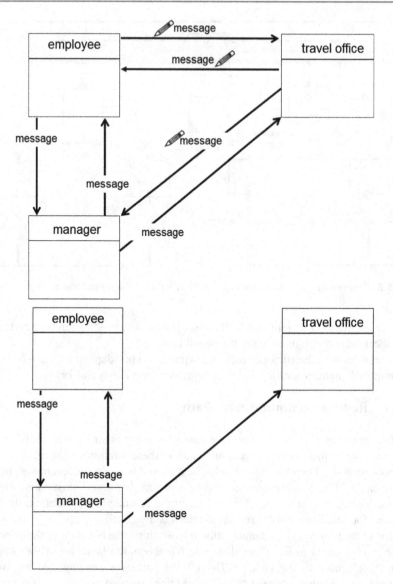

Fig. 6.7 Removing dispensable communication relationships—before and after removal

Figure 6.10 shows the customized communication structure. The general message "message" is no longer exchanged between the employee and manager subject. The employee sends the message "business trip request" to the manager, and he sends either the message "approval", or "rejection" (instead of "message") back.

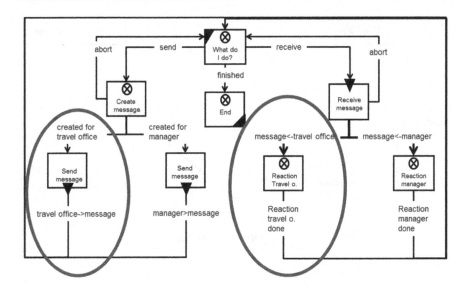

Fig. 6.8 Behavior specification prior to removal of communication links that are not required for task accomplishment

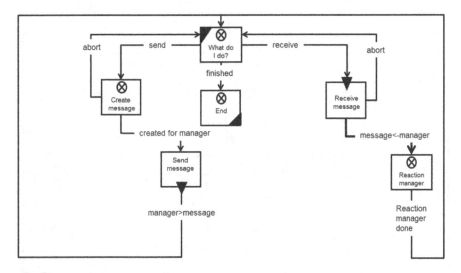

Fig. 6.9 Behavior specification after removal of dispensable communication links

When renaming or splitting the general (unified) message, the behavior of subjects has to be adapted accordingly. Figure 6.11 shows the corresponding changes. In the left half of the behavior diagram, the message with the modified

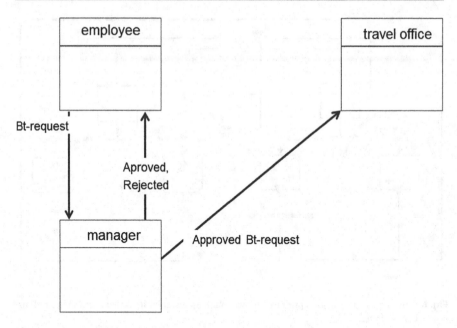

Fig. 6.10 Communication structure with application-specific message types

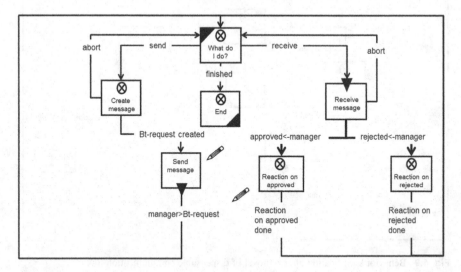

Fig. 6.11 Behavior with adapted message types

name has already been included. In the reception branch, the message type "message" has been divided into the message types "rejection" and "approval".

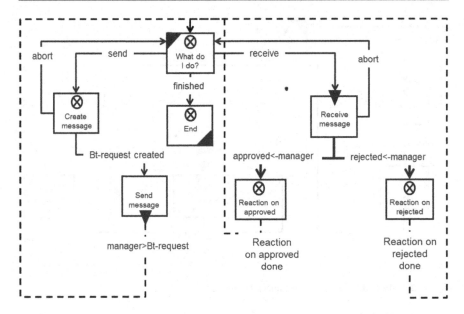

Fig. 6.12 Subject behavior including behavior paths that are not required (*dashed lines*)

6.3.4   Adapt Behavior of Subjects Accordingly

So far, all subjects in the process model could send and receive messages in any order. Thus, the subject "employee" could send the message "Bt-request" as often as desired to the subject "manager". In addition, the subject "employee" should only start waiting for a message from the subject "manager" after having sent the "Bt-request" message. After receiving the message "approval" or "rejection", the end state should be reachable.

Figure 6.12 shows the behavior of the subject "employee" in which the unnecessary behavior paths are represented as dashed lines.

The paths not required are removed and replaced with the desired behavior. After sending the message "Bt-request", the state "receive message" can be entered. The transition from the state "what do I do?" to the state "receive message" can be removed. This amendment ensures that the message "Bt-request" is sent only once, and then a corresponding answer is awaited.

The transitions from the states "reaction on rejected" and "reaction on approved" to the state "what do I do?" are also removed, and instead transitions to the state "end" are added. This modification ensures that the particular process or its instance terminates after a respective response has been received.

Figure 6.13 shows the specifically adapted behavior of the subject "employee".

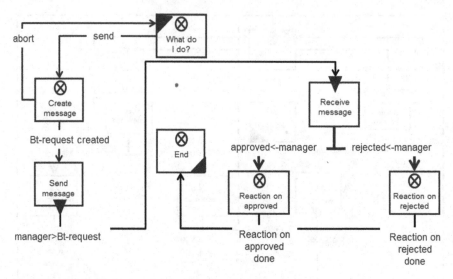

Fig. 6.13 Adjusted behavior of the subject "employee"

Field	Content
Name	
Surname	
Start trip	
Finished trip	
Customer/Destination	
Reason	

Fig. 6.14 Structure of the business object for the message type "Bt-request"

6.3.5 Specify and Refine Business Objects

When using the message type "message", a universal business object "blank sheet of paper" is transmitted. In this business object, the data to be transmitted can be entered without any formal restrictions. This informal data entry is restricted when using application-specific message types. For each message type, a business object is defined which allows the desired information to be transmitted in a certain format when the corresponding message type is transferred from sender to receiver. Figure 6.14 shows the business object that is transmitted when sending the message "Bt-request".

When using the messages "approved" or "rejected", the business object "blank sheet of paper" continues to be transferred. On demand, the manager can enter here the reasons for his decision, or any other information, without format restrictions. The example shows that the message types and business objects required for task accomplishment can be defined in parallel.

6.4   Evaluation

S-BPM is the only known approach enabling both traditional modeling by construction and innovative modeling by restriction.

Since process modeling requires some cognitive effort and methodological interventions, such as interviews and prototyping, describing processes is often accompanied by misunderstandings. The consistent use of message-based interaction helps to avoid misunderstandings by ensuring the integrity of interaction flows. The main task in comprehensive business process management is the transformation of business processes to communication relationships between work performers (subjects).

The methodical guideline represented by the six steps outlined in Sect. 6.2 provides a means for narrowing down an S-BPM-process pattern to valid patterns of interaction. This enables stringent achievement of work outcomes. This restriction, by focusing on simple interaction relations, helps to increase acceptance for the modeling of business processes and also ensures the usability of the S-BPM method.

Reference

Fleischmann, A., Stary, Ch., Whom to Talk to? A Stakeholder Perspective on Business Processes, in: Universal Access in the Information Society, Springer, Vol. 11, No. 3, 2011.

Subject-Oriented Validation of Processes and Process Models

7

7.1 To Go

Now we have a process model which describes the communication between all parties involved. The results from analysis have in fact been incorporated during modeling. But does the model behave in the way we intended? We should check this.

I took care that all of the involved parties could participate in modeling and could consider the process from their individual perspectives. During validation, they actually did a dry run of the process, which means I have organized a kind of interactive theater performance, instead of boring testing with checklists, which is only done under great pressure anyway and therefore not thoroughly enough. Selected participants have played their role in a 'process theater', following their script, or in more formal terms, according to their subject behavior.

And by playing theater, we could find out whether we achieve our objectives when executing the process?

A. Fleischmann et al., *Subject-Oriented Business Process Management*, DOI 10.1007/978-3-642-32392-8_7, © The Author(s) 2012

Yes, the theater has been a lot of fun. The fact that we have rehearsed the process according to our roles, helped us in finding out first hand whether we want to work in this way, or rather, whether we can actually achieve our objectives. We first rehearsed the process using pencil and paper, but this was quite an effort. It went smoother using IT-based role-playing. We could rehearse it several times in a short period of time, and in doing so, test several process variants— a kind of automated process theater, so to speak.

Yes, with IT-based role-playing, we had a lot of fun. Everyone tried to double-cross the process. Thus, we could identify many gaps that we were able to fix quickly. So we could test the process intensively before continuing on into implementation.

That sounds good, trying out processes before implementing them and spending a lot of money, only to find out that they don't work the way they should.

7.2   Nature of Validation

Once a process has been modeled (see Chap. 5), it is advisable to validate and optimize the process and its model, before the model is implemented in the organization and IT. In this chapter, we discuss the validation.

In process management, a validation is understood as a review of whether a business process is effective, i.e., whether it delivers the expected results, either in the form of a product or service. This is equivalent to the verification required by ISO 9001:2008, Sect. 7.5.2 (processes of production and service provision) as proof that a process is capable of meeting the required specifications and quality characteristics (cf. Schmelzer and Sesselmann 2010, p. 330). As outcome of a process, we do not only consider the process result from the view of customers but also its contribution to the implementation of corporate strategy, i.e., its value proposition (see Sect. 3.6.3.2).

The validation should ensure that a process meets its requirements ("doing the right things") and that the specification of process outcomes and procedures as acquired in the course of analysis and modeling, enables an organization to achieve its objectives with the process at hand. Validation is distinguished from optimization, where the goal is to improve the efficiency of a model through simulation ("doing things right", see Chap. 8). Otherwise, validation and optimization may coincide. Thus, in practice, in a validation workshop, recognized optimization approaches are usually also considered for implementation.

Practical experience, particularly in the new conceptual design of business processes, reveals that it is not usually possible to ensure a priori that the designed process model actually produces the intended output quality, from a customer and process owner perspective. During the review of process models, it is again observed in practice that a significant proportion of these models have formal and logical errors, insufficient descriptions, and inadequate focus on customer needs.

An accurate description is a prerequisite for validation. Moreover, it facilitates self-contained maintenance and control.

Therefore, we need to validate both the considered business process itself, including its characteristics and requirements as outlined in analysis, as well as its content and formal aspects as mapped to the specification in the course of modeling.

The concrete objects for validation are therefore the main results of analysis and modeling. They are usually more or less structured text documents, which contain process descriptions from a strategic perspective, as well as graphically presented process models with associated database records that describe model components in the form of attributes in more detail.

We subsequently introduce both the validation of acquired processes (see Sect. 7.4), as well as their mapping to a corresponding model (see Sect. 7.5), since the former is a prerequisite for coherent mapping to a business process model. Before doing so, we show, according to the basic idea of the subject orientation, how the various S-BPM stakeholders are involved in the validation (see Sect. 7.3). With this, subject-oriented validation justifies that a process typically is a highly complex structure with many implicit requirements, the fulfillment of which is best evaluated by involving all concerned parties (stakeholders).

7.3   S-BPM Stakeholders Involved in Validation

In Sect. 3.3, four groups of relevant stakeholders have been identified for Subject-oriented Business Process Management. In the following, we consider them in the context of validation.

7.3.1 Governors

In the course of validation, different Governors act at different levels. The review of the strategic aspects of a process requires knowledge of corporate strategy, critical success factors for the company, and the core processes. As Governors, members of top management (CEOs) therefore evaluate the process documentation, e.g., along the following questions:

- Does the process support the policy and strategy of the organization?
- Is the process approach aligned to the stakeholders (e.g., customers)?
- Are the process objectives clearly defined?
- What are the risks of the process?
- Has a process manager (process owner) been nominated?

The process owner is also usually involved as a Governor in the validation of the process and the process model. Because of his responsibility for the performance of the process, he pays particular attention to the coherence of the appropriate measurement system. A selection of questions he uses to address these issues, under consultation of key performance indicator (KPI) experts from controlling when appropriate, are:

- Are there meaningful metrics to evaluate the extent of target achievements?
- Are the methods of measurement of the KPIs clearly defined?
- Are the target values for the performance metrics systematically determined?
- Are the metrics documented with their attributes in the metrics sheets?
- Are there numerical data defined (e.g., frequency of occurrence of the process per unit of time, breakdown of the numbers with respect to existing process variants)?

When reviewing the process model, process owners take a superordinate perspective, however, in coordination with the Actors involved in its respective steps, while essentially pursuing the following questions:

- Is the process flow in the model clearly defined (sequence of substeps and activities within the substeps)?
- Are the responsibilities (organizational units, roles, and people) clearly defined for each substep?
- Are the relations of the process to other processes and the thereby necessary interfaces adequately described?

A specific task of the Governor in validating process models is to check whether the given conventions of modeling and description have been followed. This is usually carried out by the authority which has adopted the conventions, such as the Organization Department (see Sect. 3.6.3.4).

7.3.2 Actors

Actors (work performers) are the central element in S-BPM and as such are crucial for the validation of process models. They focus on the accuracy of contents, and thus, on the coherent mapping of process analysis data to the process information of the model. The Actors, e.g., responsible people in a respective process, typically have fundamental knowledge and experience with respect to the accomplishment of their tasks while executing the process. They dry run the process in the course of subject-oriented validation in their specific roles as involved Actors (subjects), as modeled, and thereby are able to identify any errors, inconsistencies, and shortcomings. The lessons learned are used to answer the following selected questions, which have been arranged according to key aspects of subject-oriented modeling:

Question about the subjects:

- Are the subjects described in sufficient detail, and do they correspond to the desired roles?

Questions about the interaction of subjects and the messages or business objects exchanged, respectively:

- Are the required inputs, especially information, and the suppliers of such (organizational units, roles, and people) sufficiently detailed and correctly described, i.e., as perceived in reality (see also the principle of accuracy of modeling in Sect. 3.6.3.4)?
- Are the produced results (outputs) and their recipients (organizational units, roles, and people) sufficiently detailed and correctly described, i.e., as perceived in reality (see also the principle of accuracy of the modeling in Sect. 3.6.3.4)?

Questions about the behavior of subjects:

- Are the sequences of actions to be performed in a subject clearly defined?
- Do work instructions (e.g., checklists and guidelines) for the execution of activities in each substep exist, and, if so, are they part of the context of the model?
- Are they sufficiently detailed and intelligible, so that concerned Actors can work accordingly?

Questions about business objects:

- Are the business objects and their structures clearly defined?
- Has it been clearly defined for the business objects, in which process steps which views are required?
- Are operations defined on each business object?

With the answers to such questions, the Actors are able to assess whether they can work according to the model description in a satisfactory way, or whether some simplification or loss of context has occurred in the course of modeling.

7.3.3   Experts

Experts in the role of internal or external consultants may support management on demand when validating the strategy (i.e., the compliance of its respective processes). Experts from controlling could help in assessing the performance figures of the process documentation. When testing models, Actors or the Facilitator could consult methods specialists and tool specialists. In a certain sense, especially the

Actors are experts for validation, as they operate the business. They know the process best and can therefore assess its suitability very well.

7.3.4 Facilitators

A facilitator role in the activity bundle of validation is mostly taken by representatives of middle management who are leading an S-BPM project. They coordinate the execution of tasks occurring during the validation. Specifically, they ensure, e.g., that process documentations and models resulting from analysis are reviewed by the other stakeholders (Governors, Experts, and Actors). Depending on the results of the validation, the Facilitator initiates the transition to other activity bundles. This can be, e.g., the analysis, if a need for improvement with respect to the definition of relevant process indicators and target values is identified.

If the validation, however, has confirmed the effectiveness of the process, the Facilitator triggers optimization, while possibly consulting a simulation Expert. The latter tests different resource allocations in the model, in order to specify requirements for the organization-specific implementation (see Chap. 9). The Facilitator may also decide that optimization will not be performed due to a lack of sufficient data for simulation. Then, the activity bundle concerning the organizational implementation of the process can be immediately initiated.

7.4 Validation of Processes

The basis of the validation process is usually an informal, textual description of a process from a strategic perspective. This results from analysis and includes statements regarding goals, strategy contribution, customer orientation, risks, etc. of the process.

A possible path leading to a review of this kind of process description is the largely linear sequence of the activity bundles analysis and modeling, as is the case when designing a new, not yet existent process. Here, as Facilitator, the responsible person for the organizational development project can pass on the questions for assessing the process, structured in the form of checklists, to the responsible Governors (CEO and process owner), together with the results from analysis, and along with the process model. The selected people perform their review individually and independently, and rate, possibly involving consultants (Experts), the items of the checklist.

In the next step, the Facilitator consolidates the results and attempts to resolve contradictions. Serious deviations of estimates are discussed and clarified in a workshop or in bilateral talks with the involved parties. Finally, once there is consensus about the need for action, the Actors eliminate in the bundle analysis and modeling the recognized deficiencies in an iterative loop. Then, the Facilitator distributes the revised documentation to the Governors for reevaluation of the originally recognized deficiencies.

If thereafter no more contradictions exist, the validation of the process is considered to have been successfully completed, and the Facilitator proceeds with content validation of the process model. Figure 7.1 summarizes the described multistage procedure.

A valid model requires a correct representation of the current state of affairs. It characterizes semantic correctness. This results from the consensus of domain experts and method experts once they consider a model to be accurate. Semantic correctness needs to be differentiated from syntactic validity, as the latter refers to the compliance with specified rules for documentation.

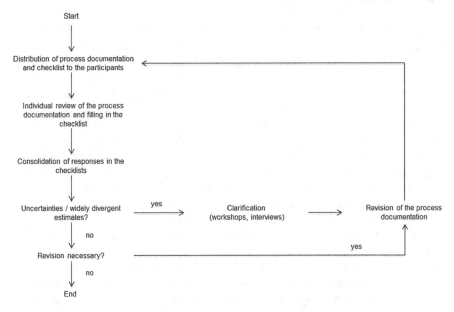

Fig. 7.1 Steps of process validation

In S-BPM, other, less linear paths may lead to the validation of a process. In particular, in case of preexisting and already running daily business processes, validation (or at least validation of specific aspects) can be triggered by an actor. If for instance, a salesperson recognizes in the sales process that an increasing number of customers no longer wants to receive sale documents on paper, but rather in digital form, he may ask the process owner as Governor to modify the process accordingly. The Governor, in turn, depending on his authorities and skills, will either check by himself whether the process design should be adapted to meet this customer need, or he will trigger validation through the superordinate Governors (e.g., management). In case of a positive decision, the process owner can subsequently, by involving a Facilitator (managing the project), analyze change options in detail and initiate their implementation.

S-BPM strives to provide long-term support for the Actors (work performers) by improving their individual situations in daily work. This is why we focus on subject behavior. The subject's inclusion in the interactive behavior, as well as the objective-oriented accomplishment of tasks, determines the conclusiveness of S-BPM Models.

7.5 Validation of Process Models

7.5.1 Formal Validation

Formal validation determines whether the means of describing a process model for its representation are used properly. This type of review requires that a formal syntax exists for the description language. The latter defines the allowed usage of description constructs. This precondition for accurate modeling is met with subject orientation, so that here the formal validation of process models is not a separate step, but rather an implicit part of the activity bundle "modeling".

In contrast to other modeling languages, subject-oriented modeling follows a clear formal syntax and semantics with subject, predicate, and object (see Chap. 12) and only uses a very limited number of symbols (see Chap. 5). An initial positive consequence is that modelers generally have less chance to generate formally incorrect models. However, its main advantage lies in the fact that a suitably designed subject-oriented modeling tool, based on the formally correct use of the notation, can help to entirely avoid formal modeling errors.

Other notations, such as EPCs or BPMN, as well as their corresponding software tools, usually provide users with a high degree of freedom when modeling, and thus increase the potential for errors. This applies to the use of language elements for task settings (e.g., what symbol represents information exchanged by e-mail) and to the arrangement of language elements for representing a specific business logic, input, output, etc. Possible consequences are ambiguities and inconsistencies in the presentation and the violation of rules with respect to the notation's use (syntax errors). The first-mentioned defects can ultimately only be avoided by a comprehensive specification of conventions and a manual or visual verification of syntax compliance.

Some errors regarding notation can be detected automatically if a tool provides the appropriate functionality. Well-known functions of modeling tools in this respect range from preventing incorrect inputs and indicating flaws to the automatic improvement of models. For example, one of these tools (ARIS) produces an error message when an event-driven process chain (EPC) does not, as provided by the syntax definition, start or end with an event or a process interface. Another tool supporting modeling according to the Business Process Model and Notation (BPMN) detects violations of fundamental notational rules, i.e., when modelers incorrectly combine activities in different pools with a sequential flow, the tool replaces it automatically with a message flow.

Despite the implied functions of these tools for supporting established modeling languages, formal model deficiencies remain undetected when using the corresponding methods such as incorrect logical connections in ARIS or BPMN. This leads, e.g., at the latest, in the course of IT implementation to problems. Measures taken by IT to eliminate the deficiencies are often not reflected back into the model. Hence, IT implementation and functional modeling are inconsistent in terms of seamless round-trip engineering (see Sect. 15.1).

In contrast, S-BPM models, which have been described using the appropriate modeling tools, are formally correct and can, after successfully validating their content (see Sect. 7.5.2), be easily implemented or transferred automatically into code (see Chap. 10). Moreover, for subject-oriented modeling, there is no need for comprehensive convention guidelines (e.g., in contrast to ARIS), in order to ensure an intelligible, consistent, and comparable model representation.

7.5.2 Content Validation

Since S-BPM differs from other major BPM approaches, due to its primary reference to subjects and their interaction relationships, it is recommended that this unique feature also be used when validating models for the sake of increased consistency and coherency. In this section, we therefore introduce a subject-specific approach aligned to semantic coherence. The core of this innovative method is its ability to dry run a process, while involving the actual participating process stakeholders to which subjects are assigned. This provides them with a script of how they should perform along a specific process.

According to this script, the process can be executed as a role play. Thus, the participants actively experience the process and get an idea of how the process works in daily business. From their respective subjective points of view, the Actors are able to assess, e.g., whether substeps assigned to their role in the model description, the associated sequence of actions, the thereby required documents, IT systems, and especially their interactions comply with the requirements for the successful completion of a process. The Facilitator organizes and moderates the interactive execution of a process.

For this comprehensive experience of a subject-oriented process, the subjects, their behavior, and the communication structure, which means the interactions of subjects with the thereby exchanged messages and business objects, in accordance with the modeling methodology already introduced in previous chapters, need to be specified. The following variations show how this can be accomplished both with a conventionally designed, as well as with an IT-based role play.

The formal part of validation captures the usage of the modeling language, while the content part represents a task-relevant test procedure. Both evaluations are required for successful validation in S-BPM.

7.5.2.1 Content Validation Using Conventional Role Plays

Conventionally, the implementation of a model in a (role) playing environment can be done as detailed in the following:

Representation of subjects:

- Actual involved stakeholders of the process (subjects) are seated at a large table in a meeting room.
- Name tags identify their roles.
- The input and output trays are represented through storage boxes.

Representation of the behavior of a subject:

- Standard-sized sheets of paper contain the steps required by each subject (sending, receiving, and other activity) according to the process model.

Representation of the subject's interaction including exchanged messages and business objects:

- Index cards (single messages) for labeling with parameters
- Forms describing the business objects used, which can be attached to messages
- Photocopy machine, for making copies of business objects.
- Before beginning, each subject obtains a sufficient number of messages and business objects for the execution of multiple instances.

Figure 7.2 shows part of a possible role playing environment.

Fig. 7.2 Conventional interactive process role play (photo: Alexandra Gerrard)

The Facilitator of the game starts the game by asking the first subject to become active, according to the process model, and to create an instance, e.g., to fill in a business trip request as an employee. The game Facilitator then monitors the further course of the game until the end of the play by checking off the activities performed by the subjects, such as sending and receiving messages or filling out a form, on a corresponding model diagram.

Both the subjects and observers not involved in the process, articulate and document their perceptions, e.g., on the following topics:

- Have Subjects been forgotten? If yes, which ones?
- Have Messages been forgotten? If yes, which ones?
- Have Business objects been forgotten? If yes, which ones?
- Are the business objects structured correctly, or are data elements missing or redundant?
- Where are redundant work tasks?
- Where are any unnecessary communication steps?
- Which subjects are not required for accomplishing tasks?

The immediate discussion and evaluation of the interaction allow the rapid identification of problems with respect to process effectiveness and efficiency and also facilitate developing possible solutions with respect to subject behavior, interactions between subjects, and the exchanged information. Identified weaknesses can be handled on the spot, i.e., by directly editing the model. An improved model can then immediately be interactively played once again.

The key advantage of the described approach is that the Actors validate the model by themselves, from their individual perspectives, by actively playing the respective roles. Using conventional methods, such as the walkthrough, originally stemming from software testing, the model is checked step by step, however, only "on paper". To do so, usually in a workshop, large-format plotted graphical models are pinned to moderation walls (see Fig. 7.3). Instead of printouts, also large beamer presentations are used, possibly supported by animation capabilities of modeling tools, which facilitate following the flow by visualizing pointer movements.

Fig. 7.3 Typical walkthrough situation (Source: binner IMS GmbH)

The workshop participants scan the process step by step using concrete examples of the mapping of the perceived reality and review it with regard to its effectiveness, as well as with respect to formal deficiencies. The detection of errors in the process or of improper process output is much more difficult with this theoretical approach than with actual "doing". This disadvantage of the conventional walkthrough is reinforced by the fact that the work performers of the process rarely participate as Actors. The walkthrough team consists mostly of process owners, and when appropriate, various consultants as content specialists, and method and tool experts with respect to formal aspects of the model. These people are not really familiar enough with the operational details of the process for them to recognize obscure deficiencies of the model on paper.

7.5.2.2 Content Validation Using IT-Supported Role Playing

Conventional role playing as described in the previous section is very useful; however, especially when used for more complex processes, it may become very costly. The materials (e.g., cards and sheets) need to be prepared, the participants need to gather simultaneously in a convenient place, the process needs to be manually recorded and analyzed, etc. It therefore obviously makes sense to support the described procedure with an IT solution.

The principle corresponds to the conventionally designed game. The difference is that the gaming environment is mapped onto an IT landscape so that a kind of distributed prototyping is enabled (cf. Schmidt and Fleischmann et al. 2009, p. 56; Fischer and Fleischmann et al. 2006, pp. 93 ff.). Consequently, executable software is generated from each subject-oriented model description, including user masks for each subject. For subject-oriented models, this is relatively easy, since the graphical notation presented in Chap. 5 is based on a formally distinct semantics, which provides a machine-interpretable representation including subject, predicate, and object (see Chap. 12).

The generated program also represents the communication relationships between subjects, and therefore, the interactions along the process flow. The stakeholders can collaborate along the process using spatially distributed computer systems, and exchange messages via an appropriate Internet server (see Fig. 7.4).

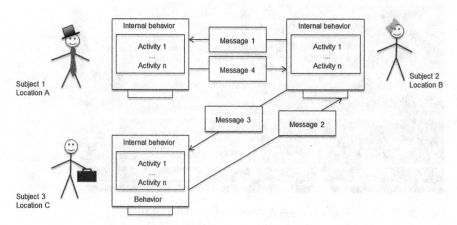

Fig. 7.4 IT-based interactive process role play

They can immediately check and evaluate its associated forms, entry fields, and dialogs in the respective steps of the process flow.

At this time, such an evaluation can be performed, independent of the IT implementation later on. For instance, when an SAP form is used in a subject behavior description, the SAP system does not have to be available with the appropriate transaction. For role playing, it is sufficient that the Actor can check at this point the behavior of the SAP system in terms of an interface, e.g., can verify whether the input data which the SAP system requires are available.

While validating, the system can automatically record all activities of the subjects and the resulting changes to objects (e.g., completed forms). In turn, the process participants capture their comments on the validation in provided masks. The analysis of the generated data can largely be performed IT based.

Regarding our example of handling business trips, a validation scenario could encompass the following subjects: employee, manager, and travel office, as part of the internal organization (e.g., a company); and the travel agent as an external subject (interface subject). The employee starts an instance of the process by completing and sending the request to the manager. After the other necessary work and communication steps have been completed, the process instance ends with the employee's (as applicant) receipt of an approval from the manager in positive cases and a rejection in negative cases.

For validation purposes, the representatives of specific subjects can be given access to the application which is automatically generated from the model. Each of them can then run at their PC workstations within a defined period of time their relevant work steps and communication procedures. If concentrated in a single location, at least the people who represent the internal subjects could come together in a room and validate the process, e.g., using mobile computers. Then, in addition to the communication provided by the process model within the validation application, the participants can also reflect personally on the process. In this way, they can especially review their interactions, which represent their interfaces for collaboration and, where applicable, adapt them accordingly.

In the case of a spatial distribution of the subject representatives, e.g., the external travel agent in our example, telephone or video conferencing can be used as additional communication channels for validation.

We will briefly explain in Sect. 13.4, how such an IT-based validation environment can be achieved.

References

Fischer, H., Fleischmann, A., Obermeier, S., Geschäftsprozesse realisieren, Wiesbaden 2006.
Schmelzer, H., Sesselmann, W.: Geschäftsprozessmanagement in der Praxis, 7. Auflage, München 2010.
Schmidt, W., Fleischmann, A. und Gilbert, O., Subjektorientiertes Geschäftsprozessmanagement, HMD – Praxis der Wirtschaftsinformatik, Heft 266, S. 52-62, 2009.

Subject-Oriented Optimization of Processes

8

8.1 To Go

My process is finished; it is modeled and validated—why should anything be improved?

By validating, we have determined that we do the right things. However, we still need to check whether we do these with the least possible effort. It may be, e.g., that we still perform unnecessary actions or communications. Then, the process should be optimized...

... in case the deficiencies cause us to either partially or even completely miss the process objectives. We want to avoid unnecessary work, if possible.

We have already considered this in the course of validation! Nobody wants to perform unnecessary tasks.

A. Fleischmann et al., *Subject-Oriented Business Process Management*,
DOI 10.1007/978-3-642-32392-8_8, © The Author(s) 2012

Validation and optimization are mutually
related. In the context of optimization, however, we
want to reduce expenses without questioning already
achieved effectiveness targets. Process managers
cannot just turn a button, in order to change the
overall behavior. Optimization is a complex process
requiring the collaboration of all subjects and actors.

8.2   The Nature of Optimization

In Chap. 7, we have described validation, which ensures the effectiveness of
business processes. Its goal is to make sure that a process delivers the results as
described by analysis. When optimizing, the efficiency of processes is at the focus
of interest, in order to achieve the desired results with the least possible expenditure
of time and resources. Efficiency targets are set in the course of analysis in the
form of reference values of performance parameters derived from a corporate
strategy. If the comparison of the recorded actual values with the target values in
the course of monitoring leads to negative deviations (see Chap. 11), optimization
measures need to be taken. Such a situation indicates that the process is not (or no
longer) meeting its requirements, and consequently, not (or no longer) achieving its
objectives.

> It is not only the selection of appropriate means for accomplishing tasks
> (effectiveness), but also their economical use (efficiency) that determines the
> success of S-BPM—the latter is ensured by optimization.

For instance, it may happen that a process has been running satisfactorily over a
long period of time, but then, for no obvious reasons, unplanned deviations, such as
an increase in process duration time, occur. In the course of optimization, the causes
for these effects need to be explored. They are often a result of changes in the
configuration limits for a process, so that perhaps more process instances need to
be run than originally planned. This in turn can mean that employees are
overburdened, or that the tools used do not meet the changed requirements. In
this case, organizational leaders (Governors) initiate optimization after an analysis,
without previously modeling and validating.

In an organizational development project following a linear approach to S-BPM,
e.g., designing a new process, the Facilitator can initiate a first optimization of the
process immediately after its modeling and validation. In this case, the validated
process model is checked to see whether, based on its current design, the process
can be improved with respect to the achievement of its defined efficiency targets.

An increase in efficiency already at this stage of an organizational development project reduces the likelihood of the necessity for subsequent adjustments during operation of the considered process.

8.3   S-BPM Optimization Stakeholders

8.3.1   Governors

Governors play an important role in the optimization. At the management level, they need to decide which processes are subject to optimization and what associated objectives should be pursued, while taking into account the respective overall goals, the positioning, and the resources of the organization (see Sect. 8.4). Moreover, the time horizon for achieving the goals, and possible intermediate objectives, needs to be defined. The process owner can also act as Governor in the context of optimization, when it comes to optimization approaches with manageable organizational changes, such as enriching existing software with additional functions to support the process.

8.3.2   Facilitators

A Facilitator initiates optimization induced by a Governor. He organizes, usually as a project manager, the individual activities within an optimization project. In particular, he coordinates the Actors, whose involvement is of crucial importance because they usually know best how processes can be improved in their area of expertise.

8.3.3   Actors

The individual Actors involved in the practical implementation of a process model know best the distinguishing characteristics of "their" process through practical experience at working with the process. They are able to identify weak spots of the process and to provide respective explanations (see Sect. 8.6.2). Problems can arise from the fact that the individual Actors possibly only optimize a process according to their subjective point of view, which can lead to significant time and resource savings, but then makes it necessary for the Facilitator to, potentially with the assistance of Experts, achieve a balanced design of the overall process and thus avoid suboptimal behavior as a result of limited individual views of process participants.

8.3.4 Experts

Experts support an optimization step by bringing in expertise where appropriate. Above all, they support the Actors in the diagnosis of weak spots and are specialists in optimization methods (see Sect. 8.6). Experts can complement local views of Actors through an expanded, holistic view. They are particularly required when processes are simulated in the context of optimization, as specialized technical knowledge and extensive experience are necessary to perform simulations and to interpret their results.

8.4   Specifying Optimization Targets

Before performing the optimization, it needs to be specified which characteristic of a process needs to be improved and which does not (cf. Best and Weth 2007, p. 95). These optimization targets should be derived from organizational and process goals. For example, it could be specified that all customer processes have to be completed within a designated period of time. For other processes, however, speed of processing is of less importance. Thus, e.g., an organization that has positioned itself with its product quality in the upper price segment will consider potential for savings, at the expense of quality, as critical.

Process transparency is the key to continuous process optimization.

In general, a process should not contain any activities, which do not stand in direct relation to its results and do not contribute to value creation. Moreover, the entire process should be operated with as little effort as possible (cf. Schmelzer and Sesselmann 2010, pp. 3). Consequently, the following points are usually referred to as traditional goals of process optimization:

- Optimization of process costs
- Optimization of process times
- Optimization of process quality

8.4.1 Process Costs

Process costs are understood as the expenses required to execute a process instance. In process cost accounting, the costs for each process activity are assigned to executing units.

Process cost accounting differentiates between performance volume-induced costs and performance volume-neutral common costs (Hans-Jürgen Kupper 2011, p. 67). Performance volume-neutral common costs are basic costs incurred for the process at all times. Volume-induced costs are instance based and play a role only when the process is executed. These include, e.g., consumption goods required for processing.

The process costs per instance are calculated by adding the volume-induced costs for an instance to the basic costs allocated to the number of instances per unit of time. An optimization of the process costs can therefore be achieved via a reduction of the performance volume-induced and/or performance volume-neutral common costs. This becomes necessary, once the actual costs of the process exceed the predefined targets.

Optimization can target both volume-induced costs and basic costs. This also applies in the case of the business trip application process. In its context, process cost components can be, among other things, the process-related personnel costs, in particular with respect to the travel office, and the software cost for process execution. The latter may contain volume-related shares, such as user-based licensing costs, and volume-independent components, such as maintenance fees. These basic costs can be reduced, e.g., by negotiating a discount on the annual maintenance fee with the provider.

8.4.2   Process Time

The process time can be measured in terms of cycle time or throughput time. The throughput time is the duration from the process start to the completion of the process results (cf. Schmelzer and Sesselmann 2010, pp. 250 ff). The cycle time includes the duration of each substep, also those running in parallel. While the cycle time is more the focus of internal analysis (e.g., cost and capacity optimization), the throughput time plays a major role in the external visibility of a process, namely as reaction time toward the customer.

As an example, an online service provider guarantees all orders to be delivered within 3 days. This can be a unique selling proposition in the marketplace and linked to promotions ("money-back guarantee"). However, if this goal is not achieved, it will not only result in a negative impact on income, but also a loss of image will be experienced. If competitors are faster in delivery, this can result in optimization pressure for the own organization.

For the business trip application, the timeframe between the submission of the application, and its subsequent processing by the travel office, can be an important indicator of process time, impacting booking of travel modalities, hotels, etc. The shorter it is, the more likely it is that early booking discounts can be claimed, and ultimately, associated costs saved. The processing time largely depends on the reaction time of the manager and the work capacities of the travel office. An optimization, for instance, could lead to a delegation scheme for cases in which a manager does not respond within a specified time period. An additional employee in the travel office could help in shortening the response time for processing. An essential prerequisite for the realization of early booking discounts is of course the timely submission of the travel request as soon as the need for the trip becomes evident. A corresponding briefing of employees in this respect could contribute to optimization.

8.4.3   Process Quality

The third optimization goal is process quality. This is measured as the quality of the process result from the perspective of the internal or external customers (cf. Tomys 1995, p. 17). For instance, if a process does not deliver its expected result, it is considered to be malfunctioning. Therefore, a quality index could be defined, such as the produced number of defects for the manufacturing of products, or the number of customer complaints for the provision of services. In addition, the meeting of deadlines, i.e., adherence to predetermined throughput times, is traditionally an important quality attribute. Such directly measurable quality criteria also influence another additionally or alternately used common measurement of process quality, namely customer satisfaction. This is determined by regular customer surveys and reflects the extent of fulfillment of customer expectations.

In the case of the business trip application, quality can be measured, e.g., by the number of erroneous travel bookings (wrong date, wrong class, etc.). When serving employees as customers, satisfaction could be extended by meeting individual demands such as a window seat reservation.

8.4.4   Target Triangle

The goals of cost, time, and quality represent a so-called magic target triangle. Optimization objectives in this triangle can have a conflicting, complementary, or neutral relationship to each other. The optimization goals specified by the responsible managers of an organization for improvement measures depend on the prioritization of overall process goals.

> The process attributes "cost," "time," and "quality" can lead to target conflicts. Prioritizing helps to avoid negative consequences of improvement activities. Governors should assess mutual relationships of process attributes, even though the reduction of process costs is a key driver of optimization efforts in daily operations.

Particularly in the case of conflicting goals, the negative impact of an improvement measure on other parameters needs to be assessed in terms of an overall optimum. Thus, the reduction of throughput time by parallel processing of process steps can lead to an increase of costs due to an associated increase in staff. In such cases, the Governor needs to intervene. He can decide on the basis of the priority of process goals, whether the improvement measure should be carried out as planned.

Ideally, an improvement in one dimension also positively affects the others. An example for this could be the shortening of processing time by transfer of competencies. Thus, a bank could shift approval competence for processing a loan offer from the department head to operations staff. By eliminating this manager approval loop, not only can time be saved, which means the customer receives the offer faster, but this also results in a reduction of the operation costs, especially with respect to the associated labor costs of the approval loop for the department head. The cost for the latter is higher than the newly incurred staff costs due to the organizational change on the operational level.

In practice, reducing process costs is often regarded as the most important optimization goal. It is also targeted by responsible management when optimizing other parameters (cf. Rosenkranz 2006, p. 257).

Optimization opportunities may not only be limited by negative effects on other predefined objectives but also through environmental conditions. For instance, an improvement option cannot be pursued, if it is not possible to alleviate deficiencies of the required knowledge and skills through appropriate personnel training, development, and recruitment activities.

8.5 Foundations of Optimization

For the pursuit of the goals addressed in Sect. 8.4, it is important to provide operational definitions—goals need to be expressed in terms of performance figures (what?), target values (how much?), time references (until when?), and organizational roles (by whom?).

As a starting point for improvement, we need the actual (as-is) performance values detailing a goal. Such values can be obtained as follows:

- Hypotheses about time and resource requirements for process execution: In this case, assumptions are made about the number of processes to be executed per time unit, as well as about the thereby required time and resources. These assumptions can be supported by more or less extensive experiences. Such a procedure is required whenever a process is introduced from scratch, or has been significantly reworked, and no reliable measurements are available yet.
- Measurements of previous process executions (see Chap. 11): The situation is simpler when a process is already in production and there are measurements available for instances, which allow calculating resource and time consumption of processes and process components.
- Benchmarks: Sometimes managers can also access and use values from comparisons with business partners (customers and suppliers), and even with competitors, or with industry averages. In order to get meaningful results in simulation when using such basic data, however, it is important to know the calculation scheme of the used benchmarks.

For optimization, as a minimum requirement, a process model should provide some orientation for optimization measures. In the process model, the appropriate assumptions about required resources and time with regard to process execution or, respectively, available measurements, can be included. They allow deriving necessary changes to the model and determining requirements for the organizational and/ or IT implementation of the process, respectively.

Process optimization can only be achieved if all key performance processes of an organization are streamlined to its global goal.

8.6   General Optimization Possibilities

After specifying the objectives of optimization, it is important to identify those elements of a process that allow reducing costs and time while increasing quality. Optimization opportunities arise mainly from the following three areas:

- Process model
- Organization-specific implementation
- IT implementation

In practice, optimization measures in these fields are not independent. A process model could support only selected organizational and technical aspects of an implementation. Conversely, organizational or technical constraints could preclude certain process specifications.

Figure 8.1 provides an overview of fundamental optimization capabilities, focusing mainly on resources and execution alternatives (cf. Bleicher 1991, p. 196; Stoger 2005, pp. 109 ff. Gadatsch 2010, p. 21). They can also be applied to the behavior and communication structures of subjects engaged in processes.

Optimization	Explanation
Omitting	Remove unnecessary steps
Outsourcing	Assignment of tasks to external service providers
Summarizing	Grouping of several work steps to one step
Parallelizing	Distributing of work steps to multiple resources so that they can be executed simultaneously
Shifting	Earlier starting of currently downstream activities
Accelerating	Providing (better) work equipment, which allows a faster completion of tasks (e.g., IT systems)
Supplementing	Adding work steps (e.g., for assurance of quality and results)

Fig. 8.1 General possibilities of process optimization

In the following sections, we discuss various methodological aspects of optimization, before going into the details of subject-oriented optimization.

8.6.1   Simulating Process Models

A simulation verifies process behavior by simulating instances, even before a process has been used in practice (cf. Tomys 1995, Harrington 1998). Thus, before productive utilization, it can be determined on the basis of a process model which processing times and resource requirements for a given quantity, i.e., a certain number of process instances per time unit, are likely to be incurred.

For example, a simulation can provide valuable information with respect to potential bottle necks if it reveals that with a certain amount of orders, congestion in subjects occurs, and their carriers (Actors) are no longer able to cope with the resulting workload on site.

For simulation, adequate parameters need to be defined. Gadatsch (2010, p. 224) distinguishes between workflow-related and resource-based variables for analysis. They are determined by time, values, and quantities, respectively (see Fig. 8.2).

Orientation \ Relation	Workflow-related	Resource-related
Time-oriented variables	Processing times Execution times Waiting times	Operating times Waiting times Downtimes
Value-oriented variables	Process cost	Used capacity costs Idle time costs
Quantity-oriented variables	Executed process steps Unexecuted process steps	Object input Object stock Object output

Fig. 8.2 Analysis parameters for the simulation of process instances

Check your points of measurement on the process. S-BPM mainly considers communication flows, along with functional task accomplishment.

In order to simulate, the mentioned variables of analysis are assigned different probability distributions. The process model is then processed in fast motion with given parameters several times. Using random number generators, the corresponding times and resource requirements are determined according to the distribution functions for each cycle and recorded for each process execution. The data are evaluated after an appropriate number of executions. In this way, it can be explored how the process performs, e.g., under execution load, in terms of time and costs.

As the simulation executes a process model in fast motion, it requires an executable process model. Simulations are frequently applied to several process variants to determine the most efficient variant in terms of cost, time, etc. We therefore also understand simulation as "systematic experimentation" (Gadatsch 2010, p. 216) using models of actual problem situations.

In the example of the business trip application, the processing time can be simulated to obtain indications for the staffing of the various processing stations. Execution times, waiting times, and communication times of the subjects are assigned values from practical experience. Then, the application process is simulated with the given resources, in the various stations, with varying numbers of submitted requests (instances) per unit of time (simultaneously). In this way, it can be determined whether the processing time increases when the number of applications per unit of time increases. This could be an indication that the human resource capacities of the travel office can only account for a certain number of cases within a specific period of time, and that bottle necks could be experienced once business travel activities increase.

The difficulty in simulation is to find appropriate parameter data. To carry out a simulation, it must be known, e.g., how many instances are to be processed per unit of time. This requires a corresponding probability distribution with parameters. In addition, for each action, it must be known how much time or how many resources are needed. These time and resource requirements are usually not only constant but also follow probability distributions with the corresponding parameters. In an ideal situation, measures from executing actual process instances exist. Otherwise, these need to be estimated.

> For S-BPM, the semantic comparison is crucial, as it provides evidence for correspondence between models. When comparing models, the semantic compatibility of their respective content needs to be considered.

Running a simulation requires special expertise, both for its preparation, and also for the evaluation of obtained results with respect to their plausibility, their interpretation, and for drawing associated conclusions regarding resource and time demands. It is the responsibility of the Facilitator to involve people with such expertise, when required.

8.6.2 Identifying Weak Spots and Root Cause Analysis

While in simulation, the efficiency of a given model is examined, regardless of its use in organizational work practice, the analysis of weak spots aims at the critical examination of the behavior of a process in productive operation. It is therefore considered, how efficiently a process runs with a given model in its organizational and technical environment. The analysis of weak spots is composed of identifying deficiencies to this respect, and subsequently determining their (root) causes.

The identification of weak spots is a result of observations in most cases. For instance, it could become evident that the processing of the business trip application currently takes much longer than it did 1 year ago. This could be a result of monitoring, if appropriate performance indicators are available. Not all weak spots can be diagnosed with metrics, especially in cases in which the maturity is low and, accordingly, no metrics have yet been defined. Such a situation is common for processes that run "somehow," i.e., without knowing the reason why they work, and without any documentation. Fischer et al. (2006, p. 39) refer to such processes as "zombie processes."

Figure 8.3 shows examples of weak spots. The table is composed of columns according to key characteristics of processes described in a subject-oriented way and rows capturing important aspects of organizational design. The listed weak spots affect in varying degrees cost, time, and quality.

Weak spots in Related to	Subject behavior	Subject integration	Business object
Organizational structure (organizational implementation of processes, see Chapter 9)	• Inadequate skills • Lack of incentives • Unclear responsibilities, inadequate responsibility of decision making and processing	• Pronounced hierarchy with official channels	
Operational structure	• Sub-optimal sequence of sub-steps • Long processing times • Duplication of work	• Unclear official channels • Long waiting times	
Operational structure	• Missing features • Lack of usability • Lack of integration at the application level (e.g., by portal)	• Lack of technical integration of communicative devices	• Media breaks • Many paper-based documents

Fig 8.3 Selected weak spots of processes

The identification of weak spots does not mean however that their source of origin has already been revealed. Deficiencies in fact point to "phenomena," the root causes of which possibly lie elsewhere than in the organization segment or perspective currently under consideration. Especially for IT-based and networked processes, the actual cause of problems is often difficult to determine.

Therefore, a sound root cause evaluation is the most important component of the weak spot analysis and should involve all stakeholders, ranging from Actors in the process to the process owners (Governors). One common method, which can be applied in this context, is the so-called Ishikawa analysis (cf. Schulte-Zurhausen 2002, p. 513). It allows identifying primary and secondary causes of a problem via the criteria "man," "machine," "environment," "material," "method," and "measuring." This is performed in work groups in which the primary problem is identified through collaboration of relevant knowledge carriers. Root cause analysis in S-BPM is therefore subject-oriented in itself. This does not mean that the subjects are the causes of a problem; it is rather assumed that subject carriers can specify best why work processes are performing poorly.

In our example of the business trip application process let's assume, e.g., that there are a high number of erroneous travel bookings, which results in the travel office not meeting the expected service quality requirements. In a joint workshop, the participants recognize that the root cause is not the human being. Rather, the material used consists of forms, which are partly filled out using a word processing application and partly manually. This procedure contains the actual cause: forms are differently interpreted and filled out. As a result, the travel office needs to check back with applicants frequently, or it wrongly interprets provided information. As a solution, the workshop group proposes automation support, whereby inquiries are delivered through business objects in a standardized form.

8.7   Optimization Aspects

In the course of subject-oriented optimization, various aspects can be tackled:

- Improvement in the behavior of subjects
- Communication between subjects
- Restructuring the behavior of subjects
- Improving business objects

The orientation toward subjects allows the immediate participation of stakeholders and facilitates activities aimed at organizational development.

8.7.1   Improvement of Subject Behavior

A first approach to optimization is the investigation of the behavior of subjects. Often, steps are rigidly anchored in the behavioral repertoire of the Actors in the process. An impetus for changing individual behavior may be interpreted as a personal attack on the stakeholder, in particular, when the subject carrier too closely identifies himself with the subject at hand. Or a "tunnel vision" is created which leaves no room for improvements in the behavior.

The Japanese method KAIZEN is an example of a method for optimizing subject behavior. According to KAIZEN, every employee is able to review his own behavior and to subject it to a continuous improvement process. Each employee must be aware of his responsibility for the optimization of processes in which he is involved. Thereby, the employee takes on a second role: he is not only an operating Actor but also an active designer. "The participation of every individual is welcome" (cf. Steinbeck 1995, p. 38, Bösing 2006). This is not a matter of checking the behavior of individuals and improving it. Rather, subject carriers review the subject as object and look for joint improvement.

This process is not controlled externally. The subject carriers themselves take over the role of optimizers. As knowledge carriers they can exchange knowledge about a possible "best practice" according to their operational behavior. This method is not necessarily self-evident and needs to become an explicit element of corporate culture. For the staff it needs to be clarified, in particular, that Kaizen does not mean that everyone can do what he thinks is right. A change in the process, for instance, requires approval from the Governor.

Although Kaizen has not been designed specifically for business process management, it can still also be used for the optimization process in S-BPM. All concerned stakeholders need to be involved, and process goals have to be measurable. Because subject orientation transparently conveys to each employee what is expected from him in which process (see Sect. 9.4.1), it is also clear that the optimization refers to the corresponding subject carrier. This can affect the behavior of the process model or the organizational and technical implementation.

In the context of the business trip application, the staff of the travel office could participate in a common Kaizen workshop. In the course of the workshop, they discover the existence of an Internet portal which, after entering a specified travel time and destination, automatically delivers the fastest means of travel and the most inexpensive hotel arrangement, and then also automatically makes the corresponding bookings on demand. The work group calculates the realistic potential for improvement and suggests the integration of the portal into its own process to the Board.

8.7.2 Communication Between Subjects

There is high potential for optimization in the communication between the subjects. Often, too much insignificant, and too little important, information is exchanged from one subject to another. The result is that the subjects can neither perform their tasks in an adequate timeframe nor deliver results meeting the required quality. This has a direct impact on time and quality. In addition, communication is always related to cost. This results in a high potential for optimization.

By changing the communication relationships between subjects, the achievement of defined goals can be facilitated. Thus, in our example, the approved business trip request could be sent directly to the travel office by the employee, without involving the manager. Such a change optimizes the organization with respect to self-responsible budgeting of time. It is accompanied by job enrichment in terms of vertical reintegration of tasks. Changes in the structure of communication result in appropriate changes in the behavior of the respective subject—in the above-mentioned job enrichment, the applicant no longer needs to seek approval from his superiors.

The modification of the communication between the subjects could also require adapting the structure and content of business objects. Certain information needs to be distributed to other business objects or can be summarized, depending on what information needs to be sent to which other subjects after the change.

In addition to the previously mentioned adjustments to the process model, it may also be necessary to improve the realization of the communication, especially through the use of a suitable communication medium. In the organizational environment, this could mean that personal or cultural barriers need to be eliminated. Cultural barriers can represent a major optimization challenge, especially in the case of cross-organizational processes. Technical aids, such as e-mail or workflow systems, can help to simplify the communication from a technical perspective. Sending a business object by e-mail involves less effort than sending a paper form. Thus, business processes and the associated communication are increasingly realized through appropriate IT infrastructure (see Chap. 10).

In the case of the business trip application process, travel documents (tickets, hotel vouchers, etc.) are sent to the employee by conventional mail. Accordingly, for each business trip request, considerable costs occur. The process could be changed in such a way that only online tickets are ordered. Hence, the tickets could then be sent to the employees much quicker and at almost no cost by e-mail.

8.7.3   Restructuring Subject Behavior

An extensive optimization approach is the complete redesign of the subject structure. The existing communication and activity structures are thereby completely dissolved and redefined. This corresponds to a radical, far-reaching reorganization of the company, which Hammer and Champy have introduced as business process reengineering (BPR) (cf. Hammer and Champy 1993). This should be applied in situations where short-term changes no longer seem adequate. A complete reorganization of business processes should enable cost and quality improvements, because single or multiple processes are rebuilt from the ground up.

However, it is usually a very radical cut in an organization. Employees partially lose their "identity" because transfers take place, responsibilities are shifted, and tasks are outsourced to external service providers, etc. In this way, a wealth of experience may be lost, and great uncertainty created within the organization. Moreover, organizations cannot be seen as bare frameworks. Processes have to fit to a certain extent to the existing organizational structure, staffing, and infrastructure. To completely rebuild all of these from the ground up would be a very expensive and a time-consuming endeavor. Moreover, it is often unrealistic. BPR is controversially discussed, as a result of the above-mentioned advantages and disadvantages (cf. Fischer and Fleischmann et al. 2006, p. 22).

> Reengineering is the rigorous redesign of subject behavior. It can lead to incompatibilities with the way of thinking and the work styles of concerned stakeholders, if they are not actively involved.

Possible reasons for a rigorous approach are:

- Due to changes in the personnel structure, certain subjects can no longer be engaged. Continuing work as usual is not possible; the subjects need to be completely reassigned.
- Qualifications of subject carriers are not sufficient to accomplish the required tasks. By reorganizing, the tasks will be widely redistributed.
- Requirements are derived from process standards for specific roles. These roles are not yet available in this form in the organization. A mapping of the current functions to the new roles seems too difficult.
- The maturity of the process has decreased and simple improvement measures are no longer sufficient—so that the management decides to redefine the process from the ground up.

In the example of the business trip application, the management could decide that processes not critical to business success, i.e., support processes, including the business trip application process, will be run via a service desk of an outsourced service provider. The consequence would be the dissolution of the travel office, and booking through travel agencies, which have been commissioned by the external service provider, but are unknown to the company. This would correspond to a far-reaching transformation of the business trip application process, involving the release and reassignment of staff, at least in the travel office.

A less rigorous form of restructuring activity and communication structures of subjects is the horizontal reintegration of subtasks (job enlargement). This leads to a change in behavior of the subjects. Some subjects then perform additional work steps, others fewer. This can lead to the complete dissolution of a subject in an associated process, namely when all of its corresponding activities can be shifted to other process participants. Such a move requires empowering other subjects to accomplish tasks new to them (e.g., through training and adequate IT support). As a result of this kind of reintegration, communication steps, interfaces, latency, etc. can be omitted.

8.7.4   Improving Business Objects

For business objects, it is already needs to be ensured in the process model that only data which are actually needed are included, and accordingly, that only data which are required for other subjects to accomplish their tasks are sent to them. The concerned data need to be correct and sufficiently detailed. By meeting these requirements, considerable effort in resolving deficiencies can be avoided.

This also applies to the layout of user interfaces of business objects, regardless of whether they are in paper or electronic form (display screens). An ergonomic design facilitates the manual collection of information for the Actor, thereby accelerating task completion. The Actors generally know exactly how forms and input dialogs can be improved. Consequently, their perspective should be shared in any case.

The way that business objects are implemented provides another approach to optimization. Here, the replacement of a paper form with an electronic counterpart could represent considerable potential for improvement. This begins with the more simple methods for filing, copying, distribution, resubmission, etc. and continues with the ability to automatically complete input fields and check entries for plausibility.

In the case of the business trip application process, the name, first name, organizational unit, and availability data of the applicant could be automatically transferred into an electronic form. Such information can be obtained using the login information from the entries of user directories. A plausibility check could prevent Actors, e.g., from entering an end date for the trip, which is prior to the start date.

References

Best, E., Weth, M., Geschäftsprozesse optimieren, Wiesbaden 2007.

Bleicher, K., Organisation: Strategien – Strukturen – Kulturen, Wiesbaden 1991.

Bosing, K.D., Ausgewählte Methoden der Prozessverbesserung, TFH Wildau, Wiss. Beiträge, Wildau 2006.

Fischer, H., Fleischmann, A., Obermeier, S., Geschäftsprozesse realisieren, Wiesbaden 2006.

Gadatsch, A., Grundkurs Geschäftsprozessmanagement, 6th edition, Wiesbaden 2010.

Champy, M., Hammer, J., Business Reengineering: Die Radikalkur für das Unternehmen, 5th edition, Frankfurt a. M./New York 1993.

Harrington J., Simulation modelling methods, An interactive guide to result-based decision, New York 1998.

Hans-Jürgen Kupper: Übungsbuch zur Kosten- und Erlösrechnung. 6th edition, Vahlen, München 2011.

Rosenkranz, F., Geschäftsprozesse, Wiesbaden 2006.

Schmelzer, H., Sesselmann, W., Geschäftsprozessmanagement in der Praxis, 7th edition, München 2010.

Schulte-Zurhausen, M., Organisation, München 2002.

Steinbeck, H.-H. (Hrsg.): CIP-KAIZEN-KVP – die kontinuierliche Verbesserung von Produkt und Prozess, Landsberg 1995.

Stoger, R., Geschäftsprozesse, Stuttgart 2005.

Tomys, A.-K., Kostenorientiertes Qualitätsmanagement, München/Wien 1995.

Organization-Specific Implementation of Subject-Oriented Processes

9

9.1 To Go

Now, we are almost done. We have a validated model and have thought about optimal process structures and utilization of resources. Now, we need to know: Who does what?

You are right. Now it comes to names. When the activities specified in a subject are carried out by a person, management and all other involved parties need to know who this person is. Instead of a single person, an entire organizational unit could also be responsible for a subject.

And at the same time, we also have the challenge that process models are used independently in several different parts of the organization. The business trip needs to be approved by the responsible supervisor, and not by just any manager.

Right. For this, we also have the ability to assign appropriate staff to a subject of a process model depending on the particular environment.

A. Fleischmann et al., *Subject-Oriented Business Process Management*,
DOI 10.1007/978-3-642-32392-8_9, © The Author(s) 2012

So I need to know the organizational context of my process.

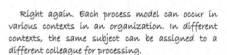
Right again. Each process model can occur in various contexts in an organization. In different contexts, the same subject can be assigned to a different colleague for processing.

What about delegation regulations? We have repeatedly had problems with them!

They are part of embedding a subject into the organization. But read for yourself!

In the previous chapters, we have described how business processes of an organization are mapped to a process model by the subject-oriented method. The result is then validated and optimized as required. The process is now specified to the extent that it can be used in the organization. This step is referred to in terms of the S-BPM process model as an organization-specific implementation. With this, abstract subjects become real-life employees, the subjects are embedded into the organization.

As part of this process, however, two different "worlds" are brought together: an abstract model, and thus an artifact, is transferred to a social system. A transfer of model structures to a living system occurs. This transition requires guidance and support. Organizational developers can help here. The subject-oriented approach also helps, because the direct relation of subject specifications to humans as Actors can be used. In addition, context-sensitive business rules can be defined.

9.2   S-BPM Stakeholders Handling the Organization-Specific Implementation

9.2.1   Actors

Employees participating in the processes under consideration were already involved in the development of the process model, including validation and optimization. They can be of great help in introducing a new or revised process. Their participation in the development of the model facilitates their individual identification with the process. In most cases, this in turn helps in achieving acceptance of the process by other affected employees. Thus, the Actors involved in modeling are an essential starting point for the organizational implementation of business processes. The other Actors become acquainted with the process and learn how to use it through these advocates.

> Work performers affected by changes need to be actively engaged in the change process, to ensure their acceptance. They play a crucial rule, as they need to internalize a process to bring it to life.

9.2.2   Governors

The Governor is in the focus of organization-specific implementations, as he needs to make decisions with respect to personnel issues. In addition, affected managers need to be involved. They need to ensure that the existing personnel can work along the process in a target-oriented way, and they have to assign the subjects to the appropriate people. The role of Governor represents the management level, which has interest in ensuring that new processes in the organization actually work and that the employees are motivated and willing to work along them. The Governor's intent is to ensure that processes become familiar, and their benefit transparent, to the entire organization.

Finally, the Governor needs to provide the necessary resources to qualify, when necessary, people taking on new tasks in processes.

9.2.3   Facilitators

A Facilitator accompanies the entire process of organization-specific implementation. He ensures, in cooperation with the Governor, that the concerned managers identify the appropriate people for a subject, and that these people are informed about their respective tasks in the process. The affected employees also need to be trained accordingly, if necessary. The development of required training programs is designed and prepared by the Facilitator, along with those Actors already involved. For this, it may also be necessary to involve Experts.

9.2.4   Experts

A key Expert in organizational implementation is the consultant for organizational
or personal development. For upcoming changes, specialists should be involved
who accompany the introduction or revision procedure. They develop measures for
informing the employees specifically about the innovation or change, and try to
motivate. Various media can support this process in a target-oriented way, such
as the use of wikis, which could store important process information available
to Actors. Furthermore, workshops can help to make employees familiar with the
process changes.

9.3   Embedding Subjects Into an Organization

9.3.1   Mapping Subjects to Subject Carriers

Subjects are abstract active resources in S-BPM. They represent Actors or systems
in a process that initially have nothing in common with actual entities, such as
people or IT systems. It is only during the implementation of a process that abstract
subjects are assigned to specific individuals, groups, or systems, termed subject
carriers in the context of subject orientation. This chapter deals with the assignment
to individuals, while the assignment to technical systems is discussed in Chap. 10.

Using the example of the business trip application, we describe for human
actors, how the three subjects "employee", "manager", and "travel office" are
embedded into the organization. We assume the simple organizational structure
as shown in Fig. 9.1.

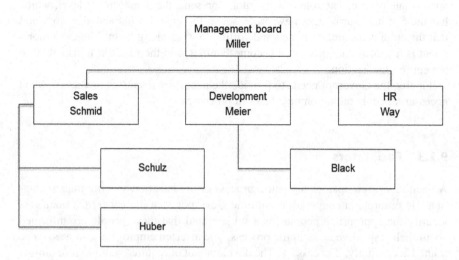

Fig. 9.1 A simple organizational chart

In this structure, e.g., Mr. Schulz from the sales department issues a business trip request. Mr. Schmid as his manager approves it, and Mr. Way as a representative of the travel office in the human resources department (HR) is responsible for organizing the trip. Figure 9.2 shows how the subjects are assigned to the respective subject carriers.

Subject	Subject behavior	Subject carrier	Organizational unit
Employee	is transferred to	Mr. Schulz	Sales
Manager	is transferred to	Mr. Schmid	Sales
Travel office	is transferred to	Mr. Way	HR

Fig. 9.2 Subject mapping table for the business trip request of Mr. Schulz

Figure 9.3 shows the processing of the process instance "business trip request" of Mr. Schulz' according to the organization-specific embedding.

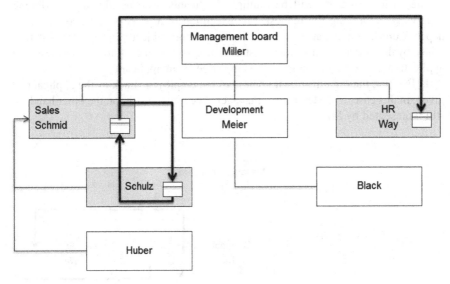

Fig. 9.3 Embedding the subjects of the business trip request of Mr. Schulz

With this, the organization-specific implementation of this simple example is initially completed. However, it quickly becomes obvious that in practice we have to consider the following aspects, which we subsequently describe in more detail:

- Firstly, the mapping reveals that only the business trip request of Mr. Huber can be handled analogously to Mr. Schulz's. In contrast to Mr. Schulz, Mr. Black's manager is Mr. Meier. Therefore, he has to be put in a different organization-specific context (see Sect. 9.3.2).

- Secondly, a direct assignment of a (single) concrete subject carrier to a subject is usually not advisable, since work overload or lack of availability could impede, or even prevent, process execution. This leads to the introduction of subject carrier groups (see Sect. 9.3.3) and delegation regulations (see Sect. 9.3.4).

> The basic principle of intelligible modeling is of crucial importance for organization-specific implementation. A model is only beneficial if it is understood by all concerned participants.

9.3.2 Considering the Organization-Specific Context of a Subject Carrier

Usually, it is not sufficient to assign only one subject carrier to a subject, because a process inherently should be able to be run by several people in different places in the organization. For example, Mr. Schulz will not be the only one who is going on business trips. So there will be multiple applicants, who usually have different supervisors approving the request. The execution of a process instance therefore depends on the organization-specific context of the subject carrier. This is determined by the initiator of the process (start subject) when instantiating a business trip application, so in our example by the employee as an applicant.

In Fig. 9.4, the organizational context of the employee Black as the applicant is given. In this case, Mr. Meier is his manager. The travel office, on the other hand, is still represented by Mr. Way.

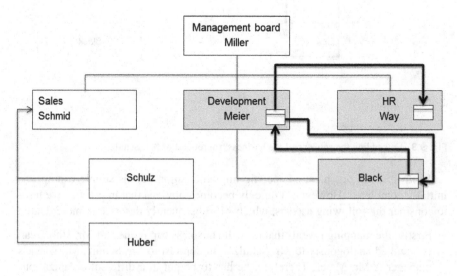

Fig. 9.4 Embedding the subjects into the business trip request of Mr. Black

The organization-specific contexts for the employees at different hierarchical levels reporting to Mr. Miller in the business trip application process (as shown in the organization chart) can be represented in tabular form (see Fig. 9.5).

Employee start subject	Manager in organizational context	Travel office in organizational context
Miller	Miller	Way
Schmid	Miller	Way
Meier	Miller	Way
Schulz	Schmid	Way
Huber	Schmid	Way
Black	Meier	Way
Way	Miller	Way

Fig. 9.5 Context table of the business trip application process for the shown organization structure

Context tables allow representing relevant rules and factors for the situation-sensitive processing of business objects in a comprehensive and structured way when embedding processes in organization-specific settings.

According to the table, Mr. Way is subject carrier for both the subject "employee" and the subject "travel office". Consequently, he himself can also apply for business trips, and he not only processes the approved applications of his colleagues but also his own. It is also apparent that Mr. Miller as CEO has, at least in this context, no superior, and therefore is allowed to approve his own business trip applications.

The example of Mr. Way shows that people are usually involved as subject carriers in multiple processes. They can have a specific context for each of these processes. Mr. Schmid and Mr. Meier also represent two subjects in the example. On the one hand, they are employees of Mr. Miller and in this context can apply for business trips with him as their superior. On the other hand, they are themselves managers of Mr. Schulz, Mr. Huber, and Mr. Black, respectively, and need to approve their requests.

9.3.3   Mapping Subjects to Subject Carrier Groups

Instead of assigning a subject specifically to a single person as subject carrier, it can also be mapped to an organizational unit, a role, a committee, or the like. In such a case, we speak of an assignment to a subject carrier group.

This possibility is important in practice, because in operational reality a process is run at any particular point in time multiple times in parallel, i.e., many process instances occur per time unit (e.g., per day). For processing these within a specified timeframe, operational managers obviously engage a number of people who can process the instances or parts thereof in parallel.

In large organizations with many business trip applications per day, assigning only a single person to the travel office would only allow processing applications sequentially and therefore lead to a bottleneck. As a consequence, applicants would have to wait a relatively long time for the feedback of the travel office with regard to the completed bookings. So instead of assigning the subject "travel office" only to the subject carrier Mr. Way, the organizational developer maps the subject to a predefined subject carrier group "employees of travel office". Besides Mr. Way, the subject carrier Mr. Longway is also part of this group (see the grayed elements in Fig. 9.6). Basically, two people are then available to process business trip applications. This enables the parallel execution of processes. The assignment of members to the subject carrier group determines its capacity, and as such, also the capacity of its assigned subject.

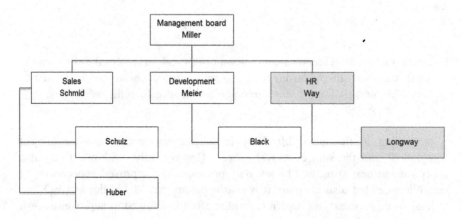

Fig. 9.6 Organization structure with subject carrier group "employees of travel office"

In order to implement this change, the operation manager only needs to replace in the context table of Fig. 9.5 in the column "travel office in organizational context" the entry for the subject carrier "Way" by the subject carrier group "employees of the travel office". In case the responsibility for processing business trips for the management board should remain exclusively with Mr. Way in the travel office, he remains as subject carrier in the row of Mr. Miller.

The outlined context tables need to be specified for each process of an organization. Since in reality individuals are involved in diverse roles in many different types of processes, subject carriers and subject carrier groups occur in many of these tables and also in different columns, respectively. Depending on their various tasks, individuals are assigned to multiple subject carrier groups.

This type of organization-specific implementation of processes is very flexible, as organizational changes, such as changing the role of a person, can easily be accomplished at a fine-grained level. For example, an employee needs only to be assigned to one of the corresponding subject carrier groups. The context table of the affected process remains unchanged.

The various context tables can be interpreted as superimposed organizational charts. Thus, this methodology enables a precise but simple mapping of the usually complex organizational structures in reality.

Still pending is the question of how to determine which individual, initially not specified subject carrier within a group, executes the associated subject behavior when an instance is created at runtime, or an instance step has to be performed. This requires the definition of rules by organizational developers. Selected examples in this regard are:

- Freedom of choice: Instances are pooled prior to the respective processing stations. Any member of the subject carrier group takes one instance, another group member takes another one, etc. The Actors coordinate their activities and decide themselves according to the principles of the subject orientation on the assignment of each case.
- Determination by dispatcher: A dispatcher as a dedicated subject carrier (Governor) inside or outside the group assigns the instances to the group members for processing. With the support of a workflow solution, a process engine takes this role (see Chap. 10). Criteria in both cases could be based on various aspects, such as the general availability or the workload of Actors and the nature of the business objects (see Sect. 9.3.5).

Each organization can consider whether it makes sense to only exclusively assign subjects to subject carrier groups which, in effect, must have at least one subject carrier as a member. This would ensure in a straightforward way from the very beginning the scalability of processing capacity. The group could accommodate additional human resources, if required. A direct mapping of a subject to a person would still be possible if the subject carrier group, as an exception, contains only one subject carrier. The only disadvantage of this approach would be an additional, actually unnecessary step in the dissolution of the organizational context at runtime (subject $\rightarrow$ subject carrier group $\rightarrow$ subject carrier, versus subject $\rightarrow$ subject carrier).

Functional roles and organizational units are implemented in S-BPM through subject carrier groups.

9.3.4 Considering Delegation Regulations

Another requirement from the practice for the organizational integration of processes is the regulation of delegations. This is particularly relevant in cases in which a subject is not assigned to a subject carrier group, but to a concrete subject carrier. The absence of people should not lead to unplanned delays in the execution of process instances. For the organization-specific implementation of a process model, it is therefore necessary to ensure that its execution does not depend on individual subject carriers, but rather is ensured by delegates in case assigned authorized people are not available. By specifying delegates, people responsible for the organization or subject carriers themselves can avoid delays in executing process instances when a subject carrier responsible for an upcoming process step is not available, e.g., due to illness.

In the example of the business trip application, a delegate of Mr. Schmid needs to be determined to act as manager. Otherwise, applications from Mr. Schulz and Mr. Huber could not be approved if Mr. Schmid is not available. Therefore, Mr. Meier is authorized as Mr. Schmid's delegate to process business trip requests, which is expressed by the dashed additions in Fig. 9.7. Alternatively, Mr. Miller can be modeled, as the next higher manager in the line organization, as the delegate of Mr. Schmid. However, this could be undesirable for business trips, because the management board would have to spend an unnecessary amount of time for such administrative tasks.

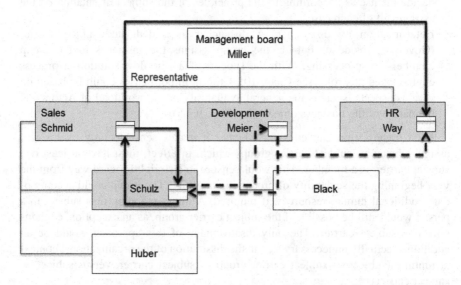

Fig. 9.7 Delegation regulation Schmid/Meier for processing business trip requests of Mr. Schulz

Since Mr. Schmid is subject carrier for several different subjects in different processes, we need to assign to him different subject carriers or groups as delegates for his tasks in each process. Mr. Schmid is already involved in the business trip application process in the form of two subjects (employee and manager). Because of his responsibility for sales, he will also represent subjects in sales processes. This needs to be reflected in the delegation regulations. His disciplinary delegate as manager for business trip requests could be Mr. Meier, as previously shown. Functionally however, e.g., in the sales process of bidding, he could be represented by a member of his organizational unit, such as Mr. Huber.

By concatenating the representation logic, we could also cover cases where not only the Actor of a functional process, but also his (primary) delegate, is not available. In such cases, the delegate of the delegate needs to step in.

For the implementation of flexible delegation regulations, the organization responsible can again utilize the instrument of subject carrier groups. It could make sense, e.g., to define a group containing all managers of a particular hierarchy level (e.g., heads of department—in the sample organization chart Mr. Schmid, Mr. Meier, and Mr. Way). In the absence of one of the three people, each of the other two would then be authorized to sign business trip applications for his employees, and thus, act as a delegate. The actual allocation at runtime can be done similarly to the procedure described in Sect. 9.3.3. In doing so, the subject carrier group "area manager" is specified, rather than Mr. Meier, as a delegate for Mr. Schmid.

The delegate regulation is another aspect of the organization-specific context of embedding subjects into an organizational structure. Finally, when implementing this structure, we need to clarify who, and under what conditions, is allowed to activate a delegation regulation. For planned absences such as vacations, business trips, or training, Actors can determine for themselves who takes their role(s) as subject carrier. For unplanned absence, e.g., due to illness, the administration needs to dynamically determine a subject carrier or a subject carrier group as a delegate.

9.3.5 Considering the Context of Business Objects

In addition to the subjects, also the content of the business objects can be considered in the course of organization-specific implementation. The subject carrier or the subject carrier group is determined in this case through values of one or more business objects occurring in the instance.

For a business trip request, it could be that an employee in the travel office, Mr. Longway, is specialized in international travel and therefore is handling respective questions (like visas, mobility, etc.). In this case, it would be useful to assign applications for business trips abroad to Mr. Longway as subject carrier. The destination country would then represent a business object context for the business trip application. The necessary information can be dynamically derived at runtime of an instance from the object (e.g., value of the data element "destination country" unequal Germany).

Figure 9.8 shows this type of embedding. Mr. Schulz applies for a trip within Germany and for a trip abroad. Both are approved by his superior, Mr. Schmid. Then, the first application is forwarded for further processing to Mr. Way, whereas Mr. Longway organizes the international travel. The path of the request for the foreign trip is marked by the dashed lines.

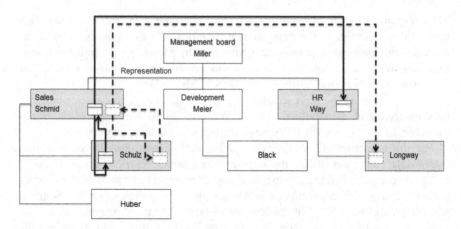

Fig. 9.8 Determining subject carriers from business object context at runtime

Such a distinction leads to a change in the context table (see Fig. 9.9). If it should apply to all applications in our example, the if-then clause needs to be inserted in all table rows. This case demonstrates the implementation of business rules relevant to

Employee (start subject)	Manager in organizational context	Travel office in organizational context
...	...	...
Schulz	Schmid	If requested destination country = Germany, then Way, otherwise Longway
...	...	...
...	...	...

Fig. 9.9 Extract of the context table including dependencies on a business object

a particular organization.

In large organizations, a further distinction between responsibilities for different countries could make sense. For example, the organization responsible for the travel office could form subject carrier groups for China, USA, etc. and assign to them proper specialized staff. In the if-then clauses, we would then need to replace the actual names of the subject carriers by the corresponding subject carrier group names.

9.4   Embedding Behavior

Subjects are defined by their behavior and communication with other subjects. This abstract behavior is transferred to actual behavior in reality. Subject carriers as holders of positions in the organizational structure implement the abstract behavior with their qualifications (skills) and suitable tools.

9.4.1 Adjustment of the Tasks in Job Descriptions

Job profiles document roles and responsibilities of employees. In the allocation plan, all activities that an organization provides are described. After having specified the real people involved in a process by assigning subjects to subject carriers, the job profile of the assigned subject carriers may need to be adjusted. Job tasks could be added or removed, which therefore needs to be documented accordingly in the job description.

For instance, in case the job profiles of the managers do not yet explicitly include the approval of business trips, because it was taken for granted, it should be added now. When the booking of business trips has previously been down by team assistants and this is no longer required due to the establishment of the travel office, this task needs to be removed from the profile of the team assistants.

The adjustments in the job description are of particular importance when salary depends on certain profiles in collective or other contracts. A change can then actually result in the assignment of a subject carrier as holder of a position to another wage group. Such environmental conditions need to be recognized when embedding a process. They can lead to a respecification of subjects, which in turn may lead to a far-reaching modification of the process itself.

> Job profiles may concern several subjects. Thus when embedding subjects, the specific capabilities of individual position holders need to be considered and coordinated accordingly.

9.4.2 Design of the Work Environment

For successful task accomplishment, an adequate working environment needs to be established. In all processes in which people, with their associated tasks and decisions, influence the results of process performance, workplace design plays a critical role. Initially, this is related to the spatial conditions (size, location, lighting, etc.) and interior design (furniture, pictures, plants, etc.). A second aspect concerns the equipment, primarily IT systems that people are provided with to perform their tasks along the process at hand (see Chap. 10). Catalysts to increase motivation and performance are especially ergonomically advanced solutions, such as intuitive, accessible user interfaces, or personalized portals with single sign-on. Compliance with government regulations is mandatory, e.g., limits for radiation from computer monitors.

When designing the work environment, the temporal dimension requires attention, i.e., appropriate measures must be taken in time, so that a smooth implementation process is not impeded. For example, it may be useful to locate people (as subject carriers) with mutually intense communication in close proximity to each other. This holds particularly true when communication occurs via traditional paper and interoffice mail.

Equipping the travel office with work supplies concerning the business trip application process could include the provision of timetables, hotel directories, city maps, etc., or, respectively a facility to access similar online sources of information.

9.4.3   Coordination of Required Competencies

In order to perform their tasks as defined in a process, subject carriers need to have certain skills. The necessary skill sets are explained in the sequel.

Functional Expertise

As characteristic feature of process specifications, different key personnel collaborate to achieve a result in terms of added value for an organization. It is usually not a goal that all people perform all the functions of the subjects, but rather that specialists cooperate for task completion. Each specialist needs specific expertise to accomplish his tasks. Even if merely an approval is requested in a process, thorough knowledge is required with respect to the concerned object for approval and potentially relevant internal and external rules and regulations, etc.

Some approaches try to incorporate, as part of a process-oriented knowledge management approach, tacit knowledge in form of context information of a process (cf. Abecker et al. 2002). In S-BPM, this knowledge is encapsulated in subjects, and as a rule, does not need to be explicitly documented. Functional expertise is certainly required in order to perform the expected subject behavior in a responsible way.

In the sample business trip application process, subject carriers of the travel office are expected to have, among other things, a sound standing knowledge of current travel legislation and associated case law.

Process Skills

Each subject carrier needs to know the fundamentals and the context of his own process. These include:

- Process overview: Each subject carrier should know the aims and importance of his process for the organization.
- Own responsibilities in the process: Each subject carrier needs to know his duties within the given process and be able to assess his contribution for completing the process.
- Communication partners: Each subject carrier must know its communication partners in process execution.
- Business objects: Each subject carrier must know the range of business objects available to him for task accomplishment.

Process skills for the business trip application process means in this sense that the employees know the purpose of an application and its procedure: What do I have to do myself, what do others do for me? To whom do I send my application? What happens with it? Which form do I use?

In such simple processes, it is usually sufficient that the Organization Department is in possession of a freely accessible process documentation, which contains the aforementioned information and makes the procedures transparent. For complex processes, additional in-house training and training-on-the-job are required so that participants can acquire process skills.

Tool Skills

In order to perform their tasks, stakeholders involved in the process are provided with information and communication technology tools, e.g., to edit and share business objects (see Chap. 10). These may be office applications, ERP systems, e-mail, telephone, or workflow management systems.

In terms of efficient task completion, the employees need skills for the appropriate use of these tools. For dealing with software and devices, e.g., they need to be adequately trained in time. In particular, software functionality should not only be taught in an isolated fashion, but also in the context of daily work routines along the process, otherwise process stakeholders may develop their own (partial) solutions with end-user tools, such as Microsoft Excel. These solutions are often defective and difficult to integrate into the overall process execution.

Communicative Competence

Each process is characterized by communication between the individually assigned subject carriers. This means that the people involved in the process need to exchange messages with each other. For each human interaction, a proper communication channel and partner has to be identified. Business communication, including e-mail or electronic forms, needs to meet minimum requirements for appreciation, clarity, style, and communicative behavior. A business trip request of an employee such as "Wonna fly to London next week!" is not very likely to be approved by the supervisor, not only due to serious flaws in the specification but also due to the choice of words.

Social Skills

A process model can be considered as a template for procedural specifications. However, during its implementation and execution, there may be interventions and disturbances, which need to be clarified. Social competence is particularly required when external disturbances need to be eliminated. In such cases, all involved process parties have to cooperatively adopt appropriate measures to nevertheless achieve the desired process result. All participants need to be willing to resolve conflicts and to hereby apply the necessary social skills (e.g., conflict resolution and ability to work in a team). They should be willing to share responsibility and to think and act in terms of the overall team perspective.

9.4.4 Change Management in S-BPM

In the course of organization-specific implementation, a model is transferred to the realities of an organization. This leads to changes in the organization; employees have to learn new behavior patterns or dismiss existing ones. Often, projects fail at this step. The inertia of the organization is sometimes so strong that the implementation of new processes fails (cf. Best et al. 2007, pp. 183 ff.).

To avoid or at least reduce problems of acceptance by those affected, which could impede a successful implementation, changes should be carefully prepared and accompanied by an appropriate change management as part of process management. Measures to this respect are, e.g., open communication, changes actively exemplified by management, and encouragement for individual initiative of employees, or in other words, contributions to the active development and promotion of an S-BPM culture (see Sect. 3.6.3.3). For details, procedures, etc. of change management, readers can refer to various resources such as Doppler (2003) and Hirzel and Kuhn (2008, pp. 247 ff.).

For acceptance, especially those Actors, who were involved in the redefinition or modification of a process, play a major role. They can most credibly convey that a new process will deliver a benefit, and therefore these Actors can represent important promoters of an organizational development project.

Usually, organizational change processes open up development fields that require special attention because of avoidance strategies. Therefore, change management needs to rationalize the reactions of employees to change. It is therefore beneficial in the process of change to start at the point of formal changes for each employee, namely with his duties and his job description. S-BPM enables this, since it moves the responsible authority of work activities to the center of change. Hence, in case a process is described in a subject-oriented way, it is much easier to identify the starting point for change processes. The direct relation between subject and work authorities supports a targeted approach.

Another advantage of the subject-oriented approach is that the subject carriers have already been involved as Actors in the previous bundles of activities. Due to this involvement, a change process is likely to be able to be completed in a socially acceptable way. The participants are already familiar with the objectives and details of the organizational development project. In most cases, this positively affects their acceptance behavior.

References

Abecker, A., Hinkelmann, K., Maus, H., Muller, H., Geschäftsprozessorientiertes Wissensmanagement, Berlin/Heidelberg 2002.
Best, E., Weth, M., Geschäftsprozesse optimieren, Wiesbaden 2007
Doppler, K., Der Change Manager, Frankfurt/Main 2003.
Hirzel, M., Kuhn, F., Gaida, I., Prozessmanagement in der Praxis, Wiesbaden 2008.

IT-Implementation of Subject-Oriented Business Processes

10

10.1 To Go

Now, I am excited! So far, everything went more or less without IT. But is it not necessary to let the process run on my systems?

I am extremely keen on mapping the process on IT systems. I see high potential for motivation and optimization. In addition, IT should guide our staff's work and support them in doing their job.

The natural language sentence semantics with subject, predicate, and object can be transferred to concepts of IT—and quite seamlessly! There is no need for employees to deal with unknown terrain; they can immediately just 'do'.

Natural language sentence semantics allows us to make use of approaches, such as service-oriented architectures, in a straightforward way. In the realm of S-BPM, SOA even takes on a new meaning. Services are ultimately the predicates a subject uses.

A. Fleischmann et al., *Subject-Oriented Business Process Management*,
DOI 10.1007/978-3-642-32392-8_10, © The Author(s) 2012

IT has achieved a high level of penetration in many organizations. Without IT support, many business processes cannot be handled in an economically beneficial way. For this reason, the careful and on-demand mapping of processes to information and communication technology is an important task. This applies for cases where employees are involved, as well as for operations in which a high degree of automation is striven for. A suitable and well-fitting software environment plays a significant role here. However, the challenge in many cases is an existing heterogeneous landscape of systems and services, in which each of the components fulfills specific tasks, and for which all of these components need to be integrated into an overall solution for adequate process support.

In this chapter, we first describe the roles of S-BPM stakeholders in the IT implementation (Sect. 10.2). Then we introduce a framework for IT implementation of subject-oriented process models (Sect. 10.3) and describe the IT implementation of subjects and their behavior (Sects. 10.4 and 10.5). Finally, we show that service orchestration is not only an effective but also efficient way to support the dynamics of S-BPM (Sect. 10.6).

10.2   S-BPM Stakeholders in IT Implementation

10.2.1 Governors

The IT manager (e.g., CIO) plays a superior Governor role in IT implementation. He calls for IT compliance of planning, development, and operation of IT solutions (see Sect. 3.6.4). This ranges from the fulfillment of legal requirements (e.g., data protection, principles of data access, and verifiability of digital documents) to the observance of standards and internal guidelines, which the organization itself has defined as binding (e.g., IT infrastructure library, IT architecture principles, IT security policies, etc.). In large organizations, particular roles need to be installed, such as IT security and data protection officer, which will also take over functions of Governors and need to be involved in the IT implementation of processes. This also applies to staff representative bodies such as the works council, which can exert Governor functions, as a result of codetermination regulations.

An important task in the Governor's activity bundle of IT deployment is the process-related assignment of permissions to subjects or subject carriers to enable access to functions and data in the solution. In these cases, the process owner can be Governor. The implementation will be performed by a system administrator in the role of an Actor.

10.2.2 Actors

Actors involved in the process represent the users of solutions for process support. As such, they play an important role in IT implementation. Their behavior specified in the model defines the functional requirements for the systems to be developed.

The Actors can be involved at an early stage of IT implementation by participating in the design of user interfaces and functionality. They can also try out prototypes. They test solutions using specific test cases and data, which they themselves have designed, eventually assisted by Experts.

With the help of Enterprise Mashups, process participants may step increasingly into the role of producing small applications to support their tasks in the process. Prerequisites are an Enterprise Mashup platform with which users can orchestrate information and application services without programming, as well as governance rules, which control and monitor these activities (Pahlke et al. 2010, pp. 302 and 307). This type of end-user computing is particularly suited for situation-specific processes with individual needs and workflows and can be "understood as the next step toward a distributed workflow management by knowledge workers" (Pahlke et al. 2010, p. 307). Given these properties, Enterprise Mashups can serve on the IT technical side as catalyst for self-organization in S-BPM.

10.2.3 Experts

Typical Experts in this bundle of activities are IT professionals, such as IT architects, software developers, database specialists, hardware specialists, and system administrators. They support the Governors, Facilitators, and Actors in building the IT infrastructure for process execution.

10.2.4 Facilitators

A key Facilitator for IT implementation is the leader of a development project. He coordinates the implementation of the domain model into a workflow and all associated tasks. In the development process, he integrates the Actors according to their demands and suggestions, the Governors with respect to their constraints, the Experts with their know-how, and if required, external resources for specific tasks (e.g., training providers).

After going into production with a solution, the responsibility for maintenance and further development is usually passed on to the IT (line) unit. It could also be outsourced to an external service provider. In both cases, troubleshooting and change requests are usually handled by a service desk. Its employees will act as Facilitators, receiving requests for small maintenance tasks or changes during operation. For major modification proposals, they address the respective process owner, who in this case initiates as a Facilitator a (change) project when appropriate.

10.3   Framework for Executing Subject-Oriented Processes

To implement IT support, a business process needs to be represented as a workflow. This is the detailed specification of a process from an IT perspective (cf. Vogler 2006, p. 40). From several conventional interpretations of existing workflow definitions (see, e.g., Becker et al. 2008, p. 56; Gadatsch 2010, pp. 46 ff.; Schmelzer et al. 2010, p. 420; WfMC 1997, p. 244), the following understanding of a workflow can be derived:

A workflow is a:

- Formal description of
- Activities which are executed by
- Communicating actors (roles/people, embedded IT systems)
- Partially or fully automated on
- Objects (inputs and outputs, including data structures)
- Following business rules
- Controlled by the business logic

A workflow is a refinement of a purely domain-specific business process with respect to implementing a strategy (what?) in terms of IT support (how?) (cf. Gadatsch 2010, p. 53).

Referring to the concepts presented in Chap. 5 concerning subject-oriented modeling, and putting these into relation with essential workflow characteristics, the relationships depicted in Fig. 10.1 can be complemented in the right column with the corresponding aspects with respect to IT implementation.

Workflow characteristic	Illustration in the subject-oriented approach	Aspect of IT implementation
Actors (roles/persons)	* Subjects/subject class * Subject carrier (result of the organizational implementation)	Implementation of subjects and subject carriers via the user management of systems (e.g., via LDAP, role and rights concepts, etc.)
Actors (IT system)		Implementation of the action behavior of mechanical subjects (integration of existing and new applications, e.g., as Web Services)
Activities controlled by business logic and rules	* Subject behavior (internal strictly sequential ⇒ orchestration) * Communication structure (subject interactions ⇒ choreography)	Implementation of the action and communication behavior of subjects as steps in Workflow Engine / Business Rule Engine with the integration of existing and new applications [e.g., as Web services]
Communication of the actors	Communication structure (subject interactions), including synchronization of message exchanges using the input pool	Implementation of the communication behavior of the subjects, e.g., by e-mail, etc.
Objects (inputs and outputs incl. data structures)	Business objects	Implementation of business objects and their manipulation in the action behavior of the subjects by user interaction (screen forms) or automated application functionality (e.g., program-triggered database transactions)

Fig. 10.1 Workflow characteristics equivalent in the subject-oriented approach and related aspects of IT implementation

Whereas for organization-specific implementation, the relation of process models to the organization, including underlying human actors (subject carriers) was discussed (see Fig. 10.2, upper part), in the context of IT implementation, the focus is placed on the relation of a process model to IT systems (Fig. 10.2, bottom part). In the course of IT implementation, also the assignment of subject carriers to subjects needs to be done according to the result of the previously performed organization-specific implementation.

Figure 10.2 shows the frame of reference (framework) integrating humans and machines in a socio-technical system for process execution. As revealed by the figure, models of business processes couple human actors with supporting IT solutions, while they control the process. If the formal model description is transformed into an interpretable language for a workflow engine, the engine can take over the control flow at runtime. It triggers people and application systems as actors according to the workflow specification, supports their individual activities and their cooperation by providing guidelines, information, etc. and documents the progress of processing.

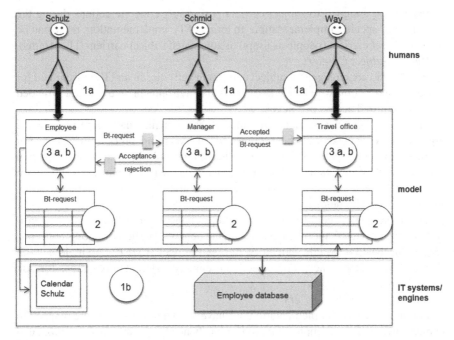

Fig. 10.2 Framework of IT implementation for a subject-oriented process model

In this context, the principle of constructing models systematically becomes essential: taking into account technical systems, such as information systems, the data and functions perspective is, in addition to the stakeholders perspective, in the focus. For IT implementation, the organization-specific implementation needs to be explored and specified in terms of data management, service architecture, and user privileges, and implemented accordingly.

The circled numbers in Fig. 10.2 represent the following aspects of an IT implementation, which are detailed in the following sections:

1. Implementation of access for subject carriers
   (a) Humans (roles/people)
   (b) IT systems/machines
2. Implementation of business objects (see 3a)
3. Implementation of subject behavior (business logic and business rules)
   (a) Behavioral action (manipulation of business objects)
   (b) Communication behavior (sending and receiving messages)

10.4   IT Implementation of Subject Carrier Access

Subjects were assigned to subject carriers performing concrete actions during the organization-specific implementation. In terms of IT implementation, these can be human subject carriers (people as users) or automated subject carriers (IT systems).

Human Subject Carriers

People who are engaged as subject carriers in activities in an IT environment for workflow support must be made known to this environment as users and provided with the required access privileges.

These privileges can be static, but can also change dynamically depending on the organizational context and the progress when executing process instances. For example, the employees of the travel office should only have access to personal data provided by applicants, as long as they work on the travel request. A short-term designated delegate must have the same system and data access privileges as the subject carrier who delegated him.

The implementers could realize user and privilege administration either specifically in the individual applications, or with the help of overall user access concepts, e.g., using the Lightweight Directory Access Protocol (LDAP). A single sign-on should be provided, as actors may need to use many different applications for task completion.

Automated Subject Carriers

For organizational implementation, we have shown how subjects are mapped to human carriers. For IT implementation, subjects need to be assigned to automated subject carriers. IT systems acting in such a process must be integrated into the workflow. To accomplish this tasks, interfaces need to be created which enable the communication between automated subject carriers and also between automated and human subject carriers. Automated subject carriers are mainly used for parts of workflows that can run with minimal human intervention.

Workflow Management Systems facilitate the straightforward implementation of those parts of subject behavior specifications that can be executed without human intervention. In S-BPM, the subject behavior specification reveals the stakeholder intervention and control requirements for task accomplishment.

10.5   IT Implementation of Subject Behavior

The modeled behavior describes the action behavior (work steps) and the communication behavior (sending and receiving) of the subjects involved in the process (see Sects. 5.5.5. and 5.5.3). The type and sequence of activities of the model determine the business logic of the process which is to be implemented.

The implementation has to create a process flow control and to integrate applications and services providing the functionality required for performing work and interaction steps. For the implementation of the process flow control, the developers may use standardized technologies, such as Java and Business Process Execution Language (BPEL) in conjunction with a workflow engine. Services can be integrated by linking, as a portlet, by calling methods, or as Web services. In this way, when required, the human users can also become part of workflows, e.g., by triggering a service to display a user interface enabling users to enter data into a business object.

The following sections detail various IT implementations of action and communication behavior, exemplifying its use.

10.5.1 Action Behavior

Action behavior includes internal functions a subject or its respective carrier executes in the course of processing a process instance. Of particular importance are operations on business objects. Business objects and possible operations on business objects, or respectively, on their instances, were introduced in the context of modeling (see Sect. 5.5.7.6). The business objects defined in a process model are transformed in the course of IT implementation into appropriate data structures that can be processed by IT systems (e.g., XML schemata).

In a further step, operations on business objects need to be implemented. Figure 10.3 shows various approaches. They are usually applied in combinations.

Subjects that perform operations as part of their behavior for creating and manipulating business objects and business object instances (as shown in the figure) can be users (human subject carriers) or applications (automated subject carriers). They require functions for creating, viewing, editing, storing, etc. of business object content.

10.5.1.1 Human Operators

If users should interactively perform operations on business objects and their instances, they need user interfaces. These can be provided either by an application managing the business object or generated from the data structure description of the business object.

- *Using the user interface (front end) of an application (IT system).* The behavioral description of a subject can define in a state that a subject carrier uses a particular application to modify business object data. For this purpose, the application's

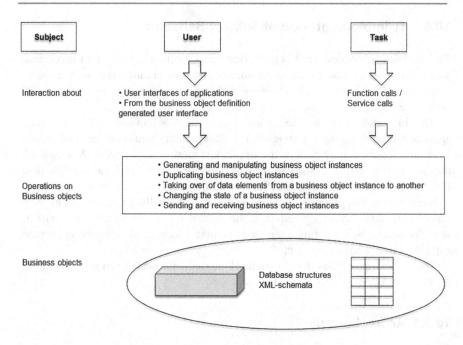

Fig. 10.3 IT implementation of operations on business objects and their instances

screens are directly activated in this state and entered data stored by way of the same. An example of this type of integration of business objects are SAP application transactions. The behavioral description controls the invocation of the transaction, which is represented and implemented in the process model by the abstract business object. In this case, the application can be considered as an encapsulated business object in which the data structure and the user interface are unified.

The technical implementation for the integration of user interfaces of such encapsulated business objects is very straightforward. The transfer of their data into other business objects and vice versa, however, is generally more complicated. This is due to the fact that the complete data structure of an encapsulated business object often remains to a great extent hidden, and only those elements displayed in the associated user interface are visible. Consequently, if elements of the business object need to be accessed without involving the user interface, transfer programs need to be developed to transfer the desired data from the encapsulated object, e.g., from an SAP database, to a target business object, and vice versa.

- *Generating the user interface from the business object definition.* For the manipulation of business objects without recourse to existing applications, the user interface can be derived from the data structure description of the business object. The elements of the business object are mapped to corresponding fields of a screen mask. In case the behavior description contains user interactions, the subject carrier is able to maintain the data by means of this screen mask. The newly entered or modified values are stored in the corresponding data elements of the business object definition.

If the implementation of the user interface is restricted to simple, table-like user dialogs, its code could automatically be generated from the business object definition using appropriate technology, e.g., http://www.ecplise.org. This also applies for static validation checks for preventing input errors. For instance, in a field that is defined as a date field, only data in a valid date format can be entered; arbitrary strings are not permitted. For a field where only certain inputs are allowed, a bulleted list of the possible values can be defined (value range).

More sophisticated designs leading to more comfortable user interfaces can be achieved through usage of dedicated design tools for user interface screens and forms. However, usually a manual mapping of data elements of the business object to (form) fields is required. Complex, dynamic plausibility checks also require more effort, e.g., due to the need for programming special tests. An example is the dependency of an input on previously entered data. For instance, an underage trainee, after entering his date of birth in the business trip application form, might subsequently be required to enter his legal guardian's data in a dynamically displayed input field.

10.5.1.2 Operations Through Application Functions or Services

Instead of being operated interactively, business objects or their instances can be manipulated automatically and without user intervention by application program functions or services. For implementation, internal functions of a subject behavior are linked to appropriate application functions or services. The flow control component of the workflow engine then invokes these when a subject carrier reaches the respective functional state.

Such functions or services could be database queries or calculation algorithms. They are forwarded business objects to be manipulated, or parts of them, as parameters. They then return results from querying and calculation, respectively, which are transferred to the business object data. The reverse path, e.g., updating data base records from a business object, can also be performed.

In the example of the business trip application, a service could automatically be triggered after an employee has entered the business trip data, in order to calculate advance payments. This service receives a part of the business object "business trip request" with the relevant data for determining the advance payment for the trip, passed on as parameters (e.g., employee number, start and end date, national/ foreign country, salary grade, amount of the advance payment [empty], etc.). Using this data, first the service accesses a database in which the expense rates are structured according to destinations and salary groups. Then, it calculates the amount according to the duration of the trip. The calculated value flows back as parameter into the appropriate field of the specific instance of the business object "business trip request".

10.5.2 Communication Behavior

Subjects interact and synchronize by exchanging messages, which often contain business objects. As described in the context of modeling, the concept of input pool is used for implementation (see Sect. 5.5.5.2). Each subject must have such an input pool. IT managers may implement a pool as parameterized service module (e.g., using Web services). It provides insertion and extraction operations and associated interfaces with which subject carriers can deposit outgoing messages and extract received messages.

The extract interface is a local internal affair of the subject and can be implemented by any technology. As a subject usually communicates with several other subjects, however, for the realization of outgoing messages, it should be noted that for sending messages to different recipients different technologies may have to be used (such as Remote Method Invocation (RMI) and Web services). If these are known, in the course of generating code for the subject behavior, the appropriate send operation can be embedded.

When sending a message that contains a business object, only a copy of the business object is created and sent. When receiving a message, the values are taken from the received business object and put into a uniform business object of the receiver. The implementation of these operations can be part of code generation for the behavior of a subject.

10.5.3 Example

The scenario in Fig. 10.4, namely registration and approval of a business trip request, illustrates the combination of the presented possibilities for manipulating business objects, which is often required in practice, as well as the communication of the involved subjects.

The subject "employee" has been linked in the course of the organizational implementation to Mr. Schulz as subject carrier. In the state "complete business trip request", he fills out an instance of the business object "business trip request". In order to complete this task, he uses the automatically generated screen mask (from the business object definition), and initially enters his personnel number into the respective entry field. In the background, a function (database query) checks automatically whether for this personnel number, forwarded as a parameter, a record in the employee database exists. It returns either an error message, or data of the person, such as name, first name, salary grade, etc., which are incorporated into the appropriate fields of the business object instance.

For entering the trip start and end date, the electronic calendar of Mr. Schulz is integrated (with a specific) user interface as encapsulated business object. The clicked dates are forwarded by an operation right from the calendar to the business object.

Further information from Mr. Schulz, with respect to destination and the intention of the trip, completes the application instance of the business trip request,

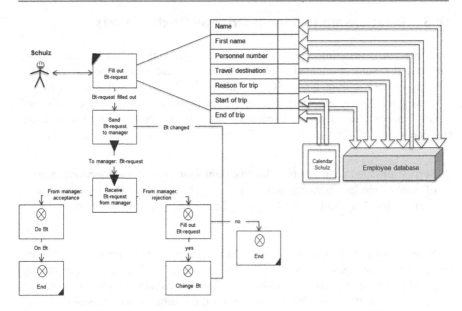

Fig. 10.4 Embedding of the subject employee in the organization-specific and IT environment

which is then sent for approval to Mr. Schmid, the organization-specific implemented manger of Mr. Schulz.

Mr. Schmid sees the arrival of the application process in his process portal and opens it. The data entered by Mr. Schulz and the automatically generated data of the request are enriched for the manager with the notice for approval (e.g., a checkbox with a remark field) and shown on the screen. Mr. Schmid approves the trip without any changes, clicks the appropriate check box, and executes thereby a state transition in accordance with his modeled behavior, namely from the function state "Business trip application—check request" behavior to the send state "Approve".

With this state transition, not only the delivery of the approved application to the applicant is achieved. The approval is also the trigger for the automatic update of a number of databases. A function call linked with the state transition results in the transfer of selected data from the business trip request (travel time, target, intention, etc.) into the employee database. Another function transmits the approved advance payment to the payroll system, which initiates the payment. At the same time, with a corresponding call, the flextime application is triggered to take over the travel dates of Mr. Schulz, which were transferred as parameters from the business object and store them in its own database including presence and absence times, working time balances, etc.

10.6   Relationship to Service-Oriented Architectures

With the use of existing and newly developed applications and services within subjects, the subject-oriented approach forms a solid foundation for building service-oriented architectures (SOA). This architectural principle for software systems provides for the representation of business logic a loosely coupling of largely independent function modules with clearly defined functional tasks (services) (cf. e.g., Krcmar 2010, pp. 345 and 494; Reinheimer et al. 2007, pp. 7).

> Service-oriented architectures allow the implementation of the functional part of subject models in a straightforward way. In S-BPM, all functions of a subject, which are linked to calls of application systems, are affected.

Subject orientation combines the two SOA management concepts of orchestration and choreography as needed (cf. Decker et al., 2007, p. 296). The strictly sequential services for the realization of the subject behavior are orchestrated. The synchronization of the parallel activities of multiple subjects with messages, possibly even across organizational boundaries, corresponds to the principle of choreography. Consequently, subjects of a process can be implemented and run on different IT platforms or workflow engines, respectively. Only the communication between them must be standardized, e.g., via an appropriate Web service agreed upon between all affected parties.

> The principle of coordination in S-BPM corresponds to the same in choreography. In contrast to orchestration, the coordination of subject behavior is achieved by direct message exchange, which simultaneously represents the control of the entire system, and as such, the organization.

Especially in historically grown, heterogeneous, and complex IT environments that are typical for many organizations, the approach thus helps to achieve the goals of SOA. These aim to make software systems more flexible and to adapt them more easily and more quickly to changing operational requirements, particularly at the level of business processes (Reinheimer et al. 2007, pp. 7 et seq.)

10.6.1 Services in Subject Orientation

In the previous sections, it was shown that subjects use services in their behavior to perform operations on business objects and to exchange messages. These services can be of different nature:

- On one hand, they can be function blocks, already developed following the principles of service orientation, which have characteristic features such as

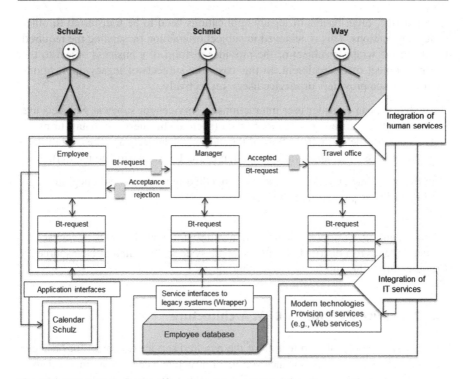

Fig. 10.5 Integration of services into the subjects of a process

abstraction (hiding function details), reuse (use by different consumers), and far-reaching autonomy (control over their own environment and resources) (cf. Erl 2008, pp. 86 et seq.)

- On the other hand, in the organization, as a rule legacy systems (applications) are in use which usually, especially for economic reasons (protection of investment, capital accumulation), cannot be easily converted in the short term into a modern, from the ground up designed service-oriented landscape (cf. e.g., Friend et al. 2008). Therefore, along the way the goal is to use mostly proven functionalities of existing systems, for instance, in that IT developers encase these functionalities using so-called wrapper programs (Legacy Wrapper). These separate functions from the monolithic structure and publish them as Web services, and so provide them as services in the sense mentioned above (cf. Mathas et al. 2008, pp. 111 ff.; Erl et al. 2008, p. 311; SOA Glossary 2011).

If access to a legacy application is preprocessed through a subject with wrapper properties, this handles the synchronous access to the functions of the application and provides the requester a usable asynchronous service. The consuming service is so less tightly coupled to the provider, compared to the case of self-contained, synchronous use of the function of the legacy system. This approach especially helps in meeting the demand for loose coupling of services.

In practice, often results of legacy applications need to be transferred to other legacy applications. This is achieved in subject orientation by sending the required data from the wrapper subject of the provider in form of a business object to the wrapper subject of the recipient. In this case, the subjects of legacy applications become service providers or service users, respectively.

• Finally, we can consider user interactions as services for subjects. Subjects use skills of their carriers, e.g., to enter data (such as, business trip data), to make decisions for the subsequent flow of the individual subjects and the overall flow of the process (e.g., approval or rejection of the business trip application).

In this way, human and IT services are bundled in a subject and integrated as a unit in a business process (see Fig. 10.5).

Implementing a service-oriented architecture for realizing S-BPM consequently leads to a distributed choreographic system. This enables IT resource optimization through flexible load sharing.

10.6.2 Service-Oriented S-BPM Architecture

SOA defines the logical architecture of the required service (bundles) for business process management. This business-oriented structure needs to be mapped to a corresponding physical infrastructure. Figure 10.6 shows an example of how this could be achieved. The dashed rectangles each represent different technical platforms.

The subject carriers use for their interactions within the process workplace computers, which are connected via proper networks to servers. These execute one or more subjects of the relevant business process, but possibly also other subjects of other processes. In the example, the subjects "employee" and "manager" run on the same physical system, while their business objects, e.g., for safety reasons, are located in separate environments, respectively. The subject "travel office" is located together with its business objects on a separate system. This could be due to the fact that for historical reasons the travel office has its own IT infrastructure, which is managed by an external partner. In addition, services required for communication among users or manipulating business objects were, e.g., for reasons of load balancing, distributed to separate systems, respectively.

Integration technologies need to be used for the interaction of solution components mapped to such a heterogeneous physical landscape. Figure 10.7 exemplifies a cross-selection of such technologies and the positions in the S-BPM architecture where they could be used. The numbers in the figure correspond to those in the subsequent explanation.

1. User interfaces are typically Web-based implementations. Here, different technologies, such as HTML, JavaScript, etc., can be used. For implementation, tools like Google Web Tool (GWT) and Flex (Adobe) are available. They offer

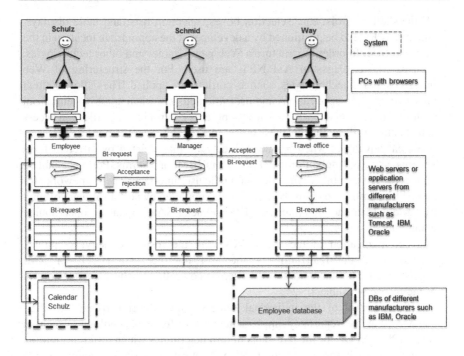

Fig. 10.6 Distribution of an S-BPM solution to multiple physical systems

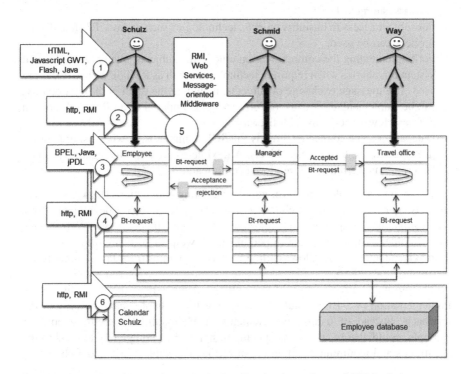

Fig. 10.7 Examples of integration technologies when implementing an S-BPM solution

off-the-shelf controls, e.g., selection boxes, selection lists, and table displays, which only have to be positioned by a developer at the appropriate location in the user interface. In order to structure a Web page, frames and other technologies, such as Master Pages in ASP.NET, are used. For the structuring of Web interfaces, portal technologies, such as portlets, are applied. They allow content presentation in an application- and user-oriented way when context stems from multiple sources. In this way, entries for process control in one portlet can access actual data for filling in a business object in a second, separate portlet. This is of particular advantage when business objects are manipulated by different form systems, such as Adobe Forms, eForm from IBM, or xForms. Portlets enable a high degree of flexibility when designing the user interface. The frameworks for assembling portlets to entire Web pages are supported by portal software offered by various manufacturers, such as IBM, Oracle, SAP, or, in the open source community, Liferay.

2. The communication of the users' PCs with the respective servers can be, depending on the realization of the user interface, via HTTP, or RMI implemented. The interaction of the users is controlled by the sequence control of the respective subject.

3. The flow control of the individual subjects and subject carriers, i.e., their behavior, can be separately implemented by different technologies, such as Java, BPEL, XPDL, or the like. This in turn determines which different runtime systems for each server are used. Web Application Servers already provide support for storing state information, for handling exceptions, or when restarting after a system crash.

4. For subject access to business objects, technologies such as Java, RMI, and Web services can be used.

5. For implementing the communication among the subjects, even across physical system boundaries when required, technologies such as RMI or Web services are used. The message exchange of subjects, including the input pool functionality, can be implemented, e.g., as a Web service. Compared to an RMI solution, in this case fewer problems with firewalls occur.

6. Databases can be connected directly via SQL commands, or when using Java via jDBC functions, to business objects. A flexible solution in this regard, based on Hibernate, is the hiding of vendor-specific features in SQL.

The type of technology used for coupling existing applications (legacy systems) strongly depends on the architecture in which they were developed. New applications usually provide an opportunity to trigger functions via Web service calls. In older systems, e.g., developed in Cobol, wrapper software may need to be used as an adapter, which allows calling COBOL programs from Java programs (cf. Herrmann et al. 2009).

The presented cross section of technologies demonstrates the flexibility in the implementation of S-BPM solutions, as well as the technological neutrality of the approach. Instead of using Java elements, a Microsoft.NET environment, for example, could also be used. The specific design can be completely aligned to the constraints and requirements of an organization. The subject-oriented architecture helps in clearly spotting relevant areas with respect to technology and thus facilitates decision making regarding the implementation of BPM solutions.

The technological flexibility is especially demonstrated by the capability to provide different IT implementations for different organizational embeddings of a subject, which means for multiple subject carriers, within a specific process. This affects all aspects of process flow control, from manipulating business objects, to exchanging messages. For instance, an employee in the German headquarters may submit his business trip request via an SAP application, whereas employees of foreign subsidiaries accomplish this task via a Web interface. The flexible combination and integration of highly diverse technologies is of particular benefit in the case of inter- and cross-organizational processes.

References

Becker, J., Kugeler, M., Rosemann, M. (Hrsg.), Prozessmanagement, 6th edition, Berlin 2008.

Decker, G., Kopp, O., Leymann, F., Weske, M., BPEL4Chor: Extending BPEL for Modeling Choreographies, IEEE International Conference on Web Services, Salt Lake City, 2007, pp. 296-303.

Erl, T., SOA – Entwurfsprinzipien für Serviceorientierte Architektur, München, 2008.

Freund, J., Götzer, K., Vom Geschäftsprozess zum Workflow, München, 2008.

Gadatsch, A., Grundkurs Geschäftsprozess-Management, Wiesbaden 2010.

Herrmann, W., Java-Wrapper für COBOL-Funktionen, http://www.computerwoche.de/software/soa-bpm/1884724/index3.html, Download 11.03.2011. 2009

Krcmar, H., Informationsmanagement, 5th edition, Heidelberg 2010.

Mathas, C., SOA intern: Praxiswissen zu serviceorientierten IT-Systemen, München 2008.

Pahlke, I., Beck, R., Wolf, M., Enterprise-Mashup-Systeme als Plattform für situative Anwendungen, Wirtschaftsinformatik 52. Jg. (2010) 5, pp. 299–310.

Reinheimer, S., Lang, F., Purucker, J., Brügmann, H., 10 Antworten zu SOA. in: HMD – Praxis der Wirtschaftsinformatik, Heft 253, 2007, pp. 7–17.

Schmelzer, H., Sesselmann, W., Geschäftsprozessmanagement in der Praxis, 7th edition, München 2010.

SOA Glossary (2011) Definitions for Service-Oriented Computing Terms, http://www.soaglossary.com/legacy_wrapper.php, Download 11.03.2011

Vogler, P., Prozess- und Systemintegration, Wiesbaden 2006.

WfMC, The Workflow Reference Model, In: Lawrence, P. (Hrsg.), Workflow Handbook 1997, Chichester 1997.

Subject-Oriented Monitoring of Processes **11**

11.1 To Go

Now, we can start. Each of my colleagues is well-informed. The IT department has done a great job—even our tried and tested systems have been integrated.

Yes, I'm also happy to get going. Now, we'll see whether our expectations can be met. Because the purpose of all of this is to help us achieve our objectives and contribute to the success of our business.

We are of course curious whether everything runs the way we have worked it out based on the models and their execution.

Yes, now we'll see whether all that we have brought together leads to the desired result. The metrics we measure are by all means aligned with the goals.

A. Fleischmann et al., *Subject-Oriented Business Process Management*,
DOI 10.1007/978-3-642-32392-8_11, © The Author(s) 2012

Through the IT-supported execution of the process with the help of our workflow engine—or better said, communication engine—we can automatically document each process step. This then allows us to extract the information we need.

Are we then totally transparent? What about data protection?

No problem, in my role as data security officer I have negotiated respective agreements; no individual-related reports are allowed.

We are interested in the overall picture, not in individual-specific data. We have a written agreement with the work council to that effect. Moreover, we have set up technical barriers so that not even management can run person-specific reports. The collected metrics are exclusively for the purpose of improving our processes.

11.2 Nature of Monitoring

Optimized and implemented processes go live after their final acceptance sign-off. This means that they are executed in the course of ongoing business operations, in the organization and IT environment described in the previous chapters. Experience reveals that process execution here is exposed over time to changes to a variety of influencing factors. These can negatively affect the process performance and thus increasingly decrease value generation, if not addressed properly. An example of such factors is the rapid, nonpredicted increase in parallel occurring instances of customer inquiries in a bidding process. This can lead to an increase in turnaround time for quotations, with the risk that potential customers switch to competitors.

A permanent, real-time monitoring of process efficiency in the key dimensions of quality, time, and cost can help to avoid such developments and also help to identify opportunities for improvement (Heß et al. 2005, p. 10). In doing so, usually IT systems with appropriate functionality record actual (as-is) values for suitable key performance indicators, compare them with predetermined target (to-be) values, report deviations outside tolerance limits, and so provide the basis for a cause analysis and subsequent actions. Addressees of the recorded data and exception reports are the work performers as Actors and the process owner as Governor. They interpret the results and take appropriate action.

> Recognize the beginnings of deviation from predetermined target behavior!—The monitoring task is to track possible deviations in a timely, causality-driven way with respect to resources and to immediately reveal these to stakeholders and operation managers.

Process Monitoring is also termed Process Performance Measurement (PPM) or Operational Process Control. It is logically the last bundle of activities of the open S-BPM life cycle. Since a performance value recorded in a running operation environment is usually interpreted arbitrarily by its receiver, monitoring is linked closely to the activity bundle of analysis. It is an essential part of the Process Performance Management (PPM), which is the planning, measurement, evaluation, and control of business processes (Schmelzer and Sesselmann 2010, p. 230). The PPM is in turn part of a company-wide Corporate Performance Management (CPM), which refers to the overall corporate performance (Heß et al. 2005, p. 11).

Schmelzer and Sesselmann distinguish between ongoing and periodic monitoring, which usually complement each other (Schmelzer and Sesselmann 2010, pp. 281 f). Figure 11.1 provides an overview of the essential characteristics of the two variants.

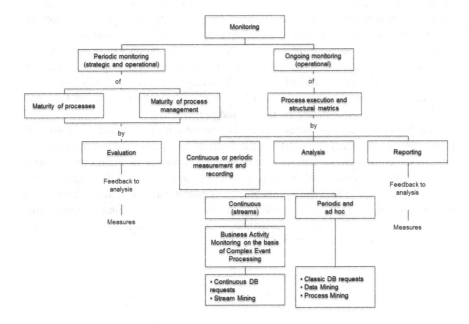

Fig. 11.1 Types of monitoring in business process management

Periodic monitoring is about capturing the maturity of both the business processes, as well as the overall business process management approach in the company, at longer intervals, e.g., quarterly or semiannually. Maturity models can serve to support in this case. Well-known examples are the Business Process Maturity Model (BPMM), which was developed by the Object Management Group, and the process assessment models for business processes (PAB) and for enterprises (PAE), which are based on the Model of the European Foundation for Quality Management (EFQM) (cf. Hogrebe and Nüttgens 2009; OMG 2008; Schmelzer and Sesselmann 2010, pp. 288 ff.).

These models include five maturity levels to assess the processes and the BPM concept, respectively. They help an organization with the evolutionary increase in process maturity by providing guidance for the prioritization of opportunities for optimization (cf. OMG 2008, p. 11). We do not hereby regard the maturity models only as a means of operational process control, like Schmelzer and Sesselmann but also as instruments of strategic process controlling which feedback control information for revising the S-BPM strategy (see Sect. 3.6.3.2) and represent a kind of link between operational and strategic process controlling.

Due to its affinity to execution, S-BPM supports all of the various variants of monitoring equally. Behavior data can be generated continuously and periodically from the flow of messages and execution of function.

Ongoing monitoring records evaluation data during process execution for each instance, calculates actual values for defined metrics (see Sect. 11.4), and prepares these for reporting to relevant stakeholders. In addition, process structure parameters, such as the available work capacity at a certain point in time, can be a matter of ongoing monitoring. For instance, in case the number of subject carriers drops under a certain threshold due to illness, managers could respond quickly to maintain the stability of critical factors, such as throughput time. The evaluation of the measured data can occur continuously, periodically at short intervals (daily and weekly), or ad hoc, depending on targets and purpose.

The following sections focus on ongoing monitoring and its main subtasks of measurement and analysis of data in the form of key performance indicators for process execution and design, and the associated reporting including preparation, delivery, and distribution of findings to relevant stakeholders (cf. Wagner et al. 2007, p. 186). Figure 11.2 shows this process of monitoring, including the essential information required for this purpose, which should be carefully and systematically defined in the form of key performance indicators (cf. Kütz 2009, pp. 47 ff.; Marx Goméz and Junker 2009, p. 131).

Procedure of monitoring		Information in the key performance indicators
	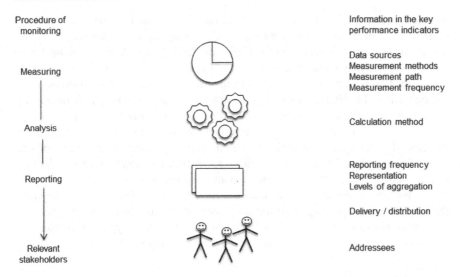	
Measuring		Data sources Measurement methods Measurement path Measurement frequency
Analysis		Calculation method
Reporting		Reporting frequency Representation Levels of aggregation
		Delivery / distribution
Relevant stakeholders		Addressees

Fig. 11.2 Procedure of process monitoring and the associated information from the key performance indicators

We will now deal first with the S-BPM stakeholders in monitoring and then, following the structure of the figure above, with the measurement of key performance indicators, and finally, with evaluation and reporting.

11.3   S-BPM Stakeholders in Monitoring

11.3.1 Governors

The Governor in monitoring is often the process owner. His role is characterized mainly by the assessment and analysis of performance indicators with target values provided for the overall process, which he has usually assisted in defining in other bundles of activities (e.g., analysis). Examples of such performance indicators are the work load of the subject carrier, the cycle and throughput times of instances, the number of instances per time unit and their temporal distribution (e.g., on weekdays), as well as the average cost per instance. The process owner is the addressee of the actual (as-is) values, which are usually automatically measured and prepared in the form of reports for key performance indicators. He analyzes and interprets them and initiates steps to eliminate problems, if required.

11.3.2 Actors

The Actors as subject carriers observe the process and identify during operation both relevant quantitative and qualitative aspects of the execution process. For example, each subject carrier notes when continuously too many or too few instances per time unit are due for his attention, or the response time of a shared IT system is not satisfactory. The first case could be an indication of deficiencies in the organization-specific implementation (insufficient work capacity), so that the Actor informs the Facilitator who then verifies this. In case Actors are not able to evaluate values for key performance indicators or identify root causes by themselves, they can contact the Facilitator, or via the Facilitator available experts. The same is true, when they identify their own deficiencies, e.g., missing know-how or IT expertise. In this case, the Facilitator can, for example, organize appropriate trainings by Experts. If Actors recognize execution deficiencies or communication problems with other stakeholders involved in the process, they can collaboratively identify causes, and in coordination with the responsible Governor, either eliminate these themselves or initiate their elimination via the Facilitator. The Actor is primarily the addressee for reporting of performance indicator values related to the (partial) process he is involved in, i.e., his behavior and interactions. Typical examples are the processing times of his steps and the latency time in his inbox.

11.3.3 Experts

Expert roles in the monitoring process could be taken by controllers and external consultants in assessing measured indicators, comparing them to benchmarks, providing explanations for poor results, and suggesting means for improving them. Also, these activities reach over into the activity bundle "analysis".

11.3.4 Facilitators

A Facilitator helps the Actors (as shown) in the assessment of perceived problems and in finding solutions. This role could be taken, e.g., by the process owner, the service desk (also as external service provider), or a quality management representative (QMR).

11.4   Measurement of Process Indicators (Key Performance Indicators)

11.4.1 Overview

Process indicators as measuring objects are, like any business metrics, scale values expressing quantifiable facts in numbers, and thus making them comparable. They need to be relevant for achieving process goals (reference to strategy), economically determinable, comprehensible for all involved, and influenceable in terms of controlling. For the application of key performance indicators, often their operationalization function (manageability of goals), target function (setting targets), control function (target/actual value comparison including variance analysis), impulse function (detection of abnormalities), and simplification control function (simplification of complex control processes) are highlighted. Indicators can only meet their target function if they have meaningful target value sets. In particular, for any new processes or those with a low level of maturity, it is often difficult to determine realistic target values for process indicators in the course of goal setting. It may be helpful to use one's own experience with other, potentially comparable transactions, estimates, and benchmarks of other organizations.

Figure 11.3 shows a differentiation of key performance indicators according to execution and structure, as well as a further distinction between business and, in terms of IT support for business processes, technical indicators.

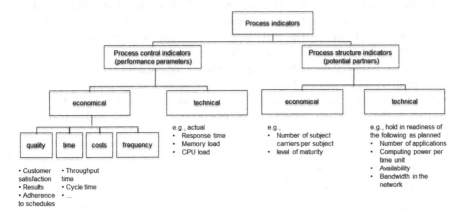

Fig. 11.3 Types of process indicators

11.4.2 Process Execution Metrics

Process execution metrics as performance parameters (Key Performance Indicators) target instances of processes. Their values are acquired dynamically, e.g., when processing a limited number of test instances in the course of validation or a large number of them during simulation in the context of optimization (see Chaps. 7 and 8). The most important application area, however, is monitoring. Hereby, actual values are recorded which are obtained when processing real process instances, i.e., concrete business cases. The term Key Performance Indicator (KPI) is assigned to a measure of particular importance for the organization, as it represents a critical success factor. In many cases, several performance parameters are subsumed as a KPI, e.g., when summarizing latency, transportation, and processing time as throughput time. Common key performance indicators are the satisfaction of external or internal customers, the quality of the process results, reliability of meeting deadlines for delivery of results, the process time (throughput time and cycle time), and the process costs (cf. Schmelzer and Sesselmann 2010, pp. 239 ff.). The partial interdependence of indicators requires their joint consideration. In addition to absolute key measures, such as totals (e.g., total cost of a process), situational measurements (e.g., average processing time), and measures of dispersion (e.g., standard deviation of processing time), often relative measures, also known as ratios, are used (e.g., number of bad credit offers per 100 offers).

> A proper business implementation of S-BPM monitoring requires the alignment of process key measures to the behavior parameters of subjects. This provides the basis for developing Key Performance Indicators.

Key measures can accommodate fixed values or probabilities, which have been defined as plan or target values in the course of analysis and modeling. For example, employees as Actors can run their own tests to determine a realistic value for the completion of a business trip application, and define, in coordination with the process owner as Governor, 5 min as maximum completion time (see Fig. 11.4). Analogously, a maximum limit for preparation of a message for sending a mail can be defined, as a conventional approach in the example, i.e., the insertion of the business trip request into an interoffice mail envelope and its deposit in the main mailbox in the office. An example of the labeling of a complete partial path of a

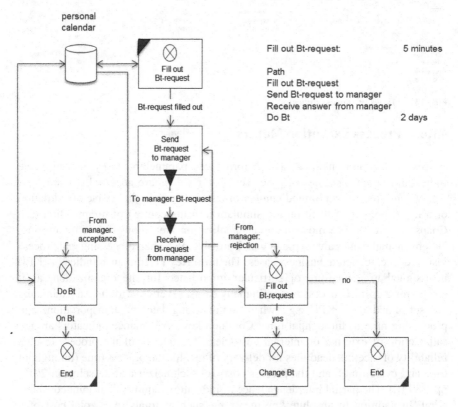

Fig. 11.4 Selected performance indicators for the behavior of the subject "employee" in the business trip application process

behavioral description of a subject with time information is also shown in the figure. Thus, the path from application to the state where the business trip can be started, takes 2 days. In this example, it might also be useful to measure real-time operation, namely how often the branch of rejecting business trip requests is executed in general, and how often with respect to each subject carrier in particular. A high or progressively increasing proportion of the total number might suggest a lack of coordination between employees and supervisors, or some potential for conflict in the individual organizational units.

An example for the specification of target values by way of a probability distribution would be the requirement that the completion time should not exceed 5 min in 80 % of all cases or the limitation of the average processing time of the whole path to 2 days.

Process execution metrics are continuously measured. This means the values are collected along the process in each run of an instance at defined positions so-called measurement points (cf. Kronz et al. 2005, p. 35). This can be done manually or automatically via sensors, counting and timing functions, etc. in workflow engines, application systems, and system software. The resulting process execution data is continuously recorded (logging).

Typical examples of entries in log files are process numbers, activity keys, time stamps for the beginning and end of activities, etc. The sum of log records is also known as an audit trail from which, among other things, can be reconstructed, who executed what steps and when of a business process instance during runtime. Using appropriate algorithms, also values can be calculated, such as the duration and cost for each activity in process steps, for process branches, or for entire processes.

Using the subject-oriented methodology, the main process execution metrics can be applied to the subject behavior and measured in terms of function, send, and receive states, as well as in their transitions. This allows the assessment of both the subject behavior and the subject interactions and provides ideas for their optimization. Figure 11.5 shows an example of how different times can be measured by recording of state transitions. We distinguish here between the time-relevant elements of processing, waiting, and latency. The individual elements can be aggregated to cycle and lead times.

S-BPM enables localizing work activities and responsibilities due to its stakeholder orientation and subject behavior models. Together with the organization-specific implementation, an entire set of data describing a certain situation is available for evaluation.

The processing time is the period of time in which a subject is in a function state processing a task. The total processing time in a process can thus be represented by the sum of all time periods subjects are in function states. In the figure, it is obvious that the processing time of the subject "manager" begins with the transition from the receive state "receive business trip request" to the state "check business trip request". It ends when one of the states "accept" or "reject" has been reached.

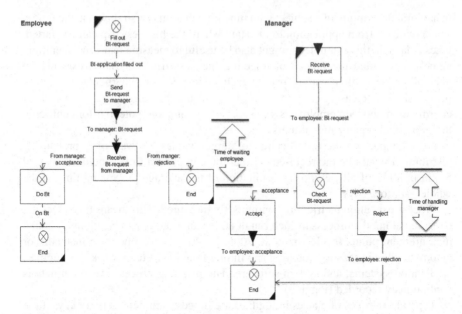

Fig. 11.5 Measurement of processing and waiting time in the subject-oriented approach

Waiting time is defined as the period of time which elapses between the moment in which a subject enters a receive state, and the time at which the expected message from the sender is actually received. The total waiting time of a process is consequently calculated by summing up the waiting times for all subjects. In the example, the waiting time of the subject "employee" starts as soon as it enters the state "receive Bt-request from manager". It ends, once the response is received from the manager ("from manager: acceptance" or "from manager: rejection").

In reality, operations cannot be processed immediately in a processing station. This results in latency time, which in subject orientation refers to the time that elapses after the arrival of a message in the input pool of the receiving subject until its processing by the subject.

A selection of business process execution metrics that are relevant for S-BPM is shown in Fig. 11.6. They usually refer to time, frequency, cost, and quality and are generally defined in the course of analysis or modeling by Actors, together with the Process Owner (Governor) and process controllers (Experts). When monitoring, the Actors measure the specified parameters on the fly in real instances, either manually or with the help of appropriate software functions. Process participants and controllers can measure time- and cost-related parameters also on test instances simulated during optimization. Sensitivity analyses performed in the course of simulation require a lot of process or methods experience to achieve improvements by parameter changes without creating local suboptima (e.g., reduction in cycle time due to additional personnel, but without overcompensating increase in costs). Here, Actors can bring in internal or external Experts having the necessary experience and qualifications.

Key indicator	Motive (awareness interest)
Time reference (for current or former instances)	
Throughput time (min., max., average)	Detection of variations and exploration of causes
Cycle time (min., max., average)	Detection of variations and exploration of causes
Processing time (duration of a process step) of all subject carriers (min., max., average)	Detection of variations and exploration of causes
Frequencies (for running instances)	
Number of open process instances per process type	Identification of bottlenecks in total and exploration of causes
Number of open process instances per process type in which a subject carrier is involved	Identification of bottlenecks of subject carriers and exploration of causes
Start times of instances per type of process (distribution)	Determining the temporal distribution of the instantiation and the distribution of instances on the individual process steps, on that basis, determining the temporal distribution of load in the further processing stations and actual timeouts, and forecasting the residual maturity, impending timeouts, and end time points
Number of instances, which are located in a particular process step	
Number of instances that have exceeded a certain period of time at a particular transition	Identification of bottlenecks of message exchange and exploration of causes
Frequencies (for completed instances)	
Number of process instances per process type and time unit	Identification of the quantity structure
Number of process instances for which the throughput time is above average	Identification of bottlenecks in total and exploration of causes
Number of subject changes of a subject carrier per time unit	Identification of the intellectual and organizational set-up times
Costs	
Total cost of the process	Identification of process costs
Cost of a subject / subject carrier in the process	Identification of the cost of a subject / subject carrier in the process
Proportions of subjects / subject carriers to the total cost of the process	Identification of the cost distribution to subject / subject carrier
Quality	
Numbers of mistakes in result	Identification of the faulty process results
Proportion of reworking correctable errors	Classification of the errors

Fig. 11.6 Selected business process execution metrics related to S-BPM

Since work performers sometimes need to adapt their behavior in processes to changing requirements, but this knowledge usually is lost, in S-BPM they are able to update their subject behavior by themselves while following agreed rules of governance in the respective models, and thus, ensure consistency between process documentation and execution.

Technical process execution parameters refer to the IT infrastructure, within which the IT support of processes is implemented. Examples are CPU utilization (per server), the number of concurrent users, main memory usage, and database response times. By capturing these parameters, IT architects and system specialists can, e.g., determine the system load and identify opportunities for virtualization.

They define such execution parameters in the course of IT implementation and specify target values, e.g., in terms of Service Level Agreements, in cooperation with the person functionally responsible for the process (typically the process owner) and based on the expected numbers (e.g., number of parallel instances and system users).

System and service programs measure actual values with real instances in the course of operation with respect to the actual performance and use of IT assets and make these accessible for evaluation by process and IT managers. In addition, users themselves recognize flaws in the system performance and articulate them, e.g., to a service desk as a Facilitator.

11.4.3 Process Structure Key Indicators

For process management, in addition to the performance parameters, the process structure key indicators are relevant as they identify potential that describes mainly the human and technical infrastructure for the execution of process instances, and thus affect the performance parameters. They are static and refer to a process or its model. Examples are the number of simultaneously available subject carriers for a subject, the number of processes in which a person is subject carrier, or the computing power of a supporting IT system in accordance with the Service Level Agreement. Process and IT executives define such indicators usually in the course of organizational and IT implementation and provide their target values. In monitoring, they compare these with the actual values obtained from the current operation. The actual available number of Actors during operation could vary from the number specified in the course of organization-specific implementation, e.g., due to illness and fluctuation. The maturity level of a process can also be regarded as a structural key indicator. As an actual value it captures the current state of a process as an overall entity, and as a target value it sets the intended (to-be) state.

The values of process structure key indicators are measured at fixed time intervals (e.g., daily calculation of the actual available work capacity in the travel office) or ad hoc on the basis of certain value constellations of process performance metrics (e.g., determining the actual work capacity when instances have to wait longer at a processing site than previously planned). The measurement is carried out when optimizing the model or when running test instances, and also during monitoring at runtime, independent of specific instances, namely on the process level. Figure 11.7 exemplifies a selection of business process structure metrics.

Key indicator	Motive (awareness interest)
Frequencies	
Planned number of subject carriers assigned to a subject	Identification of the processing capacity (plan)
Actual number of subject carriers assigned to a subject	Identification of the processing capacity (actual, i.e., at runtime)
Number and names of subjects involved in a process	Identification of the horizontal and vertical reintegration potential (too much division of work?)
Number of sent and received message types in a process	Identification of the horizontal and vertical reintegration potential
Number and names IT systems used in a process	Identification of the integration potential (too many interfaces?)
Number and names of processes / subjects who use a particular IT system	Support the design of IT architecture

Fig. 11.7 Selected business process structure key indicators

Technical process structure key indicators are defined by IT specialists in the course of IT implementation. For the existing or envisioned IT infrastructure, they specify the performance potential as gross values. Examples are the number of available application servers, their main memory capacity, and their computing power per time unit. These provide insights into the processing potential. Its consumption is measured by the above-mentioned technical process execution metrics.

11.5 Evaluation

We distinguish between different types of evaluation. We will now introduce these in the context of S-BPM.

11.5.1 Periodic and Ad hoc Evaluation

On the basis of permanently recorded and stored execution data, retrospective, periodic log file evaluations of completed process instances (store-and-analyze), i.e., every week, every month, or every quarter, are common. Hereby, Actors and/or process owners use predefined conventional database queries and calculate on the basis of statistical functions. According to the given calculation rules, where appropriate, previously determined key indicators are composed from raw data (e.g., summation of times for individual process steps to achieve the overall runtime of a process).

In this way, in addition to the usual quality-, time-, and cost-related indicators, additional information can be gained, such as the number of instances initiated per time unit and their temporal distribution, the average duration of an instance in a processing station, or the average data throughput per instance. The results obtained serve as a basis for regular reports. From these reports, conclusions can be drawn for modeling, for the organization-specific implementation, and for the IT-related implementation (e.g., on the need for additional homogeneous workstations or higher bandwidth for data transmission).

In addition to the periodically, usually automatically generated and preprogrammed analyses, individual evaluations are carried out in practice, using interactive ad hoc queries to meet specific, singular objectives. This enables subject carriers as Actors to search themselves for causes of perceived events (e.g., increased waiting time).

A special form of evaluation is represented by process mining. Hereby, the data collected in the log files of the workflow engine are analyzed together with comparable information, e.g., delivered by ERP systems. The initial aim is to generate process models out of the information accumulated in the course of process execution of multiple instances and to create transparency of process structures in this way. This is helpful for the initial creation of actual (as-is) models for the documentation and verification of lived processes. It also facilitates the analysis of discrepancies between lived processes and existing, previously documented flow schemata (target models), which may provide clues for improvement.

Such discrepancies often occur, when Actors need to adapt their behavior in the process on short term autonomously to changing demands on the process. S-BPM enables them to update their modified subject behavior themselves in the model, in accordance with the agreed governance arrangements (e.g., consultation with, and approval by, the process owner as Governor), and thus to ensure consistency between process documentation and execution.

In addition to models derived from objective facts, process mining also allows conclusions about the actual distributions of process variants (e.g., what percent of all instances have passed paths A, B, and C, respectively). Another objective is the generation of information on process performance and success by comprehensive inclusion of additional information such as the business object (e.g., customer orders), the process result (e.g., customer order completed on the requested delivery date), the subject carriers (such as acting people and systems), etc. (cf. Grob et al. 2008, pp. 269 ff.).

Process mining can be used as a diagnostic tool in monitoring and analysis, while using methods thereof, such as analytical sequence and graph-oriented procedures, Markov chains, and genetic algorithms (Grob et al. 2008, p. 270).

> Process Mining delivers useful insights with respect to distributions of process variants and provides a fundamental basis for organizational agility.

11.5.2 Continuous Business Activity Monitoring

The concept of Business Activity Monitoring (BAM) denotes the continuous, business-oriented monitoring and evaluation of business process instances in real time (cf. Heinz and Greiner 2009; Hauser 2007; Reibnegger 2008). The view taken here on BAM does not only include business-related key indicators as targets for continuous monitoring activities but also technical parameters such as database response times. Business Activity Monitoring uses the continuously acquired data, analogous to periodic and ad hoc reporting. However, it usually leads to an immediate stream-oriented analysis (stream-and-analyze) of these data, using methods of complex event processing (CEP) (cf. Heinz et al. 2009, p. 84).

Complex event processing denotes computational methods, techniques, and tools, which allow the processing of events at the time of their occurrence, i.e., in a continuous and timely manner (Eckert et al. 2009, pp. 163 ff.). It especially deals with the recognition and processing of event patterns (observed facts), which only become visible by combining several individual events (simple events) in so-called complex events (Luckham et al. 2008, pp. 5 ff.), defines a simple event in this context as "anything that happens, or is contemplated as happening" and a complex event as "an event that is an abstraction of other events called its members". It is important to conclude the likelihood of the occurrence of the complex event as soon as possible after the occurrence of the associated simple events, in order to still initiate proactive measures for preventing or limiting the consequences. Detailed information on complex event processing, in addition to the sources already mentioned, can be found in Luckham (2002), Levitt (2009), Chandy et al. (2010), and Etzion et al. (2010).

An illustrative example of the conceptual framework of CEP and its effect can be described as part of the business trip application process. The travel office tries to use the lowest available rates for train and flight tickets whenever possible. These are early booking rates, usually only available up to a certain date, e.g., seven days prior to departure. The threat of losing the early bird discount can be understood as a complex event. It is defined by the simple events "processing status: open", "current latency time of the application in a processing station", and "expected remaining processing time". A CEP application is capable of calculating on the basis of these data, by means of continuous evaluation, consolidation, and correlation of generated values of simple events, for each instance the complex event or the likelihood of its occurrence, respectively.

Moreover, the system can recognize, e.g., that for a specific business trip request, delays have occurred (e.g., due to lack of approval), and its processing by the travel office will be too late to claim the early bird discount. One consequence then could be that the IT system ranks the business trip application with highest priority, thus putting it on top of the work list of subject carriers of the travel office, or that it at least induces such a proposal, leaving the decision to the subject carriers. CEP supports S-BPM by allowing subject carriers to recognize complex relationships, assess them independently, and become active in order to avoid negative consequences for the process result.

In order to recognize previously known patterns of events, e.g., as in the case of the business trip application, event query languages are suitable (e.g., composition operators, data stream query languages, or production rules), while previously unknown patterns in data streams are tackled for identification with methods of machine learning and data mining (Eckert et al. 2009, pp. 163 f.).

The aim of Business Activity Monitoring is to automatically identify in the course of operation short-term problems and missed targets in the execution of process instances and to respond in accordance with the predefined escalation procedure. Such problems can occur both on the technical level of process support caused by IT, as well as on the basis of economic performance indicators, and may be interdependent.

In the first case, a BAM solution within operational system control will monitor and analyze mainly simple events related to the functioning and utilization of information and communication technology resources (cf. Becker et al. 2009, pp. 174 ff.). Examples of responses to detected problems could be automatic load balancing across multiple application servers, or exception messages to system administrators, e.g., when the specified maximum response time has been exceeded for database queries.

Events in the form of variations in economic performance indicators can trigger as reactions alarms to process owners. BAM could provide the prognosis for an instance of a customer order after the first half of the processing steps that the total processing time will exceed the target value (complex event) due to already accumulated delays. It informs the people in charge, so that they can take any necessary measures to accelerate the process or inform the customer about the delay.

Systems for Business Activity Monitoring, especially with CEP functionality, can be understood as an enabler of S-BPM. They relieve work performers (Actors) and process owners (Governors) of regular and continuous monitoring tasks and create spaces, e.g., for subject carriers to reflect on optimizing their behavior and interactions with partners in the process.

> Business Activity Monitoring comprises technical parameters in addition to economic key indicators for monitoring.

11.6 Reporting

Reporting covers the preparation, delivery, and distribution of evaluation results in the form of reports. It therefore follows the same pattern over time as evaluation. Figure 11.8 gives an overview of possible report types and their characteristics.

Report type	Report frequency	Trigger	Presentation	Role of receiver
Running and exception reports	Continuous	Time or event	Cockpit / dashboard with speedometer display, warning and indicator lights, traffic lights, etc.	Passive (push)
Predefined standard reports	Periodical	Time	Rather printer-friendly view of tables, business graphics, and text blocks	Passive (push)
Individual demand reports	Ad hoc	Acute awareness interest	Situational	Active (pull)

Fig. 11.8 Types of reports

Ongoing and Exception Reports

Based on the continuous evaluation of the Business Activity Monitoring, results are continuously processed and documented. The focus is on monitoring business operations, which means constant reporting on running instances in very short time intervals (minutes, seconds, etc.).

For the presentation here, so-called dashboards and cockpits are used. The metaphors for appropriate IT solutions underline the intuitive and quickly understandable display of a few, but very important parameters for control (Key Performance Indicators). Instruments such as speedometers permanently visualize values like the number of instances currently in progress. The ending of the more or less short time interval triggers refreshing of the quasi-analog display. Digital accessories such as warning lights or traffic lights can signal the presence of special situations, such as exceeding the specified maximum processing time of an instance for a subject carrier. Here, the trigger is the exceptional case.

In any case, the cockpit/dashboard system independently informs the user with a push of information, without the necessity of his proactive involvement. These instruments are often integrated into process portals. Process owners and managers in their role of Governors can take a quick look and easily grasp information like in a control station. They also can oversee the current process steps and projected trends and compare them with historical data when needed. Such portals offer Actors involved in the process personalized work environments for executing their process-related activities. In a portal area, each employee finds a list of pending, to-be-processed instances of the processes in which he is involved ("my work"). Another list shows him the range of processes he is allowed to trigger by generating an instance ("my processes"). Examples of these could be the business trip request, the request for leave, etc.

Predefined Standard Reports

The periodic evaluations provide the basis for issuing predefined standard reports, e.g., weekly, monthly, or quarterly reports. According to the previously identified information needs of the recipients, usually printer optimized versions of presentations including business graphics (bar charts, pie charts, etc.), tables, and text blocks are generated and distributed in paper form or as electronic documents by e-mail, or published on the intranet. In addition to these traditional presentation methods, for periodic reporting cockpit/dashboard systems are increasingly used. The recipient of information automatically receives the reports themselves at a defined reporting date, or the information that they are available via the process portal or elsewhere (information push).

Individually Required Reports

The evaluation using individual ad hoc queries needs to meet a very specific interest in knowledge. It usually turns into an equally individual report. It may be sufficient to display query results on the screen or to issue them informally in paper form. Evaluation and report correspond to the request and activity of a user, so that in this case we speak of an information pull.

Reporting overall, but individually required reports in particular, represent an enabler of S-BPM. Only when subject carriers have appropriate functionalities and privileges, are they able to obtain process- and instance-related information, which can be applied in a self-organized way for optimal process design and processing.

For detailed information on reporting, see, e.g., Mertens et al. (2002, pp. 69 ff.) and Gluchowski et al. (2008, pp. 205 ff.).

> Reporting requires identifying a specific target group, and possibly compressing data for measurement, e.g., in dashboards, in order to support individual subject carrier groups according to their needs.

11.7 Process Key Indicators Related to Bundles of Activities

The acquisition and compilation of data concerning running processes to support decision making when deviations from a predefined target behavior occur is the focus of monitoring. In this section, we have identified possible variants of data collection, introduced different forms of decision making, and established their relevance for S-BPM and/or illustrated it by examples.

Figure 11.9 gives a summarizing overview of the application of the discussed types of process performance indicators in the S-BPM activity bundles. It shows where they are usually defined, provided with target values, and used for simulations and analyses on the level of process, model, and instances.

Activity bundle	Analysis	Modeling	Validation	Optimization	Organization-spezific implementation	IT implementation	Monitoring
Content	Survey / documentation Cause study	Design	Validation/ Ensuring the effectiveness	Validation/ Improving the efficiency	Integration into the organizational structure	Representation as workflow	Measurement, calculation and evaluation of indicators
Process	Survey / documentation How should a process be? (Top-down approach) How is a process? (Bottom-up approach)		Feedback		Economical structure indicators (Definition and target value determination)	Technical indicators (definition and target value determination)	Economical and technical structure indicators (Actual-value detection) ── periodic analysis
Model	Execution and structural indicators (Definition and target value determination)			Structure performance indicators			
Instances	Cause study Why is the process performance worse than targeted?		Feedback	Execution performance indicators (only result) Simulation of a few test instances	Execution and structural indicators (only result) Simulation of many test instances Feedback		Economical and technical structure indicators (Actual-value detection) Permanent logging of all instances of: • Continuous real-time evaluation (Business Activity Monitoring with Complex Event Processing) • Periodic analysis • Regular reporting • Process Mining • Level of maturity

Fig. 11.9 Process performance indicators along the S-BPM bundles of activities

Feedback always leads to the activity bundle of analysis, regardless of who is analyzing (Actor, process owner as Governor, etc.). The analysis result determines the next activity. Thus, an Actor with poor performance of the IT system supporting his process steps will contact the IT service desk as Facilitator, which then itself carries out a root cause analysis or initiates it. Its result in turn leads to the activity bundle of IT implementation, in case load balancing between servers is required as a solution.

If the process owner receives an ad hoc message from monitoring that the waiting times in a subject increase significantly, he can increase on short-term notice, in consultation with line managers, the number of deployed subject carriers. This measure is part of the activity bundle organization-specific implementation.

References

Becker, J., Mathas, C., Winkelmann, Geschäftsprozessmanagement, Berlin 2009.

Chandy, K., Schulte, W., Event Processing: Designing IT Systems for Agile Companies, New York, 2010.

Eckert, M., Bry, F., Complex Event Processing (CEP), Informatik Spektrum, Band 32, Heft 2, 2009, pp. 163-167.

Etzion, O., Niblett, P., Event Processing in Action, Greenwich (Connecticut, USA), 2010.

Gluchowski, P., Dittmar, C., Gabriel, R., Management Support Systeme und Business Intelligence: Computergestützte Informationssysteme für Fach- und Führungskräfte. 2nd edition, Berlin, 2008.

Grob, H., Coners, A., Regelbasierte Steuerung von Geschäftsprozessen – Konzeption eines Ansatzes auf Basis von Process Mining, Wirtschaftsinformatik 50. Jg. (2008) 4, pp. 268-281.

Hauser, J., Business Activity Monitoring, Saarbrücken, 2007.

Heinz, C., Greiner, T. Business Activity Monitoring mit Stream Mining am Fallbeispiel der TeamBank AG, HMD – Praxis der Wirtschaftsinformatik, Heft 268, 2009, S. 82-89.

Heß, H., Von der Unternehmensstrategie zur Prozess-Performance – Was kommt nach Business Intelligence? in: Scheer, A.-W., Jost, W., Heß, H. und Kronz, A., Corporate Performance Management, Berlin 2005, pp. 7-29.

Hogrebe, F., Nüttgens, M., Business Process Maturity Model (BPMM): Konzeption, Anwendung und Nutzenpotenziale, HMD – Praxis der Wirtschaftsinformatik, Heft 266, 2009, pp. 17-25

Kronz, A., Management von Prozesskennzahlen im Rahmen der ARIS-Methodik, in: Scheer, A.-W., Jost, W., Heß, H. und Kronz, A., Corporate Performance Management, Berlin 2005, pp. 31-44.

Kütz, M., Kennzahlen in der IT, 3. Auflage, Heidelberg 2009.

Levitt, N., Complex Event Processing Poised for Growth, Computer, 42 (2009) 4, pp. 17-20.

Luckham, D., The Power of Events: An Introduction to Complex Event Processing in Distributed Enterprise Systems, Amsterdam, 2002.

Luckham, D., Schulte, R. (Hrsg.) (2008), Event Processing Glossary Version 1.1/2008, Event Processing Technical Society, http://www.complexevents.com/2008/07/15/complex-event-processing-glossary-2008, Download am 21.07.2010

Marx Goméz, J., Junker, H., Odebrecht, S., IT-Controlling, Berlin 2009.

Mertens, P., Griese, J., Integrierte Informationsverarbeitung 2, 9th edition, Wiesbaden 2002.

Object Management Group, 2008. Business Process Maturity Model (BPMM), Version 1.0, http://www.omg.org/spec/BPMM/1.0, Download 13.07.2010.

Reibnegger, C., Business Activity Monitoring als Enabler von Real-Time Enterprises: Vorgehensmodell zur Einführung von Business Activity Monitoring, Saarbrücken, 2008.

Schmelzer, H., Sesselmann, W.: Geschäftsprozessmanagement in der Praxis, 7. Auflage, München 2010.

Wagner, K., Patzak, G., Performance Excellence – der Praxisleitfaden zum effektiven Prozessmanagement, München 2007.

A Precise Description of the S-BPM Modeling Method

12.1 To Go

Now, I understand the benefit of seamless modeling and execution. It is a prerequisite for process development and optimization. However, I still struggle with the flow of communication. For instance, what happens in case I receive several messages simultaneously? Where and how is this handled?

For clarifying those issues, we have prepared a dedicated specification. It is also written in a special symbol language, which details the handling of the symbols of the S-BPM models or their diagrams.

Applying the method of Abstract State Machines allows us to eliminate all ambiguities when executing models and to precisely describe the behavior of an implementation of the models. The development of the formal language has also been guided by an orientation to natural language which should make it easy to understand after just a short briefing.

A. Fleischmann et al., *Subject-Oriented Business Process Management*,
DOI 10.1007/978-3-642-32392-8_12, © The Author(s) 2012

Well, when ambiguities occur, just look them up and you should find the answers in the precise specification. The starting issue is how input pools of subjects handle messages. Using formal S-BPM, we are able to check and specify the constraints for communication to be considered successful, namely if nothing that has been communicated gets lost.

This chapter presents a precise formulation of the S-BPM constructs discussed in the preceding chapters. We express them in the form of an abstract SBD-interpreter,[1] which yields a precise, controllable definition of the subject behavior in SBDs, the so-called semantics of SBDs. Furthermore, this definition establishes a solid scientific foundation for the S-BPM method to support a guarantee of the implementation correctness of the interpreter by the Metasonic modeling tool.[2] The correctness of the interpreter model concerns two levels: correctness of the interpreter with respect to the intended meaning of the modeling constructs (*ground model correctness*) and correctness of the interpreter implementation by the tool with respect to the interpreter (*refinement correctness*). Thus, the interpreter model represents a blueprint of the system and the double-faced correctness guarantees that the user understanding of processes and the result of their machine executions match, a feature that is crucial for reliable computer supported modeling systems.

Due to the survey character of this chapter, we only review here the main S-BPM modeling constructs and refer for a complete version of the interpreter model to the appendix.

12.2   Abstract State Machines

A precise definition of the meaning of business process modeling constructs provides a reliable basis for successful communication between the different stakeholders, namely designers and analysts on the management, development, and evaluation level, IT-specialists and programmers on the implementation level, and users on the application level. This needs a language that is common to the involved parties and allows to avoid the well-known problems of ambiguity of natural languages. This holds in particular for the S-BPM approach whose fundamental concepts—*actors*, which perform arbitrary *actions* on arbitrary *objects* and communicate with other actors—require most general heterogeneous data structures: sets of various elements with various operations and predicates (properties and relations) defined for them and agents, which execute those operations.

---

[1] SBD stands for subject behavior diagram.
[2] Such a guarantee must come in the form of a mathematical verification of appropriate interpreter and implementation properties, which is made possible by the precise character of the interpreter. This issue is not treated in this book.

The language of the so-called *Abstract State Machines* (ASMs) represents such a language. It uses only elementary If-Then-Else-rules, which are typical also for rule systems formulated in natural language, i.e., rules of the (symbolic) form

if *Condition* **then** ACTION

with arbitrary *Condition* and ACTION. The latter is usually a finite set of assignments of form $f(t_1, \ldots, t_n) := t$. The meaning of such a rule is to perform in any given state the indicated action if the indicated condition holds in this state.[3]

The unrestricted generality of the used notion of *Condition* and ACTION is guaranteed by using as ASM-*states* the so-called *Tarski structures,* i.e., arbitrary sets of arbitrary elements with arbitrary functions and relations defined on them. These structures are updatable by rules of the form above. In the case of business processes, the elements are placeholders for values of arbitrary type and the operations are typically the creation, duplication, deletion, or manipulation (value change) of objects. The so-called views are conceptually nothing else than projections (read: substructures) of such Tarski structures.

An (asynchronous, also called distributed) ASM consists of a set of agents each of which is equipped with a set of rules of the above form, called its program. Every agent can execute in an arbitrary state in one step all its rules which are executable, i.e., whose condition is true in the indicated state. For this reason, such an ASM, if it has only one agent, is also called sequential ASM. In general, each agent has its own "time" to execute a step, in particular if its step is independent of the steps of other agents;[4] in special cases multiple agents can also execute their steps simultaneously (in a synchronous manner).

This intuitive understanding of ASMs suffices to understand the definition of an SBD-interpreter given in this chapter. The subjects acting in an SBD are interpreted as agents, which at each diagram node execute their associated rules.

Without further explanations, we adopt usual notations, abbreviations, etc., for example:

if *Cond* **then** M_1 **else** M_2

instead of the equivalent ASM with two rules:

if *Cond* **then** M_1

if not *Cond* **then** M_2

Another notation used below is

let $x = t$ **in** M

---

[3] Usually, we write ASMs in capital letters as in ACTION, predicates beginning with capital followed by lower case letters as in *Condition*, and functions and terms with lower case letters as in f, t_i, t.

[4] This means that technically speaking a run of an asynchronous ASM is not a sequence of steps of an agent, but a set of such sequences defined by the involved agents, where steps m of an agent which depend on steps m' of another agent are in an order relation m *before* m' or m *after* m'.

for $M(x/a)$, where a denotes the value of t in the given state and $M(x/a)$ is obtained from M by substitution of each (free) occurrence of x in M by a.

For details of a mathematical definition of the semantics of ASMs which justifies their intuitive (rule-based or pseudo-code) understanding, we refer the reader to the AsmBook (Börger and Stärk 2003). It contains also an explanation of the so-called refinement method which we use here to define the components of the SBD-interpreter in steps—a didactical concern adopted already in the preceding chapters of this book.

12.3   Interaction View of SBD-Behavior

An S-BPM *process* (short process) is defined as set of agents each of which is equipped with an SBD so that the process behavior can be defined by the SBD-behavior of its subjects (see Sect. 5.5.5). Thus, the definition of an S-BPM process interpreter as asynchronous ASM is reduced to the definition of a sequential ASM, which represents the interpreter BEHAVIOR$_{subj}$ (D) of an arbitrary subject *subj* in an arbitrary SBD-diagram D. For the interpretation of a process, this interpreter can then be replicated (read: instantiated) with each corresponding SBD.

A subject walks from node to node along the edges of D, beginning at the start node, and executes at each node the associated *service* until it reaches an end state. Therefore, the total behavior of the *subject* in D can be defined as set of each local BEHAVIOR*(subj, node)* of the *subject* at this *node* of D:

BEHAVIOR$_{subj}$ $(D) = \{$BEHAVIOR$(subj, node)$ | $node \in Node(D)\}$

In this way, one can define SBD-computations of *subj* in the usual way as sequences $S_0, \ldots, S_n$ of (data) states of *subj* in the diagram which begin with an initial state S_0, i.e., a data state which has an initial SID-state,[5] lead to a state S_n with a final SID-state and where each state S_{i+1} is obtained from S_i with SID-state *state$_i$* by a step of BEHAVIOR*(subj, state$_i$)*.

Thus, the construction of an interpreter is decomposed into the definition of the behavior of a subject in a given state, represented in the diagram by a node, for each type of state. This directly supports the intuitive operational understanding of the single S-BPM constructs and simplifies the interpreter definition. Before proceeding to this definition in Sect. 12.3.2, we list in Sect. 12.3.1 the assumptions we make for the diagrams.

12.3.1 Diagrams

An SBD is a directed graph. Each *node* represents a state where a *subject* which is in this state performs the associated action *service(node)*. We call such a state an

---

[5] SID stands for Subject Interaction Diagram.

SID-state (Subject Interaction Diagram state) and denote it by *SID_state (subj)* since the abstract interpretation of *service (node)* refers only to the role the state plays with respect to other subjects with which *subj*ect communicates from within *D*. We speak without distinction about states as nodes.

Each SID-state has one of three types corresponding to the type of the associated *service*: *function state* (also called internal function or action state), *send state*, or *receive state*. Each SID-state is implicitly parameterized with the SBD in which it occurs, sometimes denoted by an index as in *SID_state$_D$ (subject)* and *SID_state (subject, D)*. Each SID-state is part of the encompassing so-called *data state* or simply *state* (read: the underlying Tarski structure of the SBD).

The *edge*s which enter or exit a *node* represent the SID-state transitions from the source node *source(edge)* to *node* resp. from *node* to the target node *target(edge)*. Therefore, we call the *target(outEdge)* of an *outEdge* (an element of *OutEdge (node)*) also a successor state of *node* (in the diagram an element of the set *Successor (node)*) and *source (inEdge)* of an *inEdge* ∈ *InEdge (node)* a predecessor state (an element of the set *Predecessor(node)*). A transition from a source to a target node is permitted only if the execution of the *service* associated to the source node is *Completed* so that each outgoing edge corresponds to a termination condition of the *service* and is typically indicated on the edge as *ExitCond*. We write *ExitCond$_i$* for the *ExitCond* of the *i*-th outgoing edge if there is more than one.

Each SBD is finite and has exactly one initial and one end state. Each path is required to lead to at least one end state. It is permitted that an end state may have outgoing edges; a process terminates only if each of its subjects is in an end state.

12.3.2 SID-View of State Behavior

For the definition (of the SID-view) of BEHAVIOR *(subject, state)*, see Fig. 12.1. It describes the transition *subject* has to perform from a *SID_state* with associated *service A* to a next *SID_state* with associated *service B$_i$* once the execution of *A* (using an abstract machine PERFORM) is *Completed*, where *subject* upon entering a state must START the associated *service*. The successor state *target(outEdge (state, i))* with its associated *service B$_i$* is determined via a function *select$_{Edge}$*; it can be defined by the designer or at runtime by the executing subject.

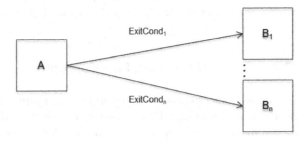

Fig. 12.1 SID-transition graph structure

The following ASM-rule provides a compact textual description where the **else**-case expresses that it may take many steps until the execution of PERFORM for *A* by the executing subject is terminated.

BEHAVIOR*(subj, state)* =
  if *SID_state (subj)* = *state* **then**
    if *Completed, (subj, service (state), state)* **then**
      let *edge* =
        select$_{Edge}$ ({*e* ∈ *OutEdge (state)* | *ExitCond (e)(subj, state)*})
          PROCEED*(subj, service (target (edge)), target (edge))*
      else PERFORM *(subj, service (state), state)*
  where
    PROCEED*(subj, X, node)* =
      SID_state (subj) := *node*
      START *(subj, X, node)*

Remark. BEHAVIOR *(subj, state)* is a scheme which comes with abstract machines PERFORM, START, and an abstract termination criterion *Completed* as components. It describes the interaction view of an SBD—that a subject upon entering a node STARTS the associated action and PERFORMS its steps until *Completed* becomes true—without providing details on how the component machines work and how they satisfy the termination criterion. The three constituents can and must be specified further to make the meaning of the performed action concrete. We do this in the next two sections for the S-BPM communication actions. The extension for the additional behavioral S-BPM constructs is given in the appendix.

12.4   Choice of Alternative Communication Steps

In this section, we define what it means to bring one step out of a set of so-called alternative communication steps to its execution. In this description, the meaning of a single such step still remains abstract and is refined in Sect. 12.5 by details of their multiprocess communication capabilities. In Sect. 12.4.1, we define the elements of the characteristic S-BPM input pool concept and formulate in Sect. 12.4.2 the first refinement of START, PERFORM, and *Completed* for sending and receiving; here the multiprocess communication capability still remains abstract. Since many definitions are symmetric in sending and receiving, we formulate them using a parameter *ComAct* for the corresponding *Communication Action*.

12.4.1 Basics of the Input Pool Concept

To support asynchronous communication, which is typical for distributed systems, each *subject* has an *inputPool(subj)* where other subjects in the sender role may deposit messages and where *subject* in the receiver rule "expects" messages (i.e., looks for messages when it is ready to receive some).

Each *inputPool* can be configured by capacity bounds for the maximal number of messages it may contain of a specific or an arbitrary type and/or from a specific or arbitrary sender. All four possible cases (read: parameter pairs of arbitrary or specific type and sender) are considered (see Sect. 5.5.5.2).

To obtain a uniform description also for synchronous communication, 0 is allowed as value for the capacity parameters of an input pool. It is interpreted as requiring that the receiver expects to receive messages of the indicated type and/or from the indicated sender only via a rendezvous with the sender.

Asynchronous communication is determined by positive natural numbers for the input pool capacity parameters. Two strategies are contemplated for the case that a sender tries to deposit a message in an input pool that has reached already its corresponding capacity:

- *Canceling send* where either (a) a message is deleted from the input pool to enable the insertion of the incoming message or (b) the incoming message is thrown away (not inserted into the input pool).
- *Blocking send* where sending the message is blocked and the sender must repeat the attempt to send this message until either (a) an appropriate place has become free in the input pool, or (b) a timeout interrupts the attempt to send the message, or (c) the sender decides to abrupt the attempt to send the message.

For the first case, two versions to cancel are contemplated, namely to delete from the input pool the message which is *Present* there for the longest resp. shortest time, as described by two functions *oldestMsg* and *youngestMsg* defined in the appendix.

Whether an attempt to send is treated by an input pool P of the receiver as canceling or blocking is a question of whether in the given state the capacity condition of P would be violated by inserting the incoming message. These conditions are given by a *constraintTable(P)* in which the i-th row indicates for a combination of *sender$_i$* and *msgType$_i$* the allowed maximal number *size$_i$* of messages of this kind, together with the *action$_i$* to be performed in case of a capacity violation:

constraintTable (inputPool) =

> $\cdots$
>
> *sender$_i$ msgType$_i$ size$_i$ action$_i$* $(1 \leq i \leq n)$

$\cdots$

where

> *action$_i$* $\in$ *{Blocking, DropYoungest, DropOldest, DropIncoming}*
> *size$_i$* $\in$ *{0,1, 2, . . .,∞ }*
> *sender$_i$* $\in$ *Subject*
> *msgType$_i$* $\in$ *MsgType*

When a sender attempts to deposit a *msg* in P the first *row* $= s\ t\ n\ a$ in *constraintTable(P)* is identified (if there is one) whose capacity bound is relevant for *msg* and would be violated by inserting *msg*:

ConstraintViolation(msg, row) iff[6]

   Match (msg, row) $\wedge$ *size ({m $\in$ P | Match (m, row)}) + 1 > n*

where

   Match(m, row) iff

      (sender(m) = s **or** *s = any)* **and** *(type(m) = t* **or** *t = any)*

If there is no such row, the message can be inserted into *P*. Otherwise the action indicated in the identified row is performed so that either this attempt to send is blocked or the message is accepted via a cancellation action (possibly by directly throwing away the message).

It is required that each row with $size_i = 0$ satisfies $action_i = Blocking$ and that if $maxSize(P) < \infty$ holds, then the *constraintTable* contains the following default-row:

   any any maxSize Blocking

Similarly, a receiver tries to transfer from its input pool into its data space an "expected" message (i.e., a message of the indicated *(msgType, sender)*) as we will see when interpreting a receive step.

In a distributed process at a given moment, multiple subjects may try to deposit a message in the input pool *P* of a same receiver, but only one subject can obtain the access to the resource *P*. Therefore, a selection mechanism is needed to determine this subject. We use a function $select_P$ which allows one to define the access predicate as follows:

CanAccess(sender, P) iff

   sender = $select_P$ ({subject | TryingToAccess(subject, P)})

12.4.2 Iteration Structure of Alternative Communication Steps

In an *alternative communication state*, a subject performs the requested communication action *ComAct* by executing, until the communication succeeds (see Sects. 5.5.4.3 and 5.5.4.4), the following three steps, where *Alternative(subj, node)* is the set of all *ComAct*-alternatives the *subj*ect finds in the given state *node*:

- Selection: Choose from *Alternative (subj, node)* an *alt*ernative communication kind.
- Preparation: Prepare a *msgToBeHandled* which corresponds to the chosen *alter*native, that is in case of *ComAct = Send* a concrete *msgToBeSent* and otherwise a concrete *expectedMsg* kind.
- *ComAct*-attempt: TRYALTERNATIVE$_{ComAct}$, i.e., try—synchronously or involving the input pool—to send the concrete *msgToBeSent* resp. to accept a message that *Match*es the *expectedMsg* kind.

The first two steps (choice and preparation of the alternative) are done by a component CHOOSE&PREPAREALTERNATIVE$_{ComAct}$ which represents the first step of TRYALTERNATIVE$_{ComAct}$ and is defined in Sect. 12.5.1.

---

[6] iff stands for: if and only if.

If the third step fails for the chosen *alt*ernative, that is if *msgToBeHandled* cannot be sent resp. received neither asynchronously nor synchronously, the subject repeats the three steps for the next *alt*ernative until:

- Either *ComAct* succeeds for some alternative and the subject can set the predicate *Completed* for the *ComAct* (i.e., the *service*) in the given state *node* to true.
- Or *TryRoundFinished* holds, that is all *alt*ernatives have been tried without success.

In the second case, after this first so-called *nonblocking* round, further rounds of *ComAct*-attempts are started which are *blocking* in the sense that they can be terminated, besides by being normally *Completed*, also by a *Timeout* or by a *UserAbruption*. *Timeout* has higher priority than *UserAbruption*.

The set *RoundAlternative* of still to be tried alternatives must be initialized for each round to *Alternative (subj, node)*. This happens:

- For the *nonblocking*-round in START.
- For the first *blocking*-round in INITIALIZEBLOCKINGTRYROUNDS, where also the *Timeout*-clock is set.
- For each further round in InitializeRoundAlternatives.

Since the blocking rounds can be interrupted, to continue the computation via PROCEED the SBD must contain at least three edges leaving *node* to be taken after a normal or a forced *ComAct*-termination. Three predicates *NormalExitCond*, *TimeoutExitCond*, and *AbruptionExitCond* determine the outgoing edge which must be taken to reach the next SID-state if COMACT is normally *Completed* or ends by a *Timeout* or a *UserAbruption*. These three predicates are initialized in START, namely to *false*.

The following definition of PERFORM *(subj, ComAct, state)* synthesizes the preceding explanations in symbolic form. We write it down in the form of a traditional flowchart in Fig. 12.2. Such diagrams represent ASMs and thus have a precise semantics [see Börger et al. (2003, p. 44) and the equivalent textual definition in the appendix, where also the other more or less obvious and therefore here not listed component machines are defined].

Macros and Components of PERFORM*(subj,ComAct, state)*. We define here START*(subj, ComAct, state)*, INTERRUPT, and ABRUPT and refer for the other components to the appendix.

START*(subj, ComAct, state)* =
    INITIALIZEROUNDALTERNATIVES*(subj, state)*
    INITIALIZEEXIT&COMPLETIONPREDICATES$_{ComAct}$*(subj, state)*
    ENTERNONBLOCKINGTRYROUND*(subj, state)*
where
    INITIALIZEROUNDALTERNATIVES *(subj, state)* =
        RoundAlternative (subj, state) := Alternative (subj, state)
    INITIALIZEEXIT&COMPLETIONPREDICATES$_{ComAct}$ *(subj, state)* =
        INITIALIZEEXITPREDICATES$_{ComAct}$ *(subj, state)*
        INITIALIZECOMPLETIONPREDICATE$_{ComAct}$ *(subj, state)*
    INITIALIZEEXITPREDICATES$_{ComAct}$ *(subj, state)* =

$NormalExitCond\ (subj, ComAct, state) := false$

$TimeoutExitCond\ (subj, ComAct, state) := false$

$AbruptionExitCond\ (subj, ComAct\ \textsc{t}, state) := false$

INITIALIZECOMPLETIONPREDICATE$_{ComAct}$ $(subj, state) =$

$Completed\ (subj, ComAct, state) := false$

ENTER[NON]BLOCKINGTRYROUND $(subj, state) =$

$tryMode\ (subj, state) := [non]blocking$

INTERRUPT $_{ComAct}$ $(subj, state) =$

SETCOMPLETIONPREDICATE$_{ComAct}$$(subj, state)$

SETTIMEOUTEXIT$_{ComAct}$ $(subj, state)$

SETCOMPLETIONPREDICATE$_{ComAct}$ $(subj, state) =$

$Completed\ (subj, ComAct, state) := true$

SETTIMEOUTEXIT$_{ComAct}$ $(subj, state) =$

$TimeoutExitCond\ (subj, ComAct, state) := true$

ABRUPT$_{ComAct}$ $(subj, state) =$

SETCOMPLETIONPREDICATE$_{ComAct}$ $(subj, state)$

SETABRUPTIONEXIT$_{ComAct}$ $(subj, state)$

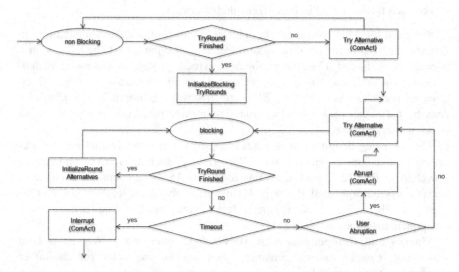

Fig. 12.2 PERFORM *(subj, ComAct, state)*

12.5   MultiProcess-Communication

In this section, we refine TRYALTERNATIVE$_{ComAct}$ (and thereby by one more level of detail also PERFORM *(subj, ComAct, state)*) by a definition of the elements which enable this component for multiprocess communication in S-BPM (see Sect. 5.6.4).

As said in Sect. 12.4.2, the first TRYALTERNATIVE$_{ComAct}$ step consists in calling the CHOOSE&PREPAREALTERNATIVE$_{ComAct}$ component, followed by a call of the component

TRY$_{ComAct}$ to execute the *ComAct* for the chosen alternative and the corresponding prepared message(s) (if this *ComAct* is possible for the message(s)). This is synthesized in symbolic form by the following definition:[7]

TRYALTERNATIVE$_{ComAct}$ *(subj, state)* =

CHOOSE&PREPAREALTERNATIVE$_{ComAct}$ *(subj, state)*

seq TRY$_{ComAct}$ *(subj, state)*

The two components define the multiprocess character of S-BPM communication. Multiprocess communication means to communicate a bundle of *mult(alt)* >1 messages belonging to the chosen multi*alt*ernative. Bundling means that to successfully execute a multi*ComAct* a subject must successfully execute the *ComAct* for exactly the bundled messages that is *mult(alt)* many, without executing in between any other communication. Thus, executing a multi*ComAct* is a multiround of single *ComAct*s and appears as detailing one iteration step TRYALTERNATIVE$_{ComAct}$ of the TryRound described in Fig. 12.2.

A further characteristics of a multi*ComAct* in S-BPM consists in the requirement that (a) all relevant messages (those in the set *MsgToBeHandled)* must be prepared together before for each of them the execution of the *ComAct*-step is attempted and that (b) when the multi*ComAct* fails—that is if the *ComAct* fails for at least one of the bundled messages—the information on which *ComAct*-executions were successful resp. unsuccessful is available so that in case of failure the procedure HANDLEMULTIROUNDFAIL$_{ComAct}$ for error handling and possibly some compensation can be called.

We define CHOOSE&PREPAREALTERNATIVE$_{ComAct}$ in Sect. 12.5.1 und TRY$_{Send}$ and TRY$_{Receive}$ in Sect. 12.5.2.

12.5.1 Selection and Preparation of Messages

A *subject* can choose a communication *alt*ernative among those possible in a *state* in a nondeterministic manner or following a priority scheme. We express this by abstract functions *select*$_{Alt}$ and *priority* which can be refined as soon as a concrete state and the selection scheme intended there become known.

For each chosen communication alternative, the corresponding message to be sent resp. the kind of the to be received message (in case of a multicommunication the elements of the set *MsgToBeHandled)* must be prepared. This is done by the component PREPAREMSG$_{ComAct}$ described below.

Additionally a MANAGEALTERNATIVEROUND-component must guarantee that (a) each possible communication *alt*ernative in *Alternative (subj, state)* is selected in each TryRound exactly once and that (b) in case of a multicommunication *alt*ernative the multiround is initialized. For (a) in each round, the static set *Alternative (subj, state)* is copied into a dynamic set *RoundAlternative*.

---

[7] We use the **seq** operator [see Börger and Stärk (2003)] to describe sequential execution order for ASMs.

This description is synthesized in symbolic form by the following definition whose component PREPAREMSG is defined below:

CHOOSE&PREPAREALTERNATIVE$_{ComAct}$ *(subj, state)* =

   let *alt = select$_{Alt}$ (RoundAlternative (subj, state), priority (state))*

     PREPAREMSG$_{ComAct}$ *(subj, state, alt)*

     MANAGEALTERNATIVEROUND *(alt, subj, state)*

   where

       MANAGEALTERNATIVEROUND *(alt, subj, state)* =

       MARKSELECTION *(subj, state, alt)*

       INITIALIZEMULTIROUND$_{ComAct}$ *(subj, state)*

       MARKSELECTION *(subj, state, alt)* =

       DELETE *(alt, RoundAlternative (subj, state))*

Before sending a message, a subject will *composeMsg* from the relevant data, that is from the values of the underlying data structures, which are accessed via an abstract function *msgData*. Similarly in a given state, a receiver chooses one message kind out of those which are possible in this state for to be expected messages, using a selection function *select$_{MsgKind}$*. The abstract functions used here represent the interface to the underlying data states and can be refined as soon as the data structures become known. We assume only that there are functions *sender (msg)*, *type (msg)*, and *receiver (msg)* to extract the indicated information from a message; thus, *composeMsg* has to insert this information. Similarly for *expectedMsgKind* and *select$_{MsgKind}$*.

The preceding description defines the component PREPAREMSG$_{Send}$ and is symbolically synthesized as follows:

PREPAREMSG$_{ComAct}$ *(subj, state, alt)* =

   forall $1 \le i \le$ *mult(alt)*

   if *ComAct = Send* **then**

     let m_i = *composeMsg (subj, msgData (subj, state, alt), i)*

     MsgToBeHandled (subj, state) := $\{m_1,.. ., m_{mult\ (alt)}\}$

   if *ComAct = Receive* **then**

     let m_i = *select$_{MsgKind\ (subj,\ state,\ alt,i)}$(ExpectedMsgKind (subj, state, alt))*

     MsgToBeHandled (subj, state) := $\{m_1,.. ., m_{mult\ (alt)}\}$

12.5.2 Sending and Receiving Messages

TRY$_{Send}$ is defined by the flowchart in Fig. 12.3, TRY$_{Receive}$ by the analogous only slightly different flowchart in Fig. 12.4.

Both diagrams describe for multicommunication nodes the multiround of a TryRound-*ComAct*-step: once a communication *alt*ernative has been selected and the corresponding set *MsgToBeHandled* has been prepared, during the multiround successively for each $m \in$ *MsgToBeHandled* an attempt is made to send resp. receive *m* performing the steps described below. After concluding the *ComAct* for an *m* (with success or failure), the subject continues the multiround for the next available $m \in$ *MsgToBeHandled*; at the end of the multiround in case of failure of

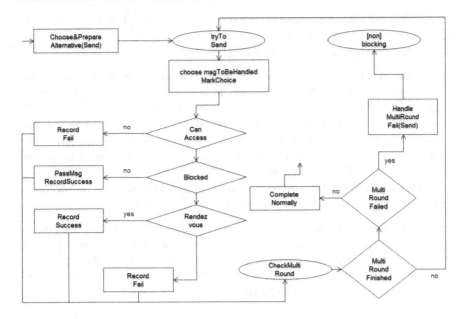

Fig. 12.3   TRYALTERNATIVE$_{Send}$

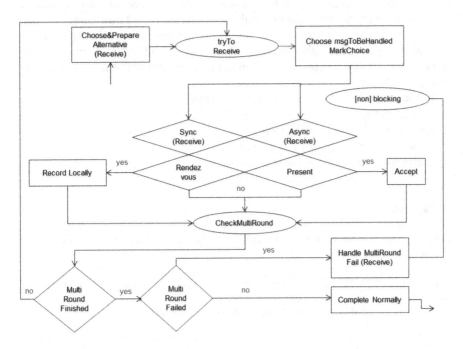

Fig. 12.4   TRYALTERNATIVE$_{Receive}$

the *ComAct*, the subject proceeds to the next *alt*ernative, resp., in case of success, it sets *Completed* for this *ComAct* in this state to true.

Here are the steps in the order of their execution:

1. A sender checks whether it can access for *m* the input pool of the receiver. If the check outcome is negative, this attempt to send *m* fails. Otherwise, the sender proceeds to the next step.
2. Sender and receiver try to communicate *m* asynchronously. If sending *m* is not *Blocked* resp. if a message matching *m* is *Present* in the input pool of the receiver, *ComAct* succeeds for this *m*. Otherwise, the sender proceeds to the next step resp. the attempt to receive *m* fails.
3. Sender and receiver try to communicate *m* synchronously. If it succeeds, *ComAct* is successful for this *m*; otherwise, it fails for this *m*.

The meaning of the here not furthermore specified predicates and component machines (like passing a message to the input pool resp. to the local data space or transferring a message from the input pool to the local data space of the receiver) should be intuitively clear so that we refer for their detailed definition to the appendix, not to disrupt the synoptic character of this chapter.

12.6 Refinement for Internal Functions

Communication yields no deadlock even in the presence of communication alternatives (TryRound) and/or multicommunication (MultiRound) if one introduces a *Timeout* systematically for each communication node. This can be done also for internal functions by introducing *Timeout* and/or *UserAbruption* there too (see Sect. 5.7.6). It comes up to refine the SID-transition scheme in the **else-**clause as follows:

> **if** *Timeout (subj, state, timeout (state))* **then**
>> INTERRUPT$_{service(state)}$ *(subj, state)*
>
> **elseif** *UserAbruption (subj, state)*
>> **then** ABRUPT$_{service(state)}$ *(subj, state)*
>> **else** PERFORM *(subj, service(state),state)*

Reference

Börger, E., Stärk R. Abstract State Machines. A Method for High-Level System Design and Analysis. Springer, 2003.

Tools for S-BPM

13

13.1 To Go

We're making great progress using the method. I think the suite of tools actually helped us very well to describe the models, to try them out, and to implement them.

The validation in particular was so much easier. We could interactively evaluate the various models without endless interviews and theoretical discussions, and without traveling around.

Using the specialized tools, it is much simpler to write down what we actually mean. It is so much more tedious with standard applications for writing and drawing. I especially enjoyed being able to immediately interactively test my specifications.

Yes, that does make everything easier and faster. I think that the direct implementation has saved us a lot of time. With the help of the simulation, we were also able to better assess how many resources we need to execute the processes.

A. Fleischmann et al., *Subject-Oriented Business Process Management*,
DOI 10.1007/978-3-642-32392-8_13, © The Author(s) 2012

I think it is important for us to respond quickly
to changes in our business environment, and the
tools allow us to do so.

Speaking for management, we are reassured that
everyone knows how they need to work. Compliance
is virtually no longer a problem, because the process
models are documented seamlessly, and the
resulting key performance indicators provide a good
overview of the company situation.

However, only after we have not only defined the
targets, but also clarified further activities for
moving forward. For Actors, this would mean that
their interventions along the process sequence have
been determined.

In the following sections, we provide insights into jBOOK, jSIM, and the Metasonic Suite, exemplifying a set of tools for each activity bundle in the development process for business process applications. jBOOK is a documentation tool to support subject-oriented analysis. jSIM can be used by Actors to simulate processes based on subject-oriented models on the computer.

The Metasonic Suite consists of a number of elements: the module "Build" supports the modeling of the subjects, their behavior, their interactions, and the thereby exchanged messages and business objects. "Proof" enables distributed, computer-aided validation and "Flow" as a process engine controls the execution of instances for all subjects involved in the process. The base module includes the "Usermanager", which allows those responsible for organization-specific implementation the assignment of users to roles and subjects.

The subsequent content is illustrated mainly with screen shots, but should not be understood as a step-by-step guide of how to use the tools. It should give rather an impression of the practical work with the tools in each activity bundle of the S-BPM process model, ranging from the analysis of a process, modeling activities, validation, optimization, and implementation as executable workflow to monitoring during operation.

13.2   Process Analysis

For analysis activities, jBOOK provides appropriate checklists and form templates supporting the documentation of results. Figure 13.1 lists, as a practical guide, the activities within the activity bundle for analysis. We explain these in more detail below.

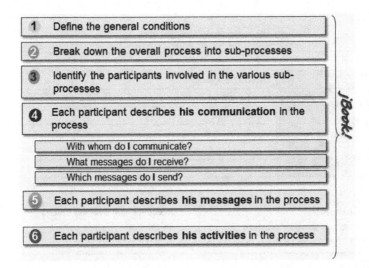

Fig. 13.1 Activities of analysis

Depending on the intensity and level of detail when performing analysis steps, the results can already include many elements of modeling. The team working on a process decides by itself, depending on the situation, to what extent details are already explored in the course of analysis, or instead should be considered later on.

The first step is to define the general conditions for accomplishing tasks in the appropriate form (see Fig. 13.2). This includes information such as name, objectives, tasks, success criteria, contribution to organizational success, and participants of the process. Furthermore, any risks are identified, described, and evaluated. These conditions should provide a brief overview of the position of an observed process in the organizational environment.

The process objectives can be refined on the basis of an overview. jBook provides a separate template to this respect, in particular, to establish criteria to measure and evaluate the achievement of objectives (see Fig. 13.3).

In the process map, it has already been specified that the process of applying for business trips poses no risk to the organization. Figure 13.4 shows a form designed to capture potential risks in detail.

Once the general conditions of the selected process are defined, the analyst can, in the second step, detail its structure. In this case, he splits the business trip handling into two subprocesses, the application process and the booking process, the latter of which is run at the travel agency.

Figure 13.5 shows the resulting structure and the messages exchanged between the subjects in the subprocesses, namely as a process network diagram (see Sect. 5.5.2).

Based on the process structure, in a third analysis step the subjects of subprocesses need to be identified and their essential activities specified (see Fig. 13.6).

1	Define the general conditions

Process name:	Business Trip Application
Process owner:	Mr. Ernst Haftig
Author:	J. Doe, E.Haftig
Date:	November 05, 2010
Company:	
Organization:	

Initial situation

Currently, applications for a business trip
will be delivered in paper form.
The approved trips are also given in paper
form to the travel office which carries out
the administrative tasks and sends the
appropriate booking orders by mail to the
travel agency.
This returns the documents by mail to the
company.

Objectives and success criteria

The throughput times or business trips
are to be reduced, and the processing
status should always be detectable for
all concerned persons.

Risks and risk reduction

As a result of the process, there are no special risks
for the company.

Process participants

Employee
Manager
Travel office
Travel agency

Fig. 13.2 General conditions form of a process

In the next step, the analyst describes the communication between subjects. To do so, he collects and documents which messages a subject receives from others, or sends to others, respectively (see Fig. 13.7).

For a more detailed specification of the messages, jBOOK provides a template for parameters as shown in Fig. 13.8.

The description of the communication between the involved parties can be included in the analysis, but this is not mandatory. It is advisable to include it, if at the time of the analysis the respective information is already available and can easily be complemented to the specification. The resulting documentation,

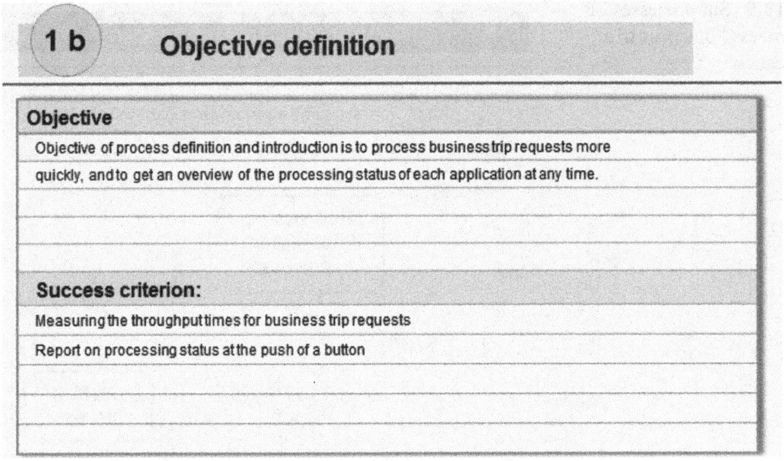

1 b   **Objective definition**

Objective

Objective of process definition and introduction is to process business trip requests more

quickly, and to get an overview of the processing status of each application at any time.

Success criterion:

Measuring the throughput times for business trip requests

Report on processing status at the push of a button

Fig. 13.3 Form for detailing objectives

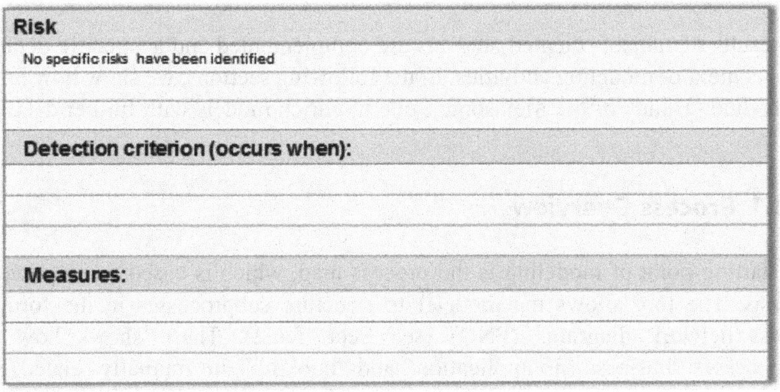

Risk

No specific risks have been identified

Detection criterion (occurs when):

Measures:

Fig. 13.4 Form for detailing risks

however, will be complete only in exceptional cases. Therefore, traditionally, information about the message exchange and the parameters of the messages is added in the course of modeling, or even right from the beginning, first collected and described in detail there.

The same statement holds analogously for the sixth step of the analysis, the description of the subject activities. The analysis usually only leads to a rough outline that needs to be refined when modeling, i.e., describing the subject behavior. A typical basic behavior description for the subject "employee" is shown in Fig. 13.9.

Fig. 13.5 Subprocesses of
the process "business trip
application"

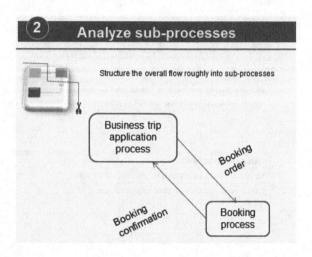

13.3 Process Modeling

The results of subject-oriented analysis are complemented and accurately detailed
in the context of modeling activities. In the following sections, we show how to use
the module "Build" of the Metasonic Suite to enrich models with further details.

13.3.1 Process Overview

The starting point of modeling is the process map, which is based on step two of
analysis. The tool allows the modeler to structure subprocesses in the form of
process network diagrams (PND) (see Sect. 5.6.2). These shows how the
subprocesses "business trip application" and "booking" are mutually related, and
the possible interactions between the concerned subjects (see Fig. 13.10).

The interactions in the overview do not yet need to correspond to individual
messages. Thus, an interaction can be refined if needed into multiple messages in
the communication view (see Sect. 13.3.2). In our example, this is not the case. The
interactions between the processes consist of single messages, the booking order,
and the booking confirmation, respectively.

13.3.2 Communication View

The refinement of the process overview leads to the communication view, which is
represented in the modeling phase by subject interaction and communication
structure diagrams (SID, CSD) (see Sect. 5.5.3). As an input the modeler can use
the information from the completed jBOOK templates gained in the analysis steps
two, three, and four (see Sect. 13.2).

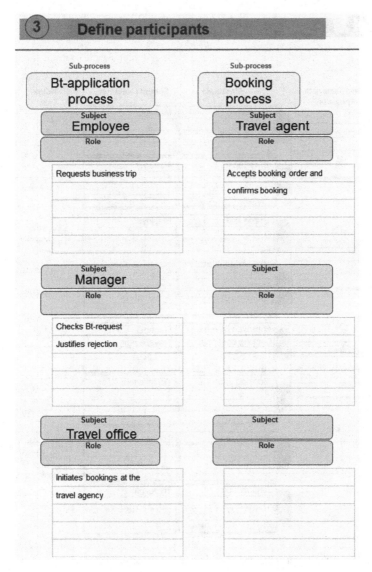

Fig. 13.6 Form for naming the subjects of subprocesses and identifying their main activities

Figure 13.11 shows how the "Build" tool displays an interaction diagram containing the subjects of the process "business trip application". The subject "travel office" is an external subject, representing a corresponding interface as part of the process "booking" (see Chap. 5.6.2).

Figure 13.12 shows the process "booking". From here, the external subject "travel office", as an interface subject, refers to the process "business trip"

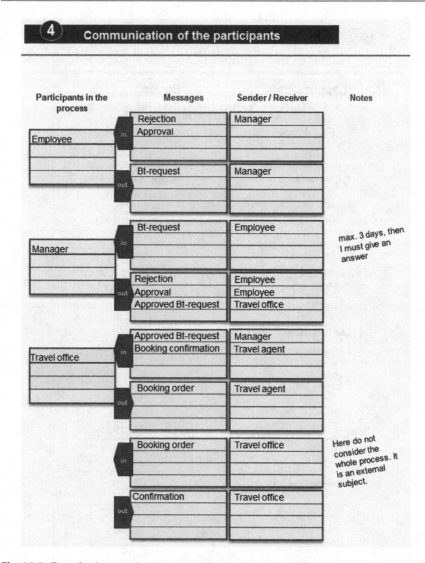

Fig. 13.7 Form for documenting the communication between subjects

application" in which it resides. The communication partner to the travel office in the process "booking" is the internal subject "travel agent".

Looking back again to the lower part of Fig. 13.11, it can be noted that the interface subject "travel agent" in the process "booking" [*Properties* tab, *Link (relative)* selection list] is termed "travel agent" (*Related Subject* selection list) rather than "travel agent". This means that the interface subject and the corresponding internal subject (in this case, in the "booking" process) need not be named identically.

Name	Bt-request		
Parameter	Type	Mand.	Medium/Remarks
First name		☐	
Name		☐	
Personnel number		☐	
Start of trip		☐	
End of trip		☐	
Reason for trip		☐	
		☐	
		☐	
		☐	
		☐	

Fig. 13.8 Form for defining messages and message parameters

⑥ Outline the sequence

What activities do I run in what order?

Subjekt: Employee

Requirements		Tools
1. Submit Bt-request in a timely manner	• Fill in Bt-request and then send it to the manager. • Wait for answer of the manager. • If rejected, possibly submit changed Bt-request. • Otherwise, make travel arrangements.	1. Intranet with form 2. Documents

Fig. 13.9 Form for describing a subject's behavior

For reasons of clarity however, identical identifiers are recommended, as with the travel office (see bottom part of Fig. 13.12). However, in practice, this is not always possible, especially in cases in which the subprocesses are located in different organizations that need to be connected via interface subjects, and there are already historically defined names for organizational units or roles.

13.3.3 Subject Behavior

The next step in modeling is the definition of subject behaviors. The methodology provides the subject behavior diagram (SBD) for this purpose (see Sect. 5.5.5). Starting point is the data collected in step six of process analysis (see Sect. 13.2).

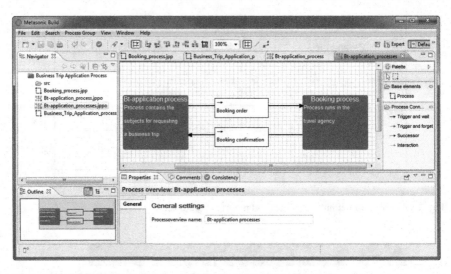

Fig. 13.10   Process network diagram "business trip application process"

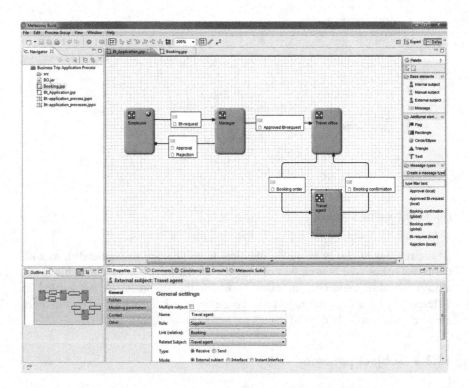

Fig. 13.11   Subject interaction diagram of the subprocess "business trip application"

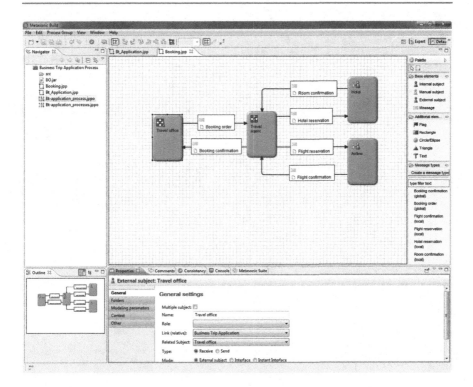

Fig. 13.12 Subject interaction diagram of the subprocess "booking"

Figure 13.13 shows the sample SBD for the subject "employee" of the "business trip application" process created using the modeling tool. Function states are characterized as rounded rectangles with a small clock icon, send and receive states with a small envelope icon with incoming or outgoing triangles, respectively. The transitions are specified using conventional rectangles with a horizontal arrow and a standardized verbal description.

This behavior reveals that the employee fills out the application form first and then sends it via "provide business trip request" to the manager. Then he waits for the response of his manager. This can be "approval" or "rejection". In the first case, the employee takes the trip and then reaches the end state. In the case of "rejection", the subject will immediately proceed to the end state.

So far, we have considered only the logical flow of the process. However, the model specification can already be executed at this stage. This means that participants are able to test the business logic in a distributed role play. Before discussing this further in the context of the validation process described in Sect. 13.4, we explain the required data modeling activities. The modeler needs

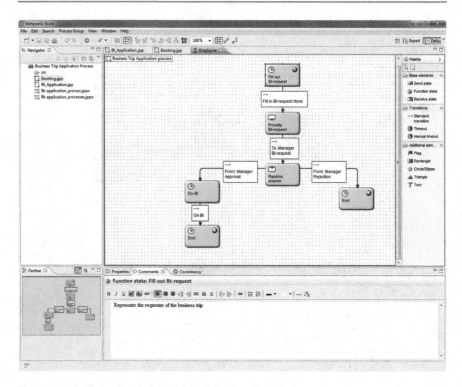

Fig. 13.13 Behavior description of the subject "employee"

to specify what data exists in each subject state, and what messages transfer it between subjects.

The S-BPM method provides business objects for this purpose. They can be a complex structure, with different statuses, views, and access rights (see Sect. 5.5.7). For their manipulation, appealing user interfaces should exist (see Sect. 10.5.1.1). The functions provided by the modeling tool for the detailed definition of business objects are discussed in Sect. 13.6.

Here, we show instead how to quickly and easily define data, in order to test in the subsequent validation, whether they are even the right data, before refining their definition. Using this straightforward approach, complex business structures with object data types, plausibility rules for entry, etc. are not yet created, but rather simple data elements, which are initially sent as parameters using messages. The definition of such primitive business objects occurs on the level of business processes. The required information may stem from the jBOOK form for describing messages, completed in step four of the analysis (see Sect. 13.2).

Figure 13.14 shows the data (parameters) required for the process "business trip application". Not all of this data is used in all subjects. However, each subject has its own set of variables for these parameters. Hence, a change of name in the subject "employee" is not visible to the other subjects. Instead, the value of this variable "name" needs to be transferred with a message containing the parameter "name" to another subject that should know the value. When accepting the message, the value of this message parameter is transmitted to the variable "name" of the receiving subject "manager". Thus, the variable "name" in the subjects "employee" and "manager" has the same content.

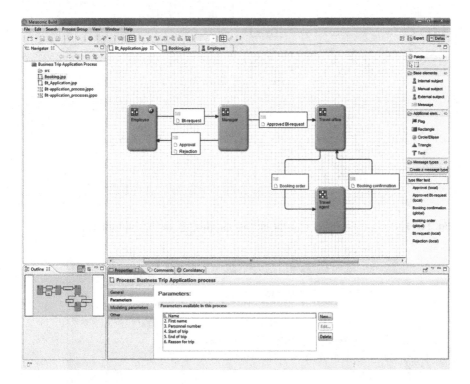

Fig. 13.14 Modeling the data of the process "business trip application"

Each subject can potentially access all process parameters, which can be filled with values by internal functions in the subject behavior. Figure 13.15 shows this for the assignment of values to the variables "name", "first name", "personnel number", "start of trip", "end of trip", and "reason for trip" in the function state "fill out business trip request".

For the transmission of parameter values between subjects, they need to be assigned to appropriate messages. Figure 13.16 shows this assignment for the message type "business trip request", sent by the employee to his manager.

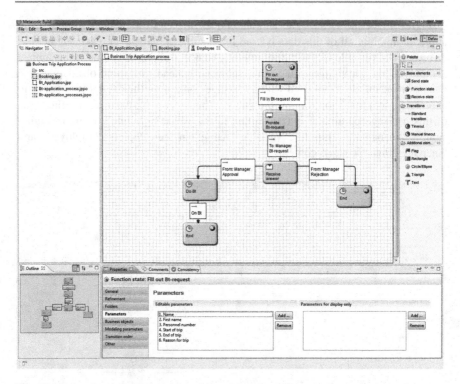

Fig. 13.15 Parameter assignment in the internal function "fill out business trip request"

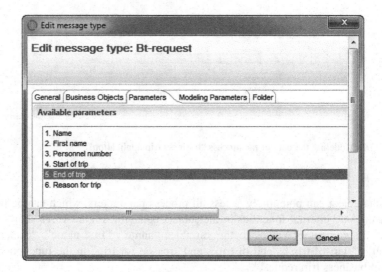

Fig. 13.16 Modeling of the parameters of the message type "business trip request"

When receiving a message, the values are transferred from the message parameters to the subject's local variables with the same name. Thus, the business trip request data is available after the receipt of the message "business trip request" by the subject "manager" for use in its internal checking function. Hereby, the data is delivered by which the supervisor in his check function decides whether the transition to "reject" or "approve" will subsequently be executed (see Fig. 13.17).

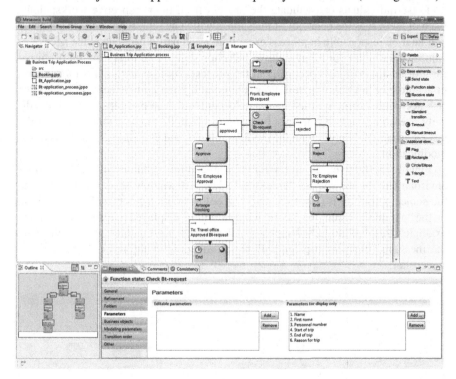

Fig. 13.17 Modeling the receipt and use of parameter values

13.4   Process Validation

The process model contains in the current status all information regarding the logical flow of the process, the data required in the process, and the data variables either being used by the subjects or being exchanged between them by sending and receiving messages. Although the business objects are currently defined only in the previously introduced primitive form, i.e., without data types, value domains, origin of values, etc., the existing model can already be tested in a role play. This involves reviewing the following two questions:

- Does the described process logic correspond to the desired way of working?
- Do the data variables meet the process objectives?

   For implementing an IT-based role playing (see Sect. 7.5.2.2), the process model is transferred by the click of a button into the appropriate execution environment in the module "Proof" of the Metasonic Suite. This environment is available via Internet or Intranet and can be accessed by a browser via its address (URL). Employees who are involved in a process can now use the subject, as it represents their share in the process: an employee applying for business trips uses the subject "employee", a manager the subject "manager", and an employee of the travel office the subject "travel office".

These individuals can validate the process from their respective workstations. Each of them sees the behavior of the subject which he represents, and for which he will later be responsible in process execution. Each participant enters the necessary values of variables for his respective behavior states, i.e., works on the primitive form of business objects occurring in the process. By exchanging this information in accordance with the process flow, they quickly notice whether parameters for task accomplishment are missing, or redundant, etc. The participants can immediately overcome such deficiencies by using the "Build" module, then restarting the test environment "Proof" with the modified model, and examining the effects of the modification.

Figure 13.18 gives an overview of the control windows of the validation environment for the subject "employee". The left window shows in which state the subject currently is (function state "fill out business trip request"). By clicking on the "parameter" icon, the middle window will be displayed to enter values. In the example, this has already happened. Closing of the input leads to delivering the message "business trip request" to the manager in the right window of the screenshot.

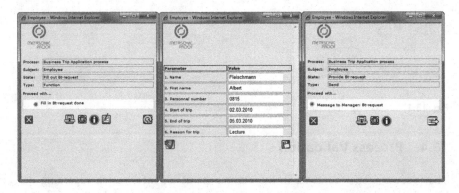

Fig. 13.18 Validation user interface of the subject "employee"

Figure 13.19 shows the interactive window for the subject "manager" indicating the receipt of a business trip request (left window). The manager accepts, by clicking on the icon with a right arrow, and changes from the receive state to the state "check business trip request" of his behavior, where he can then decide between the options "approved" or "rejected" (middle window). For decision making, he can display the trip data by clicking on the parameter icon (right window).

Fig. 13.19 Validation user interface of the subject "manager"

An iteration in such a validation session corresponds to the execution of a process instance. A recorder documents each step of a validation session. The steps can be displayed in a swim lane diagram (see Fig. 13.20).

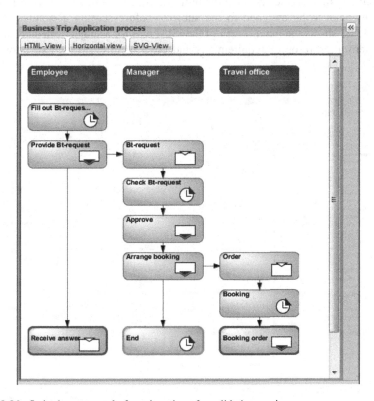

Fig. 13.20 Swim lane protocol of one iteration of a validation session

In this way, an arbitrary number of validation sessions addressing different variants of process iterations for a process model can be performed, potentially with changing participants. This allows the parties to review whether the process corresponds to the desired way of working. Through the recording of the validation iterations, the test coverage can also be estimated.

13.5   Process Optimization

The validation checks whether the described process corresponds to the intended way of working, i.e., whether the right action is taken. Optimization is on the other hand about checking whether the validated process can be performed with minimal effort (see Sect. 8.2). For an associated simulation, it is necessary to determine, or at least estimate, the time required for each activity within a subject. In addition, it needs to be known how often per time unit a corresponding process instance is created and put into execution. Since such information is usually enriched with probabilities, the parameters for probability densities need to be known. Finally, resources need to be assigned to the subjects before starting a simulation run. Figure 13.21 shows the main screen of the jSIM tool for a subject-oriented simulation determining resource requirements and costs incurred in the execution of a process.

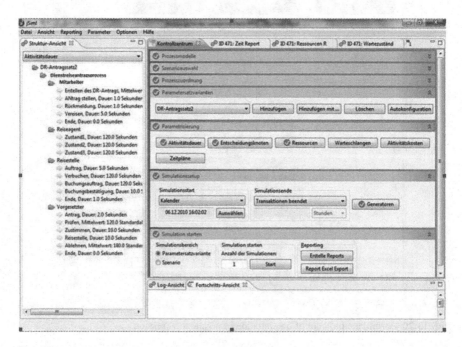

Fig. 13.21 Main screen for entering simulation parameters

In Fig. 13.22, the times required for the accomplishment of individual actions in the respective subjects are shown. Thus, the duration of creating the business trip request is distributed normally with an expected value of 180 s and a standard deviation of 40 s. For reasons of simplicity, in this example the other time parameters are assumed to be constant.

Business trip application process							
Subject/Activity	Distribution	Value1	Value2	Unit	Activity cost	Cost category
Employee							
Fill out Bt-request	normal distribution	180	40	Seconds		
Send Bt-request	constant	1		Seconds		
Receive answer	constant	1		Seconds		
Do Bt	constant	5		Seconds		
End	constant	0		Seconds		
Travel agent							
State 1	constant	120		Seconds		
State 2	constant	120		Seconds		
State 3	constant	120		Seconds		
Travel office							
Order	constant	5		Seconds		
Booking	constant	120		Seconds		
Booking order	constant	120		Seconds		
Booking confirmation	constant	10		Seconds		
End	constant	1		Seconds		
Manager							
Bt-request	constant	2		Seconds		
Check Bt-request	normal distribution	120	60	Seconds		
Approve	constant	10		Seconds		
Arrange booking	constant	10		Seconds		
Reject	normal distribution	180	60	Seconds		
End	constant	0		Seconds		

Fig. 13.22   Excerpt of simulation parameters

It becomes apparent that the determination of the parameters for the simulation is not trivial and requires extensive experience. Even after this hurdle has been taken, the interpretation of simulation results requires advanced skills. In Fig. 13.23, an excerpt of the simulation results is presented. The graph shows the minimum and maximum activity and waiting time, and the minimum and maximum resource requirements for a given instantiation of processes.

13.6   Modeling Business Objects and Integrating in Behavior Descriptions

So far, only simple parameters have been used as business objects in process models. They merely served to verify in validation that all required data was included in the model.

In Sect. 13.3.3, we have already mentioned that business objects occurring in a process subsequently require a more detailed and precise modeling specification in

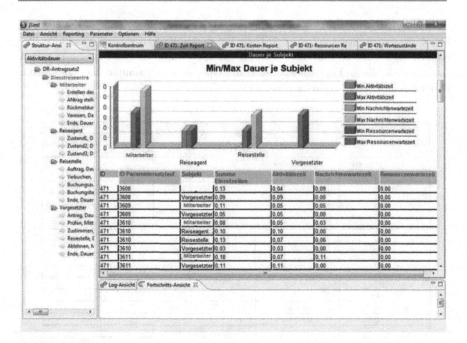

Fig. 13.23 Excerpt of simulation results

order to comply with the requirements of a workflow system being used in practice. This detailed description includes aspects that we have presented in Sect. 5.5.7. Examples here are hierarchical structuring; the definition of states, views including access rights, look-and-feel, value ranges for user input; and the coupling of programs to manipulate data elements.

In the following, we show an excerpt of the potential tool support for detailed modeling of business objects in terms of their subsequent use when executing the process in a workflow engine. The result of this detailed modeling of business objects can also be tested in the validation environment, before implementing a process in a workflow.

Figure 13.24 shows the structure of the business object "business trip request" and its defined views. The application consists of three parts: "personal data", "information on the business trip", and "processing status". Each of these three sections contains respective elements. The modeler can therefore organize a business object with the tool across various hierarchy levels, in each of which data structures and/or individual data elements can occur. For each element, different attributes can be specified, e.g., whether an element could occur multiple times (like a position of an order), whether it is a mandatory field users need to fill in, its specific data type, etc.

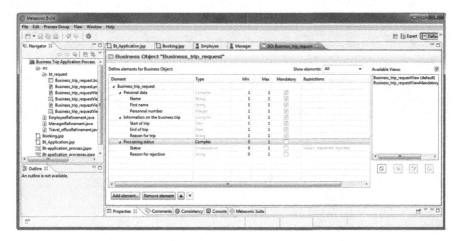

Fig. 13.24 Business object definition using the business object editor

For each business object, any number of views can be specified, each containing subsets of the elements of the object. In this way, the modeler can determine that during execution only an excerpt of a business object is displayed, processed, or transmitted in specific states. Figure 13.25 shows the view "no decision" on the business object "business trip request", which contains only the personal data and the information on the business trip. The processing status containing the approval notice is not displayed in this view.

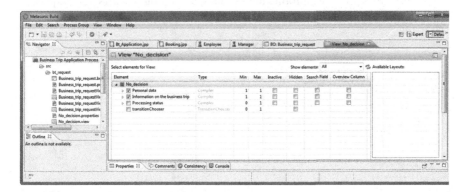

Fig. 13.25 Specification of a view using the business object editor

After having defined the structure, views, and rules (not illustrated), it has to be determined how the business object is to be displayed on the screen. Figure 13.26 shows the editor for specifying the layout.

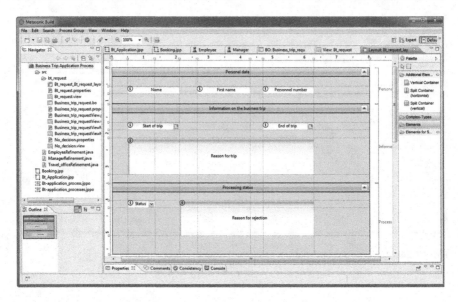

Fig. 13.26 Specification of a form using the business object editor

After completing their definition, business objects need to be inserted at appropriate positions into the behavior description of a process. To do so, the user selects in the modeling tool the state in which the business object is used, e.g., displayed and/or filled out. For this purpose, there are so-called folders. In each state, it is defined what business object types are allowed in a specific folder, and what types of operations can be executed in this state.

Figure 13.27 shows this information for the state "fill out business trip request", in which the "business trip request" can be created, displayed, and edited.

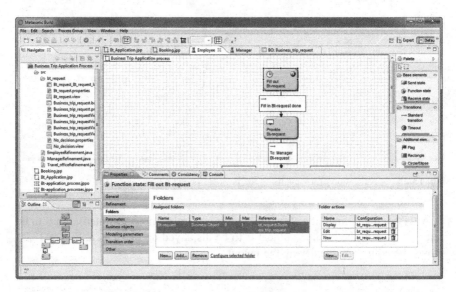

Fig. 13.27 Integration of the business object "business trip request" in the state "fill out business trip request" as part of the behavior specification of the employee

13.7 Organization-Specific Implementation

After describing the process behavior and the business objects, an active agent (subject carrier) needs to be assigned to each subject. This carrier performs the actions of the subject according to the modeled behavior (see Chap. 9).

The assignment of an active agent to a subject is performed using the tool "Usermanager" on several levels. A person (subject carrier) is part of one or more groups (subject carrier groups). One or more of these groups are assigned to a role, and a role to one or more subjects.

Figure 13.28 shows how Mr. Schulz is assigned to the group "employee group" using the "Usermanager".

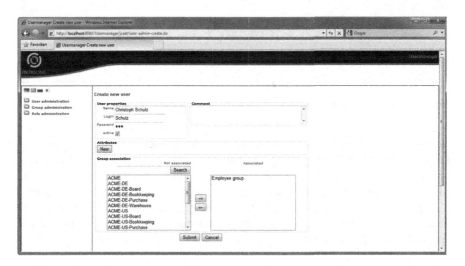

Fig. 13.28 Screenshot of the tool for managing users, groups, and roles

Analogous to the assignment of Mr. Schulz to a group, a role is assigned to a group. The assignment of roles to subjects is performed using the modeling tool. Figure 13.29 shows how the role "employee" is assigned to the subject "employee".

At the end of the outlined multiple steps, Mr. Schulz is able to submit a business trip request, since he has been assigned to the subject "employee" as subject carrier.

13.8 IT-Specific Implementation

After embedding a process in the organization, the integration of applications needs to be performed. Applications are used to retrieve business object content, to manipulate it, to store it, etc. (see Sect. 10.5.1).

The integration is realized by so-called refinements. They denote software invoked in function states within the subject behavior. Whenever a process enters a

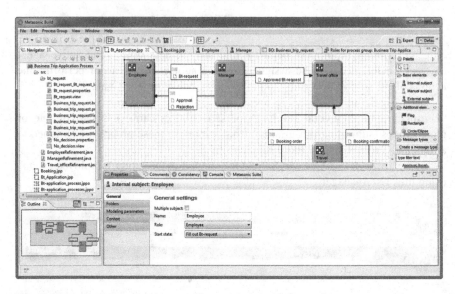

Fig. 13.29 Assignment of a role to a subject using the modeling tool

state with a refinement, the stored program is executed. Such a program may initially serve only to call an existing application having a specific user interface for editing a business object (e.g., an SAP transaction). A refinement could also be code which itself accesses business object content and manipulates it in a dialog with the user.

Figure 13.30 shows the storing of a refinement in the state "check business trip request". The implementer uses the option "Execute own refinement" to insert a specific refinement to this state.

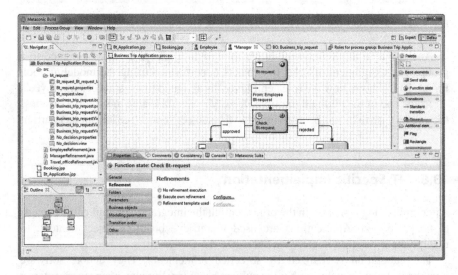

Fig. 13.30 Insert "Execute own refinement"

Figure 13.31 shows the respective potential code body.

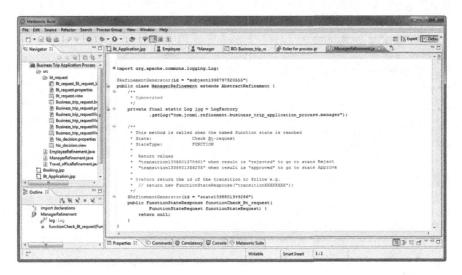

Fig. 13.31 Body of code for a refinement method

13.9   Process Execution

Once the applications running in a process have been integrated, the process can be used productively after extensive testing.

A suitable workflow engine, in our case, the module "Flow" from the Metasonic Suite, interprets the structured process model at runtime and controls the operations from its instantiation to its termination. The engine ensures that the subject carriers perform those actions in each processing step that are expected of them according to the behavioral description of their assigned subjects (internal function, send, and receive). At the designated positions in the model, the engine supplies them with the business objects to be processed and invokes the designated applications.

For instance, Mr. Schulz could log on to the workflow system and create a process instance for applying for a business trip. Figure 13.32 shows the workflow system in the initial state in which the employee submits the request. In the upper part, the respective state of the process is displayed to the user, and in the lower part the business object to be filled out.

After filling out the business object, the user triggers the transition to the next state (top right). After that, the business trip request of Mr. Schulz is transmitted by an appropriate interaction to his manager Mr. Schmid. Mr. Schmid accepts the message with the request and checks it. Figure 13.33 shows the corresponding user interaction.

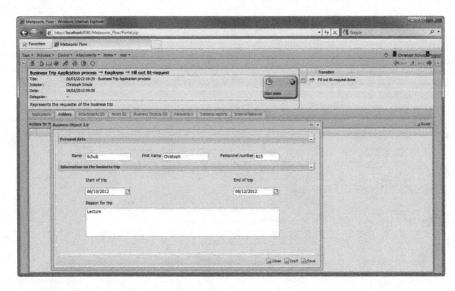

Fig. 13.32 The workflow system in the state "fill out business trip request" of the subject "employee"

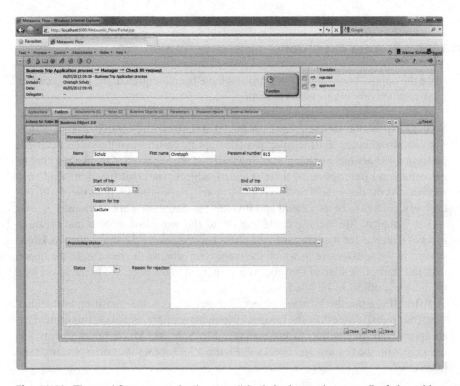

Fig. 13.33 The workflow system in the state "check business trip request" of the subject "manager"

13.10   Process Monitoring

During execution of each process instance, the workflow engine records numerous data. Examples include the state for each process instance, the point in time at which this state is reached, and much more. Such data about instances can be used to observe process executions in an organization (see Chap. 11). Executives can, for example, receive information about how many crucial process instances are currently being executed, or how each process progresses in each process instance.

Figure 13.34 exemplifies a simple list including details of running process instances. It contains the name of the process, its priority, the name of the person who created the instance, the time stamp when it was created, etc. The table includes only a small part of the recorded, and therefore available, data.

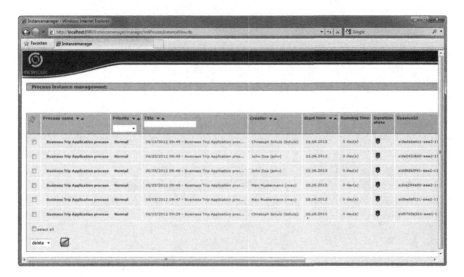

Fig. 13.34   List of process instances in the monitoring tool

Such a list representation of the processes running in an organization can quickly become overloaded once further parameters are included. Then, it can become necessary to implement a process cockpit with intelligible indicators and traffic light representations (see Sect. 11.6).

S-BPM Method by Comparison

14

14.1 To Go

I have noted with dismay that we indeed (still) have our existing data and functional models of work organization. What should we do with these?

Alignment should be easy, since S-BPM covers both structural and functional characteristics, and enriches these with the actor's perspective. This ultimately facilitates the embedding of existing specifications, such as data models, into business objects, so that all of the structures can again be found in S-BPM-models.

I suggest that we look at each model and existing specifications, and adjust them first with the respective S-BPM dimensions. In addition to the existing structural descriptions, such as data models, which can be attributed to the object perspective, we will work on the functional processes including the flow of information and communication, in order to identify subjects and predicates. In this way, we can collect all of the ingredients for integration.

A. Fleischmann et al., *Subject-Oriented Business Process Management*,
DOI 10.1007/978-3-642-32392-8_14, © The Author(s) 2012

The basis is the behavior as described in my subject diagram.

This book provides comprehensive insights into the subject-oriented methodology. In addition to deriving and justifying the concept, we have developed a subject-oriented process model for dealing with models. To complete the picture with respect to BPM, we examine the extent to which other methods also comprise subject-oriented elements. The focus on subjects while reflecting standard sentence semantics of natural language can be spotted in the canon of existing approaches for modeling business processes in various places. The following overview of essential diagrammatic or formal modeling methods for business processes shows the different links of existing approaches to the modeling categories subject, predicate, and object. The respective approaches are comparatively described.

After a review of the concepts for modeling, we follow the historical development of business process modeling and start with activity- or function-oriented approaches—they refer to the predicate. The object-oriented approaches stem from software engineering and refer to objects. The subject reference can be traced back to the theory of process-directed data processing. Finally, there are integrated approaches that include at least two of the three constituent characteristics of subject-oriented business process modeling.

14.2   Subject, Predicate, and Object in Modeling

Business processes are sequences of actions in a company that will be described by a model. Developing business processes means that a model of the existing or a new requirement for a target business process is created.

Business processes can also be interpreted as descriptions of socio-technical systems (Sinz 2010). Business process models describe the properties and behavior of process participants and their interaction with(in) the technical and organizational environment. These models can be viewed from different perspectives. The process of model construction is preceded by an analysis that leads to specific facts either being considered essential or merely supplemental (cf. Scholz and Holl 1999; Denert 1991). In Scholz and Holl (1999), crucial model elements are termed essentials and complimentary ones accidentals.

Depending on which model elements are considered essential when defining business processes, different approaches to modeling are used. Accidental elements are grouped around essential ones. The following aspects of modeling are currently being used (cf. Scholz and Holl 1999; Denert 1991):

- The functional approach focuses on functions. Examples of function-oriented models are control flow diagrams and data flow diagrams according to de-Marco (1979) or Event-driven Process Chains (EPCs).
- In data-driven approaches, accidents are grouped around data. A well-known example of data-driven modeling approaches is Entity-Relationship Diagrams.
- In the object-oriented approach, accidents are grouped around objects. Objects in computer science are data structures, encapsulated with the operations on these data structures. The object-oriented modeling approach is currently considered the most accepted. A well-known method of description is the Unified Modeling Language (UML).

A prerequisite for modeling is that the models are adequately described and documented, so that they can be understood by all and model content can be communicated or discussed. Models are used in particular in BPM for analysis of business processes with the involvement of different actors.

In the above list, some well-known languages for documenting results of process analysis have been given. Modeling, ultimately, describes part of reality using an "artificial" language. A model is thus an artifact, an artificially created structure which contains an excerpt of the reality as perceived by humans. The formalism of models for business processes is such that they can be mapped to IT. In the last few decades in computer science, a paradigm shift from flow orientation to object orientation has occurred. Applied to modeling, the essential aspects have been shifted from the predicate (batch processing, while ...do...) to the object, while subjects were treated only rudimentarily so far. Subject-oriented business process modeling puts the subject into the center of attention. Participants of the S-BPM ONE 2010 congress in Karlsruhe created the hypothesis that after 1970 and 1990, the year 2010 could mark the beginning of a new paradigm switch, namely to subject orientation (see Fig. 14.1).

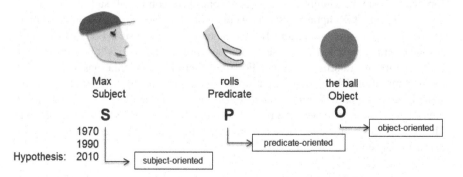

Fig. 14.1 Temporal evolution of flow orientation, object orientation, and subject orientation

14.3   Comparative Analysis

In the following, the best-known modeling approaches are presented and analyzed for their coverage of the natural language sentence semantics and the resulting impact for modeling. Finally, these are compared with the subject-oriented modeling approach.

We exemplify the different approaches using the process for applying for a business trip. It will be shown, in which models generally available for practical description and definition of application programs in computer science, which parts of the standard semantics of subject–predicate–object correspond to essential or accidental elements, and how the process can be described in the respective modeling approach.

We start out with the natural language description of the business trip application process (see Fig. 14.2). This description focuses on the elements perceived as essential aspects of the process when applying for business trips. It will now be specified using various formal or semiformal modeling methods. The relevant sections provide a brief overview of the history of the respective category of approaches, before explaining their representatives in an exemplary way.

The employee Schulz requests a business trip. The application will be reviewed by the manager. He will inform the employee of its approval or rejection. The approved request is sent to the travel office which will carry out ticketing and hotel booking.

Fig. 14.2 Natural language description of the business trip application process

14.3.1 Modeling While Focusing on Predicates

14.3.1.1 Origin
In the beginning of data processing in the 1970s, mechanical and automated processing was at the forefront. In mainframe data processing, actions were at the center of attention. Terms such as "operator" or "data or information processing" were coined at that time. Even in the first programming languages, operational constructs are in the foreground; their core consists of commands such as "while . . . do . . .". The first computer systems were built to solve complex computational problems of the time, stemming from mathematics or physics. For instance, the trained civil engineer Konrad Zuse wanted to automate his statics' calculations and built the first calculating machine. For these activities, calculations were at the focus of attention. The data were parameters of mathematical or physical formulas and played a secondary role. Likewise, the actor, or the subject, was of minor importance. The subject was the person interested in the results of the calculation. The focus was on the action, i.e., the predicate. Programming was meant to define complex sequences of actions.

14.3.1.2 Flowcharts

One of the first models for algorithmic tasks was flowcharts or program flowcharts. Flowcharts describe a sequence of operations to solve a task. A business trip application can be mapped to a flowchart (see Fig. 14.3).

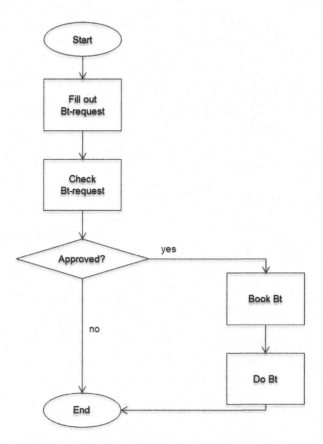

Fig. 14.3 Business trip application process as a flowchart

When flowcharts are used to describe a computational algorithm, it is clear who initiates the individual actions in the flowchart: it is the person carrying out the task, or the executing computer system. These standard subjects are not mentioned explicitly. In addition, the data required for executing a flowchart are specified only rudimentarily.

Using flowcharts, natural language supplements, such as subjects and objects, can be added, but they are not integrated in the logic of the model. Figure 14.4 shows the example extended to subjects. They were added in natural language.

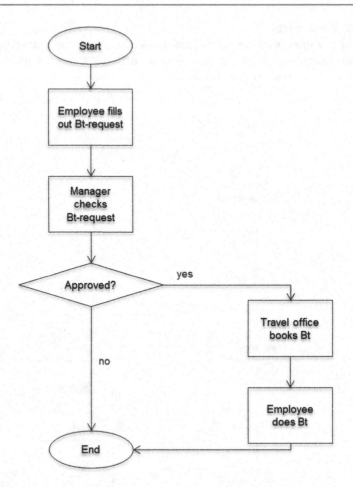

Fig. 14.4 Business trip application process as a flowchart including subjects

In advanced forms of flowcharts, in addition to the verbs, the subjects and objects are directly or indirectly represented as symbols. Figure 14.5 shows the previous flowchart after adding the subjects "employee" and "manager" indirectly by adding the symbols for the manual entry of the business trip application and the decision-making results. The modified diagram also contains an object represented by the symbol for a data set (business trip data).

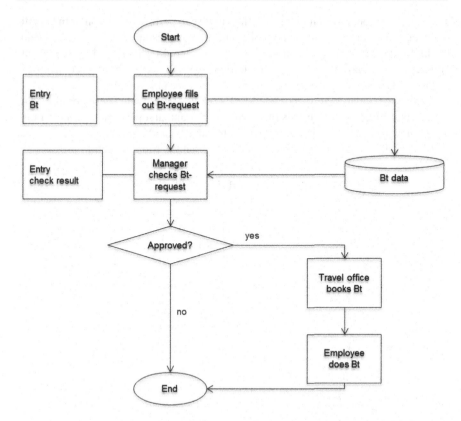

Fig. 14.5 Business trip application process as a flowchart including subjects and objects

14.3.1.3 Event-Driven Process Chains

A control-flow-based method for representing business processes is Event-driven Process Chains (EPC). Figure 14.6 shows the process of the business trip application as an EPC.

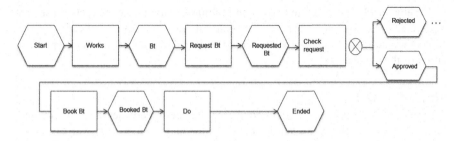

Fig. 14.6 Business trip application process as an EPC

The rectangles represent the actions of a process that may contain natural language objects for illustration purposes. The individual actions are preceded by an event (hexagons), which represents the impulse to perform an action or the result of the previous action. With the help of connectors, the results of a function can lead to different events. The action "check request" could either lead to the event "rejected" or "approved" (XOR). In addition to XOR, there are other connectors. Details of EPCs and their use are described in Scheer (1998).

In practice, today mainly extended EPCs (eEPCs) are used. These complement the original EPCs with elements of organization, data, and performance modeling. These amendments correspond essentially to subjects and objects.

Figure 14.7 shows an extended EPC of the business trip application process.

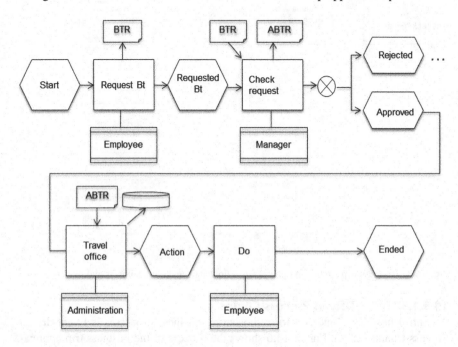

Fig. 14.7 Business trip application process as eEPC including subject, predicate, and object

Hereby, eEPCs in principle allow representing all language constructs. In such a representation, functions are still at the center of attention. An identification of the subject including its entire behavior is not possible due to the distributed representation of the subject in the diagram.

14.3.1.4 Petri Nets

An important model in theoretical computer science is Petri nets (cf. Stucky and Winand 1997). They are an action-oriented modeling method, i.e., Petri nets are predicate oriented. In contrast to control flow diagrams, they allow performing multiple actions in parallel.

In order to also support data aspects, attributed Petri nets have been developed. However, approaches to represent subjects are still missing.

Figure 14.8 shows a Petri net for the business trip application process. A Petri net consists of an initial marking, places (solid bars), transitions (ovals), and arcs (arrowed lines). Arcs connect transitions to places or places to transitions, but never places to places or transitions to transitions. In general, transitions are interpreted as actions and places as conditions for a transition. A transition can switch when in its input places there is at least one so-called token. After switching, each output place receives a token. The initial marking determines which places have tokens to start the execution. In the figure, the place "employee requests business trip" contains the token.

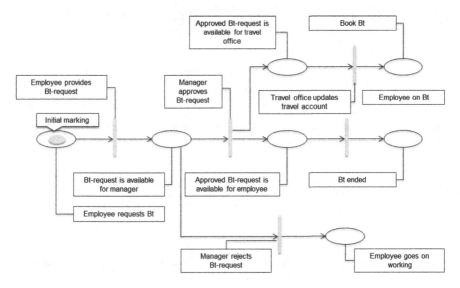

Fig. 14.8 Business trip application process as a Petri net with initial marking

After switching the transition "employee provides business trip request", the token is reassigned as shown in Fig. 14.9. The token is removed from the place "employee requests business trip" and a token appears in the place "business trip request is available for manager".

After that, either the transition "manager rejects business trip request" or the transition "manager approves business trip request" can switch. The Petri net is therefore referred to as nondeterministic. In case the transition "manager approves business trip request" switches, the places "approved business trip request is available for travel office" and "approved business trip request is available for employee" are each provided with a token (see Fig. 14.10).

The example reveals that Petri nets focus on the sequence of actions. Subjects and objects are complemented by natural language comments. In this case, this is done by selecting appropriate names for the places and transitions. The advantage of Petri nets as compared to flowcharts is that they are grounded in theory and concurrency can be represented.

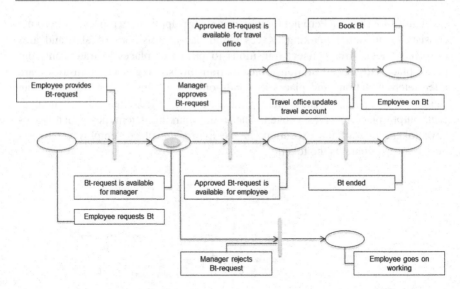

Fig. 14.9 Business trip application process as a Petri net with tokens assignment after switching "employee provides business trip request"

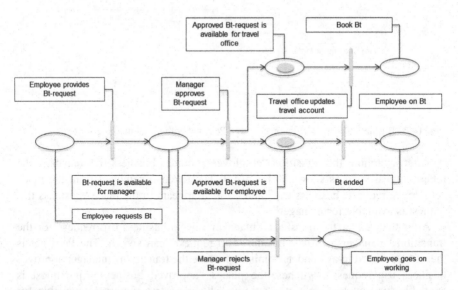

Fig. 14.10 Business trip application process as a Petri net with tokens after switching "manager approves business trip request"

14.3.2 Modeling While Focusing on Objects

14.3.2.1 Origin

With the increasing use of computer systems in industry, the aspect of data management and data processing has become increasingly important. In companies, large data sets, such as order or invoice data, need to be stored and manipulated. To meet these requirements, modeling languages have been developed which bring the target of actions, namely the objects or data, to the focus of attention.

14.3.2.2 Entity-Relationship Model

The Entity-Relationship Model (ER Model or ERM) describes data entities and their mutual relationships. ER models are usually represented graphically. Their advantage is their ability to map complex worlds using simple tools:

- Entity: object of actual world, either material or abstract (e.g., employee "Schulz", manager "Schmid").
- Relationship: semantic relationship between two or more objects (e.g., employee "Schulz" "is a staff member" of manager "Schmid").
  The model itself consists exclusively of entity types and relationship types:
- Entity type: typifying of similar entities (e.g., employee and manager), shown as a rectangle.
- Relationship type: typifying of similar relationships (e.g., "is employee of"). The semantics of the relationship between entity types is expressed in the ER diagram by a short text label on the border, while it is left up to the modeler what name he provides.

Figure 14.11 shows the ERM of the business trip application process. Each employee has exactly one manager and each manager is boss of 1 to n employees. Each employee has applied for none or up to n business trips. Each business trip request contains exactly one travel date for the beginning and the end of the business trip, respectively. A manager has to decide upon 0 to m business trip requests.

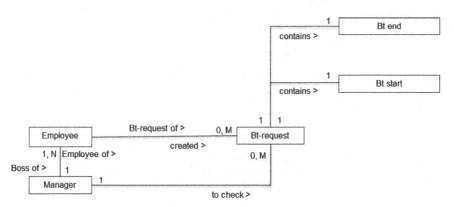

Fig. 14.11 ERM for the business trip application process

An ERM is focused on objects. Subjects and predicates are only indirectly considered, namely by the name of the relationships. In case a predicate is used to describe a relationship, a complete sentence may be the result. As demonstrated by the example, this is however not compulsory. The introduction of subject and predicate therefore depends on the discipline of the modeler. An ERM contains no control flow, so that it is not clear when and what actions are performed (predicate). Who the initiator of an action is, i.e., the subject, can only be concluded from the ER diagram when for the marking of relationships corresponding terms are used in a disciplined way.

14.3.2.3 Relational Data Model

For relational data models, analogous to the ERM, only data objects are considered, but here in the form of tables. Subject and predicate are accidentals.

As structural elements in relational data models, only those relations can be represented that can be described by tables. The rows of the tables are the data records, and the columns correspond to the data fields of the records. A data model usually consists of multiple tables. Relationships between any records, even in different tables in a model, can be constructed by using the same field content (primary and foreign keys).

Certain records are accessed via field contents. Figure 14.12 shows a data model for the business trip application. The data model consists of three tables "employees", "managers", and "business trip requests". The table "managers" includes all the supervisors; the table "employees" includes all employees with a reference to their managers in the column "M-No." The table "business trip

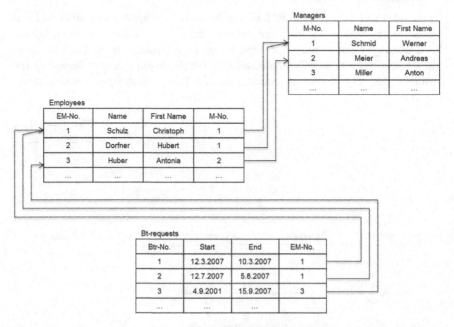

Fig. 14.12 Relational data model for the business trip application process

requests" includes all business trip requests submitted so far. The column "EM-No." in the table "business trip requests" contains a reference to the employee who has provided this business trip request.

On relational data models, logical, set-theoretic queries are defined (predicates) that are used by users (subjects). A relational data model does not include which users (subjects) are available in a certain situation or part of reality. The possible predicates that are triggered by the users are specified by the so-called query language, in general, the Structured Query Language (SQL).

In the example, the manager Werner Schmid (a user, subject) determines his subordinates by an appropriate query (predicate) from the "employees" table (objects). These are all the employees that contain a "1" in the column "M.-No." in the table "employees". Then, in the "business trip requests" table, all business trip requests are identified that contain in the "EM-No." column a number of an employee of Werner Schmid. The result set of this query therefore contains all the business trip requests of Mr. Schmid's employees, which can then be processed. Using the query language for relational databases, the predicate is present, while it is completely missing in the ERM.

Relational data models are very close to implementation. They can more or less be directly realized by a relational database, using ERM as a modeling language and the relational model already as a programming facility. In both modeling languages, however, subjects are only marginally considered. For a database application, there is always only "the" user, whoever that may be. The subject concept comes into play only in the context of authorization concepts: Which users can access which data in which way?

14.3.3 Modeling While Focusing on Predicate and Object

14.3.3.1 Origin

In the previously described modeling methods, either the subject or the predicate has been neglected. In the predicate-centered methods, the object aspect has been insufficiently described, in object-supporting methods, the predicate aspect. For databases, although there is a query language that can be used to form predicates, there is no way to define control flows (i.e., sequences of predicates). In the technical implementation of such incomplete models, missing components must be interpreted, which may lead to incorrect implementations.

It was natural, therefore, to develop modeling approaches considering action and data aspects in a balanced way, i.e., modeling languages, such as the data flow diagram, that contain predicates and objects. In this way, complete sentences can be formed in terms of the standard semantics of sentences, namely passive sentences. Passive sentences are used in natural languages, when the subject plays a minor role. A passive description of the business trip application process could be as follows: "The business trip application is filled out, the business trip request will be checked, the check result is documented, and the travel accounts of the employees (business trip directory) will be updated."

14.3.3.2 Data Flow Diagrams

Using data flow diagrams (DFD), the flow of data between functions, data repositories, and external stakeholders who are not part of the operation of the system are represented. The Structured Analysis by Tom DeMarco (DeMarco 1979) is an application of data flow diagrams for modeling.

In data flow diagrams, the following graphical elements are used:

- External interface (external partners, stakeholders, terminators): External interfaces are represented as rectangles. They denote the relations of the considered system to the outside world. They send or receive data, but do not process them. External interfaces trigger the system by the provision of data and can therefore be considered under certain restrictions as subjects.
- Function (process, task, function): Functions are shown as circles or ovals. They have the task of processing input into output data and contain the necessary algorithms. The functions correspond to predicates according to the semantics of natural language. Predicates of higher complexity can be refined by the predicates of a control flow diagram.
- Data storage (store, repository): Stores are presented as two parallel lines. They form a storage facility for data with different times of creation and use. They can be regarded as special data storage functions.
- Data flow (information flow, data flow): The data flow is represented by arrows between functions or data stores. The arrows are labeled with the name of the data flowing. In a data dictionary, the structures of all information items used are defined. The definition of data structures is done in Backus–Naur form. In this respect, an ERM could of course also be used. The data corresponds to the objects of the natural language sentence semantics.
- Context Diagram: Figure 14.13 shows the context diagram of the business trip application process. The context diagram identifies the external interfaces and illustrates the system to be developed as a function. The context diagram describes how the application receives data from an external interface and returns the result to the external interface. In this example, the external interface can be interpreted as a subject (employee). However, the manager is missing, since he is part of the system. If he and the update of the business trip data are also relocated (to the outside), virtually nothing remains from the application.

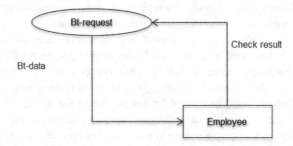

Fig. 14.13 Context diagram for the business trip application process

Figure 14.14 shows the refinement of the business trip process with the data flow between the individual functions and data stores. It is important to note that no control flow is connected to the data flow, although this might be suggested by the representation.

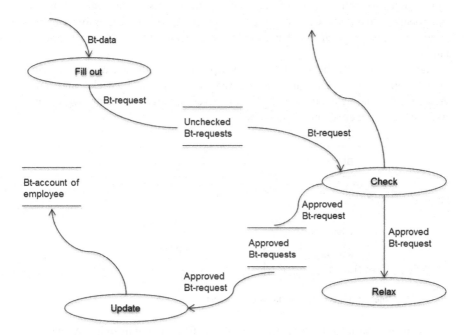

Fig. 14.14 Business trip application process as a data flow diagram

Although data flow diagrams were already developed in the 1970s, they cover predicate and object from the natural language sentence semantics. However, subjects can only be introduced via auxiliary constructions which lead to distortions. Data flow diagrams are no longer used in practice. The combination of predicate–object has evolved and led to object-oriented modeling and implementation methods.

14.3.3.3 Object Orientation

The basic idea of object-oriented programming is coupling functions (methods) that can be applied to data as closely as possible with the data being processed, including their properties, and to encapsulate them from the outside. The functions together with the data form an object in the sense of object-oriented modeling. The data of an object can only be accessed with its own methods. Objects with similar properties can be grouped into classes. Simple objects (or classes) can be developed by operations such as inheritance, polymorphism, aggregation, associations, etc. into complex structured objects and classes. For more details on the object-oriented methodology, we refer to the extensive existing literature (cf. http://www.uml.org).

Today, object orientation is the common standard for modeling and programming. Compared to approaches in which properties and functions are not considered in an integrated way, this modeling paradigm makes the claim of being able to represent the observable world more accurately than other approaches.

The object-oriented modeling approach, with objects consisting of data and functionality, covers the concepts of predicate and object according to the natural language sentence semantics. The functions correspond to the predicates and the data to the objects.

Figure 14.15 shows the object "business trip request" with the data "start of trip", "end of trip", and "check result" and the functions "fill out", "check", and "enter check result". In case the business trip is approved, the travel directory represented by the object "travel account" is updated.

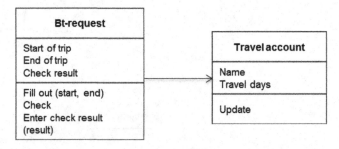

Fig. 14.15   Object or object class business trip request

The object "business trip request" now allows formulating incomplete sentences such as "fill out business trip request" or "check business trip request". To form complete sentences in the original object-oriented approaches, subjects could only be inserted into the model by natural language elements.

With the introduction of use case diagrams as contained in UML, this deficiency has been removed. UML has been developed by the Object Management Group (OMG) as a standardized language for modeling software and other systems. It includes 13 different types of diagrams (http://www.omg.org/spec/UML/2.2/). One of these diagram types is the use case diagram. The introduction of the subjects into the grammar of modeling by use case and activity diagrams will be discussed in Sect. 14.3.5.2.

14.3.4   Modeling While Focusing on Subjects

14.3.4.1   Origin

In computer science, there has long been the concept of parallel processes. A process executes actions within a given time interval to achieve a specific goal (Havey 2005). A process description defines the behavior of a process.

In the natural language sentence semantics, the subject is the starting point of activities defined by the predicate. Thus, subjects represent the active elements of reality. Subjects can execute defined sequences of actions (predicates). Subjects are mutually independent and communicate with each other, if required, i.e., they exchange information. Subjects, therefore, largely correspond to processes in computer science. Using the process concept, subjects from reality can be mapped to a corresponding construct in a model.

In the following sections, two concepts are introduced that put processes into the center of attention. For this purpose, parallel processes are defined which synchronize themselves through the exchange of messages, i.e., a process can send and receive messages by way of so-called ports. Sending and receiving are therefore the only possible predicates. Ports for message exchange can be interpreted as objects of the natural language sentence semantics.

14.3.4.2 Calculus of Communicating Systems

Calculus of Communicating Systems (CCS) is a process algebra (Milner 1980). A process algebra is used for algebraic modeling of parallel processes and consists of elementary actions and operators for joining actions. Elementary actions cannot be further detailed.

Processes can interact with the neighbors or independently perform activities in parallel. The aim of CCS is to model the communication between processes, e.g., to investigate their equivalence.

A process uses ports as enablers of communication with other processes, whereby each port has a name. A distinction is made between send and receive ports. Figure 14.16 shows the individual processes or subjects, respectively, of the business trip application process. The employee sends the business trip request to the manager. For the send port, the port name is marked with a horizontal line. The manager sends the result to the employee, and, where appropriate, the approved business trip request to the travel office.

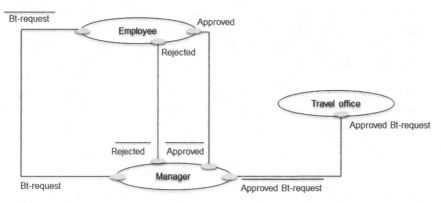

Fig. 14.16 CCS processes for business trip request

In Figure 14.16, only the involved processes and their relationships are shown. The internal behavior is not yet visible. This is described using operators. In our example, we use only a few of these operators; for a complete list, we refer to the literature (Milner 1992; Milner et al. 1992a, b; Brinksma and Mader 2003). Figure 14.17 shows the behavioral description of the individual processes and their coupling to the business trip application process.

Employee = Bt-request . (rejected + approved) . NIL

Manager = Bt-request . (rejected + approved . approved Bt-request) . NIL

Travel office = approved BT-request . NIL

Business trip application process = employee / manager / travel office

Fig. 14.17 Description of the business trip application process in CCS

In the example, the process "employee" first sends the business trip request and then waits for either the message "rejected" or "approved". Once the employee receives one of these messages, the process can be continued. In case he performs the operation NIL, the process stops. The description of the processes "manager" and "travel office" can be interpreted similarly. The last line in the figure shows the composition of the entire process using the corresponding operator.

The business trip example shows that the active element in CCS, the actor, is seen as essential, while predicate and object play a subordinate role. Thus, CCS can be considered a subject-oriented method.

14.3.4.3 Communicating Sequential Processes

Communicating Sequential Processes (CSP) is also a process algebra. It was developed by Tony Hoare (1985). CSP was first published as a programming language construct and then formalized in the following years also due to the influence of Milner (1980). In CSP, in contrast to CCS, there is initially no distinction between sending and receiving. In case processes are linked by operators, also events of the same name from the associated processes are linked.

In Figure 14.18, the business trip application process is described in CSP. For employees, the event "business trip request" is enabled, and subsequently, either the event "rejected" or "approved". The event "SKIP" describes that the process is completed. In the process "manager", also the event "business trip request" is possible and then, appropriate follow-up events. When the process "employee" is linked to the process "manager" by using the ‖ operator (see last line), they share the initial event, and in both processes the corresponding transition (arrow in row 1 and 2) is executed.

Employee   = Bt-request ⇒ (rejected ⇒ SKIP I approved ⇒ SKIP)

Manager   = Bt-request ⇒ (rejected ⇒ SKIP I approved ⇒ approval ⇒ SKIP)

Travel office   = Approval ⇒ SKIP

Business trip application process = employee ‖ manager ‖ travel office

Fig. 14.18 Description of the business trip application process in CSP

On a detailed level of CSP, it is possible to dissolve events into send and receive operations that run on ports and can transfer data. In this way, in CSP, the predicates "send" and "receive" exist, as well as objects (messages) on which these (simple) predicates can be executed.

In CSP, analogously to CCS, the subject represents the essential part. Predicate and object play a very subordinate role. Without natural language additions with respect to predicate and object, a complete model of the business trip application process cannot be created with CSP. Meaningful names are also essential for understanding processes but do not contribute to the semantics.

14.3.5 Methods Considering Subject, Predicate, and Object

14.3.5.1 Origin

In all major formal modeling methods of computer science, natural language sentences cannot be formed in the sense of natural language. Since this is always necessary for achieving a thorough understanding, the missing elements have been informally added. For instance, the rectangles for the actions in flowcharts were labeled accordingly. Instead of "fill out", the phrase "fill out business trip request" was used for labeling the action symbol. In English literature, such constructs are termed "verb–noun phrase" (Sharp and McDermott 2009, p. 45).

14.3.5.2 Use Case and Activity Diagrams in UML

UML has 13 diagram types. These are divided into six structural diagram types and seven behavior diagram types. Using the behavior diagrams, dynamic aspects of a program are described. The structure diagram types overlap in their representation aspects, whereby mutual systematic transfer is not possible. All seven diagram types include aspects of subjects, however, in an unclear form. In UML, all entities of discourse are objects. In the following, those diagram types in which the subject aspect most clearly comes to light are explained in more detail. These are the Use Case Diagram and the Activity Diagram.

Use Case Diagrams allow describing the use of a system from a user perspective. A use case shows which users (actors = subject) perform what actions (predicates) using the system. A use case describes the externally visible behavior of the considered element (system, class, etc.) and encapsulates a coherent set of actions that are executed in a fixed order. A use case does not indicate which classes and which individual operations on the actions are involved. A description of the use case is complete once the underlying processes are defined. To accomplish this, an appropriate method of UML for modeling behavior, or a natural language description, can be used.

Actors are considered special UML classes with specific properties and are not considered as being definitely active. It can therefore only be determined which actions occur between an actor and the system, but not who is the starting point of an action. However, it is advisable to consider an actor as the starting point of actions.

Figure 14.19 shows the Use Case Diagram for the business trip application process. The complete sequence of actions for "fill out request" could mean: "enter start date of business trip", "add business trip end date", and "ask manager for decision". The other use cases can be described analogously.

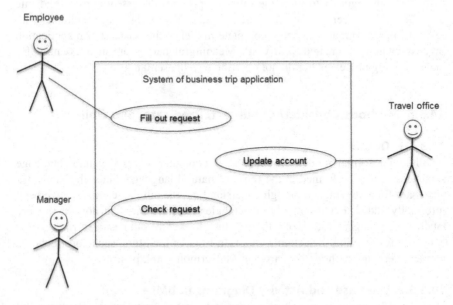

Fig. 14.19 Use case diagram for the business trip application process

Use Case Diagrams are often refined further by using activity diagrams in which elements of data flow diagrams, Petri nets, flowcharts, etc. are combined. However, the interplay of several activity diagrams by means of modeling signals and events for exchanging information is only rudimentarily possible. This means that representing the relationship between the individual use cases in our example is not possible at all on the level of Use Case Diagrams and only to a limited extent on the level of activity diagrams. An example in this respect is the alternative waiting of an employee for approval or rejection.

The following example shows an activity diagram for the business trip application (see Fig. 14.20). The individual activities have been grouped with so-called swim lanes, depending on who performs the activity. In our example, there is a dedicated swim lane for the employee, the manager, and the travel office. These lanes can be considered as subjects who carry out the assigned activities. The sequence of activities is specified by the control flow analogously to flowcharts.

It is possible to split up a single control flow by fork and join operations into parallel control flows (fork) and to rejoin them again (join). In the business trip application example, the control flow is split after the approval of the request by the manager (shown in the picture with a black bar in the swim lane of the manager). This means that the employee and the travel office obtain the approval in parallel. The parallel control flows are then joined before the end node is reached.

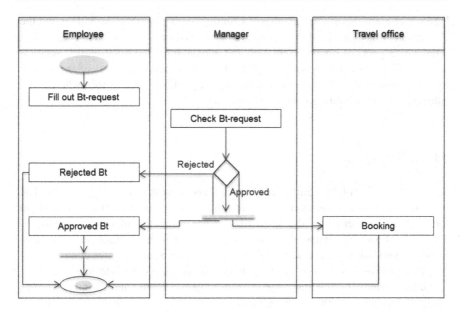

Fig. 14.20 Activity diagram of the business trip application process

The coordination of individual activities is done by shifting the control flow between the individual lanes. However, it seems unrealistic that the control flow, after completion of the business trip request by the employee, changes without further delay to the manager. Normally, process participants exchange messages when transferring the control flow. Such a transition of the control flow from one process participant to another is not obvious, and visible only with cognitive effort in an Activity Diagram.

In addition, fork and join operations in a neighboring swim lane are elusive and artificial. In fact, they are often omitted, which is even officially allowed in BPMN (http://www.omg.org/spec/BPMN/2.0) but immediately leads to semantic difficulties when using Fork, and especially Join.

Despite the identified shortcomings, UML provides with use case and activity diagrams and the other diagram types at least a limited possibility of complete sentence construction in terms of the standard sentence grammar. In UML, actors are not part of the model, so their behavior, and in particular the potential communication among stakeholders, is not considered in detail. This is also evident from the fact that the actors do not appear in the other diagram types in UML, with the exception of the time-sequence diagram.

Since the actors play an important role in business processes, UML also represents in models only a limited perspective on reality.

14.3.5.3 A Subject-Oriented Approach Using PASS

The subject-oriented methodology presented mainly in Chap. 5 of this book is based on the Parallel Activity Specification Scheme (PASS) of Fleischmann (1994).

PASS uses elements of the Calculus of Communicating Systems by Milner and the Communicating Sequential Processes by Hoare (see Sects. 14.3.4.2 and 14.3.4.3). It integrates aspects of object orientation and adds a graphical notation (cf. Schmidt et al. 2009, p. 54). In this way, S-BPM takes into account all parts of the natural language sentence semantics, including subject, predicate, and object, whereas the subject is in the role of "primus inter pares".

14.3.6 Synopsis

The table in Fig. 14.21 summarizes the findings from the previous sections. The more or less filled circle symbols express the assessment of various methods in terms of their coverage of the standard sentence semantics of natural languages. The table shows that parts of semantics are absent in many methods. We have demonstrated that these are added pragmatically by natural language comments, or by extending the basic set of symbols, to be able to form complete sentences.

Subject-oriented modeling targets active subjects (actors) and assigns activities and business objects either to them, or to their communication relationships. It thus meets the requirements of standard sentence semantics of natural language in its originally conceived sequence. Therefore, it is the only approach which can be considered complete in this respect. In addition, subject-oriented modeling is intuitive: it reduces the learning curve for modeling to the effort required for acquiring and mastering sentences of natural language.

Modeling language	Looking at			Explanation
	Subject	Predicate	Object	
Natural language	●	●	●	Description of the facts by whole sentences (who does what to what?), Exception: passive.
Control flow diagram	○	●	○	Focus on algorithms; usually natural-language extensions for objects and subjects.
(extended) Event-driven process chain	◐	●	◐	For EPCs, only predicates; extended EPCs allow the addition of subjects and objects.
Petri nets	○	●	◐	Only predicates; subjects and objects by natural-language extensions.
Entity Relationship Diagram	○	○	●	Only the structure of the object is described. No operations are possible.
Relational databases	○	◐	●	Tables as objects and SQL as language for predicates.
Data flow diagam	○	●	●	Data and data flows between various action points.
Object-oriented approaches	○	●	●	Predicates correspond to the methods that are defined on the respective data.
Calculus of Communicating Systems (CCS)	●	◐	○	Process algebra for modeling parallel systems. As a single operation, there are "send" and "receive".
Communicating Sequential Processes (CSP)	●	◐	○	Formal method for describing parallel systems that synchronize by the exchange of messages.
Unified Modeling Language	◐	●	●	Originally intended only for describing object-oriented systems (predicates and objects). In the use case diagrams, there are stakeholders as actors / subjects and the subjects of activity diagrams can be defined by swim lanes.
S-BPM based on PASS	●	●	●	Subjects interact with each other. They exchange messages and transmit thus business objects, which they edit internally.

Fig. 14.21 Model description languages in comparison with respect to standard semantics structure of sentences (based on Schmidt et al. 2009, p. 55)

References

Brinksma, E., Mader, A. Prozessalgebra, Teil 1, in: at - Automatisierungstechnik, Vol. 51, Issue 8, S. A13–A16, 2003.

DeMarco, T., Structured Analysis and System Specification, Upper Saddle River 1979.

Denert, E., Software-Engineering - Methodische Projektabwicklung, Berlin 1991.

Fleischmann, A., Distributed Systems – Software Design and Implementation, Berlin 1994.

Havey, M., Essential Business Process Modeling, Sebastopol 2005.

Hoare, C., Communicating Sequential Processes, New Jersey 1985.

Milner, R., Calculus of Communicating Systems, Berlin u.a. 1980.

Milner, R., Parrow, J., Walker, D., A Calculus for Mobile Processes, Part I. Information and Computation 100, pp. 1–40, 1992.

Milner, R., Parrow, J., Walker, D., A Calculus for Mobile Processes, Part II. Information and Computation 100, pp. 41–77, 1992.

Milner, R., Functions as processes, in: Math. Struct. in Comp. Science, vol. 2, pp. 119–141, 1992.

Sharp, A., McDermott, P., Workflow Modeling, Norwood 2009.

Scholz, M., Holl, A., Objektorientierung und Poppers Drei-Welten-Modell als Theoriekerne, in: Schütte, R. et al., Wirtschaftsinformatik und Wissenschaftstheorie. Grundpositionen und Theoriekerne, Arbeitsbericht 4 des Instituts für Produktion und industrielles Informationsmanagement an der Universität Essen, Essen 1999.

Scheer A.-W., ARIS – Modellierungsmethoden, Metamodelle, Anwendungen, Berlin 1998.

Schmidt, W., Fleischmann, A. und Gilbert, O., Subjektorientiertes Geschäftsprozessmanagement, HMD – Praxis der Wirtschaftsinformatik, Heft 266, S. 52–62, 2009.

Sinz, E.J., Konstruktionsforschung in der Wirtschaftsinformatik: Was sind die Erkenntnisziele gestaltungsorientierter Wirtschaftsinformatik-Forschung?, in: Österle, H., Winter. R., Brenner, W. (Hrsg.), Gestaltungsorientierte Wirtschaftsinformatik: Ein Plädoyer für Rigor und Relevanz, Nürnberg, S. 29–34, 2010.

Stucky, W., Winand, U. (Hrsg.), Petri-Netze zur Modellierung verteilter DV-Systeme – Erfahrungen im Rahmen des DFG-Schwerpunktprogramms "Verteilte DV-Systeme in der Betriebswirtschaft", Bericht 350, Karlsruhe 1997.

Conclusion 15

15.1 Continuous Round-Trip Engineering in Real Time

As shown in the previous chapters, continuous socio-technical system development is based on models. In case of appropriate support through modeling and implementation technology, stakeholders (i.e., all actors involved in business operations) may adjust the implementation of business process models according to their individual needs without additional development costs. This can be achieved if process descriptions are directly executable, and so enable a seamless alignment between modeling and execution.

Based on the direct implementation, not only the quality of processes but also the associated information systems can be assessed in terms of their organizational "fitness". When appropriate, a further modeling step and a subsequent additional execution step could be required. In this way, an organization can be transformed from existing (as-is) work structures to envisioned (to-be) ones. To support this, workflow management systems provide information technology tools for automated implementation of processes.

Business processes and thus, the comprehensive modeling of processes not only enable reflection and explication of knowledge about organizations and human labor but also even more so promote the communication of the respective information. Organizationally compliant process models facilitate the proper handling of economic and environmental quality requirements. Projects should not fail because participants work with unrealistic assumptions and/or develop unattainable requirements, mainly relating to the capability of an organization for change or the ability of employees to adapt. Unrealistic assumptions or requirements arise mainly from failure to reflect on developments or from delayed collection of information and its context.

In order to acquire skills in process modeling and to learn to "think in processes", the understanding and involvement of the stakeholders, both managers and work performers, for the modeling of business proceedings by means of structures such as processes, communication flows, and information flows, needs to be achieved.

A. Fleischmann et al., *Subject-Oriented Business Process Management*,
DOI 10.1007/978-3-642-32392-8_15, © The Author(s) 2012

In doing so, the focus is on the mapping of perceived facts on concrete or abstract elements of corporate structures and/or behavior. Process orientation can only be achieved by knowing existing structures in organizations and overcoming function-specific structures and procedures (Lehner et al. 2007, pp. 248 ff.).

As already mentioned, process information is represented in models, which provide the input to support systems for execution, in particular workflow management systems. Ideally, the latter can process models without further adjustment or refinement. Processes become effective via information technology in this way and form the basis of change processes in organizations with feedback loops.

Round-trip engineering in S-BPM is characterized by feedback of organizational developments becoming an integrated part of continuous (re-) design. In this context, disrupting interaction with actors and/or tools should be avoided, as a practitioner reports in http://www.wikipedia.org: "When business process modeling is performed, i.e., graphical task chains are created with a modeling tool, there is still the challenge to transfer these models to a process or workflow engine for execution. In general, a variety of technical information needs to be added by IT professionals, such as the technical invocation of an application, what parameters should be passed, what will happen in case of an error, etc. In general, the engines have restrictions, so that the model needs to be adjusted. In addition, the organizational point of view is often either insufficiently or too extensively represented in detail. In the latter case, several activities become a single one, as the rest of the tasks are executed in the invoked application.

Once the process initially designed from the perspective of the organization has been enriched technologically and is in production, execution data is logged. This is analyzed using tools from the field of business intelligence. Then, it comes to optimization, i.e., the adaptation of the processes. And hereby, the next challenge. If the technical modeling has been carried out with the tool of the process engine, there are now two models, and thus, the challenge of dual model maintenance. In case the organizational model has been created with the tool of the process engine, mainly the organization developer will be surprised about the difference to the original model.

We have tackled exactly this issue with our endeavor: subject-oriented BPM (S-BPM) minimizes the risk of reduction or the disruption of model and media, as it actively contributes to the consistency of representations and their implementation. S-BPM guides modeling from the very beginning to describe and specify processes in terms of executable entities, thereby avoiding the maintenance of multiple, possibly different models on the same issue. Each generated model can be executed without further transformation (Schatten et al. 2007). Therefore, S-BPM users do not need to rely on other developments, such as version 2.0 of the modeling language Business Process Model & Notation (BPMN—http://www.bpmn.org), which should simplify round-trip engineering. Rather, all stakeholders involved in organizational development are able to participate in integrated round-trip engineering.

15.2   Stakeholders as Key Enablers

S-BPM provides an enhancement to traditional process management in the direction of stakeholder orientation. S-BPM does not require a specific process execution language to ensure interoperability between the different tools of modeling, simulation, and execution (Sinur et al. 2005). Additionally, it does not require a BPDM (Business Process Definition Meta-model) and its associated workflow engines in order to design seamless round-trip engineering. This resolves the often uttered complaint of having to continuously switch between modeling an organizational vision, and the enrichment of data by the IT system, to run business processes [see http://www.saperionblog.com from the perspective of practitioners (Weidlich et al. 2009) from an academic point of view]. Rather, S-BPM allows the self-directed development of organizations. It enables all stakeholders to initiate development processes and to actively engage themselves.

Even the consultants of Gartner formulate in their "Seven Major Guidelines for a Successful Business Process Management Project" (http://www.gartner.com): "7. Business user engagement. If you get the people who do the actual work in a process, this can be particularly helpful."

In addition to real-time requirements for the flexible design of business processes (and thus to round-trip engineering), the stakeholder orientation is one of the biggest challenges of successful BPM (see Gartner's Trip Report of BPM2010 at http://www.gartner.com). Only a reflected approach avoids the "trivialization of dealing with processes" and lays ground for the acceptance of S-BPM [Liappas in Scheer et al. (2006)], as the stakeholders involved may become interested hereby in an effective penetration of the organization with processes.

Consequently, a language and an instrument needed to be developed enabling all stakeholders to articulate in real time their inputs toward a dynamic development of the organization, without being disturbed by modeling constructs or technology.

Subject-oriented BPM aims to provide participants and responsible actors with a methodological tool that should increase not only the acceptance but also the coherence and integrity of models of the perceived or anticipated organizational reality. Traditional surveys of work processes by means of interviews and specifications by third parties are likely to lead to incomplete representations, which become manifest later in insufficient implementations when processes are executed by means of IT (Rosenkranz and Geschäftsprozesse 2006). Hence, a stakeholder-driven, continuous round-trip, working without intermediate steps, e.g., executing process models immediately, is the primary development target.

When supported in seamless way, stakeholders are empowered to design work processes more directly, especially knowledge-based processes. The process of explication becomes more accurate due to S-BPM's intuitive usability of the modeling language. This is required when organizations implement adaptive case management, since the majority of their business processes are unpredictable. Thus, new knowledge is constantly being generated as the solution to a particular problem at hand. Finally, on the basis of such newly generated knowledge stakeholders drive the process by themselves, ad-hoc and tailored to the situation, without the otherwise often required external intervention.

References

Lehner, F., Wildner, S., Scholz M., Wirtschaftsinformatik – Eine Einführung, München 2007.
Rosenkranz, F., Geschäftsprozesse, Berlin 2006.
Schatten, A. Schiefer, J., Agile Business Process Management with Sense and Respond, in: Proceedings IEEE International Conference on e-Business Engineering (ICEBE'07), pp. 319–322, 2007.
Scheer, A.-W., Kruppke, H., Jost, W., Kindermann, H. (Hrsg.), Agilität durch ARIS-Geschäftsprozessmanagement, Jahrbuch Business Process Excellence 2006/2007, Berlin 2007.
Sinur, J., Business Process Management Suites Will Be the 'Next Big Thing', Gartner Research Note, 8 February 2005.
Weidlich, M., Weske, M., Mendling. J.: Change Propagation in Process Models using Behavioural Profiles, IEEE International Conference on Services Computing, S. 33–40, 2009.

Glossary

Abstract State Machine (ASM)

An Abstract State Machine is a machine specification according to theoretical computer science for the formal description of states. Based on the concept of the Turing machine it can be used for the formal specification to describe, e.g., programming languages. Recently, it has also been used for verifying business process models. A detailed description of the model of S-BPM can be found in the appendix of this book.

Activity

An activity is a set of actions accomplishing tasks performed by a human or automatically by a computer system when managing work. The concept is called function in function-oriented approaches. In Subject-oriented Business Process Management, we also speak of → predicates. By implementing an activity in an organization (assigned to a work performer), it becomes a concrete task.

Activity Bundle / Bundle of Activities

A bundle of activities is some part (similar to a phase) of the → S-BPM procedure model described by → activities. They are performed by the various → S-BPM stakeholders as part of an entire organizational development step. These are:
- → Analysis
- → Modeling
- → Validation
- → Optimization
- → Organization-specific implementation
- → Information Technology implementation
- → Monitoring

A. Fleischmann et al., *Subject-Oriented Business Process Management*,
DOI 10.1007/978-3-642-32392-8, © The Author(s) 2012

Actors

Actors are work performers, i.e., active participants of a work process, and represent one type of four → S-BPM stakeholders. According to the → S-BPM procedure model, they may participate in process design. They correspond to the subject carriers that take and execute the roles of subjects. Actors are also primary points of reference in the analysis, modeling, optimization, and implementation of business process models, according to the objective of S-BPM. Hence, they are active in and responsible for processes at the same time. They may be supported by → Experts and → Facilitators.

Additional Semantics

For individual subjects or states within the behavioral description, it is possible to specify an additional semantic and thus state the reasons for the existence of a subject or state within a process or for individual states in a behavior description.

Alignment → IT/BUSINESS ALIGNMENT

Analysis

Once an S-BPM project has started, the analysis is usually performed first. It involves a purposeful collection and analysis of relevant process information in preparation for the next steps. The distinguishing characteristic of the subject-oriented analysis is its focus on subjects, predicates, and objects. It implements systemic thinking by using the information about business processes to determine authorities or roles that serve as reference points. The key benefit for organizations using the method of S-BPM for analysis is that work performers (→ Actors) and managers (→ Governors) are directly involved in the collection and evaluation.

Behavior → SUBJECT BEHAVIOR

Behavior Macro

A behavior macro is a state that can be included multple times at any position in the behavior of a specific subject.

Behavior Macro Class

A behavior macro class is a behavioral description that can be included multiple times in the behavior of different subjects.

Behavior Reduction

Performance reduction refers to a simplification of the behavior of a subject to those aspects that need to be recognized by another subject who wants to communicate with the reduced subject. This other subject is only interested in the communication behavior of the partner.

Business Activity Monitoring (BAM)

The concept of Business Activity Monitoring (BAM) is the continuous, business-oriented monitoring and evaluation of business process instances in real time. BAM not only deals with financial key performance indicators, but also with technical indicators such as database response times, in the course of continuous monitoring. Business Activity Monitoring uses, along with periodic and ad hoc reports, permanently measured data. However, it immediately processes it in a stream-oriented data analysis (stream-and-analyze) using methods from → Complex Event Processing (CEP).

Business Objects

Business objects are those business-relevant components that characterize the work process. They represent data (possibly with the underlying, managed tools), which → subjects need to accomplish their tasks. In → Subject-oriented Business Process Management, those objects are represented that are relevant for the exchange of messages between subjects and for implementing the various activities of the subjects.

Business Process

A business process is a set of interrelated activities (tasks) which are handled by active entities (people or systems performing work tasks) in a logical (with respect to business) and chronological sequence, and which use resources (material, information) to work on a business object for the purpose of satisfying a customer need (to thus contribute an added value), and which have a defined start and input, as well as a defined end state and result.

Business Process Analysis → ANALYSIS

Business Process Implementation → INFORMATION-TECHNOLOGY (IT) IMPLEMENTATION, ORGANIZATION-SPECIFIC IMPLEMENTATION

Business Process Management (BPM)

The term Business Process Management (BPM) can be considered from two dimensions: The original, purely economic perspective refers to an integrated management approach in terms of documentation, design, optimization, implementation, management, and development of management, core, and support processes in organizations. It is intended to help to meet the needs of the stakeholders, especially of customers, and to achieve business objectives.

Meanwhile, in science and practice, the technical dimension of the IT support of business processes is also considered. This ranges from tools for documenting and modeling of processes, workflow engines for executing process instances using application software functionality (such as services of an ERP system), and business intelligence applications for evaluating process performance. Solutions with a high degree of coverage of these aspects are referred to as Business Process

Management Systems (BPMS) or, preferably by software vendors, as business process management suites.

Business Process Model → MODEL

Business Process Modeling → MODELING

Business Process Monitoring → MONITORING

Business Process Optimization → OPTIMIZATION

Business Process Validation → VALIDATION

Communication Structure Diagram (CSD) → SUBJECT INTERACTION DIAGRAM (SID)

Complex Event Processing (CEP)

Complex event processing denotes a set of computational methods, techniques, and tools enabling the recognition and processing of events as soon as they occur, continuously and promptly. It is increasingly about the recognition and processing of event patterns (sets of facts) that only become obvious by combining several individual events (simple events) into so-called complex events. It is important that a probable occurrence of the complex event is inferred from the occurrence of simple events as soon possible, so that proactive measures for prevention or risk reduction can be taken.

Compliance → CORPORATE COMPLIANCE

Corporate Compliance

Corporate compliance is a → governance task and denotes concepts and actions, with which organizations seek to avoid risks resulting from violations of external and internal regulations, by ensuring compliance with these requirements. It is not about the obvious compliance with any applicable law, but about possible breaches of regulations that need to be put under the regime of risk management, and that need to be addressed by appropriate organizational, technical, and personnel measures. Examples of such measures are the design and implementation of appropriate processes (such as approval workflows), increased awareness, information and staff training, and regular monitoring and documentation of regulatory compliance, including sanctions for violations. Due to the close relation of compliance to governance and risk management, the concept of the Governance Risk Compliance (GRC) triad has emerged.

Corporate Governance

Corporate governance is understood as a management system used for corporate management and monitoring, which is oriented towards the long-term creation of value, while following both legal and ethical principles. It is grounded on several acts, such as in Germany on the German Corporate Governance Code, the Law on Control and Transparency Act (KonTraG), and the Accounting Law Modernization Act (BilMoG). From corporate governance, → IT governance is derived.

Embedding

In the → organization-specific implementation, the abstract elements of the model are mapped to specific components of the organization. This mapping is also termed embedding. When → subjects are embedded, they become → subject carriers, embedding → activities leads to specific → tasks.

Exception Handling

An exception handling (also termed message guard or message control, message monitoring, message observer) is a behavioral description for a subject that is relevant when a specific exception condition occurs in the → subject behavior. A specific branch is activated, in case a corresponding → message is received and the subject is in a state in which this message is allowed to jump to exception handling.

Experts

In many situations it is necessary for → Actors to seek specialized support. For this purpose, an Expert, another → S-BPM stakeholder, is needed, and is either solicited by the → Facilitator of the development process, or by the → Governors, or by the → Actors themselves. An Expert is used for various issues as a problem solver.

External Subject

An external subject represents in a process at hand the → interface subject to an interlinked process. Mutual referencing leads to a → process network.

Facilitators

A Facilitator guides organizational development and is one of the four categories of → S-BPM stakeholders. He supports the → Actors when initiating organizational development steps and when moving from one bundle of activities to another. He accompanies the process for introducing or adapting a process. His recommendations have influence on the organizational development. In addition, the Facilitator structures and supports the communication of actors with domain experts. As such, he can be understood as a catalyst of organizational development. He could even succeed in developing other involved → S-BPM Actors professionally or personally.

Freedom of Choice

Freedom of choice refers to the right granted to a → subject carrier to make its own decisions for a variety of options in its behavior.

General Conditions

Business process management comprising the various → bundles of activities cannot be considered as being independent of the environment of an organization. It is embedded in the business environment, e.g., business system and IT environment of an organization; the vision, strategy, and culture for BPM and risk management; → Corporate Governance and → Corporate Compliance. These conditions are designed primarily by → Governors.

Governance → CORPORATE GOVERNANCE

Governance Risk Compliance (GRC) Triad
   Metaphor for the interdependence and increasing importance of → Governance / → IT Governance, Risk Management, and → Corporate Compliance / → IT Compliance.

Governors (caretakers, drivers, and responsible people)

Governors are → S-BPM stakeholders taking responsibility for all constraints of a process and having an influence on the respective work and development processes. Their job is to bridge the gap in organizational development between management responsibilities and operational business. Although, they are not in charge of the domain-specific and technical control of a process, they must ensure that processes meet the given standards: A process should always be viewed in the context of an entire organization. Therefore, for its deployment, requirements of corporate governance should exist (e.g., → Corporate Compliance, → IT Compliance). These must be followed in the course of the implementation.

Information Technology (IT) Implementation

For the realization of IT support, a business process must be designed in terms of a → Workflow, which is a detailed description of a business process from an IT perspective.

Input Pool

An input pool is a message buffer for each subject, the purpose of which is to address problems in asynchronous message exchange. It is used to buffer all messages having been sent to the subject, regardless of which communication partner they come from. The input pools are therefore "mailboxes" for flexible configuration of the message exchange between subjects. In contrast to buffers, in which always only the front message can be seen and taken, this pool solution allows removing any message.

   Instance → PROCESS INSTANCE

Interface Subject

An interface subject represents, for a link to a subject within a → process network, the subject to be referred to in the linked process. In the considered process, it is modeled as an → external subject.

IT/Business Alignment

IT/Business Alignment is the alignment of IT with business requirements to optimize IT utilization and its associated value contribution. This alignment is an essential task of → IT Governance. In the context of alignment, enabling should also be considered. This denotes the inverse relationship in which IT provides the impetus for the business, e.g., by facilitating new business models (enabling).

IT Governance

IT Governance has been derived from → Corporate Governance. It should ensure by appropriate leadership and the same organizational structures and processes that IT supports the achievement of business objectives, while resources are responsibly used and risks properly monitored.

Key Performance Indicator (KPI)

A Key Performance Indicator (KPI) is a process measure of particular importance for an organization in terms of a critical success factor. Common Key Performance Indicators are the satisfaction of external or internal customers, the quality of the process results, the adherence to deadlines for the delivery of results, the process time (throughput time, cycle time), and the process costs.

Messages

Messages are used for representing interaction relations of → subjects during process execution. They transmit simple parameters or complex information structures, such as → Business Objects.

Model

All models are, with the help of → Model Description Languages, descriptions created by humans to represent their perceived reality. Business process models are mostly diagrammatic representations of → business processes and describe the activities and communication structure of the work force, the application systems, machinery, data, and other aids or tools involved. They are a medium to build a common reference for all participants to the activities and the supporting technology. Thus, business process models should not only be intelligible to the experts creating them, but also to those who will later work according to the model (i.e., business process description), or are supposed to supplement the processes using corresponding tools. On the one hand, there are the stakeholders or users who express how they should or can perform their activities, and on the other hand, there are software developers, who integrate specific application programs into a process, and other stakeholders, who, e.g., evaluate the business process. The business process and its model allow all stakeholders to develop a common understanding of business operations. A business process model is the basic pattern, according to which process instances for specific situations are generated. For instance, a model of the process "business trip application" describes how the process works in principle, while a → process instance of the process denotes the actual execution of a business trip application of an employee according to the model.

Model Description Language

A model description language consists of a reservoir of symbols (e.g., graphical, mathematical, and natural-language characters) and a syntax for their permissible combination. On the semantic level, → modeling conventions provide for a uniform interpretation.

A modeling language exists that everyone is capable of mastering and which is generally sufficient for an initial description of business activities: the natural language. Its advantage is that it is familiar to everybody, and can be immediately understood and used by all. Task or process descriptions are therefore almost always created in their first version in natural language, enriched with diagrams.

Modeling

In general, modeling is seen as a representation which reduces the complexity of a certain part of perceived reality by using a → Model Description Language. Business process modeling is intended to capture, present, reflect, and (further) develop matters that are relevant to business processes. It is essentially meant to (re) present, which subjects (humans, machines as actors) perform what activities (tasks, functions) on which objects (usually information bound to specific carriers), using what tools (e.g., IT systems), and how they interact, in order to achieve the desired process goals and results. In the S-BPM approach, the subjects are representatives for participating agents in a process, and are as such in the center of attention. The model is constructed along the following steps in which the associated level of detail increases moving forward:

- Identification of processes in an organization: The result is a process map with the processes and their interrelationships.
- Specification of the communication structure: On the basis of the identified subjects and their interactions, in this step, the communication structure of a business process, including the messages exchanged between the subjects, can be determined (→ Subject Interaction Diagrams).
- Specification of the behavior of the subjects involved in the process: Here the work steps of the subjects and the set of rules to follow thereby are specified (→ Subject Behavior Diagrams).
- Description of the information that all subjects involved in the process edit locally and mutually exchange via messages (→ Business Objects).

Modeling by Construction

This modeling method of construction is a commonly known procedure: The starting point is a process in which nothing is initially clearly defined. It begins with a "blank sheet of paper", and then a process model is successively built. The involved subjects, their activities, and business objects need to be introduced step by step. When designing a process model, the → Actors start with the 'blank sheet of paper' already mentioned. Using the results from analysis, the process can be described step by step according to the following structure:

- Description of processes and their relationships (→ Process Network)
- Identification of the process to be described
- Identification of the subjects involved in the process
- Identification of the messages exchanged between the subjects
- Description of the behavior of the individual subjects
- Definition of business objects and their use

These activities need not be carried out in a strictly sequential way. It can occur, e.g., that it is recognized during the description of the behavior of subjects that messages need to be added or removed later on. In this way, the process model is continuously expanded. Model development by construction is also common to other modeling techniques, such as UML, BPMN, and EPCs. With these it is, however, the only possible course of action, while subject orientation additionally allows → modeling by restriction.

Modeling by Restriction

Starting point here is a "world" of subjects that can do everything at first and are able to communicate with all other subjects. Modeling starts with an open model in which all communication links between subjects are possible. The starting point for modeling by restriction corresponds to a picture in which everybody using modern communications technology can exchange any information with any partner at any place anytime. In S-BPM, the world before modeling by reduction is a "universal process", where everyone communicates with everyone. This process is restricted more and more in its possible sequences until the desired process is present. This is done by gradually omitting those components which are not needed for accomplishing the task. The method of reduction is possible only with subject orientation.

Modeling Convention

With the help of modeling conventions, the diagram types, elements, attributes to be detailed, the graphic layout, etc., to be used for modeling in an organization or a project, are defined. This ensures that even different modelers create uniform models that are suitable for each specific modeling purpose.

Monitoring

The collection and compilation of data from running processes to support decision making in case of deviation from a predefined target behavior is the subject of monitoring. A permanent, real-time monitoring of process efficiency in the key dimensions of quality, time, and cost may counteract such developments and also often allow identifying opportunities for improvement. Usually, IT systems with appropriate functionality record values for suitable key performance indicators, compare them with predetermined target values, report deviations outside of tolerance limits, and so provide the basis for an analysis of root causes and subsequent actions. Addressees of the recorded data and exception reports are initially the work performers as → Actors, and the → process owner as → Governor who interpret the results and take appropriate action. Process monitoring, which is also referred to as Process Performance Measurement or operational process control, represents the logically last→ bundle of activities of the open S-BPM development cycle. Since a value recorded in the course of ongoing operations is usually interpreted spontaneously by the addressee, monitoring is linked very closely to the activity bundle of → analysis. It is an essential part of Process Performance Management (PPM), which deals with the planning, measurement, evaluation, and control of business processes. PPM in turn is part of a company-wide Corporate Performance Management (CPM) referring to the overall business performance.

Multi-Process

A multi-process is a set of similar processes that run independently. The actual number of independent sub-processes is only determined at runtime.

Natural Language

Natural languages are used for communication between people. Natural languages have three major semantic components. These are the subject of an action as a starting point, the predicate as the performed action, and the object as the target of the action. These three elements define a complete sentence using the proper natural language sentence semantics. This facilitates the description of → business processes: In processes, there are also actors who perform actions on certain objects.

Normalization

Normalization determines, on the one hand, the coarsest grain description of a process, and on the other hand, the minimum granularity for process descriptions. The normalization of → subject behavior is also needed to determine the observable external behavior of a process.

Organizational Structure

The organizational structure of an organization determines organizational units, such as departments and job positions, as well as authorizations and decision-making responsibilities. It forms the complement to the → operational structure of an organization.

Organization-Specific Implementation

A process not only needs to be implemented technically, but also introduced into the organization. In doing so, abstract → subjects are assigned to concrete people, the → subject carriers, and → activities become → concrete tasks of employees.

Open loop S-BPM → S-BPM-PROCEDURE MODEL

Operational Structure

The operational structure of an organization comprises the processes for managing work (business processes). It can be considered complementary to the → organizational structure.

Optimization

In the framework of optimization, the efficiency of processes is the focus of the activities. Optimization includes a systematic approach for the collection of measurements and for their subsequent analysis with regards to the organization's goals. In principle, each of the → S-BPM stakeholders could contribute to optimization efforts with different methods.

Procedure Model → S-BPM PROCEDURE MODEL

Process Controlling

Process control encompasses all activities aimed at strategic and operational monitoring and control of → business processes.

Process Costs

Process costs denote the effort required for executing a → process instance. In process cost accounting, the costs of individual process activities are associated with execution units. A differentiation is made here between performance volume-induced costs and performance volume-neutral overheads. Volume-neutral overheads are basic costs incurring for a process at all times. Volume-induced costs are instance-based and play a role only when executing the process.

Process Implementation → INFORMATION TECHNOLOGY (IT) IMPLE-MENTATION → ORGANIZATION-SPECIFIC IMPLEMENTATION

Process Instance

A process instance, in contrast to a process model, is an executed occurrence of the modeled process. It comes into being when a business transaction of the associated type is triggered at runtime.

Process Model → MODEL

Process Modeling → MODELING

Process Monitoring → MONITORING

Process Network Diagram (PND)

Process network diagrams show only processes linked in a process network, and the messages exchanged across their borders. They compress → Subject Interaction Diagrams with mutual references between → interface subjects or → external subjects.

Process Networks

By linking subjects of different processes, complex process networks can be built. Relations are expressed by mutually referencing → interface subjects and → external subjects.

Process Optimization → OPTIMIZATION

Process Owner

The process owner denotes a role, position, or person that is responsible for a process within the organization. Process ownership is valid across functional borders or lines in organizational structures.

Process Performance Management → MONITORING

Process Validation → VALIDATION

Reporting

Reporting covers the preparation, delivery, and distribution of → monitoring results in the form of reports. For the presentation of results, conventional tables and graphical means, such as executive dashboards or cockpits, are used.

S-BPM → SUBJECT-ORIENTED BUSINESS PROCESS MANAGEMENT

S-BPM-Bundle of Activities → ACTIVITY BUNDLE

S-BPM Methodology → S-BPM PROCEDURE MODEL

S-BPM Procedure Model

The procedure for the implementation of subject-oriented business processes is described as S-BPM-procedure model. The objects of concern of the procedure model are business processes that are designed along the → activity bundles → analysis, → modeling, → validation, → optimization, → organization-specific implementation, → IT implementation, operation, and → monitoring. The activity bundles in S-BPM are usually performed in an open loop, controlled by the → S-BPM stakeholders in a situation-sensitive way.

S-BPM Stakeholders

Stakeholders are the actors in the → S-BPM procedure model. In a sense, in S-BPM they are meta-subjects driving the design process. Caretakers, drivers, and managers (→ Governors) create the conditions under which → Actors perform operational work, potentially in collaboration with → Experts. → Governors are also responsible for organizational development. The respective stages of development are supported by organizational development guides (→ Facilitators), potentially also involving experts. S-BPM provides no hierarchical structure of the stakeholders. It therefore requires no explicit management structures. In addition, in S-BPM the classical distinction between business and IT is dissolved. Representatives from both areas can be found in all roles.

S-BPM Tools

The following tools supporting the → S-BPM procedure model were currently available at the time this book was published: jBOOK is a documentation tool to support subject-oriented analysis. jSIM can be used to simulate processes based on subject-oriented models on the computer. The Metasonic Suite encompasses a range of tools: The module "Build" supports the modeling of subjects, their behavior, their interactions, and the thereby exchanged messages and business objects, "Proof" enables distributed, computer-aided validation, and "Flow" controls as a process engine the execution of instances with all of the participants involved in the process. The base module includes among other things the "Usermanager", which can be used by those responsible for organization specific implementation for the assignment of users to roles and subjects.

Service

Subjects use services to communicate with other subjects, or to access → business objects. In S-BPM, a service is closely linked to a subject. Hence, a → service-oriented architecture can also be constructed according to subject orientation.

Service-Oriented Architecture (SOA)

Service-oriented architectures describe software systems, which are composed of loosely coupled function components (services). Each service takes clearly defined technical tasks and encapsulates application logic and data. The entire logic of a business application can thus be distributed to many independent services. The individual services can be reused in different contexts.

Service Process

A service process is a process that has a defined result and can be used by several other processes for service provision. On the side of the service process, coupling to the calling process occurs via a so-called general-external subject which represents all potential processes using the service process. Within the calling process, the → interface subject is used as an → external subject.

States

For subjects, we distinguish between action states for accomplishing a task (function state), and communication states for interacting with other subjects (receive and send). Such a consideration leads to three different types of states for subjects:
- Performing functions (function state)
- Sending messages (send state)
- Receiving messages (receive state)

Subject

Subjects represent humans or technical systems, such as machines or computer programs, with a particular behavior. As actors in defined roles they perform their individual tasks and interact with each other in order to structure and coordinate their joint activities to achieve the desired process result. Normally, they use appropriate tools, as well as information and business objects which they access for reading or writing, and which they exchange. Subjects have an identifier referring to each specific process and a corresponding → subject behavior.

Subject Behavior

The actions of a subject in a process are called subject behavior. → States and transitions describe what actions it performs and their associated interdependencies. Besides the communication actions send and receive, a subject performs so-called internal actions / functions.

Subject Behavior Diagram (SBD)

The complete behavior of a subject is described in the subject behavior diagram (SBD). It consists of → states and transitions.

Subject Carrier

As part of the → organization-specific implementation, abstract subjects are assigned to specific people, the so-called carrier subjects.

Subject Class

A subject class is an abstract subject which is assigned a certain subject name at process execution time.

Subject Interaction Diagram (SID)

A Subject Interaction Diagram illustrates the interaction relationships between the → subjects involved in a process. These are the → messages being exchanged between the subjects. Such messages may, if necessary, contain structured information, so-called → Business Objects. The result is the Subject Interaction Diagram (SID) as a structured model for subjects with explicit communication relationships, which is synonymously referred to as the Communication Structure Diagram (CSD).

Subject Orientation

Subject orientation is understood in S-BPM as the alignment of business processes to actors, or executing IT components, which in the course of business activities are linked to other subjects by means of communication relationships. It establishes a consistent → S-BPM procedure model. The focus is on the collaborating participants in processes and owners of processes, sharing in a globally networked structure the knowledge of a company. Thus, S-BPM is a holistic approach to development of organizations – and this against the background of processes that can very easily be integrated in subject-oriented form into complex and heterogeneous IT landscapes.

Subject-Oriented Business Process Management (S-BPM)

S-BPM puts the subject of a process at the center of attention. Hence, business processes and their organizational environment are considered from a communication perspective of the involved actors.

Subject-Oriented Description of a Process

The subject-oriented description of a process starts with the identification of process-specific roles involved in the process, the → subjects, and the → messages exchanged between them. When sending messages, the data required by the receiver is transmitted as simple parameters or more complex → Business Objects. In a further refinement step, it is described which activities and interactions the subjects are performing for completing the process and in which order, i.e., the → subject behavior of individual subjects is defined. For each subject, the sequence is specified in which it sends and receives messages, and executes internal operations, as well as in what → associated states it is in(send, receive, function state). Each state and transition in a subject description is finally assigned to an operation, without further detailing it at that point in time.

Subject-Oriented Model

The essential elements of a subject-oriented model are:
- Subjects involved in the process
- Interactions occurring between them
- Messages they send or receive in every interaction
- Behavior of individual subjects

The description of a subject determines the order in which it sends and receives messages, or performs internal functions. Its behavior thus defines the order in which the subject triggers which predicates (operations). This may be the standard predicates sending or receiving, or other predicates that are defined on the corresponding objects.

Subject-Predicate-Object in Modeling

Depending on the essential model elements, different approaches to modeling can be used in the course of defining business processes. Around these essential elements, accidentals are grouped. The following aspects of modeling in software development are currently being used:
- In functional approaches, functions are central. Examples of function-oriented models are control flow diagrams and data flow diagrams according to deMarco, or event-driven process chains (EPCs).
- In data-oriented approaches, accidentals are grouped around data. A well-known example of data-driven modeling approaches are Entity-Relationship diagrams.
- In object-oriented approaches, accidentals are grouped around objects. Objects in computer science are data structures and the operations on these data structures.

The object-oriented modeling approach is currently considered to be the most accepted one. A well-known method of description is the Unified Modeling Language (UML).

Task

A task is a work step carried out by a → subject carrier in the course of its → subject behavior in a specific → process instance.

Validation

In process management, validation is considered as a review of whether a business process is effective, i.e., of whether its expected result is delivered in the form of a product or service. This understanding corresponds to ISO 9001's (processes of production and service provision) required proof that a process is capable of meeting the required specifications and quality attributes. As an output of a process, not only the process result from the customer perspective is considered, but also its contribution to the implementation of corporate strategy, i.e., its value proposition. The validation should ensure that the process meets its requirements ("doing the right things"). In addition, the specification of process results and procedures, as acquired and specified in the course of analysis and modeling, should enable an organization to meet its objectives related to the process. It differs from → optimization, where the goal is to improve the efficiency of the model through simulation ("doing things right"). Otherwise, validation and optimization may coincide. Thus, in practice, at a validation workshop, recognized optimization approaches are usually also considered.

Workflow

When implementing IT support, a business process needs to be represented as a workflow. This consists of a detailed specification of a process from an IT perspective. A workflow is a:

- Formal description of
- Activities which
- Communicating actors (roles/people, embedded IT systems) perform
- In a partially or completely automated way on
- Objects (inputs and outputs, including data structures)
- In compliance with business rules and
- Controlled by the business logic.

Hence, a workflow is a refinement of the purely functional business process for the implementation of the corporate strategy (what?), in terms of IT support (how?).

A Subject-Oriented Interpreter Model for S-BPM

We develop in this appendix a high-level subject-oriented interpreter model for the semantics of the S-BPM constructs presented in this book. To directly and faithfully reflect the basic constituents of S-BPM, namely *communicating agents*, which can perform arbitrary *actions* on arbitrary *objects,* Abstract State Machines are used which explicitly contain these three conceptual ingredients.

1   Introduction

Subject-oriented Business Process Modeling (S-BPM) is characterized by the use of three fundamental natural language concepts to describe distributed processes: actors (called *subjects*), which perform arbitrary *actions* on arbitrary *objects* and in particular communicate with other subjects in the process, computationally speaking agents, which perform abstract data type operations and send messages to and receive messages from other process agents. We provide here a mathematically precise definition for the semantics of S-BPM processes, which directly and faithfully reflects these three constituent S-BPM concepts and supports the methodological goal pursued in this book to lead the reader through a precise natural language description to a reliable understanding of S-BPM concepts and techniques.

The challenge consists in building a scientifically solid S-BPM model, which faithfully captures and links the understanding of S-BPM concepts by the different stakeholders and thus can serve as basis for the communication between them: analysts and operators on the process design and management side, IT technologists and programmers on the implementation side, users (suppliers and customers) on the application side. To make a transparent, sufficiently precise and easily maintainable documentation of the meaning of S-BPM concepts available which expresses a common understanding of the different stakeholders we have to *start from scratch,* explaining the S-BPM constructs as presented in this book without dwelling upon any extraneous (read: not business process specific) technicality of the underlying computational paradigm.

A. Fleischmann et al., *Subject-Oriented Business Process Management,*   315
DOI 10.1007/978-3-642-32392-8, © The Author(s) 2012

To brake unavoidable business process specific complexity into small units a human mind can grasp reliably, we use a *feature-based* approach, where the meaning of the involved concepts is defined itemwise, construct by construct. For each investigated construct, we provide a dedicated set of simple IF-THEN-descriptions (so-called behavior rules), which abstractly describe the operational interpretation of the construct.[1] The feature-based approach is enhanced by the systematic use of *stepwise refinement* of abstract operational descriptions.

Last but not least, to cope with the distributed and heterogeneous character of the large variety of cooperating S-BPM processes, it is crucial that the model of computation which underlies the descriptions supports both *true concurrency* (most general scheduling schemes) and *heterogeneous state* (most general data structures covering the different application domain elements).

For these reasons, we use the method of Abstract State Machines (ASMs) (Börger et al. 2003), which supports feature and refinement based descriptions[2] of heterogeneous distributed processes and in particular allows one to view interacting subjects as rule executing communicating agents (in software terms: multiple threads each executing specific actions), thus matching the fundamental view of the S-BPM approach to business processes.

Technically speaking, the ASM method expects from the reader only some experience in process-oriented thinking, which supports an understanding of so-called transition rules (also called ASM rules) of form:

if *Condition* **then** ACTION

prescribing an ACTION to be undertaken if some event happens; happening of events is expressed by corresponding *Condition*s (also called rule *guards*) becoming true. Using ASMs guarantees the needed generality of the underlying data structures because the states which are modified by executing ASM rules are so-called *Tarski structures*, i.e., sets of arbitrary elements on which arbitrary updatable functions (operations) and predicates (properties and relations) are defined. In the case of business process objects, the elements are placeholders for values of arbitrary types and the operations typically the creation, duplication, deletion, modification of objects. Views are projections (substructures) of Tarski structures.

Using such rules, we define a succinct high level and easily extendable S-BPM behavior model the business process practitioner can understand directly, without further training, and use (a) to reason about the design and (b) to hand it over to a software engineer as a binding and clear specification for a reliable and justifiably correct implementation.

---

[1] This rigorous operational character of the descriptions offers the possibility to use them as a reference model for both simulation (testing) and verification (logical analysis of properties of interest) of classes of S-BPM processes.

[2] Since ASM models support an intuitive operational understanding at both high and lower levels of abstraction, the software developer can use them to introduce in a rigorously documentable and checkable way the crucial design decisions when implementing the abstract ASM models. Technically this can be achieved using the ASM refinement concept see (Börger et al. 2003, Sect. 3.2.1).

For the sake of quick understandability and to avoid having to require from the reader some formal method expertise, we paraphrase the ASM rules by natural language explanations, adopting Knuth's literate programming (Knuth et al. 1992) idea for the development of abstract behavior models. The reader who is interested in the details of the simple foundation of the semantics of ASM rule systems, which can also be viewed as a rigorous form of pseudo-code, is referred to the ASM-Book (Börger et al. 2003). Here, it should suffice to draw the reader's attention to the fact that for a given ASM with rules R_i ($1 \leq i \leq n$) in each state all rules R_i whose guard is true in this state are executed simultaneously, in one step. This parallelism allows one to hide semantically irrelevant details of sequential implementations of independent actions.

The ASM interpreter model for the semantics of S-BPM we describe in the following sections is developed by stepwise refinement, following the gradually proceeding exposition in this book. Thus we start with an abstract interaction view model of subject behavior diagrams (Sect. 2, based upon Sect. 5.5.3, which is refined in Sect. 3 by detailed descriptions of the communication actions (send and receive) in their various forms (canceling or blocking, synchronous or asynchronous and including their multiprocess forms, based upon Sect. 5.6.4) and further refined by stepwise introduced structuring concepts: structured actions—alternative actions (Sect. 4, based upon Sect. 5.5.5, 5.7.5)—and structured processes: macros (Sect. 5.1, based upon Sect. 5.7), interaction view normalization (Sect. 5.2, based upon Sect. 5.5.6), process networks and observer view normalization (Sect. 5.3, based upon Sect. 5.6). Two concepts for model extension are defined in Sect. 6. They cover in particular the exception handling model proposed in Sect. 5.7.6, 5.7.7.

We try to keep this appendix on an S-BPM interpreter technically self-contained though all relevant definitions are supported by the explanations in the preceding chapters of the book.

2   Interaction View of Subject Behavior Diagrams

An S-BPM *process* (shortly called process) is defined by a set of subjects each equipped with a diagram, called the *subject behavior diagram* (SBD) and describing the behavior of its subject in the process. Such a process is of distributed nature and describes the overall behavior of its subjects, which interact with each other by sending or receiving messages (so-called send/receive actions) and perform certain activities on their own (so-called internal actions or functions).

2.1   Signature of Core Subject Behavior Diagrams

Mathematically speaking, a subject behavior diagram is a directed graph. Each node represents a state in which the underlying subject[3] can be in when executing

---

[3] Where needed we call an SBD a *subject*-SBD and write also $SBD_{subject}$ to indicate that it is an SBD with this underlying *subject*.

an activity associated to the node in the diagram. We call these states *SID_states* (Subject Interaction Diagram states) of the subject in the diagram because they represent the state a subject is in from the point of view of the other subjects it is interacting with in the underlying process, where it only matters whether the subject is communicating (sending or receiving a message) or busy with performing an internal function (whose details are usually not interesting for and hidden to the other subjects). The incoming and the outgoing edges represent (and are labeled by names of) the subject's SID-state transitions from *source(edge)* to *target(edge)*. The *target(outEdge)* of an *outEdge* ∈ *OutEdge(node)* is also called a successor state of *node* (element of the set *Successor(node)*), the *source(inEdge)* of an *inEdge* ∈ *InEdge(node)* a predecessor state (in the diagram an element of the set *Predecessor (node)*).

As distinguished from SID-states (and usually including them) the overall states of a subject are called *data states* or simply *states*. They are constituted by a set of interpreted (possibly abstract) data types, i.e., sets with functions and predicates defined over them, technically speaking Tarski structures, the states of Abstract State Machines. SID-states of a subject are implicitly parameterized by the diagram in which the states occur since a subject may have different diagrams belonging to different processes; if we want to make the parameter D explicit, we write $SID\_state_D(subject)$ or $SID\_state(subject, D)$.

The SID-states of a subject in a diagram can be of three types, corresponding to three fundamental types of activity associated to a node to be performed there under the control of the subject: *function states* (also called internal function or action node states), *send states*, and *receive states*. The activity (operation or method) associated to and performed under the control of the subject at a *node* (read: when the subject is in the corresponding SID-state) is called *service(node)*. We explain in Sect. 3 the detailed behavioral meaning of these services for sending resp. receiving a message (interaction via communication) and for arbitrary internal activities (e.g., activities of a human or functions in the sense of programming). In a given function state, a subject may go through many so-called internal (Finite State Machine like) control states to each of which a complex data structure may be associated, depending on the nature of the performed function. These *internal states* are hidden in the SID-level view of subject behavior in a process, also called *normalized behavior* view and described in Sect. 5.2. The semantics of the interaction view of SBDs is defined in this section by describing the meaning of the transitions between SID-states in terms of communication and abstract internal functions.

A transition from a source to a target SID-state is allowed to be taken by the subject only when the execution of the service associated to the source node has been *Completed* under the control of this subject. This completion requirement is called synchrony condition and reflects the sequential nature of the behavior of a single subject, which in the given subject behavior diagram performs a sequence of single steps. Correspondingly each arc exiting a node corresponds to a termination condition of the associated service, also called *ExitCondition* of the transition represented by the arc and usually labeling the arc; in the wording used for labeling arcs often the *ExitCondition* refers only to a special data state condition reached

Fig. B.1 SID-transition
graph structure

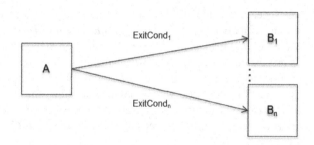

upon service completion, but it is assumed to always contain the completion requirement implicitly. In case more than one edge goes out of a node, we often write *ExitCond$_i$* for the *ExitCond*ition of the *i*-th outgoing arc.

The nodes (states) are graphically represented by rectangles and by a systematic notational abuse sometimes identified with (uniquely named) occurrences of their associated service whose names are written into the rectangle. It is implicit in the graphical representation that given a SID-state (i.e., a node in the graph), the associated service and the incoming and outgoing edges are functions of the SID-state.

Each SBD is assumed to be finite and to have exactly one *initial state* and at least one (maybe more than one) *end state*. It is assumed that each path leads to at least one end state. It is permitted that end states have outgoing edges, which the executing subject may use to proceed from this to a successor state, but each such path is assumed to lead back to at least one end state. A *process* is considered to *terminate* if each of its subjects is in one of its end states.

2.2   Semantics of Core Subject Behavior Diagram Transitions

The semantics of subject behavior diagrams *D* can be characterized essentially by a set of instances of a single SID-transition scheme BEHAVIOR(*subj, state*) defined below for the transition depicted in Fig. B.1. It expresses that when a *subj*ect in a given SID-*state* in *D* has *Completed* a given action (function, send or receive operation)—read: PERFORMing the action has been *Completed* while the *subj*ect was in the given SID-*state*, assuming that the action has been STARTED by the *subj*ect upon entering this *state*—then the *subj*ect PROCEEDS to START its next action in its successor SID-state, which is determined by an *ExitCond*ition whose value is defined by the just completed action. This simple and natural transition scheme is instantiated for the three kinds of SID-states with their corresponding action types, namely by giving the details of the meaning of STARTing an action and PERFORMing it until it is *Completed* for internal functions and for sending resp. receiving messages (see Sect. 3).

Technically speaking, the SID-transition scheme is an Abstract State Machine rule BEHAVIOR(*subj, state*) describing the transition of a *subj*ect from an SID-state with associated service *A* to a next SID-state with its associated service after (and only after) PERFORMing *A* has been *Completed* under the control of the subject.

The successor state with its associated service to be STARTED next—in Fig. B.1 one among B_i associated to the *target(outEdge(state, i))* of the *i*-th *outEdge(state, i)* outgoing *state* for $1 \leq i \leq n$—is the target of an outgoing edge *outEdge* that satisfies its associated exit condition *ExitCond(outEdge)* when the *subj*ect has *Completed* to PERFORM its action *A* in the given *SID_state*. The outgoing edge to be taken is selected by a function *select$_{Edge}$*, which may be defined by the designer or at runtime by the user. In BEHAVIOR(subj, *state*), the else-branch expresses that it may take an arbitrary a priori unknown number of steps until PERFORMing *A* is *Completed* by the *subj*ect.

```
BEHAVIOR( subj, state) =
  if SID_state (subj) = state then
    if Completed(subj, service(state), state) then
      let edge =
      select_Edge ({e ∈ OutEdge (state) | ExitCond (e)(subj,
          state)})
        PROCEED( subj,  service  (target  (edge)),  target
        (edge))
    else PERFORM (subj, service (state), state)
  where
    PROCEED(subj, X, node) =
      SID_state(subj) := node
      START(subj, X, node)
```

Remark. Each SID-transition is implicitly parameterized via the SID-states by the diagram to which the transition parameters belong, given that a (concrete) subject may be simultaneously in SID-states of subject behavior diagrams of multiple processes.

We define the BEHAVIOR$_{subject}$ (D) of a *subject* behavior diagram D as the set of all ASM transition rules BEHAVIOR(*subject, node*) for each *node* $\in$ *Node(D)*

```
BEHAVIOR_subj (D) = { BEHAVIOR (subj, node) | node ∈ Node (D) }
```

When *subj*ect is known, we write BEHAVIOR(D) instead of BEHAVIOR$_{subj}$ (D). BEHAVIOR*(D)* represents an interpreter of *D*.

This definition yields the traditional concept of (terminating) standard computations (also called *standard runs*) of a *subject* behavior diagram (from the point of view of subject interaction), namely sequences $S_0, \ldots, S_n$ of states of the subject behavior diagram where in the initial resp. final state S_0, S_n the *subject* is in the initial resp. a final SID-state and where for each intermediate S_i (with $i < n$) with SID-state say *state$_i$* its successor state S_{i+1} is obtained by applying BEHAVIOR (subject, *state$_i$*). Usually we only say "computation" or "run" omitting the "standard" attribute.

Remark. One can also spell out the SBD-BEHAVIOR rules as a general SBD-interpreter *Interpreter$_{SBD}$*, which given as input any SBD *D* of any *subject* walks through this diagram from the initial state to an end state, interpreting each diagram *node* as defined by BEHAVIOR(*subject, node*).

Remark. BEHAVIOR(*subj, state*) is a scheme which uses as basic constituents the abstract submachines PERFORM, START and the abstract completion predicate *Completed* to describe the pure interaction view for the three kinds of action in a subject behavior diagram: that an action is STARTed and PERFORMed by a subject until it is *Completed* hiding the details of how START, PERFORM, and *Completed* are defined. These constituents can be specialized further by defining a more detailed meaning for them to capture the semantics of specific internal functions and of particular send and receive patterns. Technically speaking, such specializations represent ASM-refinements [as defined in (Börger 2003)]. We use examples of such ASM-refinements to specify the precise meaning of the basic S-BPM communication constructs (see Sect. 3) and of the additional S-BPM behavior constructs (see Sect. 4). The background concepts for communication actions are described in Sect. 3.1; Sect. 3.3 and 3.4 present refinements defining the details of send and receive actions.

3   Refinements for the Semantics of Core Actions

Actions in a core subject behavior diagram are either internal functions or communication acts. Internal functions can be arbitrary manual functions performed by a human subject or functions performed by machines (e.g., represented abstractly or by finite state machine diagrams or by executable code written in some programming language) and are discussed in Sect. 3.5.

3.1   How to Perform Alternative Communication Actions

For each communication node, we refine in this section and Sects. 3.2–3.4 the abstract machines START, PERFORM, and the abstract predicate *Completed* to the corresponding concepts of STARTing and PERFORMing the communication and the meaning of its being *Completed*. Since the alternative communication version naturally subsumes the corresponding 1-message version (i.e., without alternatives where exactly one message is present to be sent or received), we give the definitions for the general case with communication action alternatives and derive from it the special 1-message case as the one where the number of alternatives is 1. The symmetries shared by the two *ComAct*ion versions *Send* and *Receive* are made explicit by parameterizing machine components of the same structure with an index *ComAct*.

In this section three concepts are described which are common to and support the detailed definition of both communication actions send and receive in Sects. 3.2.–3.4: subject interaction diagrams describing the process communication structure, input pool of subjects, and the iterative structure of alternative send/receive actions.

Subject Interaction Diagram The communication structure (signature) of a process is defined by a *Subject Interaction Diagram* (SID). These diagrams are directed graphs consisting of one node for each subject in the process (so that without loss of generality nodes of an SID can be identified with subjects) and one directed arc from node *subject₁* to node *subject₂* for each type of message, which may be sent in the process from $subject_1$ to $subject_2$ (and thereby received by $subject_2$ from $subject_1$). Thus SID-edges define the communication connections between their source and target subjects and are labeled with the message type they represent. There may be multiple edges from $subject_1$ to $subject_2$, one for each type of possibly exchanged message.

Input Pools To support the asynchronous understanding of communication, which is typical for distributed computations, each subject is assumed to be equipped with an *inputPool* where messages sent to this subject (called *receiver*) are placed by any other subject (called *sender*) and where the receiver looks for a message when it "expects" it (i.e., is ready to receive it).

An *inputPool* can be configured by the following size restrictions:

- Restricting the overall capacity of *inputPool*, i.e., the maximal number of messages of any type and from any sender, which are allowed to be *Present* at any moment in *inputPool*
- Restricting the maximal number of messages coming from an indicated *sender*, which are allowed to be *Present* at any moment in the *inputPool*
- Restricting the maximal number of messages of an indicated *type*, which are allowed to be *Present* at any moment in *inputPool*
- Restricting the maximal number of messages of an indicated *type* and coming from an indicated *sender*, which are allowed to be *Present* at any moment in the *inputPool*

For a uniform description of synchronous communication, 0 is admitted as value for input pool size parameters. It is interpreted as imposing that the *receiver* accepts messages from the indicated sender and/or of the indicated type only via a rendezvous with the *sender*.

Asynchronous communication is characterized by positive natural numbers for the input pool size parameters. In the presence of such size limits, it may happen that a sender tries to place a message of some type into an input pool, which has reached the corresponding size limit (i.e., its total capacity or its capacity for messages of this type and/or from that sender). The following two strategies are foreseen to handle this situation:

- *Canceling send* where either (a) a forced message deletion reduces the actual size of the input pool and frees a slot to insert the arriving message or (b) the incoming message is dropped (i.e., not inserted into the input pool).
- *Blocking send* where the sending is blocked and the sender repeats the attempt to send its message until either (a) the input pool becomes free for the message to be inserted or (b) a timeout has been reached triggering an interrupt of this send action or (c) the sender manually abrupts its send action.

Three canceling disciplines are considered, namely to drop the incoming message or to delete the oldest resp. the youngest message m in P, determined in terms of the *insertionTime(m, P)* of m into P.[4]

```
youngestMsg (P) =
    ι m(m ∈ P and forall m' ∈ P if m' ≠ m then
        insertionTime (m, P) > insertionTime (m', P)) // m
        came later
oldestMsg (P) =
    ι m(m ∈ P and forall m' ∈ P if m' ≠ m then
        insertionTime (m, P) < insertionTime (m', P)) // m
        came earlier
```

Whether a send action is handled by the targeted input pool P as canceling or blocking depends on whether in the given state the pool satisfies the size parameter constraints, which are formulated in a pool *constraintTable*. Each row of *constraintTable(P)* indicates for a combination of *sender* and *msgType* the allowed maximal *size* together with an *action* to be taken in case of a constraint violation:

```
constraintTable (inputPool) =
    ...
    sender_i msgType_i size_i action_i (1 ≤ i ≤ n)
    ...
where
    action_i ∈ {Blocking, DropYoungest, DropOldest,
    DropIncoming}
    size_i ∈ {0, 1, 2, ..., ∞}
    sender_i ∈ Subject
    msgType_i ∈ MsgType
```

When a sender tries to send a message *msg* to the owner of an input pool P, the first *row = s t n a* in the *constraintTable(P)* is identified whose size constraint concerns *msg* and would be violated by inserting *msg*:

```
ConstraintViolation(msg, row) iff[5]
    Match (msg, row) ∧ size ({m ∈ P | Match (m, row)}) +1 > n
    where
    Match(m, row) iff
        (sender (m) = s or s = any) and (type (m) = t or t = any)
```

If there is no such row—so that the first such element in *constraintTable(P)* is **undef**—the message can be inserted into the pool; otherwise, the action indicated in the identified row is taken, thus either blocking the sender or accepting the message (by either dropping it or inserting it into the pool at the price of deleting another pool element).

---

[4] We use Hilbert's ι -operator to express by $\iota\, x\, P(x)$ the unique element satisfying property P.
[5] iff stands for: if and only if.

It is required that in each row r with *size* $= 0$, the *action* is *Blocking* and that in case *maxSize(P)* $< \infty$, the *constraintTable* has the following last (the default) row:

```
any any maxSize Blocking
```

Similarly a (possibly blocking) receive action tries to receive a message, "expected" to be of a given kind (i.e., of a given type and/or from a given sender) and chosen out of finitely many alternatives (again either nondeterministically or respecting a given priority scheme), with possible timeout to abort unsuccessful receives (i.e., when no message of the expected kind is in the input pool) or a manual abort chosen by the subject.

Since in a distributed computation more than one subject may simultaneously try to place a message to the input pool P of a same receiver, a selection mechanism is needed (which in general will depend on P and therefore is denoted $select_p$) to determine among those subjects that are *TryingToAccess* P the one which *CanAccess* it to place the message to be sent.[6]

```
CanAccess(sender, P) if and only if
    sender = select_p ({subject | TryingToAccess (subject,
    P) })
```

Alternative Send/Receive Iteration Structure S-BPM forsees so-called *alternative* send/receive states where to perform a communication action *ComAct (Send or Receive)* the subject can do three things in order:

- Choose an *alt*ernative among finitely many *Alternatives*,[7] i.e., message kinds associated to the send/receive state
- Prepare a corresponding *msgToBeHandled*: for a send action a *msgToBeSent* and for a receive action an *expectedMsg* kind
- TRYALTERNATIVE$_{ComAct}$, i.e., try to actually send the *msgToBeSent* resp. receive a message *Match*ing the kind of *expectedMsg*

---

[6] One can formally define the *TryingToAccess* predicate, but the $select_p$ function is deliberately kept abstract. There are various criteria one could use for its further specification and various mechanisms for its implementation. A widely used interpretation of such functions in a distributed environment is that of a nondeterministic choice, which can be implemented using some locking mechanism to guarantee that at each moment at most one subject can insert a message into the input pool in question. The negative side of this interpretation is that proofs of properties of systems exhibiting nondeterministic phenomena are known to be difficult. Attempts to further specify the selection (e.g., by considering a maximal waiting time) introduce a form of global control for computing the selection function that contradicts the desired decentralized nature of an asynchronous communication mechanism (and still does not solve the problem of simultaneity in case different senders have the same waiting time). One can avoid infinite waiting of a subject (for a moment where it *CanAccess* a pool) by governing the waiting through a timeout mechanism.

[7] We consider *Alternative* as dependent on two parameters, *subject* and *state*, to prepare the ground for service processes where the choice of *Alternatives* in a *state* may depend on the subject type the client belongs to. Otherwise *Alternative* depends only on the *state*. In the currently implemented diagram notation, the *Alternatives* appear as pairs of a receiver and a message type, each labeling in the form *(to receiver, msgType)* an arc leaving the alternative send *state* in question.

The choice and preparation of an alternative is defined below by a component CHOOSE&PREPAREALTERNATIVE$_{ComAct}$ of TRYALTERNATIVE$_{ComAct}$.

If the selected *alt*ernative fails (read: could not be communicated neither asynchronously nor in a synchronous manner between sender and receiver), the subject chooses the next *alt*ernative until:

- Either one of them succeeds, implying that the send/receive action in the given state can be *Completed* normally.
- Or all *Alternative*s have been tried out but the *TryRoundFinished* unsuccessfully.

After such a first (so-called *nonblocking* because noninterruptible) TryRound a second one can be started, this time of *blocking* character in the sense that it may be interrupted by a *Timeout* or *UserAbruption*.

This implies iterations through a runtime set *RoundAlternative* of alternatives remaining to be tried out in both the first *(nonblocking)* and the other *(blocking)* TryRounds in which the subject for its present *ComAct* action has to TRYALTERNA-TIVE$_{ComAct}$. *RoundAlternative* is initialized for the first round in START, namely to the set *Alternative (subj, node)* of all alternatives of the *subj*ect at the *node* and reinitialized at the beginning of each blocking round.

Since the blocking TryRound can be interrupted by a *Timeout*-triggered INTER-RUPT or by a ("manually") *UserAbruption-triggered* ABRUPTion, there are three outgoing edges to PROCEED from a communication *node*. We use three predicates *NormalExitCond*, *TimeoutExitCond*, *AbruptionExitCond* to determine the correct *node* exit when the *ComAct* completes normally or due to the *Timeout* condition[8] or due to a *UserAbruption*. One of these three cases will eventually occur so that the corresponding exit condition then determines the next SID-state where the subject has to PROCEED with its run. To guarantee a correct behavior, these three exit conditions and the completion predicate are initialized in START to false. Since the machines are the same for the two *ComAct*ion cases *(Send* or *Receive)*, we parameterize them in the definition below by an index *ComAct*.

Since the actual blocking presents itself only if none of the possible alternatives succeeds in a first run, *blockingStartTime(subject, node)*—the timeout clock, which depends on the subject and the state *node*, not on the messages—is set only after a first round of unsuccessful sending attempts, namely in the submachine INITIALIZE-BLOCKINGTRYROUNDS. As a consequence, the *Timeout* condition guards TRYALTER-NATIVE$_{ComAct}$ only in the blocking rounds. Timeouts are considered as of higher priority than user abruptions.

This explains the following refinement of the abstract machine PERFORM to PERFORM *(subj, ComAct, state)*. The flowchart in Fig. B.2 visualizes the structure of PERFORM *(subj, ComAct, state)*.[9] The symmetry between nonblocking and

---

[8] *TimeoutExitCond* is only a name for the timeout condition we define below, namely *Timeout (msg, timeout (state))*; in the diagram, it is written as edge label of the form *Timeout : timeout*.

[9] These flowcharts represent so-called control-state ASMs which come with a precise semantics, see (Börger et al. 2003, p.44). Using the flowchart representation of control-state ASMs allow one to save some control-state guards and updates. To make this exposition self-contained, we provide

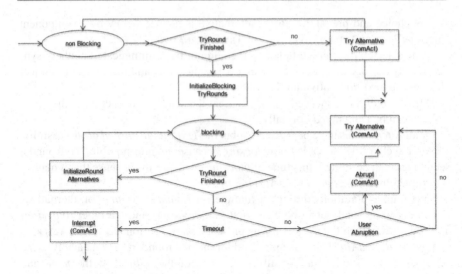

Fig. B.2 Perform (subj, ComAct, state)

blocking TryRounds is illustrated by a similar coloring of the respective components, whereas the components for the timeout and user abruption extensions are colored differently. Outgoing edges without target node denote possible exits from the flowchart. The equivalent textual definition (where we define also the components) reads as follows.

PERFORM *(subj, ComAct, state)* =
    if *NonBlockingTryRound(subj, state)* **then**
      if *TryRoundFinished(subj, state)* **then**
        INITIALIZEBLOCKINGTRYROUNDS *(subj, state)*
      else TRYALTERNATIVE$_{ComAct}$ *(subj, state)*
    if *BlockingTryRound(subj, state)* **then**
      if *TryRoundFinished (subj, state)*
      then INITIALIZEROUNDALTERNATIVES *(subj, state)*
      else
        if *Timeout (subj, state, timeout (state))*
        then INTERRUPT$_{COMACT}$ *(subj, state)*
        elseif *UserAbruption(subj, state)*
          then ABRUPT$_{ComAct}$ *(subj, state)*
          else TRYALTERNATIVE$_{ComAct}$ *(subj, state)*

---

however the full textual definition and as a consequence allow us to suppress in the flowchart some of the parameters.

Macros and Components of PERFORM (*subj, ComAct, state*) We define here also the START(*subj, ComAct, state*) machine. The function *now* used in SETTIMEOUTCLOCK is a monitored function denoting the current system time.

START(*subj, ComAct, state*) =
  INITIALIZEROUNDALTERNATIVES(*subj, state*)
  INITIALIZEEXIT&COMPLETIONPREDICATES$_{ComAct}$(*subj, state*)
  ENTERNONBLOCKINGTRYROUND(*subj, state*)
where
  INITIALIZEROUNDALTERNATIVES(*subj, state*) =
    RoundAlternative(subj, state) := Alternative (subj, state)
  INITIALIZEEXIT&COMPLETIONPREDICATES$_{ComAct}$(*subj, state*) =
    INITIALIZEEXITPREDICATES$_{ComAct}$(*subj, state*)
    INITIALIZECOMPLETIONPREDICATE$_{ComAct}$(*subj, state*)
  INITIALIZEEXITPREDICATES$_{ComAct}$(*subj, state*) =
    NormalExitCond(subj, ComAct, state) := false
    TimeoutExitCond(subj, ComAct, state) := false
    AbruptionExitCond(subj, ComAct, state) := false
  INITIALIZECOMPLETIONPREDICATE$_{ComAct}$(*subj, state*) =
    Completed(subj, ComAct, state) := false
  [Non]BlockingTryRound(subj, state) =
    tryMode(subj, state) = [non]blocking
  ENTER[NON]BLOCKINGTRYROUND(*subj, state*) =
    tryMode(subj, state) := [non]blocking
  TryRoundFinished(subj, state) =
    RoundAlternatives(subj, state) =
  INITIALIZEBLOCKINGTRYROUNDS(*subj, state*) =
    ENTERBLOCKINGTRYROUND(*subj, state*)
    INITIALIZEROUNDALTERNATIVES(*subj, state*)
    SETTIMEOUTCLOCK(*subj, state*)
  SETTIMEOUTCLOCK(*subj, state*) =
    blockingStartTime(subj, state) := now
  Timeout(subj, state, time) =
    $now \geq blockingStartTime(subj, state) + time$
  INTERRUPT$_{ComAct}$(*subj, state*) =
    SETCOMPLETITIONPREDICATE$_{ComAct}$(*subj, state*)
    SETTIMEOUTEXIT$_{ComAct}$(*subj, state*)
  SETCOMPLETITIONPREDICATE$_{ComAct}$(*subj, state*) =
    Completed(subj, ComAct, state) := true
  SETTIMEOUTEXIT$_{ComAct}$(*subj, state*) =
    TimeoutExitCond(subj, ComAct, state) := true
  ABRUPT$_{ComAct}$(*subj, state*) =
    SETCOMPLETITIONPREDICATE$_{ComAct}$(*subj, state*)
    SETABRUPTIONEXIT$_{ComAct}$(*subj, state*)

To conclude this section: an attempt to TRYALTERNATIVE$_{ComAct}$ comes in two phases: the first phase serves to CHOOSE&PREPAREALTERNATIVE and is followed by a second phase where the subject as we are going to explain in the next section will try to actually carry out the communication. If this attempt succeeds, the *ComAct* is *Completed*; otherwise the subject will try out the next send/receive alternative.

3.2   How to Try a Specific Communication Action

As explained in Sect. 3.1 subject's first step to TRYALTERNATIVE$_{ComAct}$ in [non] *blocking tryMode* is to CHOOSE&PREPAREALTERNATIVE$_{ComAct}$. Then it will TRY$_{ComAct}$ for the prepared message(s).[10]

$$\text{TRYALTERNATIVE}_{ComAct}\ (subj,\ state) =$$
$$\qquad \text{CHOOSE\&PREPAREALTERNATIVE}_{ComAct}\ (subj,\ state)$$

$$\qquad \textbf{seq}\ \text{TRY}_{ComAct}\ (subj,\ state)$$

We first explain the CHOOSE&PREPAREALTERNATIVE$_{ComAct}$ component for the elaboration of messages and then define the machines TRY$_{ComAct}$.

Elaboration of Messages Messages are objects which need to be prepared. The PREPAREMSG component of CHOOSE&PREPAREALTERNATIVE does this for each selected communication *alt*ernative. To describe the selection, which can be done either nondeterministically or following a priority scheme, we use abstract functions *select*$_{ALT}$ and *priority*. They can and will be further specified once concrete send *state*s are given in a concrete diagram.

CHOOSE&PREPAREALTERNATIVE also must MANAGEALTERNATIVEROUND, essentially meaning to MARKSELECTION—typically by deleting the selected alternative from *RoundAlternative*, to exclude the chosen candidate from a possible next AlternativeRound step, which may happen if sending/receiving the selected message is blocked.

There is one more feature to be prepared for due to the fact that S-BPM deals also with multiprocesses in the form of multiple send/receive actions, which extend single send/receive actions where only one message is sent resp. received to complete the communication act instead of *mult* many messages belonging to the chosen *alt*ernative.

In the S-BPM framework, a multiprocess is either a multiple send action (where a subject iterates finitely many times sending a message of some given kind) or a multiple receive action (where a subject expects to receive finitely many messages of a given kind). In the diagram notation, the (design-time determined) *mult*itude in question, which adds a new kind of message to communicate, appears as number of messages of some kind to be sent or to be received during a MultiSend or MultiReceive. It is assumed that *mult* $\geq$ 2. The principle of multiple send and

---

[10] Such a sequential structure is usually described using an FSM-like control state, say *tryMode*, as we do in the flowcharts below. For a succinct textual description, we use sometimes the ASM **seq** operator (see the definition in (Börger and Stärk 2003)), which allows one to hide control state guards and updates. For example in the definition of CHOOSE&PREPAREALTERNATIVE, we could skip an ENTERTRYALTERNATIVE$_{ComAct}$ update because the machine is used only as composed by **seq** (with TRY$_{ComAct}$ in TRYALTERNATIVE$_{ComAct}$).

receive actions in the presence of communication alternatives which is adopted for S-BPM is that once in a state a subject has chosen a MultiSend or MultiReceive alternative, to complete this multi-action it must send resp receive the indicated multitude of messages of the kind defined for the chosen alternative and in between will not pursue any other communication. Therefore the alternative send/receive TryRound structure (see Fig. B.2) and its START component are not affected by the multiprocess feature, but only the TRY$_{ComAct}$ component which has to provide a nested MultiRound. For MultiSend actions, it is also required that first all specimens of a *msgToBeHandled* are elaborated by the subject, as to-be-contemplated for the definition of CHOOSE&PREPAREALTERNATIVE$_{Send}$, and then they are tried to be sent one after the other.

Thus one needs a MultiRound to guarantee that if a multicommunication action has been chosen as communication *alt*ernative, then:

- Each of the *mult (alt)* many specimens belonging to the chosen message *alt*er-native is tried out exactly once.
- If for at least one of these specimens the attempt to communicate fails, the chosen *alt*ernative is considered to be failed.
- No other communication takes place within a MultiRound.

Thus each MultiRound constitutes one iteration step of the current AlternativeRound where the multicommunication action has been selected as alternative. Since single send/receive steps are the special case of multisteps where *mult (alt)* = 1 we treat single-/multicommunication actions uniformly instead of introducing them separately.[11]

In the presence of multicommunication actions for each alternative one has to INITIALIZEMULTIROUND, as done in the MANAGEALTERNATIVEROUND component of CHOOSE&PREPAREALTERNATIVE defined below.

This explains the following *ComAct*ion preparation machine a *subj*ect will execute in every communication *state* as first step of TRYALTERNATIVE$_{ComAct}$. As before the *ComAct* parameter stands for *Send* or *Receive*.

CHOOSE&PREPAREALTERNATIVE$_{ComAct}$ (subj, state) =
  let alt = select$_{Alt}$(RoundAlternative(subj,state),pri-ority(state))
    PREPAREMSG$_{ComAct}$ (subj, state, alt)
    MANAGEALTERNATIVEROUND (alt, subj, state)

---

[11] The price to pay is a small MultiRound overhead (which can later be optimized away for the single action case *mult (alt)* = 1). In an alternative model, one could introduce first single communication actions (as they are present in the current implementation) and then extend them in a purely incremental way by the multiprocess feature. Both ways to specify S-BPM clearly show that the extension of S-BPM from SingleActions to MultiActions (for both Send and Receive actions) is a *purely incremental* (in logic also called conservative) *extension*, which does only add new behavior without retracting behavior that was possible before. It supports a modular design discipline and compositional proofs of properties of the system. Notably all the other extensions defined in S-BPM are of this kind. See Sect. 6 for further explanations.

where

MANAGEALTERNATIVEROUND(alt, *subj, state*) =
    MARKSELECTION(subj, *state, alt*)
    INITIALIZEMULTIROUND $_{ComAct}$ (*subj, state*)
MARKSELECTION(subj, *state, alt*) =
    DELETE(alt, *RoundAlternative (subj, state)*)

A subject to PREPAREMSG$_{Send}$ will *composeMsg*s out of *msgData* (the values of the relevant data structure parameters) and make the result available in *MsgToBeHandled*.[12] Similarly a receiver to PREPAREMSG$_{Receive}$ may select *mult (alt)* elements from a set of *ExpectedMsgKind(alt)* using some choice function *select$_{MsgKind}$*.[13]

PREPAREMSG$_{ComAct}$ (*subj, state, alt*) =
forall $1 \leq i \leq mult$ *(alt)*
  if *ComAct = Send* **then**
    let $m_i = composeMsg(subj, msgData (subj, state, alt), i)$
        $MsgToBeHandled (subj, state) := \{m_1, \ldots, m_{mult (alt)}\}$
  if *ComAct = Receive* **then**
    let $m_i = select_{MsgKind (subj, state, alt, i)} (ExpectedMsgKind$
    (subj, state, alt))
        $MsgToBeHandled(subj, state) := \{m_1, \ldots, m_{mult (alt)}\}$

The functions *composeMsg* and *msgData* must be left abstract in this high-level model, playing the role of interfaces to the underlying data structure manipulations, because they can be further refined only once the concrete data structures are known which are used by the subject in the send state under consideration. It is however assumed that there are functions *sender(msg)*, *type(msg)*, and *receiver(msg)* to extract the corresponding information from a message so that *composeMsg* is required to put this information into a message. Similarly for the *expectedMsgKind* and *select$_{MsgKind}$* functions.

TRY$_{ComAct}$ **Components** The structure of the machines TRY$_{comAct}$ we are going to explain now is visualized by Figs. B.3 and B.4.

In TRY$_{comAct}$ the subject first chooses from *MsgToBeHandled* a message *m* (to send) or kind *m* of message (to receive) and—to exclude it from further choices—will MARKCHOICE of *m*.[14] Then the subject does the following:

---

[12] For a *Send (Multi)* alternative *mult (alt)* message specimens of the selected alternative will be composed, whereas for a *Send(Single)* action *MsgToBeHandled* will be a singleton set containing a unique element which we then denote *msgToBeSent*.

[13] In analogy to *msgToBeSent* we write also *msgKindToBeReceived* if there is a unique chosen kind of *MsgToBeHandled* by a receive action. This case is currently implemented.

[14] MARKCHOICE is the MultiRound pendant of MARKSELECTION defined in Sect. 3.1 for *AlternativeRounds*. We include into it a record of the current choice because this information is needed to describe the Rendezvous predicate for synchronous communication.

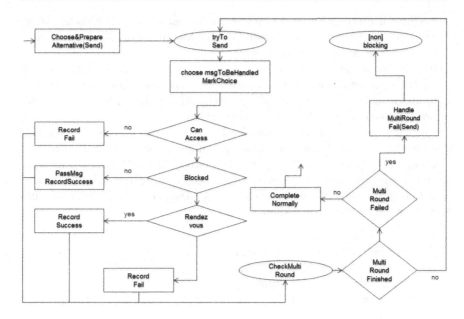

Fig. B.3 TryAlternativeSend

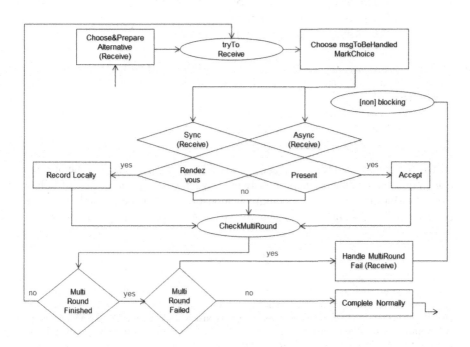

Fig. B.4 TryAlternativeReceive

- For *Send* it checks whether it *CanAccess* the input pool of the *receiver (m)* to TRY$_{Async(Send)}$ing *m* (otherwise it will CONTINUEMULTIROUNDF$_{Fail}$, which includes to RECORDFAILURE of this send attempt).
- For *Receive* it goes directly to TRY$_{Async(Receive)}$ or TRY$_{Sync(Receive)}$ a message of kind *m* depending on whether the *commMode(m)* is asynchronous (as expressed by the guard *Async(Receive)(m)*) or synchronous (as expressed by the guard *Sync (Receive)(m)*), without the *CanAccess* condition.[15]

Another slight asymmetry between send/receive actions derives from the fact that the sender tries a synchronous action only if the asynchronous one failed.

CONTINUEMULTIROUND$_{Fail}$ has a pendant CONTINUEMULTIROUND$_{Success}$ for successful communication. They record success resp. failure of the current MultiRound communication step and check whether to continue with the MultiRound or go back to the AlternativeRound.

```
TRY_ComAct (subj, state) =
    choose m ∈ MsgToBeHandled(subj, state)
      MARKCHOICE(m, subj, state)
      if ComAct = Send then
        let receiver = receiver(m), pool = inputPool
        (receiver)
        if not CanAccess(subj, pool) then
              CONTINUEMULTIROUND_Fail (subj, state, m)
        else TRY_Async(Send) (subj, state, m)
      if ComAct = Receive then
        if Async(Receive)(m) then TRY_Async(Receive) (subj,
        state, m)
        if Sync(Receive)(m) then TRY_Sync(Receive) (subj,
        state, m)
where
  MARKCOICE(m, subj, state) =
    DELETE(m, MsgToBeHandled(subj, state))
    currMsgKind(subj, state) := m
```

The components TRY$_{Async(ComAct)}$ and TRY$_{Sync(ComAct)}$ check whether the *ComAct*ion can be done asynchronously resp. synchronously and in case of failure CONTINUEMULTIROUND$_{Fail}$. If a communication turns out to be possible they use components[16] ASYNCH(*ComAct*) and SYNC(*ComAct*) which carry out the actual

---

[15] Thus the access of a *receiver* to its input *pool* (which comes up to read the pool and to possibly delete an expected message) can happen at the same time as an INSERT of a sender. One INSERT and one DELETE operation can be assumed to be executed consistently in parallel by the pool manager. An alternative would be to include the receiver into the *CanAccess* mechanism—at the price of complicating the definition of *RendezvousWithSender*.

[16] The parameter *ComAct* plays here the role of an index.

*ComAct*ion and CONTINUEMULTIROUND$_{Success}$. They are defined below together with *PossibleAsync$_{ComAct}$(subj, m)* and *PossibleSync$_{ComAct}$(subj, m)* by which they are guarded.

TRY $_{Async(ComAct)}$ *(subj, state, m)*
  if *PossibleAsync$_{ComAct}$(subj, m)* // async communication possible
    then ASYNC *(ComAct) (subj, state, m)*
    else
      if *ComAct = Receive* **then**
            CONTINUEMULTIROUND$_{Fail}$ *(subj, state, m)*
      if *ComAct = Send* **then** TRY$_{Sync(ComAct)}$ *(subj, state, m)*
TRY$_{Sync(ComAct)}$ *(subj, state, m)* =
  if *PossibleSync$_{ComAct}$(subj, m)* // sync communication possible
    then SYNC *(ComAct) (subj, state, m)*
    else CONTINUEMULTIROUND$_{Fail}$ *(subj, state, m)*

3.3 How to Actually Send a Message

In this section we define the ASYNCH(*Send*) and SYNC(*Send*) components which if the condition *PossibleAsync$_{Send}$* resp. *PossibleSync$_{Send}$* is true asynchronously or synchronously carry out the actual *Send* and CONTINUEMULTIROUND$_{Success}$.

PossibleAsync$_{Send}$(subj, m) means that *m* is not *Blocked* by the receiver's input pool so that in ASYNCH(*Send*) *subject* can send *m* asynchronously[17]: PASSMSG to the input pool and CONTINUEMULTIROUND$_{Success}$.[18]

PossibleSync$_{Send}$(subj, m) means that a *RendezvousWithReceiver* is possible for the *subj*ect whereby it can definitely send *m* synchronously via *SYNC$_{Send}$*. For the sender *subj*ect, this comes up to simply CONTINUEMULTIROUND$_{Success}$.

The prepared message becomes available through the *RendezvousWithReceiver* so that the receiver can RECORDLOCALLY it (see the definitions in Sect. 3.4).

In ASYNC(*Send*) the component PASSMSG(*msg*) is called[19] if the *msg* is not *Blocked*. Therefore *msg* insertion must take place in two cases: either *msg* violates no constraint row or it violates one and the action of the first row it violates is not

---

[17] The reader will notice that for *Send* actions the *PossibleAsync* predicate depends only on messages. We have included the *subject* parameter for reasons of uniformity, since it is needed for *PossibleAsync$_{Receive}$*.

[18] In case of a single send action, the subject will directly COMPLETENORMALLY$_{Send}$.

[19] Typically an implementation will charge the input pool manager to execute PASSMSG, even if here the machine appears as component of a *subj*-rule.

DropIncoming; in the second case also a DROP action has to be done to create in the input pool a place for the incoming *msg*.

ASYNC *(Send) (subj, state, msg)* =
    PASSMSG *(msg)*
    CONTINUEMULTIROUND$_{Success}$ *(subj, state, msg)*
where
    PASSMSG *(msg)* =
      let *pool = inputPool (receiver (msg))*
        row = first ({r ∈ constraintTable (pool) |
                            ConstraintViolation (msg, r)})
      if *row ≠* **undef and** *action (row) ≠ DropIncoming*
          then DROP *(action)*
      if *row =* **undef or** *action (row) ≠ DropIncoming* **then**
                  INSERT *(msg, pool)*
                  insertionTime (msg, pool) := now
    DROP *(action)* =
      if *action = DropYoungest* **then** DELETE *(youngestMsg (pool),*
      pool)
      if *action = DropOldest* **then** DELETE *(oldestMsg (pool), pool)*
    PossibleAsync$_{Send}$ (subj, msg) iff **not** *Blocked (msg)*
    Blocked (msg) iff
      let *row = first ({r ∈ constraintTable (inputPool (receiver*
      (msg))) |
                          ConstraintViolation (msg, r)})
            row ≠ **undef and** *action (row) = Blocking*

In SYNC(Send)*(subj, state, msg)* the *subj*ect has nothing else to do than to CONTINUEMULTIROUND$_{Success}$ because through the *RendezvousWithReceiver* the elaborated *msg* becomes available to the receiver which will RECORDLOCALLY it during its *RendezvousWithSender* (see Sect. 3.4).

SYNC *(Send) (subj, state, msg)* =
        CONTINUEMULTIROUND$_{Success}$ *(subj, state, msg)*
    PossibleSync$_{Send}$ (subj, msg) iff *RendezvousWithReceiver*
    (subj, msg)

Necessarily the following description of *RendezvousWithReceiver* refers to some details of the definitions for receive actions described in Sect. 3.4. Upon the first reading, this definition may be skipped to come back to it after having read Sect. 3.4.

For a *RendezvousWithReceiver(subj, msg)*, the receiver has to *tryToReceive* (see Fig. B.4) synchronously (i.e., the receiver has chosen a *currMsgKind*[20] which requests a synchronous message transfer, described in *Sync(Receive)*

---

[20] This MultiRound location is updated in MARKCHOICE.

(see Sect. 3.4) as *commMode (currMsgKind)* = *sync* and *subj*ect itself has to try a synchronous message transfer, i.e., the *msg* it wants to send has to be *Blocked* by the first synchronization requiring row which concerns *msg* (i.e., where *Match (msg, row)* holds) in the *constraintTable* of the receiver's input pool. Furthermore the *msg* the sender offers to send must *Match* the *currMsgKind* the receiver has currently chosen in its current *SID_state*.

```
RendezvousWithReceiver(subj, msg) iff
    tryMode(rec)   =   tryToReceive   and   Sync(Receive)
    (currMsgKind)
        and SyncSend(msg) and Match(msg, currMsgKind)
    where
    rec = receiver(msg), recstate = SID_state(rec)
    currMsgKind = currMsgKind(rec, recstate)
    blockingRow =
        first ({r ∈ constraintTable (rec) | Constraint-
        Violation (msg, r)})
    SyncSend(msg) iff size(blockingRow) = 0
```

Remark. The definition of *RendezvousWithReceiver* makes crucial use of the fact that for each subject its *SID_state* is uniquely determined so that for a subject in *tryMode tryToReceive* the selected receive alternative can be determined.

3.4   How to Actually Receive a Message

In this section we define the two ASYNC (Receive) and SYNC (Receive) components which asynchronously or synchronously carry out the actual *Receive* action and CONTINUEMULTIROUND$_{Success}$ if the conditions *PossibleAsync$_{Receive}$* resp. *PossibleSync$_{Receive}$* is satisfied.

There are four kinds of basic receive action, depending on whether the receiver for the currently chosen kind of expected messages in its current *alt*ernative is ready to receive ("expects") *any* message or a message from a particular *sender* or a message of a particular *type* or a message of a particular type from a particular sender. We describe such receive conditions by the set *ExpectedMsgKind* of triples describing the combinations of sender and message type from which the receiver may choose *mult (alt)* many for messages it will accept (see the definition of PREPAREMSG$_{Receive}$ in Sect. 3.1).

```
ExpectedMsgKind(subj, state, alt) yields a set of
3-tuples of form:
    s t commMode
where
    (s ∈ Sender or s = any) and (t ∈ MsgType or t = any)
    commMode ∈ {async, sync} // accepted communication mode
```

The communication mode decides upon whether the receiver will try to ASYNC (*Receive*) or to SYNC(*Receive*) a message of a chosen expected message kind.

Async(Receive)(m) holds if *commMode (m)* $=$ *async*. If a *subj*ect is called to ASYNC(*Receive)(subj, state, m*), it knows that a message satisfying the asynchronous receive condition *PossibleAsync$_{Receive}$(subj, m)* is *Present* in its input pool. It can then CONTINUEMULTIROUND$_{Success}$ and ACCEPT a message matching *m*. Since the input pool may contain at a given moment more than one message which matches *m*, to ACCEPT a message, one needs another selection function *select$_{ReceiveOfKind(m)}$* to determine the one message which will be received.

ASYNC *(Receive) (subj, state, msg)* $=$
  ACCEPT *(subj, msg)*
  CONTINUEMULTIROUND$_{Success}$ *(subj, state, msg)*
where
  ACCEPT *(subj, m)* $=$
   let *receivedMsg* $=$
        select$_{ReceiveOfKind(m)}$ *({msg* $\in$ *inputPool (subj)* $|$
        Match (msg, m) })
      RECORDLOCALLY *(subj, receivedMsg)*
      DELETE *(receivedMsg, inputPool (subj))*
  Async (Receive) (m) iff commMode (m) $=$ *async*
  PossibleAsync$_{Receive}$ (subj, m) iff Present (m, inputPool
  (subj))
  Present (m, pool) iff **forsome** *msg* $\in$ *pool Match (msg, m)*

When SYNC(*Receive)(subj, state*) is called, the receiver knows that there is a *sender* for a *RendezvousWithSender* (a subject which right now via a TRY$_{Send}$ action tries to and *CanAccess* the receiver's input pool with a matching message, see Sect. 3.3) to receive its *msgToBeSent*. The synchronization then succeeds: *subj*ect can RECORDLOCALLY the *msgToBeSent*, bypassing the input pool,[21] and CONTINUEMULTIROUND$_{Success}$(*subj, state, currMsgKind(subj, state)*).

SYNC *(Receive) (subj, state, msgKind)* $=$
  let *P* $=$ *inputPool (subj), sender* $=$ ι *s (CanAccess (s, P))*
  RECORDLOCALLY *(subj, msgToBeSent (sender, SID_state*
  (sender))
  CONTINUEMULTIROUND$_{Success}$ *(subj, state, msgKind)*
  Sync (Receive) (msgKind) iff commMode (msgKind) $=$ *sync*
  PossibleSyncReceive (subj, msgKind) iff
                 RendezvousWithSender (subj, msgKind)
  RendezvousWithSender (subj, msgKind) iff
    Sync (Receive) (msgKind) **and**

---

[21] The input pool is bypassed only concerning the act of passing the message from sender to receiver during the rendezvous. It is addressed however to determine the synchronization partner as the unique subject which in the given state can communicate with the receiver (whether synchronously or asynchronously), as mentioned in the footnote to the definition of TRY$_{Send}$ in Sect. 3.3.

> **let** *sender* = ι *s* (*CanAccess*(*s*, *inputPool* (*subj*))
> **let** *msgToBeSent* = *msgToBeSent*(*sender*, SID_state
> (*sender*))
>   *tryMode*(*sender*) = *tryToSend* **and** *SyncSend*(*msgToBe-*
>   *Sent*)
>   **and** *Match*(*msgToBeSent*, *msgKind*)

Remark. The definition of *RendezvousWithSender* makes crucial use of the fact that for each subject its *SID_state* is uniquely determined and therefore for a subject in *tryMode tryToSend* also the *msgToBeSent*. Thus through the rendezvous this message becomes available to the receiver to RECORDLOCALLY it.

The subcomponent structure of BEHAVIOR(*subj, state*) for *states* whose associated *service* is a *ComAct* (Send or Receive) is illustrated in Fig. B.5.

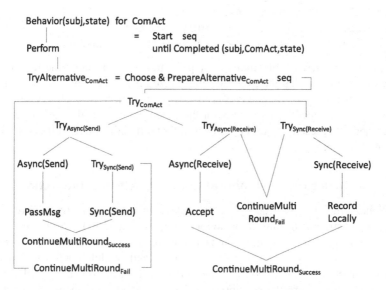

Fig. B.5 Subcomponent Structure for Communication Behavior

3.5   Internal Functions

A detailed internal BEHAVIOR of a *subject* in a *state* with internal function *A* can be defined in terms of the submachines START and PERFORM together with the completion predicate *Completed* for the parameters *(subj, A, state)* in the same manner as has been done for communication actions in Sect. 3.3 and 3.4—but only once it is known how to start, to perform and to complete *A*. For example, for Java coded functions *A* START(*subj, A, state*) could mean to call the (multithreaded) Java interpreter *execJavaThread* defined in terms of ASMs in [Stärk et al. (2001), p.101], PERFORM *(subj, A, state)* means to execute it step by step and the completion predicate coincides with the termination condition of *execJavaThread*. A still more detailed description, one step closer to executed code, can be obtained by a refinement, which replaces the computation of *execJavaThread* for *A* by a [in Stärk et al. (2001), Ch. 14] proven to be equivalent) computation of the Java Virtual Machine model (called *diligentVM$_D$* in [Stärk et al. (2001), p.303]) on *compile(A)*.

For internal *state*s with uninterpreted internal functions *A* the two submachines of BEHAVIOR(*state*) and the completion predicate remain abstract and the semantics of the SBD where they occur derives from the semantics of ASMs (Börger & Stärk 2003) for which the only requirement is that in an ASM state every function is interpreted even if the specification does not define the interpretation. The only requirement is that PERFORMing an internal action is guarded by an interrupt mechanism. This comes up to further specify the SID-transition scheme for internal actions by detailing its **else**-clause as follows:

> **if** *Timeout(subj, state, timeout (state))* **then**
>   INTERRUPT*$_{service\ (state)}$* *(subj, state)*
> **elseif** *UserAbruption(subj, state)*
>   **then** ABRUPT*$_{service(state)}$* *(subj, state)*
>   **else** PERFORM *(subj, service(state),state)*

Remark. An internal function is not permitted to represent a nested subject behavior diagram so that the SID-level normalized behavior view, the one defined by the subject behavior diagrams of a process (see Sect. 5.2), is clearly separated from the local subject behavior view for the execution of a single internal function by a subject. At present the tool permits as internal functions only self-services, no delegated service.

4   A Structured Behavioral Concept: Alternative Actions

Additional structural constructs can be introduced building upon the definitions for the core constructs of subject behavior diagrams: internal function, send, and receive. The goal is to permit compact structured representations of processes which make use of common reuse, abstraction, and modularization techniques. Such constructs can be defined by further refinements of the ASMs defined in Sect. 3 to accurately capture the semantics of the core SBD-constituents. The refined machines represent each a conservative (i.e., purely incremental) extension of the previous machines in the sense that on the core actions the two machines have the same behavior, whereas the refined version can also interpret additional constructs.

In this section we deal with a structural extension concerning the general behavior of subjects, namely alternative actions. In Sect. 5 extensions concerning the communication constructs will be explained.

The concept of alternative actions allows the designer to express the order independence of certain actions of a subject. This abstraction from the sequential execution order for specific segments in a subject behavior diagram run is realized by introducing so-called *alternative action* (also called alternative path) states, a structured version of SID-states which is added to communication and internal action states.

At an alternative action *state*, the computation of a subject splits into finitely many interleaved subcomputations of that subject, each following a (so-called alternative) subject behavior diagram *altBehDgm(state, i)* of that subject ($1 \leq i \leq m$ for some natural number m determined by the *state*). For this reason, such SID-*states* are also called *altSplit* states.

$$AltBehDgm(altSplit) = \{altBehDgm(altSplit, i) \mid 1 \leq i \leq m\}$$

Stated more precisely, to PERFORM ALTACTION—the *service* associated to an alternative action *state*—means to perform for some subset of these alternative SBDs the behavior of each subdiagram in this set, executed step by step in an arbitrarily interleaved manner.[22] Some of these subdiagram computations may be declared to be compulsory with respect to their being started respectively terminated before the ALTACTION can be *Completed*.

To guarantee for computations of alternative action states, a conceptually clear termination criterion in the presence of compulsory and optional interleaved subcomputations each altSplit *state* comes in pair with a unique *alternative action join* state *altJoin(state)*. The split and join states are decorated for each subdiagram D in *AltBehDgm(state)* with an *entryBox(D)* and an *exitBox(D)* where in the pictorial representation (see Fig. B.6) an x is put to denote the compulsory nature of entering resp. exiting the D-subcomputation via its unique *altEntry(D)* resp. *altExit(D)* state linked to the corresponding box. Declaring *altEntry(D)* and/or *altExit(D)* as *Compulsory* expresses the following constraint on the run associated to the ALTACTION split state:

- A compulsory *altEntry(D)* state must be entered during the run so that the D-subcomputation must have been started before the run can be *Completed*. It is required that every alternative action split state has at least one subdiagram with compulsory *altEntry* state.
- A compulsory *altExit(D)* state must be reached in the run, for the run to be *Completed*, if during the run a D-subcomputation has been entered at *altEntry(D)* (whether the *altEntry(D)* state is compulsory or not). It is required that every alternative action join state has at least one subdiagram with compulsory *altExit* state.[23]

When PROCEED takes the edge which leads out of *altExit(D)* to its successor state *exitBox(D)* (see Fig. B.6), the computation of the service associated to *altExit(D)* and therefore the entire D-subcomputation is completed. This does not mean yet that the entire computation of the ALTACTION state is *Completed: exitBox(D)* is a wait state to wait for all other to-be-exited subcomputations of the ALTACTION state to be completed too. Formally the *service* ALTACTIONWAIT associated to a wait state is empty and there is no isolated exit from a wait state (read: no wait action is ever *Completed* in isolation)

---

[22] It is natural to apply the interleaving policy to alternative steps of one subject. The model needs no interleaving assumption on steps of different subjects.

[23] This condition implies that if an alternative action node is entered where no subdiagram with compulsory *altExit* has a compulsory *altEntry*, the subcomputation of this alternative action is immediately *Completed*. Therefore it seems reasonable to require for alternative action nodes to have at least one subdiagram where both states *altEntry* and *altExit* are compulsory.

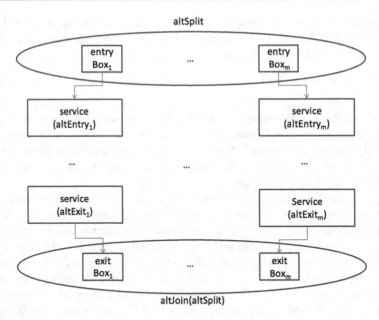

Fig. B.6 Structure of Alternative Action Nodes

but only a common EXITALTACTION from all relevant wait states once ALTACTION is *Completed* (see below). This is formalized by the following definition:

START($subj$, ALTACTIONWAIT, $exitBox$) =
    INITIALIZECOMPLETITIONPREDICATE$_{AltActionWait}$ ($subj$, $exitBox$)
PERFORM($subj$, ALTACTIONWAIT, $exitBox$) = **skip**

It is then stipulated that an ALTACTION—read: the run STARTED when entering an alternative action SID-state—is *Completed* if and only if for each subdiagram D with compulsory *altExit(D)* state the subject during the run has reached the *exitBox* *(D)* state—by construction of the diagram this can happen only through the *altExit* *(D)* after having *Completed* the *service* associated to this state and therefore the entire D-subcomputation—if in the run a subdiagram computation has been started at all at *altEntry(D)* of D.

Therefore from the SID-level point of view, the BEHAVIOR(*subj*, *node*) for an alternative action *node* is defined exactly as for standard nodes (with or without multiple (condition) exits); what is specific is the definition of STARTing and PERFORMing the steps of (read: the run defined by) an ALTACTION and the definition of when it is *Completed*. In other words we treat ALTACTION as the service associated to an alternative action state.

For the formal definition of what it means to START and to PERFORM the ALTACTION associated to an *altSplit* state, the fact is used that SID-states of a subject are (implicitly) parameterized by the diagram in which the states occur. As a result one can keep track of whether the subject is active in a subcomputation of one of the alternative subject behavior diagrams in *AltBehDgm(altSplit)* by checking whether the *SID_state(subj, D)* has been entered by the subject (formally: whether it is defined) for any of these subdiagrams D. Therefore START (*subj,* ALTACTION, *altSplit*) sets *SID_state (subj, D)* to *altEntry (D)* for each subdiagram D whose *altEntry(D)* state is *Compulsory* and guarantees that the associated *service (altEntry (D))* is STARTed. For the other subdiagrams, SID_state (subj, D) is initialized to **undef**.[24]

```
START(subj, ALTACTION, altSplit) =
   forall D ∈ AltBehDgm(altSplit)
          if Compulsory(altEntry (D)) then
              SID_state(subj, D) := altEntry(D)
              START(subj, service (altEntry (D)), altEntry D))
          else SID_state(subj, D) :=undef
```

As a consequence the computation of *subj*ect in a subdiagram D becomes active by defining the *SID_state (subj, D)* so that the formal definition of the completion condition for alternative actions nodes described above reads as follows[25]:

```
Completed(subj, ALTACTION, altSplit) iff
   forall D ∈ AltBehDgm(altSplit)
       if Compulsory(altExit (D)) and Active (subj, D)
          then SID_state(subj, D) = exitBox (D)
   where
       Active(subj, D) iff SID_state(subj, D) ≠ undef
```

Thus from the *altSplit* state, the *subj*ect reaches its unique SID-successor state *altJoin(altSplit)*,[26] where *subj*ect performs as EXITALTACTION action (with empty START) to reset *SID_state (subj, D)* for each alternative diagram D ∈ *AltBehDgm (altSplit)* and to SETCOMPLETIONPREDICATE$_{ExitAltAction}$, so that *subj*ect in the next step from here will PROCEED to a successor SID-state of the *altJoin(altSplit)* state.

```
START(subj, ExitAltAction, altJoin (altSplit)) = skip
PERFORM (subj, EXITALTACTION, altJoin) =
    forall D ∈ AltBehDgm (altSplit) SID_state (subj, D) :=
    undef
    SETCOMPLETIONPREDICATE$_{ExitAltAction}$ (subj, altJoin (altSplit))
```

---

[24] This definition of START implies that *entryBox(D)* is only a placeholder for the *Compulsory* attribute of D, whereas *exitBox(D)* is treated as a diagram state for ALTACTIONWAITing that the entire ALTACTION action is *Completed*.

[25] The completion predicate for alternative action nodes is a derived predicate, in contrast to its controlled nature for communication actions.

[26] In the diagram no direct edge connecting the two nodes is drawn, but it is implicit in the parenthesis structure formed by *altSplit* and *altJoin(altSplit)*.

To PERFORM a step of ALTACTION—a step in the subrun of an alternative action node—the subject either will PERFORMSUBDGMSTEP, i.e., will execute the BEHAVIOR as defined for its current state in any of the subdiagrams where it is active, or it will STARTNEWSUBDGM in one of the not yet active alternative behavior diagrams.

PERFORM($subj$, ALTACTION, $state$) =
  PERFORMSUBDGMSTEP($subj$, $state$)
    or STARTNEWSUBDGM($subj$, $state$)}
where
  PERFORMSUBDGMSTEP(s, n) =
    choose $D \in ActiveSubDgm(s, n)$ **in** BEHAVIOR(s, SID_state
    (s, D)))
  STARTNEWSUBDGM(s, n) =
    choose $D \in AltBehDgm(n) \setminus ActiveSubDgm(s, n)$
      $SID\_state(s, D) := altEntry(D)$
      START(s, $service(altEntry(D))$, $altEntry(D)$)
  $ActiveSubDgm(s, n) = \{D \in AltBehDgm(n) \mid Active(s, D)\}$
  R **or** $S =$ **choose** $X \in \{R, S\}$ **in** X

Remark. In each step of ALTACTION, the underlying *SID_state* is uniquely determined by the interleaving scheme: it is either the alternative action state itself (when STARTNEWSUBDGM is chosen) or the *SID_state* in the diagram chosen to PERFORMSUBDGMSTEP, so that it can be computed recursively. Therefore its use in defining *RendezvousWith...* is correct also in the presence of alternative actions.

Remark. The understanding of alternative state computations is that once the alternative clause is *Completed* none of its possibly still noncompleted subcomputations will be continued. This is guaranteed by the fact that the submachine PERFORMSUBDGMSTEP is executed (and thus performs a subdiagram step of *subj*ect) only when triggered by PERFORM in the *subj*ect's *altSplit* state, which however (by definition of BEHAVIOR(*subj, state*)) is not executed when *Completed* is true.

Remark. The tool at present does not allow nested alternative clauses, although the specification defined above also works for nested alternative clauses via the *SID_state(s, D)* notation for subdiagrams *D* which guarantees that for each diagram *D* each *subj*ect at any moment is in at most one *SID_state (subj, D)*. If the subdiagrams are properly nested (a condition that is required for alternative behavior diagrams), it is guaranteed by the definition of PERFORM for an ALTACTION that *altSplit* controls the walk of *subj* through the subdiagrams until ALTACTION is *Completed* at *altSplit* so that *subj* can PROCEED to its unique successor state *altJoin(altSplit)*; if one of the behavior subdiagrams of *altSplit* contains an alternative split state *state₁* with further alternative behavior subdiagrams, both *altSplit* and *state₁* together control the walk of *subj* through the subsubdiagrams until ALTACTION is *Completed* at *state₁*, etc.[27]

---

[27] Let SBDs $D, D_1, D_2, D_{11}, D_{12}$ be given where D is the main diagram with subdiagrams D_1, D_2 at an alternative action state *altSplit* and where D_1 contains another alternative action *state₁* with subdiagrams D_{11}, D_{12}. Then the *SID_state* of *subj* first walks through states in D (read: assumes as

Remark. The specification above makes no assumption neither on the nature or number of the states from where an alternative action node is entered nor on the number of edges leaving an alternative action node or the nature of their target states. For this reason Fig. B.6 shows no edge entering *altSplit* and no edge leaving *altJoin (altSplit)*.

Remark. Alternative action nodes can be instantiated by natural constraints on which entry/exit states are compulsory to capture two common business process constructs, namely **and** (where each entry- and exitBox has an x) and **or** (where no entry- but every exitBox has an x). A case of interest for testing purposes is **skip** (where no exitBox has an x).

5 Notational Structuring Concepts

This section deals with notational concepts to structure processes. Some of them can be described by further ASM refinements of the basic constituents of SBDs.

5.1 Macros

The idea underlying the use of macros is to describe once and for all a behavior that can be replicated by insertion of the macro into multiple places. Macros represent a notational device supporting to define processes where instead of rewriting in various places copies of some same subprocess, a short (possibly parameterized) name for this subprocess is used in the enclosing process description and the subprocess is separately defined once and for all. In the S-BPM context, it means to define SBD-macros, which can be inserted into given SBDs of possibly different (types of) subjects (participating in one process or even in different processes). The insertion must be supported by a substitution mechanism to replace (some of) the parameters of the macro-SBD by subject types or by concrete subjects that can be assumed to be known in the context of the SBD where the macro-SBD is inserted.

An SBD-macro (which for brevity will be called simply a macro) is defined to be an SBD, which is parameterized by finitely many subject types.[28] Usually the first parameter is used to specify the type of a subject into whose SBDs the macro can be inserted. The remaining parameters specify the type of possible communication partners of (subjects of the type of) the first parameter. Through these parameters what is called macro really is a scheme for various macro instances which are obtained by parameter substitution.

---

values of *SID_state (subj)* = *SID_state (subj, D)* nodes in *D*) until it reaches the *D*-node *altSplit*; *altSplit* controls the walks through *SID_state (subj, D_i)* states (for $i = 1,2$), in D_1 until *SID_state (subj, D_1)* reaches *state$_1$*. Then *altSplit* and *state$_1$* together control the walk through *SID_state(subj, D_{1j})* (for $j = 1, 2$) until the ALTACTION at node *state$_1$* is *Completed*. Then *altSplit* continues to control the walk through *SID_state (subj, D_i)* states (for $i = 1, 2$) until the ALTACTION at *altSplit* is *Completed*.

[28] This macro definition deliberately privileges the role of subjects, hiding the underlying data structure parameters of an SBD-macro.

To increase the flexibility in the use of macros, it is permitted to enter and exit an SBD-macro via finitely many *entryState*s resp. *exitEdge*s which can be specified at design time and are pictorially represented by so-called macro tables decorating so-called *macro states* (see Fig. B.7). They are required to satisfy some natural conditions (called *Macro Insertion Constraints*) to guarantee that if a *subject* during its walk through D reaches the macro state it will:

- Walk via one of the *entryState*s into the macro
- Then walk through the diagram of the macro until it reaches one of the *exitEdge*s
- Through the *exitEdge* PROCEED to a state in the enclosing diagram D

entryState$_1$	...	entryState$_n$
	M	
exitEdge$_1$	...	exitEdge$_m$

Fig. B.7 Macro Table associated to a Macro State

The macro insertion constraints are therefore about how the *entryState*s and *exitEdge*s are connected to states of the surrounding *subject* behavior diagram D if the macro name is inserted there. We formulate them as constraints for (implicitly) transforming an SBD D where a macro state appears by insertion of the macro SBD at the place of the macro state.

Macro Insertion Constraints When a *macroState* node with SBD-macro M occurs in a subject behavior diagram D, D is (implicitly) transformed into a diagram D[*macroState/M*] by inserting M for the *macroState* and redirecting the edges entering and exiting *macroState* such that the following conditions are satisfied:

1. Each D-edge targeting the *macroState* must point to exactly one *entryState* in the macro table and is redirected to target in D [*macroState/M*] this *entryState*, i,e., the state in the subject behavior diagram M where the subject has to PROCEED to upon entering the *macroState* at this *entryState*.
   - There is no other way to enter M than via its *entryState*s, i.e., in the diagram D [*macroState/M*] each edge leading into M is one of those redirected by constraint 1.
2. Each *exitEdge* in the macro table must be connected in D[*macroState/M*] to exactly one D-successor state *succ* of the *macroState*, i.e., the state in the enclosing diagram D where to PROCEED to upon exiting the macro SBD M through the *exitEdge*.
   - There is no other way to exit M than via its exitEdges, i.e., in the diagram D [*macroState/M*] each edge leaving the *macroState* node is one of those redirected to satisfy constraint 2.
3. Each *macro exit state* and no other state[29] appears in the macro table as source of one of the *exitEdge*s. A state in a macro diagram M is called macro exit state if in M there is no edge leaving that state.

---

[29] The second conjunct permits to avoid a global control of when a macro subrun terminates.

As a consequence of the macro insertion constraints, the behavior of an SBD-macro at the place of a *macroState* in an SBD is defined, namely as behavior of the inserted macro diagram.[30] This definition provides a well-defined semantics also to SBDs with well nested macros.

Remark. For defining the abstract meaning of macro behavior, it is not necessary to also consider the substitution of some macro parameters by names, which are assumed to be known in the enclosing diagram where the macro is inserted. These substitutions, which often are simply renamings, only instantiate the abstract behavior to something (often still abstract but somehow) closer to the to-be-modeled reality.

5.2   Interaction View Normalization of Subject Behavior Diagrams

Focus on communication behavior with maximal hiding of internal actions is obtained by the *interaction view* of SBDs (also called *normalized behavior view*) where not only every detail of a function state is hidden (read: its internal PERFORM steps) but also subpaths constituted by sequences of consecutive internal function nodes are compressed into one abstract internal function step. In the resulting *InteractionView(D)* of an SBD D (also called normalized SBD or function compression *FctCompression(D)*) every communication step together with each entry into and exit out of any alternative action state is kept,[31] but every sequence of consecutive function steps appears as compressed into one abstract function step. Thus an interaction view SBD shows only the following items:

- The initial state
- Transitions from internal function states to communication and/or alternative action states
- Transitions from communication or alternative action states
- The end states

Since interaction view SBDs are SBDs, their semantics is well defined by the ASM-interpreter described in the preceding sections. The resulting *interaction view runs*, i.e., runs of a normalized SBD, are distinguished from the standard runs of an SBD by the fact that each time the *subject* PERFORMs an internal action in a state, in the next state it PERFORMs a communication or alternative action (unless the run terminates).

For later use, we outline here a normalization algorithm, which transforms any SBD D by function compression into a normalized SBD *InteractionView(D)*. The idea is to walk through the diagram, beginning at the start node, along any path

---

[30] Different occurrences of the same SBD-macro M at different *macroStates* in an SBD may lead to different executions, due to the possibly different macro tables in those states.

[31] Alternative action nodes must remain visible in the interaction view of an SBD because some of their alternative behavior subdiagrams may contain communication states and others not. The other structured states need no special treatment here: multiprocess communication states remain untouched by the normalization and macros are considered to have their defining SBD to be inserted when the normalization process starts.

leading to an end node until all possible paths have been covered and to compress along the way every sequence of consecutive internal function computation steps into one internal function step. Roughly speaking in each step, say m, whenever from a given noninternal *state* through a sequence of internal function nodes a noninternal action or end state *state'* is reached, an edge from *state* to one internal function *node*—with an appropriately compressed semantically equivalent associated *service (node)*—and from there an edge to *state'* are added to *InteractionView(D)* and the algorithm proceeds in step $m + 1$ starting from every node in the set $Frontier_m$ of all such noninternal action or end nodes *state'* which have not been encountered before—until $Frontier_m$ becomes empty. Some special cases have to be considered due to the presence of alternative action nodes and to the fact that it is permitted that end nodes may have outgoing edges so that the procedure will have to consider also paths starting from end nodes or *altEntry* or *altJoin* states of alternative action subdiagrams.

Start Step. This step starts at the initial *start* state of D. *start* goes as initial state into *InteractionView(D)*. There are two cases to consider.

Case 1. *start* is not an internal function node (read: a communication or alternative action *altSplit* state[32]) or it is an end node of D. Then *start* will not be compressed with other states and therefore will be a starting point for compression rounds in the iteration step. We set $Frontier_1 := \{start\}$ for the iteration steps. If an edge from *start* to *start* is present in D, it is put into *InteractionView(D)* leaving the service associated to the *start* node in the normalized diagram unchanged.

Case 2. *start* is an internal function node. Then its function may have to be compressed with functions of successive function states. Let $Path_1$ be the set of all paths $state_1, \ldots, state_{n+1}$ in D such that $state_1 = start$ and the following **MaximalFunctionSequence** property holds for the path $state_1, \ldots, state_{n+1}$:

- For all $1 \le i \le n$, $state_i$ is an internal function node with associated service f_i and not an end state of D.
- $state_{n+1}$ is an end state of D or not an internal action state.[33]

Then each subpath $state_1, \ldots, state_n$ of a path in $Path_1$ (if there are any) is compressed into the *start* node[34] with associated service $(f_1, \ldots, f_n)$ and put into *InteractionView(D)* with one edge leading from *start* (which is then also denoted $state_{(1,\ldots,n)}$) to $state_{n+1}$. All final nodes $state_{n+1}$ of $Path_1$ elements are put into $Frontier_1$ and thus will be a starting point for iteration steps.

Iteration Step. If $Frontier_m$ is empty, the normalization procedure terminates and the obtained set *InteractionView(D)* is what is called the interaction view or normalized behavior diagram of D and denoted *InteractionView(D)*.

If $Frontier_m$ is not empty, let $state_0, \ldots, state_{n+1}$ be any element in the set $Path_{m+1}$ of all paths in D such that $state_0 \in Frontier_m$ and for the subsequence $state_1, \ldots,$

---

[32] A start state cannot be an *altJoin* (*altSplit*) state because otherwise the diagram would not be well formed.

[33] The end node clauses in these two conditions guarantee that end nodes survive the normalization.

[34] This guarantees that initial internal function states survive the compression procedure.

$state_{n+1}$ the MaximalFunctionSequence property holds. In case of an alternative action *altSplit* state in *Frontier*$_m$, as *state*$_0$ the *altEntry*$_i$ state of any alternative behavior subdiagram is taken, so that upon entering an alternative action node the normalization proceeds within the subdiagrams. The auxiliary wait action states *exitBox*$_i$ are considered as candidates for final nodes *state*$_{n+1}$ of to-be-compressed subsequences (read: not internal action nodes) so that they survive the compression and can play their role for determining the completion predicate for the alternative action node also in *InteractionView(D)*. The *altJoin (altSplit)* state is considered like a diagram start node so that it too survives the compression. This realizes that alternative action nodes remain untouched by the normalization procedure, though their subdiagrams are normalized.[35]

If the to-be-compressed internal functions subsequence contains cycles, these cycles are eliminated by replacing recursively every subcycle-free subcycle from *state*$_i$ to *state*$_i$ by one node *state*$_i$ and associated service $(f_i, \ldots, f_i)$. Then each cycle-free subsequence *state*$_1, \ldots$, *state*$_n$ obtained in this way from a path in *Path*$_{m+i}$ is further compressed into one node, say $state_{(1,\ldots,n)}$ with associated service $(f_1, \ldots, f_n)$ and is put into *InteractionView(D)* together with two edges, one leading from *state*$_0$ to $state_{(1,\ldots,n)}$ and one from there to *state*$_{n+1}$.

All final nodes *state*$_{n+1}$ of such compressed *Path*$_{m+1}$ elements, which are not in *Frontier*$_k$ for some $k \leq m$ (so that they have not been visited before by the algorithm), are put into *Frontier*$_{m+1}$ and thus may become a starting point for another iteration step. In the special case of an alternative action node: if *state*$_{n+1}$ is an *exitBox*$_i$ state, *exitBox*$_i$ is not placed into *Frontier*$_{m+1}$ because the subdiagram compression stops here. The normalization continues in the enclosing diagram by putting instead *altJoin (altSplit)* into *Frontier*$_{m+1}$.

5.3 Process Networks

This section explains a concept which permits to structure processes into hierarchies via communication structure and visibility and access right criteria for processes and/or subprocesses.

Process Networks and their Interaction Diagrams An *S-BPM process network* (shortly called process network) is defined as a set of S-BPM processes. Usually the constituent processes of a process network are focussed on the communication between partner processes and are what we call S-BPM component processes. An *S-BPM component process* (or shortly component) is defined as a pair of an S-BPM process P and a set *ExternalPartnerProc* of external partner processes, which can be addressed from within P. More precisely, *ExternalPartnerProc* consists of pairs *(caller, (P', externalSubj))* of a *caller*—a distinguished P-subject—and an S-BPM process P' with a distinguished P'-subject

---

[35] The compression algorithm can be further sharpened for alternative action nodes by compressing into one node certain groups of subdiagrams without communication or alternative action nodes.

externalSubj, the communication partner in P' which is addressed from within P by the *caller* and thus for the *caller* appears as external subject whose process typically is not known to the *caller*.

We define that two process network components (P, *(caller, (P', extSubj'))*) and $(P_1, (caller_1, (P'_1, extSubj'_1)))$ (or the corresponding subjects *caller, extSubj'*) are *communication partners* or simply partners (in the network) if the external subject which can be called by the caller in the first process is the one which can call back this caller, formally:

$P' = P_1$ **and** $extSubj' = caller_1$ **and** $P'_1 = P$ **and** $extSubj'_1 = caller$

A *service process* in a process network is a component process which is communication partner of multiple components in the network, i.e., which can be called from and call back to multiple other component processes in the network. Thus the *ExternalSubject* referenced in and representing a service process S for its clients represents a set of external subjects,[36] namely the (usually disjoint) union of sets *ExternalSubj(P, S)*, namely the *extSubjects* of the partner subjects in *caller (P, S)* which from within their process P call the partner process S by referencing *extSubj*, formally:

$$ExternalSubj (S) = \cup \ ExternalSubj (P, S)$$
$$P \in Partner (S)$$

Each communication between a client process P and a service process S implies a substitution (usually a renaming) at the service process side of its *ExternalSubj(S)* by a dedicated element *extSubj* of *ExternalSubj(S, P)* which is the *extSubj* of an element of the set *caller(P, S)* of concrete subjects calling S from the client process P.

A special class of S-BPM process networks is obtained by the decomposition of processes into a set of subprocesses. As usual various decomposition layers can be defined, leading to the concepts of horizontal subjects (those which communicate on the same layer) and vertical subjects (those which communicate with subjects in other layers) and to the application of various data sharing disciplines along a layer hierarchy.

An S-BPM process network comes with a graphical representation of its communication partner signature by the so-called *process interaction diagram* (PID), which is an analogue of an SID-diagram lifted from subjects to processes to which the communicating subjects belong. A PID for a process network is defined as a directed graph whose nodes are (names of) network components and whose arcs connect communication partners. The arcs may be labeled with the name of the message type through which the partner is addressed by the caller. A further

---

[36] For this reason it is called a general external subject.

abstraction of PIDs results if the indication of the communicating subjects is omitted and only the process names are shown.

Observer View Normalization of Subject Behavior Diagrams The interaction view normalization of SBDs defined in Sect. 5.2 can be pushed further by defining an *observer*'s *ObserverView* of the SBD of an observed *subj*ect, where not only internal functions are compressed but also communication actions of the observed *subj*ect with other partners than the *observer* subject. In defining the normalization of an SBD D into the *ObserverView (observer, D_{subj})*, some attention has to be paid to structured states, namely those with communication alternatives or multiple communication actions and states with alternative actions. To further explain the concept, we outline in the following a normalization algorithm which defines this *ObserverView (observer, D_{subj})*.

In a first step, we construct a *CommunicationHiding(observer, D_{subj})* diagram, also written $D_{subj} \downarrow observer$. It is semantically equivalent to but appears to be more abstract than D. Roughly speaking, each communication action in D between the *subj*ect and other partners than the *observer* is hidden as an abstract pseudo-internal function, whose specification hides the original content of the communication action. Then to the resulting SBD the interaction view normalization defined in Sect. 5.2 is applied (where pseudo-internal functions are treated as internal functions). The final result is the *ObserverView* of the original SBD:

$$ObserverView \ (observer, \ D_{subj}) = \\ InteractionView(D_{subj} \downarrow observer)$$

The idea for the construction of $D_{subj} \downarrow observer$ is to visit every node in the SBD of *subj*ect once, beginning at the start node and following all possible paths in D, and to hide every encountered not *observer*-related communication action of *subj*ect as a (semantically equivalent) pseudo-internal function step. Since internal function states are not affected by this, it suffices to explain what the algorithm does at (single or multi) communication nodes or at alternative action nodes. The symmetry in the model between send and receive actions permits to treat communication nodes uniformly as one case.

Case 1. The visited *state* has a send or receive action.

If the *observer* is not a possible communication partner of the *subj*ect in any communication *Alternative(subj, state)* (Case 1.1), then the entire action in *state* is declared as pseudo-internal function (with its original but hidden semantical effect). If *observer* is a possible communication partner in every communication *Alternative (subj, state)* (Case 1.2), then the communication action in *state* remains untouched with all its communication alternatives. In both cases, the algorithm visits the next state.

We explain below how to compute the property of being a possible communication partner via the type structure of the elements of *Alternative(subj, state)*.

Otherwise (Case 1.3) split *Alternative(subj, state)* following the *priority* order into alternating successive segments $alt_i(observer)$ of communication alternatives with *observer* as possible partner and $alt_{i+1}(other)$ of communication alternatives with only *other* possible partners than *observer*. Keep in a *priority* preserving way[37] the *observer* relevant elements of any $alt_i(observer)$ untouched and declare each segment alt_{i+1} *(other)* as one pseudo-internal function (with the original but hidden semantical effect of its elements) which constitutes one alternative of the *subject* in this *state* as observable by the *observer* (read: alternative in *CommunicationHiding* *(observer, D_{subj}))*. If an $alt_{i+1}(other)$ segment contains a multicommunication action, the iteration due to the *MultiAction* character of this action remains hidden to the *observer* (read: the pseudo-internal function it will belong to is defined not to be a *MultiAction* in $D_{subj} \downarrow observer$). The function $select_{Alt}$ (and in the *MultiAction* case also the respective constraints) used in this *state* have to be redefined correspondingly to maintain the semantical equivalence of the transformation.

Case 2. The visited *state* is an alternative action state *altSplit*.

Split $AltBehDgm(altSplit)$ into two subsets Alt_1 of those alternative subdiagrams, which contain a communication state with *observer* as possible communication partner and Alt_2 of the other alternative subdiagrams. If Alt_1 is empty (Case 2.1), then the entire alternative action structure between *altSplit* and *altJoin(altSplit)* (comprising the alternative subdiagrams corresponding to this *state)* is collapsed into one *state* with a pseudo-internal function, which is specified to have its original semantical effect. All edges into any *entryBox* or out of any *exitBox* become an edge into resp. out of *state* and the algorithm visits the next state. If Alt_2 is empty (Case 2.2), then the alternative action *state* remains untouched with all its alternative subdiagrams and the algorithm visits each *altEntry* state. Once the algorithm has visited each node in each subdiagram, it proceeds from the *altJoin(altSplit)* state to any of its successor states.

Otherwise (Case 1.3) the alternative action node structure formed by *altSplit* and the corresponding *altJoin (altSplit)* state remains, but the entire set Alt_2 of subdiagrams without communication with the *observer* is compressed into one new state: it is entered from an *entryBox* and exited from an *exitBox* (where all edges into resp. out of the boxes of Alt_2 elements are redirected) and has as associated service a pseudo-internal function, which is specified to have its original semantical effect. Then the algorithm visits each *altEntry* state of each Alt_1 element. Once the algorithm has visited each node in the subdiagram of each Alt_1 element, it proceeds from the *altJoin (altSplit)* state to any of its successor states.

It remains to explain how to compute whether *observer* is a possible communication partner in a communication *state* of the observed *subject* behavior diagram D_{subj}.

Case 1: *state* is a send state (whether canceling or blocking, synchronous or asynchronous, *Send (Single)* or *Send (Multi)*). Then *observer* is a possible

---

[37] In case different elements are allowed to have the same *priority*, there is a further technical complication. For the *priority* preservation, one has then to split each *alt $_j$ (other)* further into three segments of alternatives which have (a) the same priority as the last element in the preceding segment alt_{j-1} *(observer)* (if there is any) resp., (b) a higher priority than the last element in the preceding segment alt_{j-1} *(observer)* and a lower one than the first element in the successor segment alt_{j+1} *(observer)* (if there is any) resp., and (c) the same priority as the first element in alt_{j+1} *(observer)* (if it exists). Each of these three segments must be declared as a pseudo-internal function with corresponding priority.

communication partner of *subj* in this *state* if and only if *observer* = *receiver (alt)* for some *alt* ∈ *alternative (subj, state)*.

Case 2: *state* is a receive state. Then observer is a possible communication partner of *subj* in this *state* if and only if the following property holds, where D_o denotes the SBD of the *observer*:

> **forsome** *alt* ∈ *alternative (subj, state)*
> **forsome** send state *state'* ∈ D_o
> **forsome** *alt'* ∈ *alternative(observer, state')*
>   *alt* ∈ {*any, observer*} **and** *subj* ∈ *PossibleReceiver*
>   *(alt')*[38]
> **or forsome** *type (alt = type = alt'* **and** *subj* ∈ *PossibleReceiver*
> *(alt'))*
> **or forsome** *type (alt = (type, observer)* **and**
>   *alt'* ∈ {*type, (type, subj)*} **and** *subj* ∈ *PossibleReceiver*
>   *(alt'))*
> **where**
> *subj* ∈ *PossibleReceiver (alt')* if and only if
>   *alt'* = *any* **or** *receiver (alt')* = *subj*

Remark. The above algorithm makes clear that different observers may have a different view of a same diagram.

---

6   Two Model Extension Disciplines

In this section we define two composition schemes for S-BPM processes which build upon the simple logical foundation of the semantics of S-BPM exposed in the preceding sections. They support the S-BPM discipline for controlled stepwise development of complex processes out of basic modular components and offer in particular a clean methodological separation of normal and exceptional behavior. More precisely they come as rigorous methods to enrich a given S-BPM process by new features in a purely incremental manner, typically by extending a given SBD D by an SBD D' with some desired additional process behavior without withdrawing or otherwise contradicting the original $\text{BEHAVIOR}_{subj}(D)$. This conservative model extension approach permits a separate analysis of the original and the extended system behavior and thus contributes to split a complex system into a manageable composition of manageable components. The separation of given and added (possibly exception) behavior allows one also to change the implementation of the two independently of each other.

---

[38] The second conjunct implies that *observer* is not considered to be a possible communication partner of *subj* in *state* if *subj* in this *state* is ready to receive a message from the *observer* but the *observer*'s SBD has no send state with a send alternative where the *subj*ect could be the receiver of the *msgToBeSent*.

The difference between the two model extension methods is of pragmatic nature. The so-called *Interrupt Extension* has its roots in and is used like the interrupt handling mechanism known from operating systems and the exception handling pendant in high-level programming languages. The so-called *Behavior Extension* is used to stepwise extend (what is considered as) "normal" behavior by additional features. Correspondingly the two extension methods act at different levels of the S-BPM interpreter; the Interrupt Extension conditions at the SID-level the "normal" execution of BEHAVIOR *(subj, state)* by the absence of interrupting events and calls an interrupt handler if an interruption is triggered whereas the Behavior Extension enriches the "normal" execution of BEHAVIOR$_{subj}(D)$ by new ways to PROCEED from BEHAVIOR *(subj, state)* to the next state.

6.1 Interrupt Extension

The Interrupt Extension method introduces a conservative form of exception handling in the sense that it transforms any given SBD D in such a way that the behavior of the transformed diagram remains unchanged as long as no exceptions occur (read: as long as there are no interrupts), adding exception handling in case an exception event happens. To specify how exceptions are thrown (read: how interrupts are triggered), it suffices to consider here externally triggered interrupts because internal interrupt triggers concerning actions to-be-executed by a subject are explicitly modeled for communication actions Send/Receive in blocking Alternative Rounds (see Fig. 2 in Sect. 3.1) and are treated for internal functions through the specification of their PERFORM component. External interrupt triggers concerning the action currently PERFORMed by a *subj*ect are naturally integrated into the S-BPM model via a set *InterruptKind* of kinds (pairs of sender and message type) of *InterruptMsg* s arriving in *inputPool (subj)* independently of whether *subj*ect currently is ready to receive a message. It suffices to

- Guarantee that elements of *InterruptMsg* are never *Blocked* in any input pool, so that at each moment every potential *interruptOriginator*—the sender of an *interruptMsg*—can PASS(*interruptMsg*) to the input pool of the receiving subject.[39]
- Give priority to the execution of the interrupt handling procedure by the receiver *subj*ect, interrupting the PERFORMance of its current action when an *interruptMsg* arrives in the *inputPool (subj)*. This is achieved through the INTERRUPTBEHAVIOR *(subj, state)* rule defined below, which is a conservative extension of the BEHAVIOR(*subj, state*) rule defined in Sect. 2.2. This means that we can locally confine the extension, namely to an incremental modification of the interpreter rule for the new kind of interruptible SBD-states.

---

[39] In the presence of the input pool default row *any any maxSize Blocking* it suffices to require that every input pool constraint table has a penultimate default interrupt msg row of form *interrupt-Originator type (interruptMsg) maxSize Drop* with associated *Drop* action *DropYoungest* or *DropOldest*.

Thus the SBD-transformation *InterruptExtension* defined below has the following three arguments:

- A to be transformed SBD *D* with a set *InterruptState* of *D*-states s_i ($1 \leq i \leq n$) where an interrupt may happen so that for such states a new rule INTERRUPT-BEHAVIOR*(subj, state)* must be defined which incrementally extends the rule BEHAVIOR*(subj, state)*.
- A set *InterruptKind*(s_i) of indexed pairs *interrupt$_j$* ($1 \leq j \leq m$) of sender and message type of interrupt messages to which *subj*ect has to react when in state s_i .
- An interrupt handling SBD *D'* the *subj*ect is required to execute immediately when an *interruptMsg* appears in its input pool, together with a set *Interrupt-ProcEntry* of edges $arc_{i,j}$ without source node, with target node in *D'* and with associated *ExitCond* $_{i,j}$.[40]

InterruptExtension when applied to (*D, InterruptState*), *InterruptKind* and the exception procedure (*D', InterruptProcEntry*) joins the two SBDs into one graph *D**:

$$D* = D \cup D' \cup Edges_{D,D'}.$$

where $Edges_{D,D'}$ is defined as set of edges (called again) $arc_{i,j}$ connecting in *D** the source node s_i in *D* with the *target* ($arc_{i,j}$) node in *D'* where $j = indexOf$ (*e, InterruptKind*(s_i)) for any $e \in InterruptKind$. BEHAVIOR(*D**) is defined as in Sect. 2.2 from BEHAVIOR$_D$(*subj, state*) with the following extension INTERRUPT-BEHAVIOR$_{D*}$ of BEHAVIOR$_D$ (*subj, s_i*) for *InterruptState*s s_i of *D*, whereas BEHAVIOR (*subj, state*) remains unchanged for the other *D* states and for *states* of *D'*—which are assumed to be disjoint from those of *D*[41]:

BEHAVIOR$_{D*}$ *(subj, state)* = // Case of InterruptExtension(D, D')
    BEHAVIOR$_D$ *(subj, state)*   **if** *state* $\in$ *D* \ *InterruptState*
    BEHAVIOR$_{D'}$ *(subj, state)*   **if** *state* $\in$ *D'*
    INTERRUPTBEHAVIOR *(subj, state)* **if** *state* $\in$ *InterruptState*
INTERRUPTBEHAVIOR *(subj, s_i)* = // at InterruptState s_i
    if *SID_state(subj)* = s_i **then**
        if *InterruptEvent(subj, s_i)* **then**
            choose *msg* $\in$ *InterruptMsg (s_i)* $\cap$ *inputPool (subj)*
            let j = *indexOf (interruptKind(msg), InterruptKind (s_i))*
            let *handleState* = *target ($arc_{i,j}$)*

---

[40] This includes the special case $m = 1$ where the (entry into the) interrupt handling procedure depends only on the happening of an interrupt regardless of its kind. The general case with multiple entries (or equivalently multiple exception handling procedures each with one entry) prepare the ground for an easy integration of compensation procedures as part of exception handling, which typically depend on the state where the exception happens and on the kind of interrupt (pair of originator and type of the interrupt message).

[41] This does not exclude the possibility that some edges in *D'* have as target a node in *D*, as is the case when the exception handling procedure upon termination leads back to normal execution.

PROCEED(*subj, service (handleState), handleState*)
DELETE(*msg, inputPool (subj)*)
else BEHAVIOR$_D$ *(subj, s$_i$)*

where

InterruptEvent(subj, s$_i$*)* **iff**
forsome *m* ∈ *InterruptMsg (*s$_i$*) m* ∈ *inputPool (subj)*

When no confusion is to be feared we write again BEHAVIOR(*subj*, s_i) also for INTERRUPTBEHAVIOR(*subj*, s_i).

Remark. The definition of INTERRUPTBEHAVIOR implies that if during the execution of the exception handling procedure described by D' *subj*ect encounters an interrupt event in D', it will start to execute the handling procedure D'' for the new exception, similar to the exception handling mechanism in Java [Stärk et al. (2001), Fig. 6.2].

6.2   Behavior Extension

The SBD-transformation method *BehaviorExtension* has the following two arguments:

- A to be transformed SBD D with a set *ExtensionState* of D-states s_i ($1 \leq i \leq n$) where a new behavior is added to be possibly executed if selected by *select$_{Edge}$* in BEHAVIOR(*subj*, s_i) when exiting s_i upon completion of its associated service.
- An SBD D' (assumed to be disjoint from D), which describes the new behavior the *subj*ect will execute when the new behavior is selected to be executed next. To enter D' from extension states in D, we use (in analogy to *Interrupt-ProcEntry*) a set *AddedDgmEntry* of edges *arc$_i$* without source node and with target node in D' and associated *ExitCond$_i$*.

BehaviorExtension applied to (D, *ExtensionState*) and (D', *AddedDgmEntry*) joins the two SBDs into one graph D^+:

$$D^+ = D \cup D' \cup Edges_{D, D'}$$

where *Edges$_{D,D'}$* is defined as set of edges (called again) *arc$_i$* connecting in D^+ the source node s_i in D with the *target(arc$_i$)* node in D'.

BEHAVIOR(D^+) can be defined as in Sect. 2.2 from BEHAVIOR(*subj, state*) for *state*s in D resp. D' but with the selection function *select$_{Edge}$* extended for *ExtensionState* nodes s_i to include in its domain *arc$_i$* with the associated *ExitCond$_i$*. In this way new D'-behavior becomes possible which can be analyzed separately from the original D-behavior.

---

7   S-BPM Interpreter in a Nutshell

Collection of the ASM rules for the high-level subject-oriented interpreter model for the semantics of the S-BPM constructs.

7.1   Subject Behavior Diagram Interpretation

BEHAVIOR $_{subj}$ (D) = { BEHAVIOR *(subj, node)* | *node* ∈ *Node (D)* }
BEHAVIOR *(subj, state)* =

if *SID_state (subj) = state* **then**
    if *Completed, (subj, service (state), state)* **then**
      let *edge = select*$_{Edge}$ *({e* ∈ *OutEdge (state) | ExitCond
      (e) (subj, state) })*
        PROCEED *(subj, service (target (edge)), target (edge))*
    else PERFORM *(subj, service (state), state)*
where
    PROCEED *(subj, X, node) =*
    SID_state (subj) := node
    START *(subj, X, node)*

7.2   Alternative Send/Receive Round Interpretation

PERFORM *(subj, ComAct, state) =*
  if *NonBlockingTryRound (subj, state)* **then**
    if *TryRoundFinished (subj, state)* **then**
      INITIALIZEBLOCKINGTRYROUNDS *(subj, state)*
    else TRYALTERNATIVE$_{ComAct}$ *(subj, state)*
  if *BlockingTryRound (subj, state)* **then**
    if *TryRoundFinished (subj, state)*
    then INITIALIZEROUNDALTERNATIVES *(subj, state)*
    else
      if *Timeout (subj, state, timeout (state))* **then**
        INTERRUPT$_{ComAct}$ *(subj, state)*
      elseif *UserAbruption (subj, state)*
        then ABRUPT$_{ComAct}$ *(subj, state)*
        else TRYALTERNATIVE$_{ComAct}$ *(subj, state)*

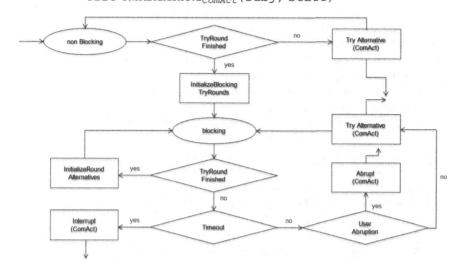

Interpretation of Auxiliary Macros

START *(subj, ComAct, state)* =
  INITIALIZEROUNDALTERNATIVES *(subj, state)*
  INITIALIZEEXIT&COMPLETIONPREDICATES$_{ComAct}$ *(subj, state)*
  ENTERNONBLOCKINGTRYROUND *(subj, state)*

where

INITIALIZEROUNDALTERNATIVES *(subj, state)* =
  RoundAlternative (subj, state) := Alternative(subj, state)

INITIALIZEEXIT&COMPLETIONPREDICATES$_{ComAct}$ *(subj, state)* =
    INITIALIZEEXITPREDICATES$_{ComAct}$ *(subj, state)*
    INITIALIZECOMPLETIONPREDICATES$_{ComAct}$ *(subj, state)*

INITIALIZEEXITPREDICATES$_{ComAct}$ *(subj, state)* =
    NormalExitCond(subj, ComAct, state) := false
    TimeoutExitCond(subj, ComAct, state) := false
    AbruptionExitCond(subj, ComAct, state) := false

INITIALIZECOMPLETIONPREDICATE$_{ComAct}$ *(subj, state)* =
    Completed (subj, ComAct, state) := false

[Non]BlockingTryRound(subj, state) =
  tryMode(subj, state) = [non]blocking

ENTER[NON]BLOCKINGTRY ROUND *(subj, state)* =
    tryMode(subj, state) := [non]blocking

TryRoundFinished(subj, state) =
    RoundAlternatives(subj, state) =

INITIALIZEBLOCKINGTRYROUNDS *(subj, state)* =
    ENTERBLOCKINGTRYROUND *(subj, state)*
    INITIALIZEROUNDALTERNATIVES *(subj, state)*
    SETTIMEOUTCLOCK *(subj, state)*

SETTIMEOUTCLOCK *(subj, state)* =
    blockingStartTime(subj, state) := now

Timeout(subj, state, time) =
  $now \geq blockingStartTime(subj, state) + time$

INTERRUPT$_{ComAct}$ *(subj, state)* =
  SETCOMPLETIONPREDICATE$_{ComAct}$ *(subj, state)*
  SETTIMEOUTEXIT $_{ComAct}$ *(subj, state)*

SETCOMPLETIONPREDICATE$_{ComAct}$ *(subj, state)* =
  Completed(subj, ComAct, state) := true

SETTIMEOUTEXIT$_{ComAct}$ *(subj, state)* =
  TimeoutExitCond(subj, ComAct, state) := true

ABRUPT $_{ComAct}$ *(subj, state)* =
  SETCOMPLETIONPREDICATE$_{ComAct}$ *(subj, state)*
  SETABRUPTIONEXIT$_{ComAct}$ *(subj, state)*

7.3 MsgElaboration Interpretation for MultiSend/Receive

TRYALTERNATIVE$_{ComAct}$ $(subj, state) =$

   CHOOSE&PREPAREALTERNATIVE$_{ComAct}$ $(subj, state)$

     seq TRYComAct $(subj, state)$

CHOOSE&PREPAREALTERNATIVE$_{ComAct}$ $(subj, state) =$

  let $alt = select_{Alt}(RoundAlternative(subj, state), priority(state))$

   PREPAREMSG$_{ComAct}$ $(subj, state, alt)$

   MANAGEALTERNATIVEROUND $(alt, subj, state)$

  where

      MANAGEALTERNATIVEROUND $(alt, subj, state) =$

       MARKSELECTION $(subj, state, alt)$

       INITIALIZEMULTIROUND$_{ComAct}$ $(subj, state)$

      MARKSELECTION $(subj, state, alt) =$

       DELETE $(alt, RoundAlternative (subj, state))$

PREPAREMSG$_{ComAct}$ $(subj, state, alt) =$

       forall $1 \leq i \leq mult (alt)$

       if $ComAct = Send$ **then**

        let $m_i = composeMsg(subj, msgData (subj, state, alt), i)$

         $MsgToBeHandled(subj, state) := \{m_1, \ldots, m_{mult}(alt)\}$

       if $ComAct = Receive$ **then**

        let $m_i = select_{MsgKind(subj, state, alt, i)} (ExpectedMsgKind (subj, state, alt))$

         $MsgToBeHandled (subj, state) := \{m_1, \ldots, m_{mult}(alt)\}$

7.4   MultiSend/Receive Round Interpretation

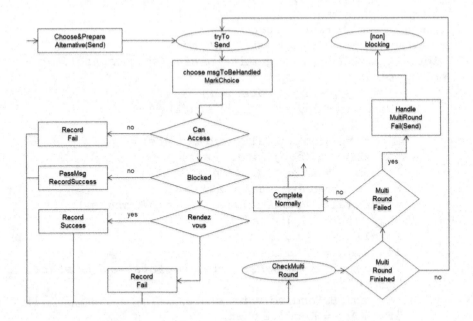

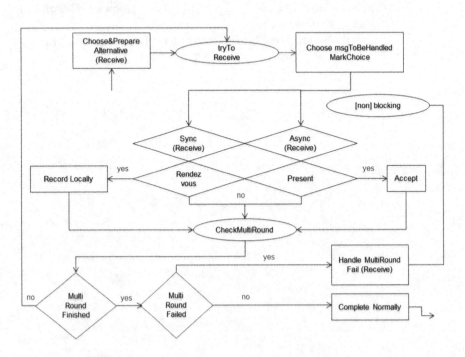

TRY_{ComAct} $(subj, state) =$
  choose $m \in MsgToBeHandled(subj, state)$
    $\text{MARKCHOICE}(m, subj, state)$
    if $ComAct = Send$ **then**
      let $receiver = receiver$ (m), $pool = inputPool$
      $(receiver)$
      if not $CanAccess$ $(subj, pool)$ **then**
        $\text{CONTINUEMULTIROUND}_{Fail}$ $(subj, state, m)$
      else $\text{TRY}_{Async\ (Send)}$ $(subj, state, m)$
    if $ComAct = Receive$ **then**
      if $Async(Receive)(m)$ **then** $\text{TRY}_{Async(Receive)}$ $(subj,$
      $state, m)$
      if $Sync(Receive)(m)$ **then** $\text{TRY}_{Sync(Receive)}$ $(subj,$
      $state, m)$
where
  MARKCHOICE $(m, subj, state) =$
    $\text{DELETE}(m, MsgToBeHandled(subj, state))$
    $currMsgKind(subj, state) := m$
$\text{TRY}_{Async(ComAct)}$ $(subj, state, m) =$
  if $PossibleAsync_{ComAct}(subj, m)$ // async communication
  possible
  then $\text{ASYNC}(ComAct)(subj, state, m)$
  else
    if $ComAct = Receive$ **then**
      $\text{CONTINUEMULTIROUND}_{Fail}$ $(subj, state, m)$
    if $ComAct = Send$ **then** $\text{TRY}_{Sync(ComAct)}$ $(subj, state, m)$
$\text{TRY}_{Sync(ComAct)}$ $(subj, state, m) =$
  if $PossibleSync_{ComAct}(subj, m)$ // sync communication
  possible
  then $\text{SYNC}(ComAct)(subj, state, m)$
  else $\text{CONTINUEMULTIROUND}_{Fail}$ $(subj, state, m)$

7.5   Actual Send Interpretation

$\text{ASYNC}(Send)(subj, state, msg) =$
  PASSMSG (msg)
  $\text{CONTINUEMULTIROUND}_{Success}$ $(subj, state, msg)$
where
  $\text{PASSMSG}(msg) =$
    let $pool = inputPool$ $(receiver (msg))$
    let $row = first$ $(\{r \in constraintTable (pool) \mid$
                $ConstraintViolation(msg, r)\})$
      if $row \neq$ **undef and** $action (row) \neq DropIncoming$
        then $\text{DROP}(action)$

$$\textbf{if } row = \textbf{undef or } action \ (row) \neq DropIncoming \textbf{ then}$$
$$\text{Insert} (msg, pool)$$
$$insertionTime(msg, pool) := now$$

$\text{Drop}(action) =$

$\quad \textbf{if } action = DropYoungest \textbf{ then } \text{Delete}(youngestMsg(pool),$
$\quad pool)$

$\quad \textbf{if } action = DropOldest \textbf{ then } \text{Delete}(oldestMsg(pool), pool)$

$PossibleAsync_{Send}(subj, msg) \textbf{ iff not } Blocked(msg)$

$Blocked(msg) \textbf{ iff}$

$\quad \textbf{let } row = first \ (\{r \in constraintTable \ (inputPool \ (receiver$
$\quad (msg))) \ |$
$$ConstraintViolation \ (msg, r)\})$$
$\quad row \neq \textbf{undef and } action \ (row) = Blocking$

$\text{Sync}(Send)(subj, state, msg) =$

$\quad \text{ContinueMultiRound}_{Success} \ (subj, state, msg)$

$PossibleSync_{Send} \ (subj, msg) \textbf{ iff } RendezvousWithReceiver$
$(subj, msg)$

$RendezvousWithReceiver \ (subj, msg) \textbf{ iff}$

$\quad tryMode(rec) \quad = \quad tryToReceive \quad \textbf{and} \quad Sync(Receive)$
$\quad (currMsgKind)$

$\quad \textbf{and } SyncSend(msg) \textbf{ and } Match(msg, currMsgKind,)$

$\quad \textbf{where}$

$\quad\quad rec = receiver(msg), recstate = SID\_state \ (rec)$
$\quad\quad currMsgKind = currMsgKind, (rec, recstate)$
$\quad\quad blockingRow =$
$\quad\quad\quad first \ (\{r \in constraintTable \ (rec) \ | \ Constraint-$
$\quad\quad\quad Violation \ (msg, r)\})$
$\quad\quad SyncSend(msg) \textbf{ iff } size \ (blockingRow) = 0$

7.6   Actual Receive Interpretation

$\text{Async}(Receive)(subj, state, msg) =$

$\quad \text{Accept}(subj, msg)$

$\quad \text{ContinueMultiRound}_{Success} \ (subj, state, msg)$

$\quad\quad \textbf{where}$

$\quad\quad \text{Accept}(subj, m) =$

$\quad\quad\quad \textbf{let } receivedMsg =$

$\quad\quad\quad\quad select_{ReceiveOfKind(m)} \ (\{msg \in inputPool \ (subj) \ |$
$\quad\quad\quad\quad Match \ (msg, m)\})$

$\quad\quad\quad \text{RecordLocally}(subj, receivedMsg)$

$\quad\quad\quad \text{Delete}(receivedMsg, inputPool \ (subj))$

$\quad\quad Async(Receive)(m) \textbf{ iff } commMode(m) = async$

$\quad\quad PossibleAsync_{Receive} \ (subj, m) \textbf{ iff } Present \ (m, inputPool$
$\quad\quad (subj))$

$\quad\quad Present(m, pool) \textbf{ iff forsome } msg \in pool \ Match \ (msg, m)$

SYNC (Receive) *(subj, state, msgKind)* =
  let *P = inputPool (subj), sender = ι s (CanAccess (s, P))*
    RECORDLOCALLY (*subj, msgToBeSent (sender, SID_state*
    (sender))
    CONTINUEMULTIROUND_{Success} *(subj, state, msgKind)*
Sync (Receive) (msgKind) iff *commMode (msgKind) = sync*
PossibleSync_{Receive} (subj, msgKind) iff
  RendezvousWithSender (subj, msgKind)
RendezvousWithSender (subj, msgKind) iff
  Sync (Receive) (msgKind) **and**
    let *sender = ι s (CanAccess (s, inputPool (subj))*
    let *msgToBeSent = msgToBeSent (sender, SID_state*
    (sender))
      tryMode (sender) = tryToSend **and** *SyncSend*
      (msgToBeSent)
      and *Match (msgToBeSent, msgKind)*

7.7 Alternative Action Interpretation

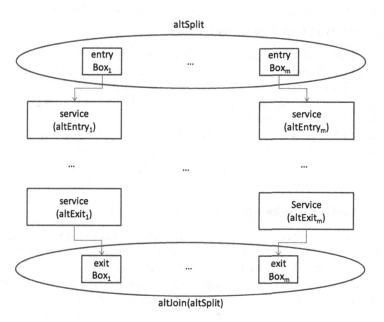

START (subj, ALTACTION, altSplit) =
  forall *D ∈ AltBehDgm (altSplit)*
    if *Compulsory (altEntry (D))* **then**
      SID_state (subj, D) := altEntry (D)
      START (subj , service (altEntry (D)), altEntry (D))

else SID_state $(subj, D)$:=**undef**
PERFORM $(subj, \text{ALTACTION}, state)$ =
  PERFORMSUBDGMSTEP $(subj, state)$
    or STARTNEWSUBDGM $(subj, state)$ }
where
  PERFORMSUBDGMSTEP (s, n) =
    choose $D \in ActiveSubDgm(s, n)$ **in** BEHAVIOR $(s, SID\_state$
    $(s, D))$
  STARTNEWSUBDGM (s, n) =
    choose $D \in AltBehDgm(n) \setminus ActiveSubDgm(s, n)$
      $SID\_state(s, D) := altEntry(D)$
      START $(s, service(altEntry(D)), altEntry(D))$
  $ActiveSubDgm(s, n) = \{D \in AltBehDgm(n) \mid Active(s, D)\}$
  R **or** S = **choose** $X \in \{R, S\}$ **in** X
$Completed (subj, \text{ALTACTION}, altSplit)$ iff
  forall $D \in AltBehDgm(altSplit)$
    if $Compulsory(altExit(D))$ **and** $Active(subj, D)$
    then $SID\_state(subj, D) = exitBox(D)$
 where
  $Active(subj, D)$ iff $SID\_state(subj, D) \neq$ **undef**

Auxiliary Wait/Exit Rule Interpretation

START $(subj, \text{ALTACTIONWAIT}, exitBox)$ =
  INITIALIZECOMPLETIONPREDICATE$_{AltActionWait}$ $(subj, exitBox)$
PERFORM $(subj, \text{ALTACTIONWAIT}, exitBox)$ = **skip**
START $(subj, \text{EXITALTACTION}, altJoin(altSplit))$ = **skip**
PERFORM $(subj, \text{EXITALTACTION}, altJoin)$ =
  forall $D \in AltBehDgm(altSplit)$ $SID\_state(subj, D)$:=
  undef
  SETCOMPLETIONPREDICATE$_{ExitAltAction}$ $(subj, altJoin(altSplit))$

---

8   Interrupt Behavior

BEHAVIOR$_{D*}$ $(subj, state)$ = // Case of InterruptExtension(D, D')
$\begin{cases} \text{BEHAVIOR}_D (subj, state) & \text{if } state \in D \setminus InterruptState \\ \text{BEHAVIOR}_{D'} (subj, state) & \text{if } state \in D' \\ \text{INTERRUPTBEHAVIOR}(subj, state) & \text{if } state \in InterruptState \end{cases}$
INTERRUPTBEHAVIOR $(subj, s_i)$ = // at InterruptState s_i
  if $SID\_state(subj) = s_i$ **then**
    if $InterruptEvent(subj, s_i)$ **then**
      choose $msg \in InterruptMsg(s_i) \cap inputPool(subj)$[42]

---

[42] Note that in each step *subj* can react only to one out of possibly multiple interrupt messages present in its *inputPool(subj)*. If one wants to establish a hierarchy among those a priority function is needed to regulate the selection procedure.

let $j = indexOf\ (interruptKind\ (msg)\,,\ InterruptKind\ (s_i))$
let $handleState = target\ (arc_{i,j})$
      PROCEED $(subj,\ service\ (handleState)\,,\ handleState)$
      DELETE $(msg,\ inputPool\ (subj))$
   else BEHAVIOR$_D$ $(subj,\ s_i)$
where
   $InterruptEvent\ (subj,\ s_i)$ **iff**
      forsome $m \in InterruptMsg\ (s_i)\ m \in.\ inputPool\ (subj)$

References for Appendix B

Börger, E.: The ASM refinement method. *Formal Aspects of Computing,* 15:237–257, 2003.

Börger, E.; Stärk, R. F.: Abstract State Machines. A Method for High-Level System Design and Analysis. Springer, 2003.

Knuth, D. E.: *Literate Programming.* Number 27 in CSLI Lecture Notes. Center for the Study of Language and Information at Stanford/California, 1992.

Stärk, R. F.; Schmid, J.; Börger, E.: Java and the Java Virtual Machine: Definition, Verification, Validation. Springer-Verlag, 2001

Meanings of the Term "Subject"

Overview

In Chap. 2, we have introduced the concept of the subject from the perspective of Subject-oriented Business Process Management and detailed in the subsequent sections. In addition, the term is used in many other disciplines and contexts in different meanings. A short glance at Wikipedia reveals the following interpretations of the German word 'Subjekt' (http://www.wikipedia.org, March 24, 2011):

- Role of a civil person:
  - Until the French Revolution: that of the Vassal
  - After the French Revolution: that of the free and self-conscious citizen
- Colloquial speech: person, often used pejoratively
- Term of philosophy:
  - Reference point within subject–object splitting
  - Position of a term in a statement of the traditional logic
- Concept of social science: individual, consciously acting person
- Concept of law: a legal entity, having rights and obligations
- Concept of international law: having rights and obligations
- Concept of Linguistics (grammar): a phrase or word
- Definition of economics: economic subject, a single economic entity acting
- Concept of the Russian Federation: federation object, administrative unit

A translation into English leads to "subject," by which "theme" is to be understood. This is evident for example in e-mail programs. Figure C.1 lists common meanings in English (http://www.websters-online-dictionary.org/definitions/subject, download March 23, 2011).

The multitude of different interpretations of the term "subject" can lead to misunderstandings. Therefore, we explain below, the understanding of the term in selected areas, such as mathematical logic and computer science, in order to single out its meaning in S-BPM.

Subjects in Mathematical Logic

The terms subject and predicate are also used in mathematical logic, but unlike in the natural language. The following discussions of the two terms in mathematical logic are mainly based on Detel (2007).

A. Fleischmann et al., *Subject-Oriented Business Process Management*,
DOI 10.1007/978-3-642-32392-8, © The Author(s) 2012

1. The subject matter of a conversation or discussion; "he didn't want to discuss that subject"; "it was a very sensitive topic"; "his letters were always on the theme of love".

2. Some situation or event that is thought about; "he kept drifting off the topic"; "he had been thinking about the subject for several years"; "it is a matter for the police".

3. A branch of knowledge; "in what discipline is his doctorate?"; "teachers should be well trained in their subject"; "anthropology is the study of human beings".

4. Something (a person or object or scene) selected by an artist or photographer for graphic representation; "a moving picture of a train is more dramatic than a still picture of the same subject".

5. A person who is subjected to experimental or other observational procedures; someone who is an object of investigation; "the subjects for this investigation were selected randomly"; "the cases the we studied were drawn from two different communities".

6. A person who owes allegiance to that nation; "a monarch has a duty to this subjects".

7. (linguistics) one of the two main constituents of a sentence; the grammatical constituent about which something is predicated.

8. (logic) the first term of a proposition.

Fig. C.1 Possible meanings of 'subject' in English

"Logic is a special theory of argumentation" (Detel 2007). The logic examines the validity of an argumentation in terms of its structure without referring to the content of statements. Statements are sentences dominated by descriptive use and their truth values. True and the false, abbreviated as t and f are called truth values. Sentences used for description aim to transmit information and the statement of facts (Detel 2007).

In comparison, sentences used with an expressive intention mainly transmit feelings, while sentences with evocative transmit appeals. Speech acts denote the nature and manner how sentences are used. The predication is a speech act, namely, a statement that specific items have a particular property or relationships to each other. A predication is performed in two steps: first, an item is picked out, and in a second step it is classified by assigning a property. In predication, two types of words are used.

One type helps single out objects. These words are termed nominators or, in older treatises on logic, referred to as subjects (Detel 2007). The second part of speech items helps classifying objects with specific properties. These words are denoted as predicators or, in older philosophical texts, as predicates (Detel 2007). There is a difference between single- and multipredicators. Multipredicators refer to relationships between multiple objects.

The meaning of the terms subject and predicate in logic is completely different from the grammatical categories of the same name. Some nouns, all verbs, and all adjectives are predicators. Nouns are also reserved terms and consequently, nominators. Labels and demonstrative pronouns are different types of nominators. "The predication-theoretical distinction between different types of nominators and between single- and multipredicators has no correspondence in the grammar" (Detel 2007).

Since Subject-oriented BPM is inspired by the concept of subjects in the grammar of natural languages, the terms subject, predicate, and object of S-BPM have nothing in common with the same concepts in logic, and derived from this, the Semantic Web.

> **Subject:** In subject-oriented programming, a **subject** is a collection of classes or class fragments whose class hierarchy models its domain in its own, subjective way. A **subject** may be a complete application in itself, or it may be an incomplete fragment that must be composed with other subjects to produce a complete application. **Subject** composition combines class hierarchies to produce new subjects that incorporate functionality from existing subjects.
> (1999-08-31) Source: The free On-line Dictionary of Computing.

Fig. C.2 Definition of subject-oriented programming (http://www.websters-online-dictionary. org/definitions/subject)

Subjects in Computer Science

Subjects in Subject-Oriented Programming

In computer science, the word "subject" in connection with the subject-oriented programming has a special meaning. This is shown in Fig. C.2.

The German translation is "subjekt-orientierte Programmierung", although the English word "subject" rather refers to the German term "theme" (wikipedia http://de.wikipedia.org/wiki/Subjektorientierte_Programmierung, download May 08, 2008).

Subject-oriented programming is an extension of object-oriented programming and was first published in 1993 by William Harrison and Harold Osher (Harrison et al. 1993). It has the goal to compensate the deficiencies of object-oriented programming in the development of large applications and when merging independently developed applications. In addition, different views on a program (subjective views) are supported. The theme "subject-oriented programming", however, has not been pursued in research. At least there are no publications after 2000. The issue seems to be more or less absorbed by aspect-oriented programming.

Subjects in the Semantic Web

Another meaning of "subject" in computer science exists in the context of the Semantic Web. The data on the Web are currently interpreted by humans exclusively. However, they are increasingly overloaded due to the flood of information available on the Internet. The aim is therefore to increasingly let machines interpret and process information. This requires the so-called Semantic Web, in which data is structured and prepared in a form allowing computers to relate it and to process it as an overall entity, similar to the database query.

In order to achieve that, the available knowledge needs to be represented formally. This allows the retrieval and processing by computer programs. An important concept in computer science in this context is ontology. Ontologies define relevant objects in a particular field of knowledge, their properties, and mutual relationships.

Ontologies are now often described with the language RDF (Resource Definition Framework). The central idea of RDF is to describe binary relations between clearly identified resources "Stuckenschmidt 2011". These binary relations are represented as a triple with subject, predicate, and object. Here, the predicate describes the relation between specified resources, denoted as subject or object. Hence, the predicate in RDF corresponds to a binary predicator from logic, and the subject or object in RDF is nominator. The use of the terms subject, predicate, and object in the field of the Semantic Web, the terms correspond to their use in mathematical logic.

References for Appendix C

Detel, W.: Grundkurs Philosophie, Band 1, Logik, Ditzingen 2007

Harrison W., Osher, H.: Subject-Oriented Programming – A Critique of Pure Objects, Proceedings of the 1993 Conference on Object-Oriented Programming Systems, Languages, and Applications, Washington 1993

Stuckenschmidt, H.: Ontologien – Konzepte, Technologien und Anwendungen, 2nd Edn. Heidelberg 2011

Modeling Tool Kit

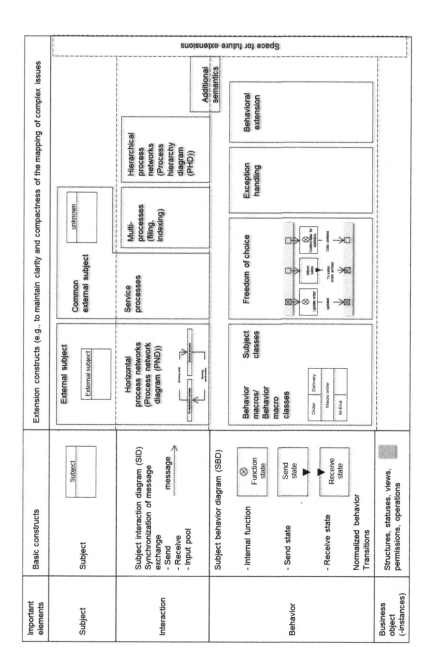

A. Fleischmann et al., *Subject-Oriented Business Process Management*,
DOI 10.1007/978-3-642-32392-8, © The Author(s) 2012

Index